CW00530888

The Girl From Ukraine

Vera Smereka

Edited by
Roman Revkniv

CONTRAFLOW MEDIA

Published by Contraflow Media 2008
10 9 8 7 6 5 4 3 2

Contraflow Media
4 Fearnville Avenue
Leeds LS8 3DG
England

Editorial Assistant: Janice Deane
Book Design and Typesetting: Roman Revkniv
Pre-Print Production Assistant: John Wheelhouse
Pre-Print Production Assistant: Nigel Linsan Colley
Cover Model: Yana Velikhovska-Potapchuk
Cover Backdrop: Bradford Odeon and Bradford Alhambra

A catalogue record for this book is available from
The British Library

ISBN: 978-0-9560811-0-0

Copyright © 2008 Vera Smereka

The right of Vera Smereka to be identified as the author of
this work has been asserted by her in accordance with
The Copyright, Designs and Patents Act 1988

All rights reserved.

No part of this publication may be reproduced, transmitted,
or stored in a retrieval system, in any form or by any means,
without permission in writing from
Contraflow Media

www.contraflowmedia.com

To

My dear father and mother
Rev Fr Stefan Nipot
and
Yevhenia Nipot, née Cherniavksa
With great love and admiration

Wm Thornhill FRC SDO
Ophthalmic Consultant Surgeon
With gratitude for inspiration

Miss Margaret Hudson SRN
Senior Operating Theatre Sister in Charge
With gratitude and great respect

Mrs Julia Reynell
A wonderful neighbour
With gratitude for the transcription of the manuscripts with
corrections, and for the advice and efforts to publish

Roman Revkniv
A good and sincere friend
With special acknowledgement and thanks for all the hard
work without which this book would not have been published

Chapter 1

I was born on the 19th of January – the day when Our Lord Jesus Christ was baptised, according to the New Gregorian Calendar. It was one of the coldest days of the year and the temperature in Ukraine had plummeted to about minus thirty degrees centigrade. Everything was covered with snow and ice, but despite the cold it continued to be one of the happiest times of the year. Christmas celebrations had lasted for two weeks, and it was the final festive day of the season. Throughout the village, every house had been cleaned in preparation for the traditional blessing with Holy Water, and every kitchen had been filled with the most nourishing foods available. Outdoors, horses and sledges stood decorated with coloured ribbons, paper flowers and rugs, ready for the day's traditional races.

Everyone went to church, and at the end of the service the whole village made its way to the river for the blessing of the water. The procession was led by the priest who was closely followed by the choir, and then the elder men who carried a large cross, a very large Bible and Holy Icons. On a carpet of white, glittering snow, hundreds of people followed them. They were all dressed in their best, winter clothes.

The river had completely frozen over, but a few feet from the bank a large, round hole had been cut. Over the hole stood an altar and two crosses which had been carved from huge pieces of ice. These works of seasonal art were all the more impressive as they had been stained maroon with beetroot juice. Set against winter's natural backdrop, they formed a scene which could only be described as one of Ukraine's most beautiful.

The priest, who was dressed in shiny, golden vestments, dipped his gold cross into the water three times. With the service over, everyone hurried with a container to take the blessed water directly from the river. Pigeons were then released from a cage to fly symbolically into the pale-blue sky. Then, somewhere in the distance, celebratory gun shots could be heard. It was the signal for the men to test their bravery by jumping into the ice-cold water.

The day's festivities continued with horse racing through the streets where the crowds enthusiastically cheered the competitors. Then, by late afternoon, the priest began to make his way to each and every house to bless everyone and everything inside them. He wished the villagers good health and happiness for the New Year ahead and thereby brought the Christmas season to a close.

I was born on that Feast of the Epiphany in 1923. My nineteen-year-old mother had gone into labour, so my father took her to Grandma's house in a neighbouring village. Mother was told by an elderly and experienced midwife that I would be born at six o'clock in the morning. She went to sleep. Then sure enough, at six o'clock in the morning, I arrived.

My father was the priest. He was of the Ukrainian Orthodox faith and had to serve the early Epiphany mass. So it was later, when he returned home, that he was presented with his first child. Joyously, he blessed both me and my mother and dutifully returned to the church to continue his work with the late service. I was told this story so many times that it felt as though I had witnessed my own coming into the world.

Chapter 2

I had a happy childhood with as much love and care a girl could have wished for. I had my mother, my father, grandmothers, grandfathers, aunts and uncles. I also had a brother called Anatoly who was just one year younger than me, and a sister called Nadiya who was three years younger.

We always went to church on Sundays where Nadiya and I wore white dresses. We had hats which were decorated with ribbons, and Mother would always take us to the front of the congregation where the grown-ups would look at us with admiration. She also made sure she embroidered Ukrainian blouses and dressed us in national costume on special religious feast days. We wore royal-blue skirts with straps over our shoulders and re-used the ribbons, but this time in our hair. We looked lovely, and people again responded by praising us. They also gave us sweets. I was a brunette and Nadiya was a blonde. Anatoly had auburn hair, and his eyes were big and brown, so Mother nearly always dressed him in brown clothes. He was a handsome, little boy. His face was rounded with a slightly tanned complexion which he had inherited from Father.

We played together, and we fought each other, just like all children do. We went swimming in the summer, and in the early autumn we would go to the woods to pick mushrooms. In winter, we went sledging and made lots of snowmen. We were happy, but little by little other things were starting to happen around us: strange events of which we knew very little. We were aware that something was happening because we noticed how Father and Mother were becoming more and more worried and sad.

As a family, we never settled down for any long period of time because we were not allowed to live in the same house. We made journeys, from one village to another, to wherever a church was still open. I can remember when I was just six years old. We lived in a single room inside a large house which had once belonged to a priest, but it had now been taken over by the Silrada – the Soviet Ukrainian Village Council. The room was small, but Mother made it cosy and comfortable. Our icons were placed in the corner and were adorned with colourful Ukrainian embroidery. On the evening of every religious feast day, a small, red lamp burned in front of them without fail.

We had a traditional Ukrainian stove called a pich, where Mother cooked our dinners. It had a stone platform immediately above it, and this doubled up as a small, centrally heated room of its own. We loved to play there, especially in winter, as it was guaranteed to be warm. We had the use of a large yard and a garden. We kept two cows and had plenty of milk and butter, and cheese which Mother made.

We also kept a pig, and in winter, just before Christmas, a man from the village would come to kill it. The blood was collected to make black pudding, and the intestines were cleaned to make sausages. The bacon was regarded as the most precious part and was cut into squares and then salted to preserve it. Winter was the ideal time for this small ritual. Outside, the frost froze everything and acted as a natural refrigerator. It was traditional in Ukraine for the dead pig to be placed over a straw bonfire to singe all of its hair. It was scraped with a knife and rinsed with cold water. The process continued until it had turned to a golden colour with the hair all gone. The fire and water made the skin crispy and clean. Later, in the fresh, morning air, the gold-coloured pig was cut up. Inside, our fresh bacon was fried, and friends came to taste it. Families described themselves as "re-nourished" because, in those days, pork was considered to be an essential food. Cats and dogs even had a "feast" of their own and received odd scraps of meat during the cutting. They instinctively knew what was going on and quickly surrounded the place.

On the following day, we made kovbasa – traditional Ukrainian sausage. It was made from the best pork and spices and was considered to be our greatest delicacy. We saved it for religious feast days. There were other dishes made from every remaining edible meat which helped us to get through the persistently cold days of winter. Hot beetroot soup – borshch – was cooked every day using the bones and ribs, and it was particularly delicious when pickled tomatoes and cream were added. We always made a roast pork and potato casserole – known as zharkoye. In the cellar, we also had plenty of pickled cucumbers and cabbage. We also stored delicious pickled apples which floated in large barrels. They replaced autumn's fresh produce and ensured our supply of vitamins throughout the winter. Every so often, we were given bliny – pancakes which were either eaten with pieces of fried, seasoned bacon, or with cream.

Winter had many special attractions which all children loved, and our parents typically found it difficult to keep us indoors. Most of the time, we wanted to be outside. We went sledging, skiing, or making snowmen which, incidentally, are known in Ukraine as "snow women". We threw snowballs at each other. We laughed and we screamed, and we always came home red-faced and happy, but those days of happiness, however, were numbered.

We lived in a village called Ivankiv. The church was taxed there. It was then taxed again, and then Father was taxed for everything he owned. Very soon, our cows, pig and hens were taken away and we were no longer allowed to use the garden or surrounding land. All of our household possessions were also confiscated. In the end, we were not allowed to live in the cosy single room. We were forced to leave.

Father managed to rent us a house on the outskirts of the village, and so we moved there. It was small and had a clay floor and whitewashed walls, but it was extremely cold. There was no way we could stay there for any length of time. Meanwhile, the village church had been closed down. Locals said that it had been "sealed up" because a lock with a seal was put on the door by an official from the Village Council. We knew we had to leave the village behind, and there would be no turning back.

Father typically went to look for a place where a church was still open: he would always be needed there. He found such a church in a village called Lushnyky on the other side of the Desna River. At his very first service there, twelve couples were waiting together to be married for what would become a magnificent village celebration. They liked my father and they were grateful to see him, so without hesitation they asked him to move there and stay with them.

By this time, we had already made many long journeys by horse and carriage. This always upset my parents, but there was also some joy for us young ones as we enjoyed seeing and discovering new places. Through the dark nights, those places appeared to be strange, and the people we met were almost always strangers, but they were always very kind. They would give us sweets, nuts and biscuits. Nadiya cried for much of the time, so Mother had to take care of her. Meanwhile, Father's face would look worried:

'Poor children,' he would say to us, 'there's no home for you, but God will help us.'

He would cheer us up, smile at us and stroke our heads, and then he would go away to deal with his other worries. I saw Mother crying, even though she tried to hide her face from me. She then always tried to smile whenever she had to face us.

When we crossed the Desna River, the water was dark, deep and fast-running. It frightened us. We had to cross on a parom – a huge floating platform pulled by a rope across the water. We were safe on the cart, and the horses stood perfectly still until we reached the other side. Father paid the fare to the two men who had pulled us. It was the usual way of crossing the river, except you had to know exactly where the parom was stationed when you needed it.

When we arrived, the new village looked picturesque and very beautiful. It was on a hill, and was surrounded by woodlands which stretched all the way down to the river. Tucked into a valley, it had a small stream flowing through it, with overgrown willow trees gently bathing their branches in the water. At one end of the valley there was a lake, and at the other end was the river which we had just crossed. The roads were all coloured white with soft sand, and in the middle of the village there was a beautiful, white church. It had a green roof and a huge, golden dome with a cross which glinted in the sunlight. It was also surrounded by a large garden which had huge, orchard trees. A stone wall, painted white, separated it from the road.

We made our way there and entered the churchyard, and were then shown a small house which had once belonged to the caretaker. No one in the village was allowed to rent a house to a priest, and not even a room. For the time being, however, this law was ignored by the locals, and the house would become our new home. It consisted of one room with two small windows set in thick, stone walls. This, too, had a large stove by the door where we were immediately made to sit down and warm ourselves. It was autumn, and we were cold and hungry from our long journey. As usual, Mother made the fire and cooked, and we ate our first dinner there with a healthy appetite: we were healthy children.

The next chapter in our family life began, and we soon grew to like it very much indeed. The large garden surrounding the church became our playground. There were graves there, and we soon became familiar with every one of them. We soon knew every tree in the orchard, too. There were different kinds growing there: apple trees, pear trees and cherry trees. We also learned when it was the best time to eat the fruit, and when to pick it for winter storage. The white, brick wall, with gaps in the shape of crosses, was one of our favourite climbing places. A tall pear tree grew near to the doorway of the house, and Father made a bench and placed it there. We learned to love sitting outside, especially on summer evenings. Bats flew round the church's high dome, and the air was always fresh from the valley. It was sweetened by the scent of summer flowers which Mother grew nearby. She had magnolias, night-scented sweet peas and a vast array of nasturtiums.

During winter, we would be snowed-in. This meant Father had the task of digging a tunnel and clearing two paths – one to the gate and the other to the church. The pear tree by the house creaked in the wind, but we were safe, and we trusted our parents' judgments: we never felt frightened.

The stove burned brightly, and we sat with Mother to listen to her stories. Father, meanwhile, sat at the table reading and writing. He was always busy with his papers, and occasionally he would come to us, smiling cheerfully. He also told us lovely stories – usually from the lives of the Saints, but he too, would eventually end up reminiscing about his own childhood.

When spring came, the Desna burst its banks and water flooded half of the village. Fortunately, it never touched the church or our little house because we were higher up in the valley. Grown-ups had their reasons to worry about such events, but for us youngsters it was fun. Together, with other children from the village, we had an excuse to go everywhere by boat. We floated slowly between the houses and trees, and we even gathered fish roe which was caught in the bushes. We sang and shouted across the water, and then we floated into houses with our friends to collect food from the shelves that their mothers had asked them to retrieve. Teenage girls went boating with their boyfriends. They would decorate the boats by covering the seats with rugs, and then added the finishing touches with flowers. They were dressed in colourful skirts and embroidered blouses, and they looked adorable on the calm surface of the water. The echoes from their singing filled the evening air with added charm.

High above the water, and the village of Lushnyky, and seemingly everything else on Earth, stood the magnificent, white church of Our Lady. It was also known as St Peter and St Paul as it had two places of worship on its two levels. When the vast expanse of water reflected the golden sunset, the church seemed to turn pink. The gold cross shone high above for everyone to see, and when the religious festivals came, the bells rang out. They were powerful, and could be heard for many distant miles across the countryside. Nadiya, Anatoly and I used to sit outside with Mother on the high steps of the church, and we watched many glorious sunsets across the water. From where we sat, the bells indeed were very loud, but we lived in peace and harmony deep inside Ukraine's natural environment. Most of all, we were happy together as a Ukrainian family.

Chapter 3

I knew Father was having trouble with some superiors. I did not understand with whom, or for what reasons exactly. I only knew they were against the work of the Church and were imposing large taxes on the parish. Many parishioners then consulted my father, and large sums of money were collected, but just as soon as this was done, somebody else "up above" increased the taxes yet again. No one could pay, so the church would have to be closed and our family would soon have to move on again. We would never be fully settled, so we tried to make the most of any time we could spend together.

The Village Council held its meetings in the former vicarage, just across the road from where we were living. Father was repeatedly asked to go there, and the authorities would detain him for a long time. I would wait for him, and looked through the crosses in the wall, until he'd come out. He often looked pale and worried, so I would cling to him, and he would put his hand on my head. Then, hand-in-hand, we would go back inside. Slowly, we would begin to feel happy again, but then more trouble was always on its way.

It was now more and more usual for Mother and Father to whisper when we went to bed, but I could not understand why they were so worried. I had heard people in the street talking about "change". They said: "It will not last long. Someone abroad, somewhere in the world, will come and help change life back to normal. Then life will be all right again".

I wondered what kind of "change" people were talking about, and asked myself what they meant by "back to normal". I tried to picture various scenes of how this "change" would arrive. Would someone suddenly just shout? Or, would all the people gather together and do something to "change" something? What? What sort of life would follow? I didn't know. I simply couldn't see it. All I wanted was for Mother and Father to be happy, and with these thoughts I eventually fell asleep. I had desperately tried to understand things which I could not even possibly imagine.

Chapter 4

I was just seven years old when my parents sent me to the Primary School in Lushnyky. It was in September 1930. The starting age was eight years, but I was accepted because Mother had already taught me how to read and write. My first day was turned into a special occasion by both of my parents. I had to wear my best embroidered blouse and royal-blue pinafore. The family gathered in front of the icons and the red lamp – which was still lit, and Father – who was dressed in his vestments, said a long prayer. He blessed me, and then presented his gold cross for everyone to kiss. Mother then took me to school where I was left to fend for myself.

To the surprise of both of my parents, I befriended and sat on the same bench as Halya who was the daughter of the Secretary of the Village Council. She was a lively, little girl who nearly always dressed in pink. She had lovely big, brown eyes and auburn hair which she tied in short plaits. I liked her immediately.

I loved school from the very beginning. I learned things quickly, and when we played games I was the one chosen to be the leader and I had to choose which game to play. Girls then started to "bribe" me by giving me sweets and apples to bring them into play. Then, one day, an older girl told me that I was doing wrong by accepting these "bribes" and I should try to be honest by choosing everyone equally and fairly. I had not yet thought of that, and I realised for the first time that there were right and wrong ways to behave. I became much wiser from then on, so I chose my friends and partners in play more fairly. In fact, I began to choose everybody. Gradually, therefore, more and more of the children asked me to organise games, and not the teacher. The older girl who had remarked upon my behaviour then began to smile at me. I was pleased. I was good at regular schoolwork, too. My homework was always done, my reading and writing improved, and I could learn and recite poetry with ease. My teacher then made me stand on a chair in front of the whole class. Sometimes, it would be at a parents' meeting, or at a gathering with the whole of the school where I would recite loudly and confidently. I never showed the slightest bit of fear. Everybody applauded, and I was pleased.

The river was just across the road from the school, and in winter, when it had frozen over, we played there and slid on the ice. There was danger, however, as the ice had holes. Women would rinse their washing there, because that's how the washing was done, but it was subsequently easy for children to fall through into the water. As a result, our parents and teachers would forbid us to play there. But we loved it, so we would not listen to what any of them had to say. Consequently, nearly every day, someone fell through one of the holes. Usually, we would rescue the unfortunate victim, and they'd be returned home with their clothes soaking wet. A punishment invariably awaited them. One day, I fell into one of those holes, and although the girls pulled me out very quickly, my coat had completely soaked through. I was not very frightened of what my father might do to me, but I did not want to displease him, so I spread my coat by the fireplace in the classroom and dried it. I returned in the hope that nobody would notice anything wrong. That evening, however, a woman came to see my mother and she told her that I had fallen into the river. I felt numb, not from fear, but from the disgrace of not having obeyed my parents in the first place. To try and save myself, I went to bed early, and when Father and Mother came to see me, I pretended to be asleep. Anxiously, they looked at me and touched me. They wondered if I would develop a fever, and then left me. I had escaped from what would have been my first ever scolding.

The pupils continued to love winter. There were many snow storms, so the roads would be covered with thick snow. Parents organised horses and sledges to bring us home, and groups of us would be packed on board. The horses pulled us through the village, and we screamed and laughed all the way. To return to the warm house, where my mother was anxiously waiting with a hot dinner, was such a welcoming feeling. We didn't sit quietly, and continued by endlessly and excitedly recounting our adventures.

In the early winter, everyone prepared for Christmas. Lent began six weeks before Christmas and Mother restricted her cooking to the customary meatless dishes. She made her very tasty borshch, but at this time of year she made it with fish and mushrooms. There were also many other dishes, and we enjoyed eating them all. We were kept busy by making decorations for the Christmas tree, and we learned to sing carols. When Christmas finally arrived, we were fully prepared for all of the festivities.

With the first star visible in the sky on Christmas Eve, Father brought a Christmas tree into the house. It was dark-green and had traces of snow and frost on its branches. It was also freshly scented. We were really happy when we decorated it. We placed hay upon the table, where the icons stood, and next to them we added Christmas puddings made from wheat or rice, with nuts and raisins and boiled, juicy fruits. Mother set the table with a candle in the middle. Then, she served us the traditional twelve dishes. We sang the carols and danced round the tree. It did not matter to us that our house was so small. The two little windows looked out over a dark and stormy night. Cut off in our own little world, happiness filled our home.

On Christmas Day we went to church. Mother sang in the choir, and I stood by her side. I loved it there: the choir's beautiful singing; Father dressed in his shining chasuble; the congregation in their best clothes. The whole world seemed to be a great festive place where all people showed goodness and kindness. After the service, we ate a rich Christmas dinner – with all of the meats we had missed over the past six weeks. Father and Mother were in a festive mood and smiled happily. We were happy too. In the evening, we went out carol singing. Groups of children went from one house to the next, knocking at the windows to ask for the owners' blessings to sing. It was a joy to be welcomed and received at each and every home. We were given sweets, nuts and money. Some people gave us pyrohy – Ukrainian pasties, or pieces of hot sausage, and pancakes or buns. By the end of the evening, we came home with many pennies in our pockets and the many gifts that people had given to us. Most of all, we returned with a joy in our hearts that would live with us until the end of our days.

Spring, too, brought its own special beauty. The slushy snow gradually gave way to the first patches of green grass. We sang and skipped around. The older girls in the village knew the traditional spring songs, and we could hear them singing on Sundays in the square in front of the church. Seven weeks before Easter, it was Lent. Each day, the church bells rang out with what I remember to be sad but very melodious tunes. Every evening, Father prepared himself for the service which would take place the following morning. It was then such a delight to see him return home. He would wear a long, brown cassock with his gold cross on his chest. His auburn hair was nearly always slightly curled over his inspired and serene face, and his big, brown eyes shone with a heavenly light. He would kiss us all, and the scent of incense from the church added to the special joy we would feel.

People wore dark garments during Lent, and they went to church very quietly. They prepared themselves for Confession and Holy Communion on Saturdays, but they still brought sweets and homemade biscuits for us whilst we played in the garden. They were all so very kind, and we loved to see them arrive.

The last week before Easter was about preparations that had to be done. Mother baked the paska – Ukrainian Easter cake – and she did this twice: once on Monday and once on Thursday. It was almost an all-day procedure as paska was made with yeast and had to be rich and very soft. If it was successfully baked, it indicated a happy, new season ahead. These cakes were many and were baked in different moulds. Mother cooked twice because she had no other time available during the week. She gave most of the cakes to the poor and lonely people on Easter Saturday. In exchange, she would ask them to remember our dead relatives in their prayers. Everything in the house also had to be cleaned. It was the time for a very thorough spring cleaning where all the covers had to be washed, and everything in the house had to be decorated with bright, new trimmings.

The festivities started fully on Thursday night – Maundy Thursday. Special candles were made for each member of the family. They were large, yellow, wax candles trimmed with white paper to stop the wax from dripping onto the floor, and they were in the shape of flowers. Everyone then had to wear clean clothes in order to remain symbolically clean for the year ahead. It was a solemn occasion, and we went into the dark and quiet church where a high pulpit had been erected in the centre. Father was dressed in black and silver vestments and read the twelve verses of the Passion and Crucifixion of Christ. Between each verse, the choir sang the Maundy Thursday psalms, and everyone in the church prayed with their candle in their hands. The service lasted a very long time. At the end, the candles were not put out but were carried home through the dark. It was considered to be good luck to bring a lit candle home. On the doorstep, and in each room, the candles were then made into crosses to keep the family safe from evil powers. The rest of the night was then spent quietly in a solemn and religious mood.

The next day was Good Friday, and there were church services in the morning and the afternoon. They were beautiful. At the end of each of these services, it was the custom to pray and ask God to grant a certain favour. As an offering, some people placed money on the collection plate, and some brought small gifts.

Saturday's preparations for Easter Sunday would then last all day. Homes now had to be so clean that surfaces sparkled; food had to be baked and roasted; Easter eggs had to be painted, and the best food for the blessing of the Easter breakfast basket had to be ready. Once this work had been done, Mother went to the Easter Saturday morning service. She was happy when she returned and said: 'They sang the psalm about Jesus Christ, the risen Lord.' She then added the final touches to the basket which looked splendid with its paska, coloured eggs, kovbasa, roast meat, ham cheese, butter and salt. The blessing was at Sunday morning's early service.

I shall never forget my earliest memories of an Easter service. An all-night service was usually held in the Ukrainian Orthodox Church from midnight. I begged my mother to take me there, but she refused. After continually pleading, she promised to wake me up and take me there later in the night. Having given me her promise, she kissed me good night and I went to sleep.

Sometime later, I woke up. The house was quiet, and only the little, red night-light was burning. I began to think that my mother had not kept her promise, so I got out of bed, dressed myself and decided to go to the church by myself.

I tried the door, but it was locked. A padlock was hanging

on the outside, and I realised that to open the door I would need a key. I went to the drawer where I found a whole bunch. There was a space beside the door and I pushed my little hand into it and tried to fit the key into the lock. It was difficult and I tried my best, but I struggled. How long I was there, hopelessly attempting to get out, I do not know, but I was trying to do the impossible as I had not chosen the right key. At the time, I thought that any key could open any lock. Suddenly, I heard my mother cry out from the other side. She unlocked the padlock and opened the door to see me standing on a stool.

'Why didn't you take me to the church?' I cried, as she carried me back across the room.

'My poor darling,' she whispered so as not to wake my brother and sister, 'I did not want to wake you up. Come. We will now go to church together.' She then dressed me properly, looked at my brother and sister who were both fast asleep, and then led me quietly from the house.

'I thought you were a burglar at the door,' she said, once we were outside, 'you gave me such a shock!' She held my hand gently. Even in the dark, I could see she was smiling. She was happy because I was safe.

The Easter service which I then saw for the first time in my life was magnificent. There were bright lights, embroidered cloths, clouds of incense, and in the middle of the church in front of the altar stood a carved and triumphant figure of the risen Jesus Christ. He had an expression of goodness on his face. Father was dressed in silvery-white vestments and went round the church with a shining, gold censer. He greeted everyone with the Easter message: 'Christ has risen!' They all replied: 'Indeed He has risen!' It was wonderful. The choir sang joyful psalms and I did not feel in the slightest bit sleepy all night. The whole experience of that evening was so wonderful, it still lives with me. I loved the cheerful Easter psalms and learned them all. Later, whenever I felt sad, I sang them and felt better for it, and whenever anything good happened in my life I sang them again. From that night onwards, I felt Easter was the most wonderful religious festival of the year.

At home, we waited for Father to return. Anatoly and Nadiya had woken up and were dressed in their best clothes.

Mother lit the candle on the table, and burned incense by the icons. The house was soon full of the mixed scent of incense, food and the freshness of spring. In those early hours of the morning, we ate our blessed Easter breakfast together. We started with the eggs and paska, and we were allowed to eat as much as we wanted. We had a short sleep and then played out all day, taking the Easter eggs with us. We met our friends in the village, and climbed the bell tower where any one of several bell ringers would play the joyful melodies of Easter Day. People then came to the evening service and gave us more Easter eggs and sweets. The whole day seemed to be an endless festival.

Spring had arrived bringing all the gifts of nature: the warmth of the sun, a gentle breeze, and the first flowers. After such a long winter, we were delighted to be out in the garden again. We ran around and climbed up the steps. I read the names on the tombstones again, and we played happily between them. The church itself stood like a citadel, protecting and guarding us, but it was not for long.

Sad and disturbing times were closing in. When the parishioners came to visit my father, they had troubled faces and asked him what they should do. Father was helpless. People were being arrested, their properties were being confiscated, and such exorbitant taxes were being demanded that nobody could pay them. My friends at school whispered sad stories about their fathers, and they often cried. I was beginning to see for myself how property and possessions were being taken away from the villagers by the Village Council. The cows – the main source of human nourishment – were now being led away. People went after them, pleading to have them given back, but all was in vain. These early impressions of people suffering filled us with sorrow, but the joys of life somehow prevailed: innocence still safeguarded our happy childhood.

Chapter 5

Spring turned into summer and we were soon celebrating Whit Sunday. The church and each village house had to be decorated with green branches which were cut from maple, oak or other local trees. Our floor was covered with scented grass, and the whole house itself began to look like a glorious garden. My mother's mother, Grandma Nadiya, came to stay with us, and I watched as they baked together. Our family was happily gathered. The church service which followed was long, and at the end there was a procession round the church for which everyone had brought flowers. Father was dressed in Whit Sunday's traditional, green vestments, and stood surrounded by a raised sea of flowers which he would then bless. This was one of the most beautiful images I will never forget. Some people then dried their flowers for use in times of illness: others kept them in the house to guard them against evil spirits. Whit Sunday's festivities lasted for two days, and people were happy to enjoy the break from their springtime work in the fields.

One of the main festivals of the summer soon followed: the Festival of St John the Baptist – known as Ivana Kupala, in Ukraine. During the morning of the 7th of July, all the girls would go to the rye and wheat fields to pick wild flowers – especially the cornflowers. I went with them and gathered big bunches and made garlands from them. In the evening, the boys and girls would meet each other on all the streets. In the old days, they used to make a small bonfire to jump over, but in my time we had to make do with jumping over a tall nettle instead. We laughed and joked and sang our favourite songs, and we jumped over the nettle until late into the evening.

The previous evening had been equally memorable and enchanting. Girls went to the river to drop their garlands into the water to foretell their future. If the water took the garland away, it meant that the girl would be married somewhere away from the place where she lived, but if the garland sank, it was a bad omen. Gorse was in bloom and anyone who picked the flowers at night would go on to find hidden treasures. Having heard all of the stories, my young imagination conjured up pictures of dark woods, a miraculous flower, a hand stretched out to pick it, and an open treasure chest glittering with gold, silver, diamonds and rubies – such as I had never seen in my life. The events of St John the Baptist's Festival live like a fairytale in my memory, and each time I think back to those summer evenings, I feel so happy that I again think of the fairytale coming true.

Every summer, we would go to visit Grandma Nadiya. It

was thirty kilometres to Krolevets Town where she and Grandpa Ivan lived. Grandpa – Fr Ivan Cherniavsky – was also an Orthodox priest. The journeys there were wonderful. Father took the reins and drove us, whilst the rest of us would sit on the cart of freshly-cut hay. Our grandparents lived in a beautiful house which had somehow stayed free from ruin and confiscation. By visiting them I was able to glimpse another kind of life where beauty and prosperity had not only been created, it had been maintained, too.

Times were hard and all grown-ups were worried, but as far as we – the children – were concerned, Grandma and Grandpa still had a beautiful home. They had tasty food, the most elegant crockery and silver cutlery. They also had beautiful furniture in spacious rooms. Their garden was full of flowers, and a river even flowed through the end of it. It was such a great joy for us to run around and play by that river, and to then go sailing in a boat with Grandpa, that we always looked forward to our visits there with great excitement.

Our home was on the other side of the Desna, and when it was time to go to our grandparents for another visit, Father told us that we would be going there by ship. It sounded so unusual. We would have to go to the shore with him and wait until the ship arrived. He would then return home by himself because he was needed in the parish. Mother packed everything for the journey and off we went, but no ship came, and nobody knew when the next one was due.

We returned to the river on the following day, and then again on the day after that, until finally, one fine afternoon, a little steamer appeared in the distance. We ran to the edge of the river and began waving our handkerchiefs until it came ashore. We ran across to it, and the sailors carefully placed a plank between the vessel and the steep river bank. One of them helped us on board, and we waved goodbye to Father. We then sailed away on the Desna's fast-flowing water.

It was fun to be aboard. We ran up and down, and explored every corner of every room. We made friends with other children, and when we rested, we watched the other passengers. We carried on until nightfall. Then, Mother put us to sleep on benches. She woke us up at dawn with the news that it was time to go ashore. The steamer moved across to one of the steep banks and stopped. The plank was extended, and before long, we were back on firm ground, standing in front of a wood.

The sun was only just rising, and the first birds were happily singing their morning songs. There was no one around, but as luck would have it, we disembarked on the wrong side of the river. We therefore had to cross back again. Even the parom was on the other side, so Mother started to call across the water until two men finally appeared and pulled the platform to our side. Despite this minor setback, I sensed that Mother was worried. She was a woman, alone with three small children, somewhere far from home. It was early in the morning, and there was nobody else around. It was dangerous. The men came to us without saying a word, but then helped us safely across. Mother paid them, and they then showed us where we could find a lift on a horse and cart for the rest of our journey. I carried the images of summer's distant sunrise, Mother's loneliness and worry, and the woodland by the river bank as an artistic picture in my memory. It had a sense of adventure and danger, and it also had a happy ending.

Grandma Nadiya welcomed us with open arms and was amazed to hear about our journey. She was a lovely woman – tall and stately and with grey hair which was now turning white. She pinned it up in a coil. Her long skirts were always dark, and her blouses were trimmed with lace. She was in charge of the house and home where Grandpa only seemed to play a small part. He came back and went out again, but he always spoke to us kindly. His hobby was to go fishing, and when the parish was not taking up his time, he could always be found sitting by the riverside with his rod.

Grandma made wonderful dinners. Her plates, cups and saucers were so beautiful that I would never forget them. Many years later, when I ended my journey in England, I thought I saw them again in a large store in Bradford called Brown Muff. I was poor when I arrived, but I went into that store a few more times just to look at them to remember Grandma Nadiya. Unlike the crockery, I always knew she was unique and irreplaceable.

The week we spent with our grandparents was one of the happiest of my life. We ran around and explored every room of their house, and we explored their garden, too. We had entered another world where we met and received gifts from some of the finest people that came to dinner and supper with them. Each glimpse into a different person's life became a fragmented memory for the rest of my own, and these glimpses had made me feel as though everything was fine and beautiful. I was inspired to make my own home in Grandma's style, even though it would be a very long time before I could afford to have anything like she ever had. I would always aspire to this and I admired other peoples' homes, too. Grandpa Ivan died shortly after our visit and left Grandma Nadiya to live on her own for many more years. I was her favourite granddaughter and she promised to give me all her precious possessions. I loved her and Grandpa, very much. They were always with me somewhere in the background of my whole existence, and they remained the inspiration behind so many of my creative ideas.

Our return journey home was as adventurous as our arrival. In the early hours of the morning we went to the Desna, but we spent all day waiting for the steamer to arrive. Grandma and Mother sat on the shore whilst we ran and played with the local children. We disappeared into their gardens for apples and cucumbers, and watched out just in case the steamer suddenly appeared. It was almost sunset when a little ship could be seen puffing a cloud of smoke, and it came rapidly towards us. We screamed with joy and waved until it turned its nose in our direction. The sun was setting, and in its golden light, Grandma was left by herself on the steep bank of the river. She stood there in her dark-grey dress and waved her white handkerchief at us. We floated further away, deeper and deeper into the night.

We sailed for many hours, and hoped to be home by morning. Father had already made plans to meet us at the shore. Just before dawn, however, we came to a sudden, bumpy stop. We soon learned that we had run aground and had become stuck in shallow water. Originally, the ship had been built for the vast Dnipro River and was very large and heavy. A recent drought had also made the Desna's water shallower than usual. We now had to wait until a smaller boat could rescue us, and Mother had no extra supply of food as she had expected to be home by morning. There was also no food on board the ship, so we became hungry. Some of the men swam ashore and went to the nearest town which was Korop. They brought back some bread and milk, and as we were the only children on board, they gave some to us. Mother wanted to pay them but they refused to accept her money. Meanwhile, everyone else was worried about how long we would have to stay there, and they were also concerned about us – the children. The night had been long, and now the day, too. It also became very hot, so some of the men went swimming whilst others waded across parts of the river to make a show of how shallow the water was.

In the evening, we went to sleep and it was still dark when Mother woke us up to say that another ship was finally coming to the rescue. Everyone rushed, disembarked and then climbed aboard that smaller ship which, I remember, was called The Pioneer. The people were considerate to Mother with her small children, and they helped us to make our way safely across. The Pioneer could not take all the passengers, but with its lighter load it could move away from the shallow water and slide back into the Desna's deeper current.

It was dawn when we woke up again, and the ship approached the shore. Father was waiting for us. He waved, and then helped us to disembark. How glad we were to see him. He took little Nadiya in his arms and carried her all the way home. The rest of us walked sleepily and listened to Mother explaining what had happened. In turn, Father told us of his evening's wait with his friend, and how he had returned again and again during the day, wondering what had happened to us. He had spent a second night by the river, hoping to see us arrive, and had even made a bonfire so that the ship's captain would be able to see where to stop. Then he told us we had been beaten there by a fox which was picking at egg shells. Listening to Father's story, I imagined the bonfire at the dead of night with the river flowing on one side and the dense, black forest on the other. I tried to imagine what the fox had looked like as I had never seen one before, and I wondered if Father and his friend had been frightened. The picture in my mind became vivid – as though I had been there with them.

It was a lovely feeling to be home again. Our little house seemed so comfortable, so neat and so dear that the thoughts of Grandma's beautiful home soon faded away. I was happy to return to our one room where our possessions were nothing more than bare necessities. I began to understand that happiness could be found in a small and poor place, just as long as there was room for love there, too. I loved Grandma's house, but I was happy to be at home in ours where I could feel Mother and Father's caring hands when they undressed us, washed us, fed us and put us to bed. I could see their loving glances and hear their quiet whispers, all in that peaceful room where the little, red lamp would burn. The following day, our life went on as usual. We met our friends and told them about the fox. The story fascinated everyone. We then ran around the garden again, and picked ripe apples and pears.

Autumn approached, and the leaves began to turn golden-yellow. It was the time of year when mushrooms began to grow in the forest. The villagers collected them and talked about them endlessly. We, too, went to pick them. Mother prepared the baskets the night before, and then early in the morning Father woke me up. After I was fully dressed and had eaten some breakfast, we went.

The morning was bright, the sun was rising in the East and the air was cool. We walked all the way to the river and entered the forest through the first trees – which I thought looked like the gates to a sleeping palace. The tall, straight, scented pines had already laid a soft carpet beneath our feet. The forest was so enchanting, that even if we would find no mushrooms, it was a pleasure just to be there. We eventually found plenty, and it was a joy to see their heads poking up through the pine needles. We picked them and carefully placed them in our baskets, and there were so many of them. We were there very early, and nobody else was out gathering that morning. We kept getting lost so we shouted to each other and joyously listened to our echoes in the vast surrounds. Higher up the hillside we were again able to see the Desna in full flow. The dawn chorus was in full song, and above us the sun continued to rise higher and higher. With baskets full, we happily returned home.

Father began to prepare a bonfire in the garden, and Mother washed the mushrooms. She then fried them over the fire. Anatoly and Nadiya, meanwhile, began to jump around, and before long, we were having a picnic. The wild mushrooms were so tasty, so nourishing and so appetising that we could have carried on eating them late into night.

Autumn also delivered plenty of apples and pears. Mother pickled them in a barrel for winter and would frequently stew them to make a tasty dessert. Pickled apples also tasted lovely on their own, especially on frosty days. They were kept in the cellar and were made to last until the end of winter.

The villagers liked my father and it was a custom to bring gifts to the priest, especially before the religious festivals. Our life in the little caretaker's house by the church reminded people that it was difficult to bring up three little children, so they sympathised with both of my parents. They often brought spare eggs, cuts of meat from their freshly-killed pig, cheese, or even a piece of butter – which was considered to be a great luxury.

Mother added all the extra touches to make our life comfortable. Meals were plentiful and the occasions were joyous. We all sat together at the table and chatted about the day's events. Usually, I spoke about my school and my friends as I loved school, and I was proud of my good marks and my teacher's praise. During winter's evenings, Mother continued to read stories. She nearly always sat us by the fireplace – by the warm walls of the stove, and read from a big book. Sometimes, she'd just tell them by heart. I loved to hear them and begged her to tell us more. Father would be busy writing at the table, but he was with us. He was close-by, graceful and calm. We felt protected and happy, but then the really bad times, which had threatened us for so long, finally arrived.

Chapter 6

I was nine years old when the famine of 1932-33 began in Ukraine. It was not a famine that happened by natural causes. It was death by deliberate starvation, and Ukrainians call it The Holodomor. It was murder. And it was murder on a massive scale. I remember hearing that we were being shown "a new and better way of life", but everyone knew it was a lie: nothing ever became better, and instead of seeing a better life, we began to see death. People who did not fit in with the Soviets' plans were imprisoned, deported or killed. The victims included women and children, and not just the men. Whole families perished. We could have been one of them. And the Holodomor of 1932-33 did not end so quickly, either. Death by starvation remained until the spring of 1934.

Ukraine's village life was being destroyed, and most of the things we had ever known and loved began to rapidly disappear. Of course, I was too young to understand exactly why it was all happening. After the harvest of 1932, we were able to buy bread then a wave of terror swept through the village.

Small groups of Communists went from house to house taking everything edible. All the crops were confiscated, as were the farm animals, domestic animals, vegetables, corn and flour. Even the mixed dough, which was used to bake the bread, was thrown out onto the mud in order to leave the villagers with nothing.

Many well-established farmers were made homeless, and in the middle of the winter they were thrown out of their homes. All other villagers were forbidden from giving them shelter. Many families were sent to Siberia, where most of them perished. How many cries I heard, how many sights I saw, how much despair and heartbreak I watched – I would never wish it upon anyone. Little children, younger than me, were thrown out into the snow. After them came their mothers who desperately clung to their remaining hard-earned possessions. They were pushed violently to the frozen ground by the Communists. Weeping and lamenting, the women begged to be left some food, but they were sent out to die following the insults or indifference of the mighty "Party Apparachiks". I can still clearly remember their faces – big, red and fat, with glassy eyes and powerful stares. Everyone feared them, and everyone knew of the injustice they were doing as they could clearly be seen taking the property of others for themselves. Their sheds were full of hens and geese, cows, pigs, sheep and horses. "They ate and drank until the fat was running down their chins". At least, that is what I heard people say, and as I walked through the streets of the village, my imagination even tried to picture those men with fat dripping from their mouths.

Terror reigned in the village, and the Communists continued to eat and drink, and they did so without any consideration for anyone but themselves. Armed with revolvers, they went through the village to petrify and intimidate everyone. In the evenings, people were afraid to put their lights on, and they did not dare to open their doors for fear of their lives. Nonetheless, the gangs would not hesitate to kick the doors down and step up their terror. They went to houses, seemingly at random, and searched for gold and silver, food and grain. They also searched for leather from which people made their shoes and boots. They also looked for anything else of value that may have been hidden away or stored. Everything now had to be handed over to the State. They beat people for personal pleasure, and played Russian roulette with the barrels of their revolvers, putting them into the mouths of their helpless victims. They took fathers and elderly grandfathers outside their homes to stand barefooted, dressed only in their nightclothes. The bitter cold was at least minus twenty degrees centigrade, and in many places the snow was as high as the houses were. In these conditions, the Communists demanded to be shown where grain was hidden. The cries and laments of the families could be heard across the whole village. Their terror continued, and there was no escaping from it.

The children at school began to tell stories to each other of how "they" – the Communists – had tortured their fathers. Some fathers had been killed, and others had been taken away. Some of the children then cried, but the teacher was too frightened to console them. Some children were even taken away from the classroom. In the middle of a lesson, one of the Communists would typically push his way through the door without knocking. He would call the name of a child. Without a single word to the teacher, he would take the child away. We knew it meant the child's family was being deported to Siberia. The children were put onto a sledge with their parents, and in the cold and harsh conditions, they were driven to the nearest railway station some 30 kilometres away. They were then packed into a freight train for the long and exhausting journey to Siberia which was about 1,000 kilometres from where we lived. Most of those people died on their journey. Many fathers died, forced to do hard labour in mines or forests. Mothers perished with them whilst trying to provide shelter for their children. It was most probable that nearly all of them perished before the end of their first winter there.

I had a friend called Halya whose big, brown eyes had always reminded me of two ripe cherries. She was taken from the classroom and sent to Siberia with her father, mother and two little sisters. Her mother died there, and one of her sisters, too. Halya grew up there, but then disappeared. I never saw her again, and I never saw her sister, either. Her father came back to the village some years later, and it was only his physical strength that had saved him. He was strong, and it was almost as though the hardship had strengthened him still further, but his black hair had now turned grey, and the look in his eyes was impersonal. He looked vacantly at the village, and as though not finding anything more in his native place of birth, he went away and nobody ever saw him again. When I think of his wonderful family and his orderly yard full of animals and his lovely, little house on the corner of two main roads, I then also remember how the best, the wisest and most capable people were so cruelly ruined and destroyed by the Soviet Communists and their system.

One evening, a storm was brewing. The wind grew stronger, and outside I could see the snow being swept up into dense clouds. Heaven and Earth seemed to entwine in a devilish dance. Finally, when darkness fell, "they" came to us.

Mother was just about to serve supper when the door was opened and a tall, dark man wearing a grey, fur hat appeared from the cold. He had a sharp and evil stare. He moved his hand slowly and took a revolver from his inside pocket. Mother, who was holding my little sister in her arms, screamed. I started to cry, and Anatoly, not understanding what was happening, also screamed from fear. Pointing the gun at Father, the man ordered him to get out of the house, but Father stood tall and noble, and remained dignified in the face of this cruel threat. He then looked at us, made the sign of the cross, and went outside. Mother screamed again, but her screams were lost in the wailing of the wind. There was nowhere we could go, so she grabbed us and fell to her knees in front of the icons in the corner of the room.

29

'Pray for Father, pray my dear, little children. Only God can save him now. Dear God, please save him!'

'God, dear God, please save our father,' we repeated again and again.

Set amongst the icons was a large picture of Jesus Christ. He was praying on his knees in the Garden of Gethsemane before his arrest, torture and crucifixion. In answer to His prayers, a chalice appeared in Heaven foretelling of His future suffering. The picture was brightly-coloured and beautiful. The light from the little, red lamp shone onto the face of Jesus, and His face seemed to be alive – gentle and humble, yet expectant of mercy nonetheless. We stayed on our knees, and I lost track of time when suddenly, we heard the door open and our dear father came back into the house. He was pale and shaking. We ran to him, and Mother cried:

'You are alive! Oh, God, you are still alive!'

'Daddy, Daddy!' We cried, putting our arms round his knees.

'It's the icon,' Mother pointed to the picture of Jesus, 'it must have saved you. It has saved you, thank God!'

'We prayed, Daddy, we prayed and prayed,' I whispered.

'My dears,' Father said quietly, 'I thought I would never see you again.'

He sat on a chair and told us how he had miraculously stayed alive. The Communist had taken him to the wall of the church. There was a rope hanging from the bell tower, so Father attempted to ring the bells to alert the villagers, but the man shouted at him and said that more of his men were standing nearby, so nobody would be able to save him. Then, he pushed Father against the church wall and raised his gun:

'It is now the end for you,' he said. Father asked him for his permission to pray.

'You have prayed enough,' hissed the Communist with anger. 'Your God cannot help you. Now say goodbye to your life. Nobody wants to see you in the village any longer.'

He then shoved the barrel of the revolver into my father's mouth. It was the usual way of doing things. My school friends had already told me similar stories.

Father trembled as he told us what happened next. He continued quietly:

'I prayed with all my soul, and all of that time I thought

about you. I thought it was the end, but when he pulled the trigger nothing happened. He pulled it again and then started swearing: "It's because of the stormy weather!" He hissed, and then swore again and pushed me away from the wall. "Go!" he shouted, "but you must quit the village within twenty-four hours!" I can't remember how I came back to the house: I can't. I thought he would then try to shoot me in the back, but he only shouted again: "You must leave the village within twenty-four hours! Do you hear me? Twenty-four hours!" Then, when I came inside and I saw you praying, I realised that God must have saved me.'

He paused, and then added: 'We must leave the village tomorrow.' He put his hands on our heads and sighed: 'Poor children, what will happen to you next? What fate awaits you?'

Little Nadiya, who had been asleep in her cradle, suddenly began to cry. Mother went to comfort her and took Anatoly with her. Father took me in his arms and carried me to my bed. His hands were so gentle. I put my arms round his neck. It was dark but we dared not put the light on.

'Let us hope he will not come back here again,' Mother said.

'You must go to sleep.' Father said to me, as he gently lowered me to my bed. 'Don't worry. God will help us.'

My father then went back to the icons where the lamp continued to burn, lighting the face of Jesus and the golden chalice in the dark sky. He prayed, and I looked at him. He was so dignified, and he was always so full of goodness. What had he done to be threatened with a pistol on this dark and stormy night? Why did someone want to shoot him? Why had this happened when people liked and loved him so much, and when he had never done anything wrong to anyone? How I liked to see him whenever he came home from church after a service. The lingering scent of the church was so sweet and holy that it never failed to wrap me in its spiritual comfort. Father always looked so serene. His big, brown eyes shone with his goodness, and he greeted everybody with his gentle smile. He would bend down and kiss us, and other children, too. Often, other people from the village would wait for him and he would sit on his chair by the icons and talk to them about their needs and troubles. His eyes looked at everybody

31

with great love and understanding, and from time to time they would also look upwards as though seeing a greater light and purpose in life. He was dedicated to serving God and God's people. Now, those awful people – the Communists, who were hated by everybody else around us, were stopping him from performing his daily duties.

'Daddy,' I said aloud, 'what will happen to us?'

My voice surprised him. He came to me and put his warm hand on my head and replied without hesitation:

'God will help us. Go to sleep my dear. Strengthen yourself with a good sleep.'

He then kissed me gently on the forehead and went back to his books. He began putting them all together, ready to be packed.

I could not sleep. After Nadiya fell asleep again, Anatoly lay there silently, then Mother put out the small night-light and the room went dark and very quiet. Although it was late, I had the feeling that my mother and father were still sitting together. Indeed, I was soon able to hear them whispering. They were discussing our future plans. I could not tell what they were saying, but I knew that our life was about to change yet again. I surrendered myself to the dark and let my imagination take hold. I now knew that the life we were living was not normal. I then tried to picture what a normal life was, but my mind no longer had a picture to show me.

Why did we have to go? Where could we go? Recently, I had heard Father say that there were no more churches open. All the priests were being deported. One of Father's friends was a priest in the neighbouring village, and I remembered him. He had once lifted me high above his head, and we laughed together. He was now dead. The Communists crushed him under a very heavy log. They sat on the log one by one to add more weight to it, and in the process they laughed together until he died. When I tried to picture that horrible scene, I became frightened. He had been such a kind and happy priest. He had talked to Father so knowledgeably, so peacefully and wisely, that he had left Father full of praise for him. So why had he been killed? My mind was tormented. I turned restlessly in my bed until Mother came to me to ask why I couldn't sleep. I did not tell her of my thoughts. I just clung to her and sobbed. She comforted me until I was quiet.

Then, she gently placed my head back on the pillow and stayed with me until all the events of the past day began to disappear. With my thoughts still unsettled, sleep eventually did take hold.

We left the village of Lushnyky and went to live in the village of Podolov where my father's parents – Granny Agathea and Granddad Ivan – were both living. Podolov, too, was not free from any of these troubles, but news soon came about the people we had left behind in Lushnyky. They could take no more of the cruelty and suffering there and had successfully managed to bring five or six of the Communists to trial. Amongst them was the man who would have killed my father. His name was Kulyk and he worked in the Village Council. A man called Mynka – the head of the collective farm also had to stand trial, as did one of his committee members – a man called Denys. The trial lasted for about a week. It was held in the Village Council's building and the court officials arrived from the district town of Shostka. The men were charged and found guilty of "znushchennya" – cruelty and mockery, and they were each given a prison sentence of up to two years: they only served a few months.

Father decided we should return to Lushnyky as new officials had been put in charge there, but little else had changed. We had no bread and the potatoes had all been eaten, and there was nothing left there for Mother to cook. The other villagers had no food either. Gone, too, were their small, beautiful and generous gifts that we were used to seeing. They had nothing left to give.

With the first signs of spring, we had no choice other than to begin gathering leaves from the trees, or the edible grass and weeds from the fields. We searched for sorrel leaves, and we ate the leaves from linden trees as they were not bitter. Mother checked our fingers to see if they were swelling. It was a danger sign, but she never said anything more about them and continued to boil large pans of thin soup. We ate but we remained hungry from the lack of proper food. Our bellies began to swell and we looked disfigured.

I was very thin, so my parents decided to send me back to my grandparents in Podolov village. They had a cow there and it was hoped that I would recover on fresh milk. After arriving at Granny Agathea's, I soon discovered that she had no food in her house, and the cow was no longer producing milk that spring because it was barren. Granddad Ivan was a noble and hardworking farmer, but he had now lost all of his land, including all the produce from the last harvest: everything had been confiscated and taken by the State to a collective farm. My father's sister, Auntie Chrystyna, lived with them, and she took me to the valley to collect some herbs and leaves with which Granny could boil some soup. There was nothing, and no sorrel leaves either as people had now gathered them to the very last. They had been the best remaining ingredient for soup. Without sorrel leaves, or potatoes, or any kind of meat, the soup was just water and weeds. It was tasteless, and it was of little use for our survival.

Auntie Chrystyna collected some tiny apples from the apple trees and chopped them into little pieces to put into the soup, but Granny was so devout that she would not have the apples in the pan as it was forbidden to eat apples until the Harvest Festival on the 19th of August, and that was a very long time away. It was especially forbidden for mothers who had lost a child. Granny had married at sixteen years of age and had lost eleven of her thirteen children, so she refused to touch an apple or a pear before then. That is how it was with her, and that is how she would always insist on doing things, even in that time of starvation. I had to admire her piety and her strength of character. She had once been a proud housewife with plenty of food and nourishing meals to put on the table for her family: now she had nothing. No matter how much she wanted to please me, she could find no food. She had the weed soup, and I had the soup with the added bits of apple.

I longed to go home to my parents, but Granny and Auntie Chrystyna begged me to stay for Whit Sunday, which was also the day of the Patron Saint of their village. Granny promised to cook something special for that day, something she had saved for the Harvest Festival. I therefore agreed to stay, but there were no more services in their once beautiful church. Festivals were something from the distant past, and starving people who wandered and strayed in search of food were to be seen everywhere. I remembered Whit Sunday from the years before, the long services in church, many

34

visiting priests, and hundreds upon hundreds of people – all well-dressed, festive and happy. I recalled the toys and sweets for sale at stalls near to the church. There were houses full of rich guests, parties… and dinners. Those days had gone, and seemingly forever. Village life had almost completely died. The weather was wet and cloudy, and it was as though Heaven was grey, and sad, and in tune with the fate of the land and its people.

Granny eventually managed to squeeze a small amount of milk from the cow, and having saved some corn flour she made a vermicelli pudding. It was the most delicious meal I had ever eaten. What had gone wrong in the lives of the adults? Once upon a time, I used to eat Granny's nutritious meals, cooked and served on a large table in the dining room. Now the food had gone. Even her wardrobe had been confiscated and taken away because of "unpaid taxes", and then "even more taxes". Granddad was now becoming weak and indifferent. He sat on the stove smoking his home-grown tobacco, and he looked through the window into the far distance. He seemed to have given in, unable to understand what was happening around him. Granny understood everything, but her greatest worry remained the cooking: there was nothing to eat, and nowhere to find food.

I wanted to go back to my parents. I missed them so much, and I hoped that I would receive something to eat at home. It rained constantly, so Granny refused to let me go. Day after day, I sat by the window watching as the rain made bubbles in the streams which ran across the yard. I wished for it to stop, but Granny told me not to worry, and to stay a little longer.

Finally, it stopped raining. Auntie Chrystyna took me to the market in town and we found the driver of a horse and cart from our village who agreed to take me home. Sitting on the soft hay in the cart, I thought about Granny. She had cried when she said goodbye to me, and she had called me her "poor child". Why did she call me "poor"? I had no idea. I was that innocent. I only knew that I was very, very hungry.

That was the last time I saw Granddad: he died in the coming winter, having never recovered from the starvation and ruin. Granny and Auntie Chrystyna were then forced to leave their home, as they could no longer pay their taxes, and they moved to Krolevets Town where they found a small room. They survived there in squalid, impoverished conditions. Even now, their room makes me shiver when I think about it. It was small, dark and cold, and full of smoke from the stove which was faulty. Their lovely house, with large rooms and big windows, surrounded by an orchard which Granddad had planted himself, had now gone. As children, we witnessed these events and always wondered why they were happening.

When I arrived home, Mother was shocked when she saw me because I was now even thinner than before. She cried and gave me some kind of a scone. It was made from a mixture of tree leaves and weeds. It was bitter and tasted horrible. I couldn't eat it. I can remember the taste, even now. The red flame still flickered in front of the icons in the corner, and Father still sat at the table with his books. From time to time, he looked up, helplessly, at his starving family. I went to bed hungry, and I cried quietly by burying my face in the pillow.

The very next morning, I heard many stories about those who had died from hunger. The whole village seemed to be quiet and submerged in sadness. Children were out gathering herbs and weeds for their mothers to cook. The only meal now available to anyone was a big pan of thin, herbal soup. I wanted to see a friend, but her father was very weak and unwell. So Mother would not let me. She did not want me to go into his house. She guarded us from seeing terrible sights such as people dying, or the grief and desperation that people were going through. Like any other mother, she wanted our childhood to be unspoilt – even in those desperate times. Father buried parishioners, but they could not pay him because they simply had nothing left to give. I understood, even in those early years of my life, how dependent we are on communal life, and upon each other, yet the "communal life" of collectivisation and Communism only brought death. From that moment onwards, every "normal" villager I knew became dearer to me. We had to leave Lushnyky again, and we moved to Chepliyivka, but life in Chepliyivka was no better and Father was forced to move out yet again.

It was winter, early in 1934. I woke up one morning and saw the house empty and bare. The icons, pictures and curtains had all gone. Mother was carefully wrapping the mirror in some linen to place in a case. Anatoly was moving about collecting nails from the floor, and Nadiya was playing with a metal tray. Anatoly was the first to notice that I was awake. Full of excitement he exclaimed:

'We are going to live in a town! There are many shops and they have cars there!'

Mother came to me, but I hardly recognised her. She had cried so much that her face was swollen. Her eyes were still wet with her tears.

'Get up, my dear,' she said, 'we didn't want to wake you as you were so tired. Get washed and dressed. There is some breakfast in the oven. Then you can help me.'

'Oh, Mama, you have been crying. Where are we going? What will happen to us now?'

'We have to leave, today,' she explained. 'The church has been locked and sealed, and the keys have been taken from the church caretaker. The building will no longer be open, and we have to leave for another village. It is final. Nobody can help us, and we must leave before dark. Father has gone out to look for a horse and a sledge.'

As though in answer to her words, a gust of wind blew some snow against our little window. The weather was stormy, and the house was dark from the surrounding heavy clouds.

'Mama, will we be able to travel in this weather?' I asked.

'We will have to, my dear,' she replied. 'You had better get up. It is getting late, and Father will be back soon with the horse.'

'But where are we going?' I asked, as I dressed.

'We will go to Krolevets,' Mother replied. 'Father has some friends there, and they may be able to help us. Grandma lives there, too, but I don't think there will be enough room for us. We shall have to find somewhere else.'

She sighed and turned away to continue packing. She didn't want me to see her tears. I helped her, and before long, Father returned. He was pale and looked disturbed.

'Nobody wants to take us. Not in this weather. They are all too frightened, and they don't want to travel in a snowstorm. What are we to do?' He lifted his eyes to the corner where the icons once hung. They had gone. Then he looked at us:

'My poor children, what will become of you?'

This time, Mother found her courage and replied calmly: 'Have something to eat and then you can try again and find someone. We will have finished packing everything by then. It is only eleven o'clock. The day is long, and we will manage to get to Krolevets by nightfall.'

Father drank some tea and continued: 'The people are terrified. Several families were visited last night. The church caretaker now says the days of the Church here are finally over, and he is frightened, too. Dear God!' He sighed and made the sign of the cross. He then left the house.

It was late in the afternoon before he returned. He announced that he had found a farmer who was willing to take us to Krolevets, and the horse and sledge would arrive at any minute. We had a drink of warm tea, and Mother dressed us in our warmest clothes. A man came inside the house and helped Father to take the cases and boxes. The sledge was full of hay. We snuggled in and Mother sat beside us. The baggage was fastened with a rope and our beds were put on top. A bucket of water was hanging from the side of the sledge for the horse to drink. We were ready to go.

For one final time, Father looked at the village church which would gradually fade from view in the storm. He made the sign of the cross again, and strode alongside the sledge. The farmer sat at the front and steered. I noticed how two tears fell from Father's eyes. They dropped onto his beard and froze, instantly.

'Where are you going, Father Stefan?' the villagers asked.

'Why are you leaving us?'

'Who are you leaving us for?'

As the villagers enquired, I noticed that they were also looking round. They were frightened should someone hear them. I, too, looked at the church for as long as I could. Standing alone, and surrounded by the snow, it seemed to have been abandoned, like an orphan. It was a beautiful creation, made by people, yet forbidden to exist in peace for those people. A sharp gust of wind then blew some snow into my eyes and made me forget about everything except my very existence.

Nadiya was a very frail child so Mother held her in her arms. She wrapped her and covered her face to shield her from the biting wind and snow. She also wrapped Anatoly, and then me, and begged us to protect ourselves to avoid getting frozen hands and feet. We had to shield our faces from the wind. Father walked beside the sledge, but only as far as the last house of the village. Then he turned around, made the sign of the cross one final time and bowed as though saying a thank you and goodbye to everything that he had loved so dearly. He then jumped onto the sledge and looked at us with love and compassion. My heart was with him completely.

'Wrap up well, children!' he said loudly. 'With God's help we will survive!' He pushed some hay towards us, protectively and unselfishly. His beard was already white and frozen with snow and icicles; his big eyebrows, too.

As we passed the fields, the wind blew harder and sharper. The road became increasingly difficult for the horse to walk, but the kind farmer encouraged us: 'Don't you worry! We will arrive before nightfall.'

I looked at him, sitting with his back to us. He was a large man and was dressed in a black coat and a worn-out, fur cap which covered his ears. Today, the farmer was our private driver. I knew him. His daughter went to school with me, and we often played together. He had many children and he was neither rich nor poor. He had not joined the collective farm, but he had managed to keep his horse. It was very good of him to help us, and he was not frightened. I was reassured that there were good people as well as bad, and there was a way to help people, even if it meant endangering oneself. How good our fellow Ukrainians were, I thought. They were simple, hardworking people. They had been farmers all of their lives, and they simply worked the land to earn food.

It was bitterly cold, and the journey we faced was long. Krolevets was approximately thirty kilometres away. We had been there often when visiting Father's parents who lived in Podolov, nearby. We had also shopped there, and had visited friends. We passed through the empty fields where the wind cut furrows in the snowdrifts. In the distance, a dark forest came into view and the farmer whipped his horse to go faster.

He spoke loudly, and with concern. He warned us: 'Let us hope there are no wolves around!'

I became very frightened. I had heard of wolves attacking people in winter, especially in snowstorms when they become very hungry. There were many wolves in the forest. They moved in packs and often came near to the village for their prey. People used to have guns to defend themselves, but nobody was allowed to have a gun now, and the only possible weapon would be flames from a fire. Even then, how could we make a fire in such a snowstorm?

As I thought about it, we reached the forest. The wind became quieter and the forest seemed to be made of two dark walls standing high over the road. I looked at the pine trees and felt calmer. I knew I had to be as strong as they were. Father was walking beside the sledge again, so I jumped into the snow and walked beside him.

'It's warmer walking than sitting on the sledge, my dear. Are you all right?' He took my hand.

'I'm not frightened!' I shouted through the wind.

Suddenly the farmer stopped. He pointed with his whip to his right-hand side, to where the forest was ending, and where little, black dots could be seen in the snow.

'Those are the wolves,' he said. 'For sure, they're the devils. You'd better all sit together and wrap yourselves in the hay! Hold on tight! I'll make the horse go faster!'

As soon as we were on the sledge he cracked his whip, and indeed, he made the horse run faster. The little, black dots were getting closer, and I soon recognised the four-legged, black animals which looked like big, wild dogs.

'My God!' exclaimed Mother. 'Don't let us perish!'

The pack of wolves came out onto the road and stood waiting for our arrival. The horse sensed the danger and became nervous. It kept lifting its head and whinnied in protest.

'It's all right! All right, my dear! Let's get closer,' said the farmer raising his whip. 'It is we who are going to frighten them!'

As he spoke to the horse, he pulled out a long stick from beneath his seat and wrapped a bundle of hay around the end. He then took a bottle of kerosene from his pocket and doused the bundle. He rubbed two stones together – a homemade lighter – that produced sparks which lit the hay. Holding the torch high above his head, he started to shout. The horse stood still, and we all sat quietly. I held my breath: Father prayed, and it seemed to be for ages. I did not dare to look from my hiding place, but in the end I heard a shot, and then the farmer's voice:

'There's someone hiding in the woods. It must be a runaway man with a gun. So, someone is still defending us? Thank God! The wolves have gone. Those devils! We're safe. Let's hope they don't come back again!'

As the horse moved on again, a man came out from the forest. He was dressed in rags. His face was unshaven and he carried a gun by his side. He came up to us and asked who we were. Seeing my father, he bowed his head and then looked at us with pity.

'Damn them for sending you out of the village in this weather. The scoundrels! We'll show them yet!'

'Are you alone?' asked the farmer. 'How do you manage to survive?'

'Better than in Siberia, that's for sure, but do you have any bread?'

Mother had some bread in her basket. Father gave it to the man and thanked him for saving us from the wolves. I noticed a faint smile on the man's face when he looked at me, and my brother and sister. His huge ragged figure bowed to Father again, and then disappeared into the forest.

'He's a hero,' said Father. 'We need them at times like these. He saved us, thank God. And so did you, Platon, with your fire. You'd thought of everything. Thank you. I won't ever forget you.'

Father then turned around: 'Are you all right, children? We will soon be out of the forest and let's hope we don't see any more wolves! Are you frozen? Rub your hands and don't forget your noses as well! We shall be all right, I promise you!' My father's optimism would live with me always.

Somehow, we finally arrived in Krolevets. It was almost dark, and we were all freezing, even though the storm had now subsided. The sky covered the town like a dark-blue carpet. It was full of silver stars, and a big moon was rising from behind the houses. The roads were clear and our sledge travelled quickly. At last we stopped, and Father asked us all

41

to wait as he knocked at the door of a small but pretty house with high steps at the front. The door opened and he went inside. A few minutes later, he reappeared with a stout man.

'Come inside, come in!' the man called. 'It is no good freezing outside! We will have to put the sledge in the neighbour's yard. These times are dangerous. I will ask the neighbour to let the farmer sleep in his house. It will be better that way.' He looked at me: 'Come on, girl!'

The man helped me up the steps. My feet were so cold I could no longer feel them. Mother carried Nadiya, and Father carried Anatoly to the doorway.

A beautiful blonde girl who was standing inside the doorway took my hand and then led me into the living room. She took my frozen garments from me. I glanced around. Where was I? Was I in paradise? Was I in a dream? It was such a beautiful house. The room was full of fresh, green flowers in shining plant pots, and the floor was red and covered with long, white rugs. There were exquisite pieces of furniture: a glass cupboard; a dresser full of ornaments and china; a large mirror; lovely, red, velvet curtains hanging all the way down to the floor. I stood there in a daze. It was as though I was dreaming, and the kind, beautiful girl looked like an angel. She asked me if any part of my body was still frozen. Mother then came in:

'She is bewildered by what she sees. Don't be surprised. She has never seen normal life. We have wandered from place to place and have recently lived in farmers' rooms or a caretaker's house. We lead a different life,' she sighed, 'but now, even our right to life is being denied. Come, my dear. Come and have something to eat.'

Mother took me by my hand and led me to the kitchen. There were rows of shining pans hanging on hooks over a large stove. A tall lady was serving soup to Anatoly and Nadiya, and she was speaking to Father:

'We told you to quit your vocation, a long time ago. It cannot lead to anything good in times like these. You see, we were right all along. What will you do now with three small children?'

Even I felt her reproach, and Mother looked down and responded quietly: 'We have hands, so we will use them to earn our living.'

'Thank you for giving us shelter for the night,' replied Father. He must have felt their reproaches most of all. 'We will find somewhere else to live tomorrow.'

'These are hard times,' repeated his friend, who smoked a pipe continuously. 'We don't want to get into trouble, and it is difficult with children.'

His three lovely daughters stood by and watched us eat the remains of their supper. They wore warm dresses and looked happy.

After supper, Mother rubbed our bodies with some oil in case we had been bitten by the frost. She wrapped us in blankets, and put us to sleep on top of the warm stove in the kitchen. Nadiya and Anatoly soon drifted off to sleep, but I could not. When everyone began to leave the room, I lifted my head and watched through the open door. I could see into a big bedroom where the three lovely daughters were getting ready to go to bed. They were like princesses.

Suddenly, I felt so sorry for us. Why did my parents have to go through such perils and so much suffering? Why couldn't we live comfortably like these people did? I assumed it was only because of Father's way of life. He wanted to serve God and His people and we had to follow him wherever he went to carry on with his life's work. Frightened again, I thought of the long journey through the storm with the wolves in the forest, and the man in rags who had saved us. Everything had been so terribly frightening. I started to cry, and I buried my face in the pillow. I continued crying quietly. Everything became mixed up, and it all felt like a wave gradually submerging me. One minute I was somewhere thinking of the past, and the next moment I was somewhere in the future thinking about the unknown life that lay ahead. The thoughts hammered on in my head for a long time until finally, sleep overcame me.

Chapter 7

Father woke up early, again knowing he would have to find a place for us to live. By dinner time he returned. He was a happier man and announced that he had found a house which was ready to move into. Our kind friends were glad to see us leave. They were frightened. We left their warm, hospitable

43

home and moved on to an empty, tiny, old house. As expected, for the middle of winter, the house was cold and damp. Father had already bought a cartload of firewood from the market, so Mother promptly lit the stove. Our possessions were brought inside by the farmer. We then caught up with our sleep. The following day, we cleaned the house and painted the walls. Mother decorated the room in her usual manner with our icons and pictures, and she placed the embroideries wherever there was a suitable space. She was good at restoring the visual comforts which we were used to seeing. After having registered us at the Town Council as newly-arrived residents, Father returned with some bread. It was 1934, and bread could only be obtained by using ration cards.

'We won't die from hunger now,' he said cheerfully, and he promptly gave us a piece of the "town bread", as he called it. We ate it eagerly on that first occasion.

As soon as we had settled, Mother took me and Anatoly to school. I was in the fifth class, and he was in the third. We were greeted by a tall, stern teacher who happened to be an old friend of my mother's from her high school. We were accepted. This was a town school and my classmates were cheekier and less disciplined than those in the villages, but the teaching was more advanced. With some amusement I observed everyone and made a new friend. She was a quiet, demure girl called Marusya. She had a pale face, and gentle, grey eyes which matched her pinafore dress. I liked her from the very start. I was confident, and if I liked someone, I made them my friend. I then stayed friends with Marusya throughout my school years, and into adulthood.

I studied hard. I noticed that my new school friends were more academically advanced than I was. Nevertheless, I soon progressed and came top of the class. I became leader in all the physical activities, and once again at breaktimes I organised the games. After school, I also took part in all of the social functions: I joined the choir; I learned to dance; I joined the drama group; I recited poems. I learned many songs, and we gave concerts and performed plays. On New Year's Day and May Day we held parties. We often danced and sang during breaktimes, and we ran joyfully after each other in the school grounds where there were trees, and flower beds, and plenty of open space. I was one of the most active pupils in the school, but I also wanted to be the best.

I enjoyed life there, but I looked with envy at the girls whose background allowed them to have beautiful dresses, bicycles, watches, guitars and all the other lovely things that young girls dream of. I knew I could never have them. My father and mother were poor. They were deprived people in this new society. My conscience told me it was unfair, especially as Father served God and His people, but I had to accept it. As well as that, I never dared to mention anything to anyone about who he really was.

My parents were like foreigners in their own land. They had no vote, and no one would employ them. They had no savings and so they had nothing to spend. Mother thus sold anything of value that she owned at the market, and she was able to feed us, but only just. Bread and potatoes became our everyday food, otherwise soups and borshch would fill our hungry stomachs. We never had anything luxurious. Socially, we could not ask Father for any money to go to the cinema or to a concert, and we were glad for any clothes that could be bought for us. I looked again at the girls in their lovely dresses. They talked about their figures, their hairstyle and their appearance. It seemed that it was not going to be something I could do, yet my ambition was strong. All my pleasure came from learning, and all I was interested in was acquiring more knowledge. My reward would be to know that I was the first, and the best.

Marusya sat next to me, and I shared my thoughts with her. She was a modest pupil but one of the brightest. I was proud to know her, and I grew to like her more and more. From those early days, her quiet personality had such an influence on me that I, too, became quieter and more reserved in the years that followed. I had been filled with a new and personal power which had to be quietly protected and not shown to most others. My power was all about my hard work. It was a pleasure for me to learn, know, and discover anything new: I went to the library; I borrowed books; I read and I became more and more familiar with many aspects of life.

After a long search for work, Mother met an old friend again from her school years – from before the Revolution.

She was a former priest's daughter and had married well, although her husband was now dead. She was called Maria Ivanivna, and she had two children to look after, as well as an ailing mother who had just had a heart attack. Hearing Mother's sad story, Maria offered her a job to look after her elderly mother for ten roubles a week. Mother was glad to accept it and went to work the very next morning. At first, I took little notice of where she was working as I was always busy reading my books. Eventually, I began to pay more attention to her stories.

She complained of how spoilt Maria's children were. Their house and garden used to belong to a rich owner who had been sent to prison – most probably to Siberia – just for being rich, and his family had been evicted. They had a large orchard full of apple, pear and cherry trees, as well as currant, gooseberry and raspberry bushes. Mother was asked if we would go to help them to pick the fruits in the summer. It was such a contrast of lifestyles. I sat with my books open and imagined a rich household where I could go and pick berries for the owners. With all my soul I protested against it, but I did not say a word aloud to my parents. Mother again mentioned how arrogant and unapproachable the two children were, and how ladylike their grandma was. She then told us how well Maria's family used to live. She went to visit them once as a young girl and recalled:

'It was Maria's birthday and they had a big party for her because she was the only daughter. Someone presented Maria with a box of chocolates, but she didn't like them. She threw the box to the floor in front of all the guests. The box burst open and the sweets rolled across the room. Everyone was embarrassed, and the maid was called in to pick them up.'

After the Revolution, Maria married a Communist. He was killed in a skirmish during collectivisation, and Maria, with her two small children, subsequently received a special widow's privilege from the new system. Her father died after the destruction of the churches, but she was allowed to keep all of his possessions. Krolevets Town Council then gave her the house that had belonged to the wealthy family. She then became a teacher and lived comfortably: 'More than comfortably,' Mother added. I could hear a grudge in her voice: 'They live like lords!'

The old lady became well again and ruled the house like a queen of old. Knowing of Mother's hopeless situation she treated her as a servant, and I often noticed how Mother sometimes cried after returning home. She would also try to heal the cracked skin on her hands – the result of her labour at the house.

When summer came, Mother told us to go and work in the orchard. Reluctantly, I went along with Anatoly who was now a brave boy of thirteen. He had Father's big, brown eyes as well as Father's disobedient hair which fell across his forehead, and his face was now handsomely rounded. He was quickly developing into a man with an independent outlook on life.

When we arrived, we entered the kitchen of the big, white house, but nobody greeted us. Eventually, an old-fashioned lady made an appearance. She was wearing long skirts which swept the floor behind her. She looked at us and then told us to sit at the kitchen table which was bare. She then brought us a bowl of soup and two wooden spoons and left the room, leaving the adjacent dining-room door open. Through the door I could see a huge table with a steaming samovar – a kettle, on a silver tray. There were plates of white bread and butter, and beautiful cups and saucers. At the end of the table, a tall youth was eating his breakfast. He never once tried to look at us. He had blue eyes, blonde hair, and long facial features. His shirt was white and spotless.

The room faced East, and the morning sun shone brightly upon the expensive furniture and pictures on the walls. Anatoly and I shared our bowl of plain soup. We were both hungry, and when the old lady brought us a piece of bread we ate it eagerly. The white bread and butter with tea which was being served in the other room, was a luxury. Everything about the scene fascinated me. It was like a dream, but in reality, Mother's descriptions of this wealthy household were now coming to life.

After we had finished eating, the old lady told us to go into the garden to pick the raspberries, blackcurrants, redcurrants, and cherries. The way she spoke immediately made me feel like a slave, and for the first time in my life I experienced humiliation. I wanted to run to our poor, little house and to my poor but loving parents. Anatoly was more practical, however. He looked at their luxurious lifestyle with contempt. His eyes showed his injury and revolt, but he responded with the necessary obedience. He took my hand and led me into the garden where the old lady gave us baskets. She told us where to pick the fruit and then hobbled back to the house. Anatoly looked back at her and said:

'She's a real barynia – a baroness, straight from the books of the last century.'

My brother had a passion for books and he read so many of them so quickly, people said they burned in his hands. Yet, to hear him say those words surprised me.

'Tsh! Quiet!' I exclaimed. 'She'll hear you!'

'So, let her hear me,' he replied. 'Who does she think she is? She is the same class as us. If she had a heart and any understanding she would have treated us differently. Just because her daughter married a Communist she thinks she can treat us like servants.'

Anatoly put some juicy strawberries into his mouth. His reddened lips smiled but they failed to hide his wounded pride. I felt hurt, too.

We worked all day, without a break, but we ate as many berries as we liked because no one came near us. As soon as a basket was full we took it to the house. We then emptied it into a very large bowl, and went back to gather more. Towards evening, we moved to the cherry orchard at the top of the sloping hill. We had almost finished when the youth appeared. He was wearing white trousers and a white shirt with short sleeves. Tall but shapely, he walked towards us. The sun was setting, and the golden rays which fell upon him made him look ghostly. The orchard was quiet, the temperature was cool, and the air was full of the sweet scents of summer. It was a beautiful evening.

The youth approached us, and without saying a word he started to pick the cherries. He could reach the higher branches, but we had to climb into the trees. The branch on which I was standing suddenly cracked. I held onto the trunk but dropped the basket. The cherries fell down like a shower of large, red raindrops. I climbed down looking guilty. The youth came up to me, looked down at the ground and said:

'Look what you've done!'

He turned and went away, and then reappeared a few

minutes later with a ladder. I was still picking up the cherries, trying to save as many as possible.

'Here,' he said, 'use the ladder.'

He looked at me in my blue-spotted dress. My hands were now red with cherry juice, and my face must have looked a bit bewildered. Of course, I didn't dare to ask him why we hadn't been given a ladder in the first place. It was much easier than climbing the trees.

All three of us gathered cherries until dusk. We noticed that "he" did not climb the ladder on the taller trees. Maybe he was frightened of falling, or maybe he did not want to do a job which was not his to do, but he did at least carry the ladder from tree to tree, and he picked the cherries at ground level. When the light was poor, he told us to finish.

The evening soon grew much cooler and the birds stopped singing. At the bottom of the hill, the golden, electric lights of the town were glimmering. Anatoly helped me to carry the baskets of cherries. In the large yard a bonfire was burning, and the old lady was making jam in a large, copper bowl. A big dog barked at us and had to be ordered back to its kennel. The lady went into the house and reappeared with a bowl of cherries which she gave to us to take back to Mother. She also gave us one rouble each.

'Nicholas!' she called to the youth. 'Take them to the gate in case the dog jumps up at them.' She then dismissed us, turned around and quietly went back to her jam.

"Nicholas" took us to the gate and held the dog to prevent it from attacking us. I looked at the beautiful, white house with its garden; the large yard and bonfire; the old-fashioned lady in her long, black skirts; the tall youth dressed in white. This was another world, I thought. Perhaps it was the "normal life" of which we had been deprived.

We arrived home and gave Mother the bowl of cherries, and we gave Father our first, hard-earned roubles. We told them what we thought, and there was no end of discussion about the way in which we had been treated that day.

Chapter 8

I was fourteen years old, and I soon forgot about the big house, the orchard, the old-fashioned lady and the proud youth – Nicholas. Mother continued to tell us stories about the way in which they lived, but I no longer took any notice. I had just finished the school year and my timetable had been full. I had passed all my exams with top marks, and that was all I needed to know.

'Thank you,' said Father, when he held my certificate.

I was aware that my friends had received presents from their parents at the end of the school year, even though their marks were lower than mine. But it was unfair for me to expect something similar from my father. There was too little money coming into our home. Father was badly paid, and the factory job he was now doing was worse than any job could be in this new society where nobody else would employ him. We were only just surviving. Nonetheless, I was happy and I enjoyed the end of term. A school party was held where I was presented with certificates for "The Best Pupil in Class" and a "Diploma of Honour". Father framed the diploma and praised me. That sufficed.

The question soon arose about which choice to make concerning my further education. I could go to a technical college, or learn a trade and start earning some money, or I could go to the Grammar School. Fortunately for us, the law changed and it allowed Father to become financially more secure. It meant I had the option of a higher education. After many discussions and advice from our friends (but mostly from teachers), my parents decided that I should go to the Grammar School. I was delighted. It was a large, yellow building in the centre of town and was surrounded by newly-planted pines and birches. Mother used to go there when it was known as a gymnasium – the old name for a grammar school before the Revolution. The building was beautiful both inside and out. It was the pride of the town, and it was now called The Model Grammar School.

When I first entered the building it appeared to be enormous. The staircase was wide, and the walls displayed a selection of classical paintings. The classrooms on the first floor were spacious and bright. The big windows allowed plenty of light inside, and the tops of the saplings were visible from the desks.

The assembly hall was magnificent. It had beautiful, ornate, cream walls with pink cornices, large windows, and glass doors leading out to sheltered balustrades. In my mother's time, there were four large portraits on the walls. On the East Wall there were icons of Jesus Christ and Our Lady in engraved frames, and on the West Wall there were pictures of Tsar Nicholas and Tsarina Alexandra – the last reigning monarchs of Russia. All I could see, and all I had ever seen, were large portraits of Lenin, Stalin, Marx and Engels. There was also a huge stage with dark, red curtains and a polished floor ready to receive enthusiastic dancers. I would eventually see many other fabulous halls in my life, but the hall in Krolevets Model Grammar School would remain the most wonderful.

I arrived with a Grade 5 certificate – the highest grade, so I was put in Form A. My friend, Marusya, was with me and we were happy to be together. We made sure we arrived early in order to choose the best places – not too close to the teacher, but not too far away from the blackboard, either. That 1st day of September 1937 was a bright day. The first lesson started, and our teacher was just getting to know us when, suddenly, the door opened and the whole class burst out laughing. A tall boy entered the classroom. He had blonde hair, an oblong face, and blue eyes.

'Nicholas!' I nearly jumped out of my seat and whispered to Marusya: 'I know him.'

He walked in, turned his shoulders, ignored the laughter and sat at the back of the class where he had seen an empty desk.

'You are late,' said the teacher rather softly, and with a gentle smile.

Nicholas did not answer. He looked at everybody as though he was in charge, and as though nothing else mattered. The laughter stopped.

'He's always late,' I heard someone whisper.

At break time, I played in the school grounds with Marusya, by the trees, but when we heard the bell and went back to the classroom we found Nicholas sitting at our desk. Our books had also been moved to a desk at the back of the

51

room. We protested and told him off, but he simply sat there and took no notice. The teacher entered and would not help us when we explained what had happened. Nicholas stubbornly and arrogantly refused to move. We called him names and protested loudly, but to our surprise he simply ignored us and continued sitting where he was and read a book. We remained seated at the back, by the window, and watched everybody, especially him – our new rival. He stretched his long legs across the gap between the rows of desks. He was huge compared to the other boys, and he was the tallest by far. He was also serious, as though the eldest and wisest, too. The teachers appeared to respect him and some boys talked to him. The rest of the class scoffed and called him a snob, and he took no notice of them, either.

'Mama, Mama!' I called, when I got home from school. 'Do you know who is in my class? You'll never guess. It's Nicholas.' I sounded too overjoyed.

'What's so special about that?' replied Mother calmly. 'After all, he is the same age as you.'

'Actually, I thought he was older than me.'

I could not hide my feelings. To be in the same class as that boy was now a challenge. Mother said no more, but I was gradually waking up to something new.

In the eighth form, literature was taught by a very handsome middle-aged man called Alexander Ivanovych. He was tall with ginger hair, and he had wise, blue eyes. He loved literature passionately, and he poured his heart into his lessons. We were deep in nineteenth century Russian literature and were studying the works of the great masters – Turgenev, Lermontov and Pushkin. They fascinated us, especially the way Alexander Ivanovych introduced them in his lectures. Literature quickly replaced mathematics as my favourite subject. I listened to his lectures and was spellbound: the fine life; the beautiful ladies; the gallant gentlemen. I caught glimpses of lives of which I knew absolutely nothing. Nicholas would become the symbol of that life. I imagined him as a gentleman gallantly approaching his lady. I could see him riding beside the carriage in which the beautiful lady of his heart was travelling along dangerous roads. He was attentive and handsome, and he dressed in the clothes of a gentleman of the nineteenth century.

I laughed and felt happy to be alive, and I talked to Marusya about my imagination, but she tried to stop me and told me not to talk nonsense. I then started to keep my thoughts to myself. Something new was stirring inside me, though I did not yet realise what it was. Nicholas was becoming my hero, my dream, my ambition, my every thing. He came first in the class in every subject, so I too, had to be the best – at least from amongst the girls. From then on, my nights were spent doing homework. My rewards were the mornings when I came to school triumphantly because my homework had been done. Nicholas could successfully finish a difficult mathematical assignment – even though everybody knew that his Mother had helped him. There was also a boy called John, and we actually called him "the brainy one". He was a poor widow's son who also completed his mathematics homework. Between the three of us, there were three different ways of solving the same difficult numerical problems.

I noticed the surprised looks Nicholas gave me, but even then he never spoke to me. It was either because we had fallen out over the desks from the very beginning, or because he felt that I was someone of lesser importance. After all, Mother worked for his family. But then, neither did I approach him, even though I never took my eyes off him from the back of the class. I observed every move he made, but I did not say a single word to him. Nonetheless, there was a change inside of me and I noticed it. Everything around me appeared to be very beautiful.

Nicholas played the piano and the clarinet in the orchestra, so he could always be found in the hall at our social functions. He always sat in the middle, and I danced to the very end of every melody. After school, I would run home and waited for the next day when I could return to do everything all over again. School became my whole life.

I worked hard, and at the end of half term I came second in the class after Nicholas. There was no end of learning still to be done, and there was no end of the wish to be as good as he was, but he still took very little notice of me. As time passed, he became an unapproachable ideal, secretly hidden in my heart. Everything that was great and noble, beautiful and rich, endlessly wished for, unknown and impossible, was embodied in him. My whole being was waking up to new desires, to the new and wonderful world in which I lived and breathed, and to a new understanding of the whole of life. From a careless, happy and sometimes bossy girl from an impoverished background, I had changed into a dreamy, quiet and thoughtful young lady. I looked around as though waking from sleep to discover the beauty of a new spring, the quiet flow of the river under the bridge by his house, and the starry sky in the evenings where thousands of planets looked back from across eternity. I fell in love with poetry, music and novels. I read until late at night, and I learned everything that came my way. Life was wonderful, people were interesting, and everything was bright and happy, and I aimed to keep it that way forever.

It did not matter to me that we were so poor – that we hardly had any food or new clothing. This aspect of life had nothing to do with Nicholas. Mother still cried after working hard, and Father was becoming thin and grey, but life remained a canvas upon which a wonderful pattern was being woven. Nicholas was at the centre of that pattern. Everywhere I went, I wished he could see me. Everything I did, I wished he would admire. He practically lived with me in all of my thoughts, my consciousness and feelings. Marusya was very annoyed with me because she openly disliked him, and my sister somehow learned about my feelings and teased me. So, I then stopped talking to everyone about my feelings. I withdrew but remained full of inner vitality. I thought my secret would never be shared with anyone ever again.

I suffered, too. The days when Nicholas was absent from school were dark and empty for me. My heart ached and I felt dead inside, and on the day when he came back to school I was bright and happy again. I became excited when I caught his first glance at me, or when he gave me a long and studious look in the classroom. He also gave me glances whenever I answered the teacher's questions. I knew these looks and glances were only for me. Deep down, I was sure of my right to this happiness.

I started to write a diary. Then one day, Mother found it and read some of the pages in which I described my feelings. She talked to Father about it and then asked me very plainly:

'What do you see in him?'

How could I tell my mother what I thought about

Nicholas? I just said nothing. I thought about it all day, and I wanted to talk to her the following evening, but she never mentioned the subject again, so I didn't say anything, either. At school, however, there was a porter – a lady called Nina. She was tall, pretty and very intelligent. She was a woman who was described as having "class from the old times". The girls confided in her and often told her their secrets. She smiled at them and always said the same thing:

'Girls! Girls! Girls! That is not love! You just don't have any idea of what love is!'

I never confided in Nina but below my breath I replied: 'And what would you know? You've never even known love yourself!'

In winter, we used to go skiing. The snow on the roads of the town was compacted and shone under the light of the lanterns. I hoped to meet Nicholas on these outings, but it was usual for the boys to stay in groups of their own. Nicholas then usually broke away and would only ever ski with one other boy. It was only after making our way back to the town centre that we could all meet, make jokes and laugh.

One frosty evening, on my way home I looked at the sky. It was beautiful – dark-blue with thousands of bright, shining stars. The moon was so big and clear that it hung over the town and intensified the glistening beauty below. The whole world was like a fairytale kingdom in which I could ski somewhere between Heaven and Earth. I went past Nicholas's house – the centre of my world. I recited some of Lermontov's poetry. The words were so beautiful and the night so pure that I forgot about the past and stopped thinking of the future. I continued to live in the present, and I loved it.

Chapter 9

Winter again brought its many festivities. At school, we prepared for the New Year's Eve party. It was an annual fancy dress ball inside the hall with a Christmas tree in the middle. I had no suitable costume to wear and was surprised when one of my friends, Tanya, asked if I would like to join her, but on the condition that her mother could make my dress. I was delighted. Tanya was a shy girl and she had already made plans to wear a traditional Ukrainian costume, but she did not want to go to the ball alone. Naturally, I accepted her offer, and after finishing school I hurried home, gulped my dinner, grabbed my skis, and made my way to her house on the other side of the town. I was very excited.

The sun was still shining brightly and my skis slid smoothly and rapidly across the top of the valley, down the hilly slopes, and then finally to the road that led to Tanya's. On arrival, Tanya's mother gave me a warm welcome. She was not only a dressmaker, but an artist, too. They were a good family with a grey-haired, stately grandfather, and a grandmother who immediately insisted that I should eat a wholesome meal. Tanya's father also greeted me with a polite and very friendly smile. I didn't realise it at the time, but they treated me so kindly because they, too, were living in fear, and were opposed to the Communist government.

Tanya's mother worked on my costume all afternoon, and by evening I was dressed in a wonderful, pink and white dress. It was fit for a princess. She even made me a diadem from old beads sewn onto a royal-blue, velvet ribbon. Tanya found some bracelets and rings, and her mother finished my makeover with a black mask to wear over my face. When I looked in the mirror, I nearly cried with joy. Tanya's father was also very pleasantly surprised by the transformation. He joked:

'Aha! Now that you look like a princess, you will have to behave like one!'

Tanya stood by my side. She had dressed in her beautifully embroidered Ukrainian costume. It was clean and cut to perfection. We were a very pretty sight together.

Tanya's father then gave us some halva – a rare luxury in those days. We put on our coats and walked the whole of the way back to school. The air was frosty, but as clean and pure as the joy we were feeling inside. When we arrived, we quietly made our way to an empty classroom. We took off our coats, tidied our hair and put on our masks. We then made our way down to the crowded hall.

Our entrance caused a surprising stir. Everybody looked at us and asked: 'Who are they?' Tanya was quickly recognised because of her tall figure and blonde hair, but they continued to point at me and asked: 'But who's she?'

Everybody surrounded me and admired my costume.

When I looked in a large mirror on the wall, I too, was still amazed at how pretty I looked. The long, pink, satin dress was also trimmed with white ribbons and glittering, silvery beads. The diadem rested upon the curls of my brown hair. From under the black mask, I could see my face – white and pink with a large forehead and rounded chin. My neck and shoulders were half-covered, and for the first time I noticed how delicately the lines of my face, neck and shoulders combined with each other. Could clothes really do so much for a person? I looked at the girls around me. Indeed, they thought I looked like a princess.

'I know who it is!' one of them exclaimed 'I'd know those eyes anywhere!'

'What a lovely dress,' remarked a senior girl who was now standing next to me. 'Did it once belong to your mother?'

'It's a Tsar's-period outfit,' someone else added.

'Well, actually,' I replied, 'Tanya's mother made it for me.'

Everybody liked Tanya. She was shy and quiet, and she was not the brightest pupil, but she was always modest and very polite. She was tall and well-built, and on that night she looked attractive in her Ukrainian national costume. I took her hand and led her closer to the Christmas tree. It had been decorated with coloured lights and shining balls, colourful toys and paper chains. It stood tall, bright and magnificent and reached to the ceiling. Music started to play so I danced with her.

Everybody danced. The band was playing a waltz, which had always been my favourite dance. The other girls were wearing a wide selection of fancy dress costumes: a newspaper; the night; a chimney sweep; a gypsy; a Russian maid, and all were wearing masks. When the music stopped, a tall boy came up to me and asked if I would like to dance with him. It was Michael – a handsome and popular boy from my class. I loved dancing, so we were soon whirling round the hall, and much faster than anyone else. Someone then proposed that we should all hold hands round the tree to dance and sing to the music. The atmosphere became electrifying. The singing and stamping of feet overpowered the orchestra. We became ecstatic, and in the middle of that ecstasy I could feel the chain of hands being broken. It was Nicholas, and my hand now rested in his. We whirled together round the tree until the orchestra changed its tune. The chain of hands broke, the singing stopped and everyone began to dance in pairs once more. I was now dancing in Nicholas's arms. He held me delicately, as though frightened to come too close. We danced on, regardless of the others around us.

'Look, look, Nicholas is dancing!' I heard some of the girls point out in surprise.

'I've never seen him dance before!'

'I never knew he could!'

'And look who he's dancing with!'

This dance round the tree was an unforgettable moment. I was in the arms of the one I had been dreaming of. It was the eve of 1939. I look back now and ask myself how many years have passed since then; how many events have happened in my life and in the lives of millions of others across the world. Yet those minutes still remain in my heart like the tree – a symbol of life and joy. Did it matter that we danced for only a few minutes before he returned to play in the orchestra? His eyes followed me everywhere. I danced with others that night, but I still continued to dance with him in my heart and in the whole of my being. Later in life, whenever I danced, I would always remember that time.

Later in the evening we took our masks off, and when midnight approached we all stood still and listened for the clock on the radio. When the twelve strokes had sounded we hugged and kissed each other, and with tears in our eyes we wished each other a happy New Year. The orchestra played another joyful tune, and once again we sang and held hands round the tree.

Nicholas did not come to wish me a happy New Year. Neither did anybody else, nor did I go to him. One dance had not given me the right to be familiar with him. I understood that it was for him to come to me, but he did not come. Only the dance was left with me, like a wonderful dream or fairy tale. Like Cinderella I had come to the ball by the magic of my friend's mother, and I had danced with my prince. How I wished to be that Cinderella just one more time.

Chapter 10

We took our winter break, so I did not see Nicholas for ten days. Christmas Eve came on the 6th of January, and we had our own little tree in the house. The candles shone brightly on its fresh, green branches. Father said grace, and Mother served the twelve traditional dishes which symbolised the twelve apostles and the twelve months of the year. This Holy Night retained its sense of magic. My auntie was with us, and we sang some new carols which she had recently taught us.

We were happy, and although we were poor we still changed into our best clothes. The house was spotless throughout, and the smell of the pine needles and Mother's cooking helped to rekindle the Christmas spirit. Father's festive greetings and Mother's happy smiles warmed us. We were all loved. All of the festival's joyous touches were there, yet part of me was not. All I could see was the huge Christmas tree in the school hall, the glitter, and my dance as a princess in the arms of my prince. My brother was stern with me. It was as though he had noticed that something was written on my face, and at times my sister was scornful. I was aware of what was happening. I was taking part in these traditional festivities, but I felt like an actor taking part in a play. I was the eldest daughter and I was supposed to be serious, studious and wise. Father had consulted with me many times and treated me as a grown-up, so I continued to remain self-assured and confident.

In that ill-fated year of 1939, there were no church services in Ukraine. They had all been closed, demolished, or turned into storehouses or clubs. On feast days, before going to work, my ever faithful father would get up early, pray and quietly sing the whole Liturgy by the icons in the corner of the room. The red lamp continued to burn, hanging on thin chains from the ceiling. The chains cast their shadows. I used to lie and watch them move across the ceiling each time Father made his sign of the cross and bowed his head in prayer. His thin, now slightly bent, figure remained his outwardly-visible tower of strength, righteousness and honour. I admired his sincerity and his dedication, and I knew how much he had suffered. Most of all, I admired his great faith and his constant trust in the will of God despite all of life's upheavals. I loved him very much. He had made a happy family of us. Love and care were better than all the other normal luxuries and riches a girl of sixteen could expect. I did not miss those things, I did not know of them, and not knowing of them, I did not particularly want to know of them. The only other thing I cared for was knowledge, but I also wanted to be noticed by one other person – Nicholas.

The splendour of high society and its trappings were substituted by the beauty I could see in nature. When spring came, I breathed the soft and gentle, warm air which swept across the land. There could be no better perfume in the world. I stood for what seemed like an age on top of the hill where our house stood, and I admired the valley and the river below. In the evening, I watched the wonders of the changing sky – especially the stars that shone high above. No pearls or diamonds would ever replace them. They had found a home within me.

I read a lot. From my books I learned about different lives; truth and faithfulness; sacrifice and dedication; the beauty of love. I hid myself amongst the trees of the nearby forest and read one particular book with a passion: "The Wandering Stars". It told the story of two childhood friends who loved each other, but the girl was snatched away by gypsies. All their lives they searched for each other. I imagined the book was telling me that we would become wandering stars throughout our lives on Earth. Youths dreamt and fell in love, but around them life was very cruel and harsh. There was unrest and fear across the country. Every night people would disappear – never to be seen or heard of again, and for no good reason. They were often charged with subversion. In truth, 1938 had been a dreadful year in Ukraine, and 1939 was about to be no better.

After the New Year's ball, my relationship with Nicholas did not change. Everything remained like a dream – a short moment that had existed and disappeared, never to be repeated. Nicholas was unapproachable. He did not seem to notice me, and I was too proud to approach him. We sat in the same classroom nearly every day; we listened to our lessons; we answered the teachers' questions; we submitted our homework; we were told the results; we played at break time, but we were as far apart as any two planets in the sky. I knew about his background and his private life, and he knew about mine. We were from two different social classes. Sometimes, when I went past his lovely, white house where I could hear the sound of his piano playing through the open windows, I desperately wanted to overturn life's rules so that he would know me, but only fate could ever bring us together again.

Nicholas was the editor of the school newspaper. It was a hand-written publication and was hung on the wall in the entrance hall. It had to be written in the best possible handwriting, and to my great surprise I was chosen to write it. Nicholas had already prepared a heading on a large sheet of paper. I had to copy the articles onto long strips which he would then stick onto the big sheet to make into columns. We worked together in the school library. I was very shy but behaved properly. In fact, I almost failed to recognise myself. From a girl who had once been forceful and bossy, I was now meek and very quiet. The upheaval in my family's life, the awareness of my father's position, and my perception of being poor compared to Nicholas, made me as withdrawn and unapproachable as he was with his sense of superiority.

It took us a few days to finish the newspaper. We were excused from some lessons and worked quietly together in the library. It was a large and lovely room with a high ceiling and book shelves running along the outer walls. They held many hundreds of books. We worked at a huge table in the middle. When the sound of soft distant music could be heard I felt happy, and Nicholas seemed to smile. The paper was very neatly written. It had colourful pictures and artistic headings, and everybody read and admired it. Two names were written at the bottom – Nicholas and Vera, and it made me feel very happy.

I began to work harder. My homework often took until late at night to complete, and the room was often so cold that I had to wrap myself in a blanket. I used a small oil lamp for my light as our house had no electricity, but my homework (especially the algebra, trigonometry and science) was always done.

Sometimes only Nicholas's homework and mine had been successfully completed; sometimes only John's and mine. John – "the brainy one" – was becoming increasingly friendly with me. Naturally, I felt friendly towards him. He was a widow's son from a poor background and he did not want to join the Comsomols – the Communist Youth League. We often sat together on a bench and discussed our homework. We went through every subject and felt as equals, and we were close. Our friends started to tease us. Deep down, I smiled at the situation. I knew that John was my friend, but my dream was sitting at the opposite side of the classroom looking back at both of us.

There was one beautiful young woman in our class, a lovely and friendly girl called Lydia. She had brown eyes, auburn hair and a slim, white face. She could sing, and Nicholas accompanied her on the piano. I often heard them practicing together, and it made me jealous. I envied Lydia. She had a lovely voice and a friendly manner, and I wished I could be like her. I wished I could sing so that Nicholas would accompany me. Although my mother had a lovely voice and had sung on the radio once or twice, I had not been encouraged to sing. Our life had changed so drastically that we had no time for such activities. Our life was about existence, and luxuries such as singing, playing musical instruments, learning languages, and taking holidays were far beyond our means. Nevertheless, I loved music, poetry and drama. I wished, many times, that I could open the door of the hall where Lydia sang, and I wished I would be welcomed by Nicholas instead of her. I wished someone could have helped me to develop my hidden talents. I never spoke about this to anyone. I was short of a good, guiding friend.

I hardly ever saw my mother and father as they were always at work, and my brother and sister were younger than I was. Granny Agathea and Auntie Chrystyna came to live with us, but Auntie would work constantly, too. They loved and admired me but they were unable to help. I now felt more educated than they were, and I told them about all the things I had learned at school. Auntie Chrystyna loved listening to me. Astronomy, which we had just started to learn, fascinated me so I told her about the stars and the planets. In return, she told me love stories and talked about boys and girls she had known, and what had happened to them, as an example for my future happiness.

I have always blessed my dear Auntie Chrystyna. She was alone in life and loved me as though I was her daughter.

She was once the village beauty and had married a rich man. She would have been happy with him had times been normal, but he was arrested just for being rich and his property was confiscated by the State. He was never heard of again and probably perished with the many thousands of others in Siberia. She also buried her father, Granddad Ivan, during the Holodomor. After having had their house confiscated by the State, and after living with Grandmother in squalid rooms, she finally came to live with us.

Granny Agathea was even more modest. She looked up to me as a learned, young lady, and on Sundays, when she wore her best clothes, she would come and sit next to me and tell me stories from her youth. She was born into serfdom, but her beauty had been noticed by the master of the village who started to take her for rides in his carriage. This frightened her father, however, so he arranged for her to be married when she was only sixteen. She worked hard and had thirteen children of whom only Father and Auntie now survived.

Listening to Granny Agathea and Auntie Chrystyna I knew that I would never be able to confide in them, and I had no other relatives. Mother's father, Fr Ivan, had died when I was only six years old, and Mother's mother – my highly respected Grandma Nadiya whom we had visited during "the good times", now lived far away from us, so we could not visit her any more. I lived alone with my hidden dreams and desires. I always carried a book in my hand and would walk with Auntie Chrystyna. My hair was cut short – in a modern style, with a fringe over my forehead. I appeared not to be interested in boys, though deep down I was hiding the truth.

I thought I was educating my auntie when I spoke to her, but she had other ideas about me – her niece of seventeen years. In her view, it was natural for a girl of my age to have a boyfriend, and to get married and start a family. She hinted at this when she told me the stories of the girls she had known, and the happy lives they continued to lead with the men they had married. Was marriage for me? Marriage was seemingly as far away as Heaven was from Earth. I wanted to learn and to be someone. Where might my dream lead me to? Life seemed to be an endless road of achievements which I had to master, and only then could I begin to think of the ideals of love, marriage and happiness.

63

As the years passed, the girls around me found boyfriends. Marusya knew a boy outside of school. She had feelings for him and secretly told me that her parents were arranging her marriage, but she would not hear of it.

Other girls fell in love – often with boys in school, and often from the same class. Some girls went out with them openly. Boys fell in love with Lydia, but she was serious as well as friendly. One of the boys fell hopelessly in love with her and started to drink. Then, a young teacher of modern history fell in love with her, but she refused to go out with him. War with Finland had just broken out so he volunteered to go but never returned. We all presumed he had been killed and were sorry for him. Nicholas often sat at the same desk as Lydia, and they talked and laughed like friends. It made me feel jealous, and I really felt it. Occasionally, Nicholas would give me a warm look with his blue eyes and I would feel reassured and happy again. After all, I was also friends with John and had no special feelings for him, so why shouldn't Nicholas be the same with Lydia. It was like an unspoken play between us all, and it continued through the rest of our school days.

Once, we were given a lecture on the subject of "Love and Friendship". The senior forms gathered in the hall and the headmaster spoke broadly about the subject. We were then allowed to ask questions, orally or in writing. Many questions were asked, and I saw Nicholas sending him a piece of paper. The headmaster unfolded it and read it aloud: 'Can love be unspoken?'

The whole senior school burst out laughing. Of course, I was the only one who didn't laugh and watched Nicholas lower his head. It had made him feel very uneasy. When the laughter stopped, the headmaster gave his answer in a soft and gentle voice:

'At your age, this is probably the best kind of love you can have.'

Everyone fell silent. I watched as Nicholas raised his head again. He was reassured. I wanted to squeeze Marusya's hand, but I kept still. I was numb. Nobody should know about the great secret I had. It was so pure and wonderful. It was mine and mine alone. It was my treasure, and I would keep it to myself. Neither Marusya nor anyone else had even noticed whose question the headmaster had read. So, nothing more was said about it and my secret was safe. It became all the more precious to me.

We often had meetings at school and gathered in the largest classroom and took a place wherever we liked. I always sat with Marusya. Nicholas would come in late and looked around as if he was trying to find someone. He would come and sit behind us and if that seat was occupied, he would move away the person who was sitting there. As the meeting continued, we had to ask questions. I would whisper a question or an answer to Marusya, not daring to say anything in a raised voice. To my surprise, Nicholas would repeat aloud anything I had said. I felt numb, but Marusya gave him angry looks. This became our game. Whenever we had such a meeting, we played it. Nicholas received appreciation from the teacher and the students, and I felt a secret and hidden joy.

There were more dances in the school hall. Nicholas continued to play in the orchestra, and I continued to dance beneath his gaze. I was happy, and I was always the last to leave the dance floor. I then always walked home alone, and I never expected him to accompany me.

Then on one occasion, after a meeting, we walked home in a group. The others eventually went their separate ways, and Nicholas and I were left to complete the journey in the same direction. The night was frosty, the moon shone brightly and the thousands of stars glittered high above. The road was white and reflected the light. Our feet crunched through the snow, and we spoke casual, unimportant words. It was as though we were frightened of each other, but that evening stayed with me in my memory. Later in life, I wrote a poem about it. The shining stars were like the many ideas in our hearts and minds – everything that was noble and best; our lives were full of purpose and we were dedicated; our wishes were beautiful, pure and everlasting. We did not say what we wanted, for like the stars, what we wanted was untouchable.

Chapter 11

My daydreaming protected me from the harsh and horrific realities Ukraine was facing. Everybody knew what was happening, but everybody also kept silent from fear. Stalin's purges had long since taken hold, but the terror continued into 1939. Father was always worried whenever a car stopped near to our house, and he looked anxiously through the gap in the curtains whenever people just walked past. Arrests were being made all around us, and he was always glad when the night was over. He would get up early, light the fire, put the samovar on to boil and call us cheerfully to greet another day.

'Let us give thanks to God; the night has passed,' he would say, as he carried the boiling water to the table.

There was no sugar in the shops, so Father drank his tea with some bread and salt. In fact, there was no food in the shops at all. Long queues formed for bread, but there was never enough for everyone. Mother worried continually about our health. Finally, she took her very last belongings to the market and exchange them for a piece of bacon which had to last for the whole week.

'Even if you eat meat just once a week, you will survive,' Father announced. He said he had read it somewhere.

The piece of bacon was divided into small pieces to be fried with onions and then mixed with potatoes. A pot of baked, seasoned potatoes was ready in the oven each day before Mother went to work. Perhaps that explained why we had been such a healthy family. Despite all of those hard times, I can never once recall Mother or Father being ill and we – the children – were also admired by other parents. Anxious mothers asked my mother: 'What do you feed your children on? They look so well.'

'I don't know what they eat all day,' my mother replied.

Some mothers complained that their daughters would not eat anything they had been given, and this would leave them looking pale and thin. The doctor advised them to take a holiday in the pine forests. Mother smiled, and said nothing. I knew the truth of the matter. She would get up hours before going to work, and day after day she would cook us a hot breakfast, and prepare meals for the rest of the day. I realised that to work hard you had to be well-nourished, and to be well-nourished you had to work hard. I admired Mother for her endless devotion to her duty: our survival.

I noticed the purges and persecution of innocent people, and I could see the hardship our family was enduring. I was also very aware of the worries and fears that my parents were living with. I was aware of almost everything around me. It was a horrific, outer backdrop to my everyday life at school, where I was encased with my concerns about my homework, learning and progress. I wanted to emerge from there and reach out for a new life of my own, and I wanted to do so with all the power and strength my youth could give me.

At school, we had heard that war had started somewhere. We were made to go on public show to welcome the annexation of West Ukraine, which was previously occupied and governed by Poland. We collected books and pencils for the supposedly poor people in that half of the country. Meanwhile, we knew very little of Fascism, territorial expansion or Hitler's war in Europe.

We held literary evenings, and for one of them I had to make a speech around Lermontov's poem "Hero of Our Days". Also, I recited poetry by other great writers such as Pushkin, and I was allowed to call personally selected friends to assist with the evening's programme. It was a great success, and from that day on, I continued to make speeches at most of the school's special occasions.

On May Day, I had to read another speech and was just about to begin when the school's electricity was suddenly cut off. At first, there was panic, and then there was laughter when a teacher brought a candle to help me to read. Order was soon restored and everybody listened in an atmosphere that remained tense. We all wondered what might happen next. At the very end of my speech, the electricity supply was restored. Perhaps it had been disconnected deliberately.

I used to prepare my speeches carefully and was influenced by some of the articles in the newspapers and periodicals. I didn't believe everything I read, but when the electricity failed, it made me begin to think about those who opposed the statements made in the official publications.

I saw Nicholas at the dance that followed. He was silent and appeared to be moody. Did he approve of my speech? Perhaps he knew something about the power failure. I did not know. He was very serious, and remained withdrawn all night.

In the end, Father remained the least unscathed by the purges. We all lived quietly together and worked hard. He and Mother would be out all day, so it was not until evening time that we could find happiness together. Granny remained at home all day, but she was ailing, and had to be left with no one to look after her. Anyone who worked was never allowed to be late or absent because heavy penalties would be imposed upon them. Then, one day, when I came home from school, I looked at Granny Agathea: she was dead.

Shocked by my discovery I cried, and I ran to Father's workplace, and then to Mother and to Auntie. They were all allowed to come home. Auntie cried aloud, but Father proceeded immediately with the funeral arrangements.

There were no functioning priests or churches open, so Father had to read the funeral service in the house, behind drawn curtains. It was May, so I brought back bunches of lilacs and other spring flowers and decorated the coffin. Granny was dressed in clothes she had prepared a long time ago. I had never once seen her look like so grand. Soon, our little house was filled with visitors. Relatives came from the villages. They were dressed poorly, but those were very hard times, and I had never realised we had so many of them. I could not cry. I stood silently and watched. Mother was worried about me as I hardly spoke to anyone. For the first time in my life I had encountered death in the family, and I tried to grapple with the meaning of our lives. The coffin, with the body of my lovely grandmother, was taken to the cemetery and was buried next to my grandfather. All her life, Granny had loved the Church. Her Christian faith had been open and strong, yet she now had to be buried in a shroud of secrecy: she had no proper service. Father blessed her grave and prayed in silence with our mourning relatives and friends.

Everybody at school knew of my grandmother's death, and I wanted Nicholas to sympathise with me, but he only looked at me and said nothing. I wanted to tell him about her. I wanted to tell him that she had once been a well-established householder. She had been a woman from a wealthy background. She had a beautiful garden and a yard full of animals and pets. She also had land with a kiln in which the local supply of bricks had been made. She did well through hard work. I wanted to tell him that she had been a great believer in God, in our traditional form of worship with its rich customs, and how everything had now been taken away from her. I wanted to tell him that her dear hardworking husband had died from the famine imposed by the new Communist regime and that her only son – for whom she had sacrificed everything in his mission to become a priest – had lost everything: his life's mission, his goals and his ambitions. I wanted to tell him that there had been no church funeral, and no official priest at the graveside where a simple cross was not even allowed to be placed on the grave. I longed to tell Nicholas all of this, for he was of this new world, he was of the new regime of his father – the representative of all that was supposed to be better for the future.

The May Day parade came. The sky was blue, the sun shone, and people dressed in their best clothes. Everyone was full of joy. As a young woman I wanted to shut out all of the horrible and difficult times we had been through, and were still going through. I was young and rejoiced in the natural beauty of the spring, and there was the added bonus of marching in the same column as Nicholas. It was wonderful. Then rationality finally took a firm hold of me. There was one major aspect of Nicholas's behaviour that I was not prepared to tolerate any longer.

Perhaps it was because of my grandparents, who had lived through serfdom in the previous century, or perhaps it was because of the poor life we were leading at that time, but I always associated with plain and ordinary people, and I willingly spoke in Ukrainian. It was the national language of our country, and by associating with plain and ordinary Ukrainians I was determined to speak only in Ukrainian. All the subjects in our school were still taught in Ukrainian, and at break, amongst ourselves we spoke in Ukrainian. We had two hours each week of Russian language education, and two hours of Russian literature. Nicholas would only ever speak in Russian and he never spoke Ukrainian to anyone except in lessons. Even then, he seemed to be annoyed at having to do so. For that reason, my annoyance with him began to grow. Who or what did he think he was? Did he think he could be a lord on our land? Did he think he could be a rich, upper-class gentleman in our Socialist society? Did he think he could put himself above ordinary people? Whether he thought so or not, he behaved in that way. He would never associate with anyone in the school who was from a poor or persecuted family. Neither would he associate with anyone who had low marks in class, nor with anyone who was in the slightest bit shy or timid. To tell you the truth, he did look like an upper-class snob. Although he was the cleverest, the tallest and the most active in our school's social life, and although he made friends with some of the teachers who looked favourably upon him, I was no longer proud to be associated with him. I had already been through so much in my life that had made me feel inferior, and I was not inferior, and I would no longer allow myself to be pulled down to his level.

Gifted senior pupils in the school were appointed to work with junior pupils. They would teach them singing, dancing and drama on a voluntary basis, and thus gain some teaching experience. That spring, I was asked to teach singing and was allocated the third form – a group of very lively boys and girls who had to stay behind after school hours. I set a target for them and organised a social evening at which they would perform in front of their parents and teachers. Perhaps it was because I was serious and determined about everything I did, or perhaps it was because I had a talent for encouraging children: my group became the best trained. They loved me and tried their very best, and by the time we were ready, our programme was so full that I was asked to shorten it. I was advised to ask Nicholas to accompany my singers at the next performance, but that was no longer a reward for me. The children and their parents enjoyed the programme, and I was praised. Typically, Nicholas said nothing. He just folded his music and went out as though everything we had just done was of no interest to him and was too far below his status.

Working with the children did not stop me from learning. I found time for most things, and the only activity I had little time for was going out, but I did not really long to do that anyway. There was no one else I would have gone out with. My life was made up of study and work with the children. My only remaining pleasure was to go to the school's dances.

In the summer holidays, I began teaching pupils who had

failed their exams. They were allowed to retake them before the new term started, and no matter how badly they had performed, I succeeded in helping every one of them to pass. As well as paying me (which came as a great help to my mother and father), grateful parents also rewarded me with boxes of sweets. On one occasion, I coached a girl whose parents were once in Nicholas's mother's class. Her mother sent praise to my mother because she was amazed that I could successfully teach mathematics to one of her "backward" children. I hoped Nicholas would hear about it. I was becoming very popular as a teacher of "backward" children.

I continued to work hard for my own final exams. The conditions were such that if you passed all the exams with Grade 5 marks, entry to a university was free and you could study anywhere in the country. However, if there was only one lower mark you had to take a university's entrance exam. To sit such exams you would have to live in an unknown city for a whole month, without a grant. If it came to that, I knew my parents would not be able to support me. They already hoped that I would start work, or at least they hoped I would go into some sort of training to earn some money. Father often had to borrow money to buy the food before his wages came at the end of each month. Even then, his wage was delayed, but I would not hear of work or training. I wanted to study. My desire was so strong that I was willing to face any hardship.

I studied each day and night, and when the time came, I passed all of my exams with the required highest marks. Then I received a shock. When my certificate arrived I found that two of my results had been downgraded: one for my written Russian exam, and the other for Mathematics – a subject in which I had always excelled. The teachers had the power to decide who could have an open road to future studies. I was heartbroken. I had no money to go and live in Kyiv, which was where I wanted to go. To live there for a whole month, and to start studying again for entrance exams was unthinkable. That afternoon, I went into the valley; into the fields; far away from everything. Surrounded by wild flowers, I eventually threw myself down onto a patch of soft grass and began to cry. I cried and cried until I had no tears left. I had been denied my lifetime's ambition. Exhausted, I fell asleep.

I woke up much more relaxed. I was calm and determined: I would still go to Kyiv, even if I had to take more exams. I told Father of my plans, and my family's subsequent protests did nothing to change my mind.

Nicholas had also passed all of his exams with top marks and was awarded a praiseworthy diploma. How I would have loved to have had his opportunity. None of the other girls in our class received such a diploma, either. But then, just as Nicholas was planning to continue with his studies, a new law came in which forced all male grammar school graduates to enlist in the army. We had no idea that World War II was just one year away from Ukraine. Our final school days were thus upsetting, but we also remained exuberant and continued to make plans for the future.

We attended the traditional farewell party to formally mark the end of our school life together. It was a supper and dance which was held in the hall and the event was prepared by our parents and the school's committee. I looked forward to it and put hope into our final gathering. Mother and Auntie made sure they found me a special dress. It was white with little pink roses, and it fitted me perfectly. I dressed like the girls I had read about. Nadiya brought me a fresh pink rose from the garden and pinned it in my hair. My family admired me and wished me a happy farewell party. Even Father looked on with approval and smiled at me on my way out. Anatoly escorted me there.

The tables had been beautifully laid out with food and wine. Everybody took their place: the teachers, the parents' committee, and we – the proudly dressed, excited and happy graduates of Krolevets Model Grammar School. Bottles of wine were allowed at the tables, but the boys also brought vodka. When the wine was poured for the toast, the boys added the vodka, and the headmaster made his speech. He spoke about the difficulties of life, about its struggles and how hard it would be to achieve what we wanted. We thought he was blundering. Which difficulties was he referring to when life was so wonderful, so full of promise and happiness? We didn't take much notice of him but lifted our glasses and burst out into a popular song of the day: "The Far Away Land". It was a new song, and it told the story of leaving home; of long and hard journeys through life; of the return to where one's loved ones had waited in a white house. We all loved that song and sang in unison with such sincerity and volume that nobody could stop us. The headmaster did not know how to react, and the teachers all smiled.

When we finished, we raised our glasses and drank a toast to the future. The wine and vodka which I drank, transformed me into a talkative, joyful and witty person. I was no longer shy and quiet. The boys surrounded me and asked me to dance. Of course, only Nicholas wasn't there to dance with me. He played his silver clarinet one last time, and one last time his eyes followed me round the dance floor.

We danced and we laughed, and we talked and sang until dawn, sending the dark night away from the large windows of the school hall. It was customary for the graduates to greet the sunrise after the farewell party, so when dawn came the dancing stopped. We all held hands and made our way out into the still morning air. From the outskirts of the sleeping town we could see the sun rising above the horizon. We continued to hold hands and sang another song. Large and golden, round and bright, the sun smiled down upon us, sending its greetings and blessing for the life which lay ahead. We were happy, young and hopeful, and we wanted our future to remain that way.

As I made my way home I was unhappy with myself for not having said goodbye to Nicholas, but then he hadn't said goodbye to me. Neither one of us had wished the other good luck for the future. We parted like strangers – like two distant stars that would never meet.

The cherry trees blossomed and I buried my face in the petals and cried. My dreams and everything I had ever wanted from life, I would continue to take with me. I would reach for everything that was noble, magnificent and splendid, and then hold it dearly, forever. I was deeply in love with life, and I wanted more from life: I became all the more determined to live it.

Chapter 12

Summer was passing quickly, so I began to work diligently in preparation for Kyiv University's entrance exam. I spent my days outside in the garden where Father had made a table and benches. They were nestled neatly between a couple of lilac trees and a jasmine bush. I was never parted from my books wherever I went, whether this was to the riverside where Anatoly fished, or to the woodlands where Nadiya collected wild strawberries, or back at the house where everybody enjoyed the warm summer evenings by the open windows. I planned well and divided each subject into sub-categories, and I gave myself time to revise everything.

By the beginning of August, I felt I was ready to sit the exam. Father blessed me, and Mother prepared a special dinner. The whole family gathered in their best clothes, including Auntie Chrystyna who wore a pretty blouse which she had from before the Revolution. Everybody wished me good luck. I had little idea of what was awaiting and I thought only about the exam. Father had borrowed 50 roubles for my journey and stay in Kyiv. Although it would be hard to support me, it would be an honour for him to have a daughter who was at university. He would now have something to speak favourably of, despite all of his suffering.

Both of my parents looked sad when I looked at them from the carriage of the express train. I would do anything for them because they were allowing me to lead my own life. When the train finally moved off and we had finished waving our goodbyes, I put my head out of the window. I enjoyed the wind in my face, the train's velocity, and my journey into the future. The harder the wind blew, the more I liked it. I felt strong and powerful. I was like a young eagle that had left its nest, and I was learning to fly, testing my strength in an unknown and undiscovered world.

It was nighttime when I arrived in Ukraine's capital city. I had never been in a big city before: there were so many lights, people, trams and cars. The noise was also something new. It must be wonderful to live here, I thought.

An old school friend called Halya met me at the station. She had promised to help me as her brother lived there. Her dark, reassuring eyes smiled at me confidently. She had been to Kyiv before and my fascination amused her. We travelled by tram and then crossed the Dnipro River by boat. The huge arch of the city's power station stood in the distance, and I felt proud of this grand Ukrainian construction. Its lights reflected in the water to form a second dazzling rainbow.

The journey was short but fascinating, unforgettable but also slightly frightening. I knew nobody here except Halya, and I did not even know her that well as she had always been in another class at school. We were potentially open to abuse from the many strangers nearby. I put my thoughts aside and tried to enjoy the journey. The river was wide, and it took a long time to reach the far side. With trust, I gave my hand to Halya and disembarked. She then took me to a hostel where her brother lived.

I knew Halya came from a family that used to be wealthy but who were now hiding in Krolevets. They had a little house on the outskirts where her father worked as a labourer. I went to visit her once, and I was impressed by their lifestyle. Their home was orderly, organised and laid out in good taste. Until that time, I had never met her brother Ihor, but when he greeted us I was impressed by his kindness, and his handsome face. He was dark like Halya, tall and slim and with brown eyes. He was quiet but intelligent. Ihor welcomed me to Kyiv and poured some tea. I unpacked my food and we had supper together. Halya told me about their parents, and Ihor listened quietly. He then showed us where we could sleep. It was in a recreation room called Red Corner. There were no beds, but he gave us some blankets and pillows and we made ourselves comfortable on the floor. As I lay awake, I wondered if Halya wanted me to get to know her brother and if that was why she had offered to help me. She had told me he was well-educated but he was working as a labourer to avoid attention from the authorities. Many thoughts crossed my mind. They gradually became more distant, and then very unreal.

After breakfast, Ihor hired a boat and took us back across the Dnipro River. He was quiet and hardly said a word until finally shaking my hand to say goodbye. He looked at me kindly. I could see he had been wronged in life and I felt sorry for him. He then told us to come again if we needed any help. Halya was taking an exam at the Medical Institute, so we wished each other success and parted. I was now completely alone.

Kyiv was just right for me. I enjoyed seeing the wide city streets, the trees, and the morning's rush of cars, trams and people. I loved it. The sun shone brightly, the sky was pale-blue and the morning's breeze seemed to greet me tenderly. I felt as though I belonged there.

When I found the University, the grand building and its pillars were so large and overpowering that I felt very small and insignificant. Dozens of students were making their way in and out, and I was just another. I soon found my way around and dealt with a succession of offices, application forms, questions, and then finally the entrance examination itself. I was allocated a place at a student hostel on the other side of the city which meant I would have to travel back and forth each day. This was no problem as I enjoyed the tram rides and the views.

In the evenings before taking the exams, I loved to go to Kyiv's central street – Khreshchatyk. It was wide, spacious, and with hundreds of people. The crowds moved in endless waves. Above them, in the green branches of the trees, were round, white lanterns which hung like shining roses under the dark-blue sky. I would mingle with this crowd and walked until late at night. I enjoyed the feeling of being one of a huge number of my own people. I enjoyed the summer's warmth, and I felt happy to be young and with prospects ahead of me.

I went to see all of the historic sights with some local girls. We visited churches and monasteries, and although these were closed for services, they were still used as museums. From St Volodymyr's Hill we looked across at the river, at the golden domes, the wide fields and meadows, and the green hills covered with forests. On one occasion we relaxed by the river where hundreds of people were enjoying the sandy beaches, the sunshine and swimming. Children paddled in the shallower waters, screaming and laughing the whole of the time.

My early thoughts of Ukraine's busy capital were rose-tinted. Watching the day trippers on the shores of the Dnipro, or the evening's crowds on Khreshchatyk, it was easy to think that these people had no worries, problems or fears, and no thoughts of one people's domination over another. At least, on the surface they appeared to be peaceful and happy. However, it was not long before I ran into a barrier which made me change my mind about belonging there.

I was well-prepared for the exams, and I was so confident of being successful that I had no worries. I had spent the whole summer studying and could even afford to help the other girls who were taking their exams at the same time, but history was about to repeat itself. When the results were announced, I was not accepted. I suffered it: I felt great pain, and I cried many tears yet again. My dreams had been shattered, and my whole world began to turn dark.

My money had almost run out and I had nothing to eat. Bread, sugar and water were all I could afford, and I did not want to return home to be seen as a failure. I struggled through each day in the hope of gaining entry to another university, but there were too many applicants in Kyiv – perhaps eight or nine for any remaining place. I had no doubts about influence or the ranks of fathers in the final selection process. I was unimportant, unknown, and my good marks had not helped me at all. I scribbled on one of the windowsills in the long corridor where I stood alone: "Goodbye, great building of science", and I cried again.

Representatives from other universities had arrived in Kyiv to take a number of students to fill their respective vacant places. I had just written an application to Kharkiv University. It was a page long and I poured my heart into it. I thought about it, and I thought about God and religion – subjects which were forbidden at school. They were never mentioned, except to be ridiculed or denied: 'God, if you exist, then please help me now,' I prayed.

I heard that representatives from Lviv University had just arrived and that they were about to interview candidates. I therefore handed them my application which was addressed to Kharkiv University. I had no time to rewrite it and I knew that I had little hope of being accepted. I also enclosed the certificate with my marks from the Grammar School and waited patiently.

A crowd of applicants were waiting by the door of the rector's office where the interviews were being held. I knew I had very little hope of being called so I stood at the back. In front of me were well-dressed girls who predicted that they would be called first as their fathers held good positions, and they would be chosen as suitable representatives to go to West Ukraine. I wore a simple white dress and my hairstyle was plain. I said my father's occupation was a clerk. Of course, I could not tell anyone who he really was.

When the interviews started there was silence. The door opened and a young man was called first, but then I heard my name being called. I could not believe my ears. Girls pushed me forward until I went through the door and stood in front of an elderly man who had a friendly smile. He was looking at my application and school certificate and at the letter in which I had poured my heart out. Within a couple of minutes he welcomed me as a student of Ukrainian Philology at Lviv University. I could not believe it. I wanted to kiss everyone around me. I had overcome the first and perhaps most difficult task that life had thrown at me.

Kyiv University informed me that if I wanted to travel on to Lviv, I would have to get permission from the local police in Krolevets. I then realised that I had too little money to make the return journey home. I searched, desperately, for a solution. Everyone I knew from Krolevets had returned home already, and the hostel where I had been staying was empty.

I noticed the cleaners who were busily preparing for the arrival of the new term's students. They were throwing out textbooks left by the applicants after their exams. I thought that if I collected the books I could sell them and raise some money. I gathered two bundles and took them to a bookshop in the centre of Kyiv. They were accepted, but the money I was given was not enough: I was still one rouble short for my ticket home.

There was no sense in staying longer than I could afford. So, I then went to the station and handed the money over to the woman in the ticket office. I knew I was short, but pretended that I did not know. What else could I do?

'Then, please give me a ticket to the next nearest station,' I said calmly. I was blushing nervously.

'Here is a rouble. Please take it.' I heard a gentleman's voice behind me, and he placed a rouble on the counter.

'Thank you, but how can I repay you?' I asked, looking at a tall, smiling gentleman. 'Will you give me your address?'

'It's all right. Really, it is.'

He smiled, and prepared the money for his own ticket. I thanked him again and made my way to the train. My faith in human nature had been restored. I had a ticket, and I could go home to where Father would try to help me again: of that, I was always sure.

I returned triumphantly. I had successfully gained entrance to Lviv University in the heart of West Ukraine. Lviv was considered to be a European city. It had been under Polish occupation until 1939, so in the minds of our local people it meant that I was virtually going to study abroad. Many of them whispered: 'That's her! She's the one going to Lviv!' Some girls envied me and others wanted to be my friend.

My only concern was that term had already started, and I had to move quickly. The police, however, delayed giving me their permission to leave. Krolevets seemed to be empty. Nicholas was also away. His certificate had failed to help him. However, he found a university willing to accept him on the condition that he passed its entrance exam, but he refused to take any further exams and was therefore not allowed to proceed any further. Meanwhile, my close friend Marusya had failed to gain entrance to Kyiv's Medical Institute, but she enrolled at a chemical institute in another town. Many of my other friends failed in their attempts to gain university places and stayed at home feeling bitter. They had no idea what to do next. Krolevets now seemed different, and I wanted to leave, as soon as possible.

After five days of waiting I was called to the Police Headquarters. An intimidating officer questioned me. I should have known why the police were not allowing me to go to Lviv. At that time, Ukrainian Nationalism was on the rise there, although most of us in East Ukraine were kept in the dark and knew relatively little about it. So, there I stood – the daughter of a man who had been deprived of his rights to work as a priest; having had the top marks in the Grammar School which had been downgraded to keep me down; now asking for my right to go and live in the heart of Nationalist Ukraine. It was so completely unheard of.

The officer remained very grim and measured me up and down with his eyes. I looked back at him. He looked back at me. There was a long pause. Finally, in a stern voice he said:

'Well, go and represent us in West Ukraine.'

He stamped a piece of paper and handed it over to me. It was my permit to travel there. It was now five o'clock in the afternoon. I ran home immediately.

'I've got it!' I shouted when I arrived. 'I've got it! I'm going! Tonight! Tonight!'

Mother knew she could not stop me. As I packed, she boiled some eggs and cobs of corn for the journey and wrapped up any other food she could spare. We knew it would be a long journey of almost two days. At half past seven my father, mother, brother and sister took me to the station.

The overnight express to Kyiv arrived on time at eight o'clock. I climbed up the steep steps and was the only passenger boarding at the station. Within minutes my dear family were left standing on the platform alone. I was again travelling into the unknown, and nothing in the whole world would stop me.

The train raced on through the golden evening and stopped only at the bigger stations. I did not think of the difficulties of the journey ahead such as changing trains in Kyiv, but luck was with me when I met other students who were also travelling to Kyiv. They took me to a student hostel where I could stay until the only train to Lviv arrived the following day.

I slept well, and in the morning I crept out so that no one in authority noticed I had stayed. I was escorted by some of the students. The early morning sun was bright and smiled down on us. The streets were clean. Tall poplars and huge chestnut trees lined the avenues. Crowds of students – beautiful, healthy young women, and handsome young men – were making their way to the University.

I still felt like an outsider in this beautiful capital city which I would always call "my capital city". Somehow, I knew that I would find no other city as beautiful and lively anywhere else in the world.

Although I deserved to be there, the road ahead would be a very long one, and Kyiv, like the first love in my life, would be forever in my heart.

Chapter 13

I boarded the train to Lviv, but slept uncomfortably that night as I had to sit upright for the entire journey. It lasted for just over a day. Lviv's station was huge and full of people who dressed differently. They spoke mostly in Polish – a language I found difficult to understand. I knew no one in the city, so the only thing for me to do was to make my way to the University. After some initial confusion, I met a man who spoke Ukrainian and who pointed me in the right direction.

The University looked like a palace with its tall pillars and wide flights of steps and it stood across the road from a big park. Inside, there was a spacious hall with soft lights and a large staircase leading to the upper floors. I loved what I saw at first sight, and I was delighted to be there.

I was so preoccupied with my sense of adventure, and with the novelty of everything around me, that I forgot to consider how I looked. Upon entering the beautiful foyer, before my interview in the rector's office, I caught a glimpse of myself in a large mirror. I looked poor and plain in my white, floral dress. My hairstyle was nondescript, and I had just come straight from a train not expecting to be in a place as beautiful as this. Some students waited with me. They were all well-dressed in the latest Polish fashions. Their standard of living had been higher than ours for at least twenty years.

The interviewers were also slightly surprised by my appearance, but my confident answers soon won them over. I was registered and given a place to stay in a student hostel. I was a late arrival, so the hostel was almost full to capacity and the only available place was on the fifth floor with two Jewish students. They greeted me kindly and introduced themselves. One was a girl called Bella who had dark, shining eyes. She was reading history. The other was called Hannah and she was reading European Philology. She was tall with brown hair and an oblong face.

The girls watched me unpack my modest possessions. I knew little about jewellery, perfume or makeup. Those sorts of things had not been encouraged at our school, so I read some strange looks on the girls' faces, but I took no notice. I began my studies, and encountered a whole new way of life.

Although I was five days late, nobody asked me any questions. The University's large lecture room finally opened its doors to me. I felt so small and insignificant, but if I had once felt reverence upon entering a church, then this was the new holiest of holy places for me. The room was like an amphitheatre. I immediately chose to climb to the highest seat to look down and met the inquisitive eyes of many students. Many of them were mature – judging by the large number of bald heads I could see, and most of the students were local West Ukrainians. They all looked different to our girls and boys. They were more serious and pale, but they were all well-dressed. When the professor came in, everybody stood up and the lecture on general philology began. I was captivated. I wrote notes, but then noticed that not everybody else was doing so. Some of the girls were flirting with the boys and this negated my first positive impressions. I continued as I had started, knowing that I had gone there to study and learn.

The lecturers changed. Some professors spoke several languages, yet, ironically they could not speak Ukrainian. The lectures were in Polish which I soon started to learn and understand. Polish is a Slavic language with a Latin alphabet, but with a different grammar. I made my notes in Ukrainian, and somehow managed. I quickly made friends and my life as a student began to feel normal.

I had found what I had wanted. I worked hard and succeeded. I was the first to answer questions, and my written work was always done on time. I also noticed that some of the girls did not study as much as I did, and they were not fully prepared for tests. They were usually the beautiful and well-dressed daughters of Communist Party officials, and they were enjoying their stay in Lviv by dressing well and having romantic flings with fellow students and lecturers.

My greatest joy was to go to the library and spend the entire evening reading the recommended books. Shelf after shelf was filled with them. In the middle of the room there were dozens of separate tables with individual reading lamps. The furniture was beautifully polished and it was always clean and shiny. Everything was tidy, well-organised and quiet. The large reading room was warm and inviting, and the visitors would pour over their books under the round, white lampshades. I marvelled at the thousands of books around me and enjoyed reading under my own lamp. I stayed there until closing time. At least in the library, nobody could see my simple and unfashionable dress. And for that matter, they would not have guessed how hungry I was, either.

The money my father had given me was soon spent, and I could only afford to spend one rouble a day. When the lectures were over, I calculated the best buy. It would perhaps be a plate of soup, or a delicious bakery bun, or a piece of gateau. Any of these alone would cost one rouble. Often, I would buy a delicious piece of cake instead of soup, to satisfy my hunger, but to have more than one item was totally out of the question.

Eventually, I heard rumours that a grant might be awarded to poorer students. I applied, and to my surprise I was awarded a sum of money which lasted for one month. I immediately bought myself a cardigan and skirt, and when I entered the University's reading room, all eyes turned towards me. The boys began to greet me with some respect, and the girls began to smile at me. I was upset by their change in attitude.

'I see, so you now want to greet my new outfit and not me, do you?'

I did not say that aloud, but I was becoming cynical. I could hear a new form of humour trying to find its way out. I began to smile and laugh and flirt, but without associating with anyone from this crowd. I no longer respected them.

I attracted more attention from the male students. One poet even fell in love with me. He walked with me, reciting his poetry. I listened, but inside I was laughing. I could not possibly fall in love with him or with anybody else. Nicholas was still in my heart, and he seemed to be well and truly locked in there. Nonetheless, I enjoyed the friendly attention from the boys, and I flirted with them. A second local student with big, blue eyes and blonde hair also fell in love with me. Unlike the first, he was shy and modest and could not find the words with which to tell me, but some of the girls made it quite clear to me that he wanted to marry me.

'Marry me?' I thought, 'Never! I have more important things to attend to, such as studying.' I then avoided the man as much as I possibly could.

The first term was ending, and my marks were all "of the highest grades, but a big blow followed. A new law was passed doing away with grants altogether. Compulsory payments were introduced for all studies. It came as a shock to me and to many others. I telegraphed home and Father replied simply: 'I cannot afford to pay.'

I cried, and did not know what to do. The law was then amended and it stated that grants would be cancelled for students who failed to attain the highest grades in their half term exams. I decided to stay on, but for the time being I had to search for a part-time job.

I had no luck. Nobody would employ me, and my money was quickly running out. My friends knew of my situation, and a local boy approached me and told me that he was leaving the University to teach in a village. He planned to continue his studies by correspondence. He then asked me if I would like to go with him and work as a teacher, too.

'No, I'm sorry,' I replied, 'I could never leave like that.'

So we parted, and he left the University. Many others left too, but I persevered with my search for work. There was probably not one office left in the whole of Lviv where I had not asked for work. Wherever I saw an office I went inside and enquired, but I was being very naïve. I received many surprised looks. From one point of view I was a poorly-dressed student from East Ukraine, and from another, it was considered to be degrading for a Soviet student to look for part-time work in former Polish-governed territory.

During my search, I discovered more of Lviv. It was a clean city where houses were surrounded by trees, and it was busy but orderly. In all my life I had never seen such shops: the butchers had row upon row of freshly-made kovbasa; the fishmongers even had live fish in an aquarium; the bakers had freshly-baked bread and all kinds of buns and cakes to make my mouth water; then there were huge shops with materials, clothes, stockings and shoes. People could choose to buy whatever they wanted.

I learned that Lviv received the largest supply of goods in the Soviet Union and was second only to Moscow. It was wonderful. Back at home we could only barter for goods and that was without the money. The quality and choice was limited and we were glad to get hold of anything we could.

Lviv's shops and markets, meanwhile, were full of everything.

The main street was so beautiful, rich and full of life that it was a pleasure just to walk there. Shops lined both of its sides and tall, mature trees stood in the middle forming a quiet promenade. There were benches where pedestrians could rest and enjoy the bustle of life around them. I admired St George's Cathedral, the many churches and the marvellously ornate buildings – each of which had a beauty and style I had not yet seen. I realised that I was as good as in the West of Europe – in a land different from the one I had left behind, yet I was still in Ukraine. In this land of two halves, my life was now very hard. I was struggling without money. My budget of one rouble a day had almost run out, and just one plate of soup was costing me between 70 and 90 kopeks. Very thankfully, I finally stumbled upon some good luck: I was offered a job.

A waitress was needed in the student canteen and the wages there were the price of a dinner and a supper every day. Visibly, I was already beginning to look unwell. I took the job. I attended lectures in the morning, but left early and would rush back to the hostel to change into a white apron. I would then make my way to the canteen where I would be given a dinner. By the time the students arrived I was relaxed, casual and talkative again.

I felt embarrassed at first, but I was helping to provide a service, so I got used to it. I learned to smile, exchange jokes and to speak in Polish. After dinner, I was free to return to the library and would sit and study until eight o'clock. I then hurried back to the canteen to serve supper, for which I was given a good meal. My worry about food was over.

I worked hard in the library, and within its quiet walls I felt more like myself. I was happy. I was eighteen and remained aware that boyfriends, clothes and luxuries had to be secondary to study, books and hard work. The attendants let me sit in peace, and I sat there happily all afternoon.

I became a favoured student in the auditorium and the professors praised my work. Another poet fell in love with me, but I did not take to him either. He was well-built, dark and very thoughtful. Naturally, he recited his poems to me, but poetry, which had been almost sacred to me, seemed to lose its attraction as I did not like the poet himself. I was not even flattered by his attention. I remained fully independent.

At the end of the first term, I received top grade marks again, so I qualified for another grant. I was overjoyed. I stopped working in the canteen, and at the same time, Father was able to send me some extra money. Knowing that I would be financially secure for the following term, I decided to go home for a holiday during the winter break which would last for two weeks. I packed my case and made the twenty-seven hour return journey to Kyiv, and then the final four hours to my dear, native home town of Krolevets.

I arrived at night, and it was approximately one kilometre from the station to the house, so I decided to walk. My homecoming was very dear to me. It had snowed and everything was so quiet and peaceful that I could have listened to the very movement of the stars. Alas, I would never feel so secure and confident along that path again. It would be my last walk through the town in peacetime.

I alarmed my parents when I knocked at the door, but they were delighted to welcome me back. Joy and happiness radiated through our home. I gave them some gifts, and we retired early. I was exhausted and had not realised how much I had missed the comfort of sleep in my own bed.

The two weeks I spent at home were wonderful. Mother would get up at five o'clock, as usual, to cook the day's dinner. She then went to work. Father got up even earlier to light the samovar. He would call us as he sat drinking his hot, steaming tea. We never drank tea with milk – that was unheard of. We used a lemon if we had one, or just drank it with sugar – if there was any of that. Tea drinking was a ceremonious occasion in our family. We all sat at the table together and looked into each others eyes. We smiled and blew the steam to cool the tea. Mother also cooked breakfast, and my favourite was pancakes with fried bacon and sour cream. My parents then went to work. Anatoly and Nadiya were both on holiday from school, so we went sledging and skiing in the valley just outside of town. I went to visit my friends, and people again pointed at me and gossiped, saying: 'That's her! She's the one who lives abroad!'

My old teachers wanted to talk to me, and everybody wanted to know what life was like "abroad". Could I tell them about the wonderful shops such as they had never seen, or of a life so different from the one they knew? I told them about everything except for the financial difficulties I had faced there. I didn't mention them to anyone, not even to my parents. I wanted to be successful in their eyes. I felt happy, and I even tried to act in a western manner with which I had now become familiar.

I would have been happy to have met Nicholas. I knew he was at home after his lack of progress to university. He was disappointed and frustrated and deliberately avoided other people. I knew that news of my arrival would reach him. In my heart I knew that I was now the victorious one. I was receiving a university education. I had caught up with him, and I had overtaken him.

I returned to Lviv happily rejuvenated. I continued to work hard. The lectures, the library and the books were again central to my goals. I watched as my friends fell in love. They, too, were very happy.

'Why are you so happy?' the porter of our hostel asked one of the girls. She smiled back at him radiantly and replied:

'It's because I am young, in love, and much loved.'

I looked at her lovely face. She was indeed a woman in love, and I wondered if I would ever look that way. There was nobody I fancied there. Perhaps life would be different in the near future.

I continued to live in the room with the two Jewish girls and grew to like them very much. Bella was the elder, and she smiled with her beautiful, dark eyes each time she looked at me. She, too, took her studies seriously, and I respected her for that. Hannah was younger, green-eyed and plain, but she also worked hard. Both of the girls came from West Ukraine. They had western ways of behaviour, and their wardrobes were full of beautiful clothes. We often had long discussions, late into the night. They, too, had no boyfriends and carried no excessive emotional baggage. Neither did they indulge in an abundance of luxuries, unlike some of the other students I knew. They smiled sincerely and laughed heartily, but never falsely. I admired them and they accepted me as a visitor from afar. My two friends were positive, I liked them, and I was influenced by them and continued being studious.

I also made friends with someone called Anya. She was

the most beautiful woman I had ever met: surprisingly, she was also the unhappiest. Anya was a student of history. She was a mature student who was married and had come to Lviv University, not from school like most of us had, but from self-tuition. She always wore a stylish, red coat and had a beautiful, red hat to match. She was slim and graceful, and she always drew the attention of everyone she passed in the street. Her face was oblong, with a perfectly-proportioned forehead which was covered with soft, auburn hair. Her eyes were brown and her lips were ruby-red. Her skin was white and her small, delicate features were like the petals of a flower. Even when she spoke, she had the voice of an angel.

The day I met her, Anya had bought some apples, but her bag suddenly burst open and the apples rolled across the pavement. A gentleman picked them up and handed them to her. He lifted his hat and said in amazement:

'Excuse me madam, but I have never met a woman as beautiful as you in my whole life.'

Anya smiled, and replied politely: 'Thank you. I have never received a compliment like that before.'

She then saw me come out from a shop and said to me in Ukrainian: 'How polite people are here. They acknowledge you, but they never pester you.'

We walked to the hostel together, and Anya shared some of her thoughts with me. She did not enjoy her studies at the University. There was too much political talk, and politics failed to interest her. For the first time, I realised that university life was not the ideal I had once thought it was. I must have been a good listener because Anya continued to talk. Perhaps she trusted me because I dressed simply and therefore was not from the world of political officialdom. I never mentioned my background, though if I had to, I would say my father was a factory worker. We continued to talk.

Anya was a child of kulaks – private land owners. Her parents had been sent to Siberia and all their property had been confiscated by the State. She was snatched back by an aunt when her parents were about to make their journey, and she grew up with her. When she was sixteen, she married, but the marriage did not last, and the couple divorced. Then, Anya married again, but not finding satisfaction or happiness in her second marriage, she decided to catch up and learn everything that she had missed at school. With some private tuition she passed grammar school exams, and with her good grades she was accepted by Lviv University. Her husband worshipped her and financed her, yet she was not happy with him. She wanted to die, and wished to disappear. She loathed the State's festivities such as May Day and The October Revolution:

'False, false, false,' she whispered to me, as we walked amongst the people.

Anya made me think. Until now, I had looked at everything idealistically, and did things without questioning. Now, I was again reminded that not everything was right. She gave me new ideas, new thoughts, and a new outlook on life.

Anya's parents died in Siberia and she never heard of them again. She never received any of their property and even had to continue hiding the fact that she was the daughter of kulaks. Did those wrongs and the power of hatred lead her to become so tormented and unhappy? She confided more and more in me, but never mentioned her husband. He must have been sending her money as she was able to live and dress well. She thought she would find happiness through study, but she remained very unhappy.

Comparing Anya to Bella, who was also beautiful, I could see the difference between the two. Study meant everything to Bella, and her life remained free from emotional complexities. We never talked about her feelings. She knew she was very pretty, and occasionally she would tease Hannah about having an advantage over her when it came to encountering men in shops: 'It's all in the eyes, Hannah,' she would say, smiling. 'It's all in the eyes.'

I did not know everything about Bella's background. There had been conditions that prevented her from going to school, so I admired her subsequent dedication to her studies. Yet I would listen more to Anya because I wanted to understand her negative attitude to life. The more she talked to me, the more I was aware that, beautiful as she was, her soul was a dark and unhappy place. I could see that beauty was not everything, neither was money. There was more to life for a woman, and my sober young heart no longer wanted to learn the facts of life from books alone.

Another friend of mine was a carefree young student

called Valya. She came from Central Ukraine, and when I first met her she had thick, black plaits but she then changed her style. She let a mass of curls fall upon her slender shoulders. Her skin was olive-coloured and her eyes were big and brown. She nearly always wore an embroidered blouse or a touch of embroidery on her dress. She was a very pretty Ukrainian woman. Her smile was always friendly and unpretentious. I liked Valya very much and saw her every day in the auditorium. She was in the same faculty and year as I was. We studied and often walked together, and we were often joined by Anya.

Valya had a sister, living in Lviv, who was married to a high-ranking military officer, and they had children. She would go to visit them, but she would never talk about them, and it puzzled me. Her answers in tests were poor and her homework was rarely done well. I liked her, however, as she did not make a show of her beauty or her expensive dresses. She was simple, sincere and friendly. My appreciation of philosophy, meanwhile, began to grow, and I studied all of the nineteenth century's philosophers and their ideas.

Finally, spring began to arrive. The first warm breezes and bright sunlight brought smiles to most people's faces. Ladies in the streets wore flowers in their buttonholes. First thing in the morning, the smell from the bakeries would make me feel happy: brown bread, white bread, buns, cobs and zwiebacks. At the end of the day, Valya, Anya and I would wander through the shops in a group and we would admire everything. In the larger stores I wondered who could afford to pay 10 roubles for 100 grams of cocoa. Would I ever be able to afford such a luxury?

I also like going to the flea market. The girls did not always accompany me, but I was interested to see all the antique articles that people were selling there when they were short of money. I could never afford to buy anything, but it brought back memories from my childhood.

Meanwhile, I remained unaware of world events. I did know about the War which had started in Europe on the 3rd of September 1939. I was not that interested in politics, and I had no idea of what was happening beyond the border. Some of the girls who were going out with soldiers talked about it, but I took no notice. The most important things were my next exams, the emerging spring, and the beautiful shops.

At night I resumed my reading, and I often saw how the sky was illuminated by searchlights. It was unsettling to see the big powerful lines of light cut through the dark, but they were fascinating, too. They were like long narrow roads above the city. I paid little attention to the watchful eyes of the military and their preparations for defence. I was naïve to never have thought about life beyond Ukraine.

May was quickly coming to an end, and Lviv was in full bloom. The trees were covered with fresh, green leaves, and the local people were happy. We walked through Kostiushko Park, opposite the University, and enjoyed the beauty of the lake, the flower beds and the stretches of grass where children played merrily. Their mothers sat on the benches and smiled.

On Sundays I would visit Lviv's many churches. At least here, they were all open. I admired the large congregations and wonderful choirs. The traditions were slightly different to ours and I wished my father could have seen them. I wanted him to share my experience. People were praying, whilst at home it was forbidden. What was so wrong with coming together to create a beautiful expression, to lift hearts and to raise human spirit? No philosopher at university, no lecture and no book could give me such a spiritual uplift as I felt in church.

I studied intensively, until the day of the first exam: the Foundations of Marxism and Leninism. I passed with flying colours, tidied up, rested, and prepared for the next one: Russian Language. Again I passed with ease. I achieved the same result for General History and Ukrainian Language. Of all my tutors, I particularly liked Professor Pushk from the Faculty of Ukrainian Philology. We had a chat after the exam and he appreciated the efforts I had made. He wished me success for the future. I returned to my room, tired but happy. There were two whole days before the next exams, so I decided to do the washing, tidy my books and have an early night.

Chapter 14

It was getting late by the time I had washed and tidied, so I was tired. I thought about my studies, and had a strange premonition that I would not be able to continue with them. It lasted momentarily. I then fell into a deep sleep, but not for long because somewhere along the corridors I thought I could hear the girls running up and down. I could hear their voices. There was some sort of commotion. It was long after midnight, and Bella came into the room.

'Why aren't that lot asleep?' I asked grumpily. 'And what is all that noise about?'

'They're talking about war,' replied Bella, but without her usual smile.

'War! What war?' I was angry. 'They'd better go to sleep, and let me get some sleep. I'm really tired.'

Bella said nothing, and didn't go to bed. Again, I heard noises in the corridor, and frightened whispers: 'Bombowtsi! Bombowtsi!' I recognised the voice of a girl who was alarmed about bombers.

'Why doesn't she go to sleep?' I asked Bella. At that very moment there was a tremendously loud bang: then another, and another.

'They're bombs,' said Bella calmly. 'We had better go downstairs.'

I had no idea how my life was about to change. If someone had poured a bucket of cold water over me I would not have been as shocked and surprised as I was at that very moment. "War" was a word I had never used. "War" had started and the girls were absolutely right.

I knew so little about the situation in the world. Memories came flooding back to me. I recalled that when I was a little girl I was actually frightened of one thing – the word "war" itself. What it actually was, or what it would come to mean was never clear to me, yet each time I would hear the word I started to cry. Children in the street soon learned of my fear, and anytime they wanted to tease me, all they had to do was shout "war". I'd scream and run to my mother, and it would be a long time before she'd reassure me that there was going to be no war.

I was terrified of soldiers, too. The sight of the military, of strict and fierce-looking men with guns used to make me feel so frightened that I would start to cry. I would hide away so as not to see them. For this reason, Mother rarely took me to town where soldiers were stationed. Occasionally, we saw them in the village. Now the word "war" had become reality.

It was Sunday the 21st of June 1941, and at about four o'clock in the morning the first German bombs began to fall on Lviv. It was still dark outside. Calmly, I made my way downstairs to the basement dining room where everyone was gathering. Some of the girls were crying, some were trembling, and others were giving orders. It was pitch-black, and someone told us to be quiet. As soon as there was an audible cry or whisper, a harsh and very nervous hiss of 'Tsh! Tsh!' would answer back. It lasted all night. That sound of someone's 'Tsh!' still terrifies me now, as I think about it.

In the morning an "all clear" was sounded and we left the basement. I went to my room and packed my case. My two companions also packed their bags and disappeared and left some of their belongings. They were both nervous and frightened. Bella, who was usually calm, was now becoming distressed. It alarmed me. Hannah was now red-faced and trembling. We shook hands and kissed each other. Then they parted. I remembered my Grandma telling me never to take even a nail from a site after a fire. It meant never to take anything from someone else's misfortune. So I didn't touch a thing. The girls left their handkerchiefs which were still drying by the window.

I finished packing my case and calmly stepped out into the streets. Everywhere, there were people, soldiers, guns, tanks. Everything and everyone was moving or running chaotically. I reached the University and hoped to say a final goodbye. It was closed, and there was nobody there. I wandered on through the streets, lost and bewildered, until I finally returned to the hostel. Some of the girls were still in the recreation room and were listening to the radio. At twelve o'clock Soviet Foreign Minister Molotov announced that war with Germany had officially started. Valya and I fell into each other's arms and cried. Other girls sobbed on each others shoulders. Some were just numb.

'Let's go into the nursing service,' Valya said decisively. 'We will help to defend our country.'

'Yes,' I agreed, 'let's go!'

'You know,' Valya continued, 'we can take our cases to my sister's home, and then we can enlist. My brother-in-law will help us.'

'All right,' I said, 'let's do that.'

Anya smiled at us, disbelievingly. 'I'm going back to my husband,' she said.

I said goodbye to Anya, and would never see her again. We went upstairs to fetch our suitcases, but as soon as we came down again there was another alarm. Bombs were falling nearby, and the building shook. We sat wherever we thought it was safe. Some students had already crawled under the table. We were all frightened, and some of girls were hysterical: they ran from one side of the room to the other.

Everything went quiet again, and then smoke and the smell of burning came in from the street. Valya and I took our cases and quickly headed to where her sister lived. We genuinely wanted to leave our things safely in her care and enlist as nurses. As we made our way through the streets people shouted at us: 'Russians, go home!'

I took no notice as neither I nor Valya were Russian. I had no idea that I had been looked upon in that way.

The apartment of Valya's sister was large, beautiful, and full of many fine pieces of furniture. I had never been in an apartment quite like it. So that's how they live, I thought. Valya did not even have time to introduce me to her sister before another alarm could be heard. We were in a house which was several storeys high and had to make our way down to the basement. There were many Jewish families living there, and they were well-dressed and well-fed. They were visibly very wealthy. I could not help noticing that with them they had purses which were full of money. I had lived on one rouble a day for the past year, and I could see that they were fully on top of their financial affairs. Although many bombs continued to fall nearby, I was no longer frightened. I was now more taken aback by this other world of wealthy and, until now, happy people.

Valya's brother-in-law arrived. He was a tall soldier and immediately ordered his wife and children to get into his car. Valya joined them and asked if I could come with them. He looked at me and said: 'There's one place. Then you can take a train home.'

He put our suitcases in the back of the car and off we drove through the streets of Lviv. Houses were burning and people were crying. The car headed rapidly to the railway station. We remained silent about our intention to enlist as nurses. Valya did not seem to be brave enough to mention it, so I stayed quiet, too. I was there only because of her kindness.

There was a train at the station, but it was packed with people and had no standing room at all. We looked to where we could see another train, but that was packed, too. We were fortunate not to have found any room on those trains. We heard later on that they had both been bombed and that there were many casualties. In a third train, Valya's brother-in-law found room for his family, but there was no place for me. I was left alone and thanked them for bringing me there. Valya had earlier asked me to pay for the car. I gave her all the money I had, even though I thought she really would not need it. We parted and never saw each other again.

With my suitcase and my winter coat tied up in a bundle I went to look for a place on yet another train. Although it was packed, I somehow managed to climb up the steps to one of the carriages and squeezed my way inside. There were no tickets and no conductors. People pushed and squeezed past each other, but everybody was glad just to be on board. Without a whistle or any other warning the train moved off and we were heading eastwards. Everybody sighed with relief.

People began to talk and described the beautiful homes they had made in Lviv. They were sorry to leave. Communist Party members with their wives and children, families of military personnel, and wealthy Jewish families must have arrived early as they all had reserved seats. They sat comfortably by the windows chatting about the "good life" they had led. They had plenty to eat and drink, and those who had to stand looked down at them, enviously. The train travelled on and on. There was no water or food, and we passed stations without stopping. As time went by, the passengers became hungry and very thirsty.

Suddenly, the train stopped in the middle of the countryside. We were all ordered outside. Planes were heard flying overhead. The Germans were following the railroad and were bombing the trains. We ran into the fields looking for somewhere to take cover. There was a small wood not far away, so everyone ran there. We fell to the ground and waited. Night was falling, and when the planes had passed we were ordered back. I could not remember which carriage I had been in, yet I still found my bundle: nobody had taken it. I recalled again my Grandma's words: "Never take anything from a disaster, and you will not lose that which is yours".

The train set off again and gained speed, and we moved on quickly through the night. By morning, having had no sleep and still standing on our feet, we became even thirstier. When the train stopped to refuel, we went to find water. There was only one bottle available and it had to be shared by all. We decided that the children should have the first drink, but then a huge man pushed everyone aside and grabbed the bottle for himself. He began to drink and everyone began to shout at him. For the first time, I was seeing the selfishness of people in the struggle for their survival. The children, the women and the elderly were all ignored. We travelled on and lost track of time, and we hoped to survive – not because of a lack of water, but because of several more attempts to bomb the train.

From Kyiv, there was no longer a connection to Krolevets. I waited for a long time until I finally jumped on board the Kyiv-Moscow express. I had climbed inadvertently into a first class carriage. I had never travelled first class before, and was frightened of the consequences of being found there. I was just about to leave when an elderly lady invited me to sit with her.

'It is wartime my dear, and it doesn't matter which class you travel in,' she said politely. 'Come sit here next to me.'

I was bewildered. I had never seen such a luxurious train, and this delicate old lady seemed to have stepped straight out of a book. The compartment was draped in green velvet. Clean mirrors sparkled on the walls and the polished mahogany wood shone as new. I knew so little of the lives of others in our society, of those who lived on the other side of life. The old lady was very kind, and she asked where I had just come from and where I was going. On learning that I was making my way back from Lviv she became more sympathetic and asked me about life there. Perhaps she was a writer. I looked into her intelligent eyes. I never found out, but I never forgot her either. She had made me feel at home in another world.

The train stopped at Konotop station, where it was terminating. I parted company from the old lady and stood on the platform. There were soldiers everywhere. Amongst them I recognised an old face from school. It was a young man now leaving to go to war. We exchanged greetings. Both of us were tired, dusty and lost somewhere on one of the most difficult journeys of our lives. We now felt like strangers in a world of danger. He was the only person I recognised from amongst hundreds of strangers on the long journey home. It was reassuring to see him and I knew he was glad to see me too, but we had to quickly say our goodbyes and part.

I waited for a long time for a local train to Krolevets, and I finally arrived late in the afternoon. The station was full of people and the noise of arriving trains. I had not lost anything on that tiring journey and was just pulling my suitcase from the train when I heard my father's voice:

'My dear, you have come! I knew you would!'

I was in my father's loving arms again, happier beyond any feeling I can describe.

'I have been to the station every day, since all of this started,' he said. 'Mother has been crying, thinking you would never make it back.'

Father did not want to use the word "war". He particularly did not want to mention it at the time of our reunion. 'Let us give thanks to God! You're safe, you've returned, and we are all together.'

It was wonderful to come home. Mother cried tears of joy. Nadiya was delighted to see me again, Anatoly smiled, and Auntie came and kissed me.

'I'm no longer frightened of dying,' Mother said, 'not now we're all together again.'

At least another "holiday" of some sort had started: it was a glorious sunny, summer month in Ukraine. War was still distant, somewhere beyond the horizon, and we did not think it would reach us. Nadiya, Anatoly and I went on picnics in the woods. I enjoyed the outings, not knowing that they would be my last taste of Ukraine. I loved our majestic and silent forests where the pines created a natural shelter. I even scratched Nicholas's name on a silver birch, for I had never done that, and I had failed to meet anyone else who had touched my heart. I gathered flowers with Nadiya and rolled in the valley's soft, green grass. Anatoly came with us, so we were never frightened of going anywhere. We went to the river where the water was clean and warm, and we swam for as long as we wanted. We jumped from the trees and splashed into the water below. We then collected water lilies, made necklaces and looked like water nymphs.

We hired a boat and drifted along the river singing, and thoroughly enjoyed the summer's evening air. The peaceful river banks were full of flowers and we dangled our fingers over the side of the boat. We came home hungry and happy, and Mother had dinner ready for us. We had borshch cooked with salt, onions and seasoning, and occasionally there would be a little bit of fried bacon. We never minded what we ate because everything that Mother cooked was always good.

One day, I went to see an old school friend Oksana, who lived in a village not far from the town. She was a tall, young woman with thick, chestnut-coloured hair and brown eyes. She greeted me happily and introduced me to her parents. She was their only daughter, and they worshipped her. We ate together, and then her father showed me around their beautiful garden which had recently been confiscated by the Village Council. They had left him with just a few trees by the house, and a small patch of soil.

'I planted all of those trees myself,' he said to me, wanting to talk to someone who understood, 'and now look at them!'

He showed me a tree which had fallen: 'They took the land, but they don't look after it.'

He chose his words carefully, and looked over his shoulder just in case somebody was listening. I looked at the large orchard with the beautiful fruit trees and felt sorry for him. This was now the normal way of life in East Ukraine. I had long since been used to it, and said little in reply.

Oksana then took me to the river. Ukrainian rivers are deep, wide and long and occasionally have sandy beaches, and they are overlooked by miles of green valleys on either side. Weeping willows can be seen dotted along the banks, and dense, green shrubbery surrounds the water. We swam, and then rowed a boat belonging to Oksana'a father. A young man called Andriy – a friend of Oksana's – turned up and joined us. He was jolly and friendly and made us laugh. I was usually shy and reserved with strangers, but on that day I found a side to my personality I never knew existed. I laughed and joked and talked and told stories. I felt light-headed and friendly as though there had never been a serious girl inside of me.

We had a happy day. We drifted along the river and stopped to swim at the sandy beaches. We became sunburnt, and though the skin soon peeled from our backs, we laughed. We went swimming again. The water was clear and deep. Andriy dived and swam and brought us water lilies and white stones from the river bed. Oksana put yellow flowers in her hair and looked beautiful. We stayed by the river until the pink sky reflected back from the water. The birds sang their final songs, and the sun set peacefully beyond the horizon. I had discovered my real personality and I had finally woken up from childhood's long and protective sleep. I had enjoyed life in its simplest unspoilt form – with nature, pleasant people, and good health. Oksana and Andriy were both farmers' children and they were very much at home with nature. They had made me feel at home with them. Later that evening, they took me to the bus station and I said goodbye to them. Deep down, I knew that a happy day like this would happen very rarely, and perhaps I would never see either of them again: sadly, I was right.

The days passed, and news came of the approaching Front Line: 'Surely they won't come here!' came the cries of disbelief.

Men were mobilised, and day after day, women were left behind to cry in the centre of town. Our neighbour was called up, and his mother packed some dry bread into his bag. She had absolutely nothing else to give him.

My father sighed: 'How can he be expected to fight? He has nothing to eat.'

We watched sadly as the tall and handsome young man said goodbye to his mother. He had worked in the local factory, but for all his efforts, his family's little house now had no food inside. Shadows from the surrounding trees made his house appear dark. His elderly mother blessed him and cried bitterly after he had gone.

The alarms rang out and the first planes appeared in the cloudless summer sky. I looked up bravely and tried to count them. When the first bombs fell, I thought about war songs that I had read about. I was not in the least bit frightened. My parents sat in the cellar and called me to come down. I obeyed, just to keep my mother calm, and I reassured everyone else in a confident voice. I carried a first aid bag on my shoulder, and I was ready to help as a nurse. That was my intention – romantically influenced by the books I had read. Then, I received my first true opportunity to be that nurse.

Gun shots were being fired from planes nearby, and then a bomb fell. Bang! The earth in the cellar seemed to shake and debris and dust fell upon our heads. I heard a cry nearby, and then everything went quiet again. I went outside despite Mother's protests, and in our yard, under the young poplar tree, I could hear someone groaning. I went closer and saw the pallid face of a young man looking back at me helplessly. Holding his hands across his middle he hid his wound. Blood was pouring out from under his white shirt. His soft, blue eyes looked at me gently, but by the time I had thought of what to do, a man came through the gate, took him under his arms, and dragged him away from the yard.

I was angry with myself. I had been too slow and failed to help. I had panicked. I froze. I realised that learning was one thing, but practice was another. I had never seen a wound, or blood, before. I had never helped anyone in danger. I was sorry for the man. I wondered who he was and what he was doing in our street in the first place, but I had been too slow. There was no end to the remorse I felt.

The alarms continued to sound, and more and more refugees came to the town. Food became rare, and people stood in long queues at shops until the next alarm sounded. Then they ran to take cover. After that, I could see they were simply glad to be alive. They hurried home to their families without any bread, and simply hoped that everybody at home was also alive. Panic began to spread through the town. The Communists and Jews began to flee, and formal documents were burned.

At the end of the summer, at the beginning of the new

school term, I found a job as a teacher in the neighbouring village of Buyvalovo, but I only just began to teach when the schoolmaster and the other teachers were called up for military action. The Front Line was coming closer. Hurriedly, they burned all of the school's registers.

The evening was cloudy but warm, so we sat quietly on a bench by the school. Thick smoke rose from the chimney where the papers were burning. The records of so many people's hard work were vanishing. The headmaster's young wife was crying. She was six months pregnant and had an old mother-in-law living with her. Another teacher's wife had two small children, and her husband had also been called up. Then, the headmaster came out of the school and said:

'That's it, that's all. Everything has now been burned. They'll not find anything. Our school year has ended. Comrades, you can all go home.'

We did not want to go home. We sat beneath the trees for a few more hours. In the distance, we could hear the sound of guns. Everything else around us was quiet. We had to confront our personal fears. Finally, the headmaster came out: 'Good night!'

'Good night.' We replied quietly.

I had been happy at that school, in my first days of professional employment. I thought about it as I walked the seven kilometres back home. Many students had returned to the town with the outbreak of war, and many had applied to teach, but only a few were given jobs, and I had been one of the lucky ones. My old teachers were on the selection committee and remembered my successes. I then recalled what some of the girls told me about my new school's headmaster:

'Oh, he is a wonderful man. He's just your type. He's so like you!'

'But he's married!' I protested.

'So, he is just the right man for you,' the girls echoed.

I was amazed at such talk, and it was not long after that when I first met him – a tall, slim and very handsome man. He was a bit shy, but he had wise and friendly eyes. His wife would wear an embroidered blouse, and she was also tall. She was well-built and had strong features, and a powerful character. They were both very friendly with me and helped me to find a room in a family home.

It was a lovely and spacious room, and it had a bed, a table, pictures on the walls, and icons, too. I ate with the family and they did the cleaning and washing for me. They were very kind, and I liked them. They had three children. Their father was fighting in the War and they had no recent news of him. I taught the children at school and they were always polite. My landlady had a good sense of humour and would make us all laugh. I helped them in the house, and we lived as one family except that I had been given their best room – the living room. The children slept in a small room by the stove, and the landlady slept on top of it.

The headmaster's wife often called in to see me, and we went for walks in the forest. I wondered if one of the girls had told her something about matching me up with her husband. I smiled and remembered the looks in his eyes. He had a quiet and attentive nature. Once we were alone in his office, and he suddenly said to me: 'You have a lovely personality.'

I looked at him in surprise, but I did not answer. I felt his presence and understood why the girls had said what they had said. We were alike, and his wife was not. She was strong, domineering, and perhaps a little bit aggressive. She was also pregnant, so I would never encourage my friendship with him to develop. I understood that not every marriage was happy, and that it takes more than marriage itself to make a happy and successful relationship between a husband and wife. I understood so much from that brief encounter.

When my work at the village school was over, I knew that the girls were right. I could have liked the headmaster, and in the end I could have fallen in love with him. With a sigh, I remembered his last handshake, his long affectionate look, and his words of farewell before he was sent on to his unknown destiny. He went, and his wife Natalya gave me the address of her parents where she was going to live. She asked me to come and see her. It underlined our friendship, and it came as a surprise, but I accepted her invitation to visit her.

Years later, when I remembered that particular episode in my life, I wondered why I had become so involved in the life of these two strangers, and why I had forgotten my previous thoughts about Nicholas. I went to see Natalya after her baby boy was born. Her parents worked on the railway and lived in a little house by the line outside of the town. They greeted me warmly and we had tea together. Natalya took me to the cradle to show me her baby. She left me for a few seconds, and as I stood there the thought crossed my mind that it was the baby of a man who could even have been mine. He was a man I could have loved, even though he belonged to someone else. Was it always going to be like this in my life? It was only for a split second that the thought crossed my mind. Then, as though realising it, Natalya suddenly grabbed the baby and took him away to another room. I saw the animosity in her look. She seemed to sense something and I never went back to their house again. All the same, her mother-in-law befriended me. Apparently, Natalya did not want to know her either, and left her to become a lonely and poor woman. I empathised with her.

As I completed my walk back to Krolevets, heavy clouds began to come in from the West. It started to rain. It was the kind of rain that comes before a storm: a few big drops, one at a time, and then eventually a torrential downpour from the sky. The clouds did not come my way, however. They were blown towards the centre of the town. The road stayed dusty, and the air stayed warm. Then, arrows of lightning began to cut through the dark sky followed by a loud rumble of thunder. Then, from somewhere in the town, there was a tremendous explosion followed by gunfire. There were huge flames, and smoke quickly spiralled upwards and merged with the thick dark storm clouds.

'Dear God!' I exclaimed aloud.

Krolevets centre appeared to be on fire. I forgot everything I had just been thinking of. The rain began to fall and the wind blew in my face, but I ran forward until I met the first people coming out in the opposite direction:

'It's an ammunition train at the station which has caught fire. It's burning and exploding, that's why it sounds like gunfire.'

I breathed a deep sigh of relief and walked into the next street. I was wet but calm. It was so warm that even the rain failed to cool the air. Krolevets was engulfed in large sheets of orange flames rising high into the sky. It was eerily dark.

I returned home, and when I opened the door everybody was shocked to see me so wet and tired. My family was frightened. The fire was huge and extremely dangerous, and some people had already been accused of sabotage. I reassured Mother who was crying, and spoke calmly to Father. I now assumed more authority in the family as the eldest child, and as an adult. I was also a student and a teacher with a calm and composed character capable of dealing with the dangers of war. I was trusted as the one who knew best, and I told my father what I had heard on the way home:

'The Front Line is still far off.'

'For that we should be grateful, and I'm so happy to see you,' he replied.

Mother wiped her tears: 'We all want to be together at a time like this. We have no idea what will happen next.' She sighed and went into the kitchen to make some supper.

'We shall put our trust in the will of God,' Father added optimistically, ever strong in his faith.

The ammunition train burned all night, and we heard more explosions from time to time, but we did not worry. We slept well as no further alarms were sounded.

Chapter 15

The following day, the town was deserted. The officials had all disappeared, as had most of the Jewish population – particularly those who had occupied higher positions. Offices were closing down, as were the shops, bakeries and every other place used for keeping the population fed, supplied or governed. The majority were left to fend for themselves, and once they had realised what was happening, they too, instinctively began to fight for their lives.

Although I was the eldest in the family and was considered to be wise and serious, I was not altogether practical. I was more of a dreamy idealist. Anatoly and Nadiya, however, made a very good match as brother and sister, and as close friends. Anatoly was now a handsome, young man. He was strong and active, and although my sister was small and delicate, she was sharp and practical in all her words and deeds. They began to bring food home from the shops which had been broken into by mobs. We ate everything they brought as there was no other food. We also moved from our own cellar to the cellar of a detached house across the road as my parents thought it would be safer there.

Day after day, people continued to leave town. The sound of gunfire came closer and closer. Mother became very uneasy. It was in her nature to be calm and gentle but she could never even stand the sound of thunder. Now the gunfire was frightening her. She crouched in a corner of the cellar and put her fingers in her ears. She was also anxious for all of us. She begged us not to go outside whenever we wanted to know what was going on, especially when the firing had ceased for a while. Meanwhile, Father always remained brave having fully placed his trust in God.

'It is all in God's will,' he would repeat calmly to Mother, whenever she pleaded with him not to go outside. 'We are completely in God's hands,' he said. He passed this message to the neighbours.

I never saw fear in his eyes. They shone with an inner light – with faith and submission to God's power.

Our neighbours sat in the cellar and talked. A candle burned in the middle of the floor, and long shadows swept across the walls whenever someone stood up. Stories were told from the Bible, about the times when people ran to the mountains to seek protection. Each time the firing started, everyone held their breath and made the sign of the cross. Children cried, and the firing went on through the night.

'It's the Front Line,' said an elderly man who had seen World War I. 'It has reached us.'

He was correct. By the early hours of the morning, the noise became worse. Shells fell nearby, and the firing of rifles continued. Then it all stopped. We sat motionless. We were very frightened, but we were glad to be alive.

It was late afternoon before some of the men dared to go outside. Low clouds rolled over the town, and the wind blew the first yellow leaves from the trees. Someone in the street said the Germans were in the town, so some people ran to the main road to see if they could be seen. It all felt unnatural. It was as though one way of life had stopped and died, and another strange, unknown and unwanted new life had begun.

As I stood by the main road with dozens of neighbours, I watched the columns of German soldiers roll past us on their motorcycles. They looked fierce, and I realised that we were a powerless people who would have no option other than to submit to their power. All my life, I would dislike motorcycles as they would remind me of the fear I felt on that day when the German army arrived.

We lived under German occupation and the days began to pass. Rumours spread that the German soldiers were picking up good-looking Ukrainian girls at night and were having their way with them. Father therefore insisted that I should dress in the worst clothes I had, and wear a white scarf on my head to look like a peasant girl. Mother found me an old, grey skirt and a white blouse, and Auntie gave me a plain, white scarf. Even when wearing that outfit, my parents hid me inside the house as soon as a German soldier appeared in the street.

Our street was away from the main road. A small stream ran down the middle, and weeping willows dipped their branches into the water. The pavements were muddy, and would have looked unattractive to any German passers-by. Nonetheless, we could still hear shooting not too far in the distance, and we disliked their presence. We wondered how far it would all go.

As time went by, I became braver and went out of the house to meet my friends in town. I also queued for some bones which the Germans began to sell to the locals from the abattoir. Local's cows and pigs were taken and killed, and sausages were made, but only for the occupying army.

As autumn progressed, more alarms were sounded. Some said it was because of British planes, though others said they were Russian. The bombs fell, all the same. One sunny morning when I went to our allotment with Auntie Chrystyna to dig up the potatoes an alarm could be heard across the town. We were some distance away but could see everything from the hill where we stood. Bombs fell, and they seemed to fall right over our street. The trees which grew along the river appeared to provide useful cover for the army and their ammunition. We began to run home, but the planes then appeared from the sky above. They swooped down and opened fire. There were also other women in the field. The planes then circled and fired again. I never made sense of it. Why would they shoot at elderly women and girls like me?

We ran and zigzagged from one place to another, and we

fell to the ground, terrified, and in tears. I do not know how they failed to kill us. We remained uninjured, but we were very frightened. We forgot about the potatoes and hurried home. Massive clouds of smoke were rising over the town. As we approached our street a woman was crying loudly. She tried to say something to me: I was not sure what.

I ran home but found nobody there. Everyone was in the cellar across the road. I ran there and was told that a neighbour's daughter had been killed by a bomb. It was her mother who had been crying outside. She had been picking potatoes in the garden and had received no warning of the raid. She and her daughter fell to the ground. Although the girl tried to cover her head with an empty bucket, the bomb fell next to her and killed her instantly. The mother was shocked and wounded, and was now also going out of her mind in despair. Her daughter was a lovely girl called Olya. She was only fifteen, and we had played together in the street. Ironically, her father was still fighting somewhere on the Front Line. We brought her mother inside:

'Why! Why did it have to be my daughter? My Olya! My only child, why have you left me? Oh, God!' She cried. There was no end to her despair.

The planes returned, and people were again frightened by what was going on outside. Nobody promised to help the poor woman bury her child, but in the end, she was buried in the cemetery by the ruined church. Then, every time she came back to the cellar and saw girls there, she started to cry aloud again and repeated: 'Why? Oh, why was it her, my dear Olya?' We all cried with her.

The bombing became heavier, so we could not possibly leave the cellar. We started to sleep there, and it seemed to be worse than what we had seen outside. I dreamt, again and again, but I never spoke to anyone about it. I found myself being transported to the world's strangest, enchanting and most wonderful cities. They were full of large shops and crowds of people. They say you dream of the things you desire, but I had never wanted for anything other than to stay alive and be with my family. Yet my dreams kept coming back. Years later, in England, I would see some of those wonderful shops and cities for real, and I would have flashbacks to those initial dreams in the cellar.

Life in the cellar was about survival: there were no shops; there was no food; there were no other commodities. Anatoly was the bravest amongst us. Despite Mother's protests he would go in search of food. The dairy had been ransacked, but he still found some half-processed bryndza – sheep's cheese. It was very salty, and we were able to pick a few fresh cucumbers from the garden. We were glad to be able to eat anything.

Gradually, the raids became less distressing. We stepped out into the bright, autumnal light, and made our way to the town centre in search of supplies. All the shops had been bombed. The quaint store, where we used to buy our pencils and paper, was the latest to stand in ruins. German soldiers in heavy boots were rummaging there in search of valuables: they left with teddy bears and ink pens. Just as soon as they had finished, other people rushed in and took anything they could lay their hands on. I watched with sadness as the small treasures of our school days were being snatched away. I could not touch anything. It felt sacrilegious for me to do so. Then, Anatoly brought me some face powder from the ransacked cosmetic store. Although I never used face powder, he told me I should. I could not touch it. It felt wrong, even though it was very costly. I admired the beautiful box and smelt the powder with delight, but I did not take it.

Later, when the alarms temporarily stopped sounding, I ventured to the centre of town again. Everybody's goal was to find food, but every last scrap of food had now been taken. Anatoly, however, still knew where to find something.

I went to visit my friends, and to my surprise I discovered some of the girls were going out with German soldiers. They dressed well and wore makeup in the way I had seen girls wear it in Lviv. I don't know who showed them because we had never used makeup before the War. Nonetheless, they looked beautiful and elegant. The Germans picked the prettiest.

A restaurant had opened which was supposed to be for the public, but when my sister and I went there we were only allowed to eat soup. As we sat there, a group of Germans came in with some of the local girls. They walked passed us and went into another room where a large meal was served for them. The women who sat at our table called the girls names and openly scorned them. It saddened me, too. How could these girls go out with German soldiers? They were good-looking, but with Germans? Some mothers even proudly said that their daughters were liked by the Germans and would be going to Germany to be married, and they were going to live in big houses. I couldn't understand them. I thought of Nicholas who was in the navy fighting somewhere on the Black Sea. I had seen his mother and sister. They told me about him and were worried. This was a war in which everyone's fate was unknown.

Autumn leaves had covered the roads. I decided to call in to Nicholas's house. His sister Nina had invited me many times, but I never had the courage to go. Nicholas was away, and I was a university student and a temporary teacher. At a recent conference, I was the youngest teacher present and Nicholas's mother had acknowledged me with a warm and friendly smile. I walked along the path familiar to me from childhood. So much had happened since then, yet I still felt my earlier feelings of inferiority creeping up on me again. I knocked on the door.

Nicholas's mother came out. She greeted me so warmly that I was completely taken by surprise.

'Come in. Come in,' she said with a smile. 'How nice it is of you to come and visit us.'

She took me inside and showed me the kitchen and rooms as though I was now a member of their family. She then led me into a bedroom where the grandmother sat on a sofa, dressed in an old-fashioned, long skirt and a black blouse with lace.

'This is my mother,' she explained: 'Mother, this is Maria Vasylivna's granddaughter. You remember them, don't you?'

'My dear, let me look at you.' Nicholas's grandmother lifted her golden pince-nez and looked at me. 'Oh, what a lovely girl you are! Come here.' She invited me to sit next to her: 'Tell me, how is Maria Vasylivna?'

'She lives alone in Sosnytsia,' I replied quietly. 'We used to visit her but her husband, Father Gregory, is dead.'

'Dear, dear, what a pity,' said the old lady. 'What lovely people they were. Theirs was the best household in the town. They had such wonderful parties.' Then, she began to tell me all about the people she had known in the old days, and how they had lived such a wonderful life.

I sat there listening to her, but I was puzzled. Why was she only talking about it now? She didn't remember all this when I went with my brother to pick the cherries. She knew who we were then, yet she had treated us like servants. Why was she treating me differently now? Yes, Nicholas's mother had married a Communist and had adapted to the new regime, but had they changed yet again? I sat there listening, but my thoughts drifted, and my questions remained unanswered.

The door opened and Nina appeared. She smiled and begged me to come with her as she had a special visitor. I followed her into the study where Nicholas's piano stood by the window. A German soldier was sitting at the table which had been covered with a lace tablecloth. It had a vase of dahlias placed in the middle.

'Come in, come in!' Nina beckoned me. 'You can speak German, so we'll be able to talk together.'

I knew Nina was working as an interpreter for the Germans as she knew the language, but to entertain a German soldier in the room where Nicholas's books and piano still stood whilst he himself was fighting the Germans – it was unforgivable. It was horrible, inconsiderate and even cruel.

'No, I cannot speak German,' I said in a cold and condemning voice as I looked at her.

'How is that?' replied Nina. 'You took German at school and at university.' She smiled all the time, but I detected her guilt: 'Surely you can speak German?'

'No, Nina, I can not,' I replied firmly, 'I learned German at school, but I never spoke German, and I cannot speak it fluently. I think I had better go now, you have a guest.'

Despite all her protests nothing would make me stay there a minute longer. I could not forgive them for suddenly treating me so differently, and for entertaining a German soldier in Nicholas's room. I left the house a different person from the one who had trembled at the thought of going there. I now felt superior.

I stopped on the bridge over the river that divided our two homes. My thoughts were like the water – a never ending flow, always moving somewhere new. I could not get over the way in which I had been treated, and I wondered why that family could not be honest, sincere and true to each other.

Darkness fell, and the first star appeared in the sky. I looked at its reflection. The water flowed on through the valley, but the star remained positioned in the same place. I looked and stared until I could find some kind of understanding. No matter how much the water flowed, truth, like the star, would always remain. As though finding a satisfactory first answer to my question, I went home slightly wiser.

To my surprise, I found a cart outside the house. The horses had been tied to a tree in the yard. They were calmly eating grain from their bag. Their smell reminded me of something from my distant childhood.

'Who has come to visit us?' I asked Mother as soon as I opened the door.

There was silence. Father sat by the table with folded arms – it was a sign of his thoughtfulness and indecision. I knew him so well. The next day was Our Lady's Day, and the house had been cleaned. The best tablecloth had already been laid. Fresh flowers stood in the vase, and the little, red oil-lamp was burning in front of the icons.

Mother gently approached me and asked: 'Where have you been my dear? We were worried about you. You should not be out so late during times like these.'

'Oh, Mother!' I exclaimed, having already forgotten about the horses. 'I have been to Nina's house. It's nearby.'

'But why did you go there?' She asked in surprise. 'After the way they used to treat us. We're not the same sort of people as they are!'

'Oh, Mother!' I put my arms round her neck. 'Why do you say we're not the same sort of people? Why did you never tell me about your father's house, and about your mother, Maria Vasylivna? I never knew they were such honourable people. What a wonderful family you come from, and what lovely parties your parents gave!' I started to cry.

'Who told you about all that?' She asked. My mother was surprised but calm.

'The grandmother – the old lady you used to look after. Why didn't she say all this sooner? Why did they treat us like servants? We were looked down upon! You should have seen them this evening. They greeted me as though I was one of their own, and they had a guest – a German soldier, and Nina was entertaining him in Nicholas's room where his piano is.'

I cried and talked at the same time. I wanted to tell my mother what had been in my heart for the last few hours. She remained silent, and so did my father.

'Don't cry my dear.' Mother sat me down on a chair. 'It's all in the past.' After a while, in an uncertain voice, she added: 'Some people from the village have come to take Father back to the parish – to our parish.'

'What!' I was shocked. 'No! Never! No! What if "they" come back again? It will be the end of all of us. No, Papa! No!' I went to my father and begged him. I pleaded with him, and I cried.

'Please, please don't do it, Papa, we will all be finished!

For the last seven years at school, I had been continually hurt by my father's forbidden occupation. Was everything about to happen all over again? I forgot about all the previous events of the evening.

He stood up and put his hands on the table. He then looked at me with such an air of power and authority that I had to stop crying: 'For you, my dear, and for your brother and your sister, I have done everything. I brought you up. Now, you have all grown up and are starting to go your own ways. Let me lead the rest of my life in the most fitting manner. I want to serve God and His people. No matter what happens to me, let it be God's will. I shall be going back to my parish in the morning.'

Having spoken, Father turned to face the icons in the corner. He then adjusted the lamp to brighten the room. He started praying. I understood there would be no further discussion of the matter. He was returning to the village of Chepliyivka.

My brother and sister came into the room.

'Everything is all right,' Anatoly said with responsibility in his voice. 'They're going to sleep next door as they want to set off early. Nadiya will arrange their supper.'

'Good,' Father affirmed.

I fell onto my bed and began to cry again. I begged Father, again. I tried to warn him not to return to his work in these dangerous and uncertain times, but my pleading was in vain. He was ready to travel the dangerous roads that lay ahead. He would probably sacrifice his life for his faith and his people. Then, through my tears, I could see that he was being true to himself and to us. He loved his work and had kept his faith through every hardship he had ever faced.

I stopped crying and joined him in the peaceful room where he prayed. The shadows flickered in time with my thoughts. He was a truthful man – the ideal that I was looking for in another, and he was my father.

At dawn, the horses pulled the noisy, rattling cart through the sleepy streets of Krolevets. They headed towards the fields and then towards the partisan-filled forests. The cart's fresh hay was covered with a white rug upon which my father was sitting. Only the early birds were singing.

Chapter 16

My conscious thought had been burdened with so many of life's impressions that my behaviour began to change. Deeper down, I was in touch with my soul which I believed was a seed the Creator had planted in me from the beginning of my existence. That seed had grown and developed and was now entering into a struggle with the visible, outer world. Father was taking the road to his destiny, and I, with my changing consciousness, opposed him. I knew I was right, and I believed I was right, so I fell out with him. For a long time, I knew nothing of what had happened to him. After he returned to his parish, I packed my belongings and left home. The schools were reopening, so I took up my old post in the village of Buyvalovo and returned to live with the same family.

As teachers, we had to perform a balancing act. On the one hand there was a change of political system, and on the other there were the children. They rightly wanted to know why only two months earlier they were being taught one way of thinking, and now they were being taught another.

'Does God exist after all?'

'Have the Germans brought God from Berlin?'

'Why are the names of Lenin and Stalin being scribbled out of our textbooks?'

I gave them the best explanations I could. I taught the third class. They were mostly farmers' sons and daughters –

healthy, robust children, good-looking and well-behaved. I coped with ease, and they liked me.

All the textbooks had to be "corrected", with all names and references to our recent political history erased. In the evenings, I had to sit until very late with a thick, black pen and cross out the names of Stalin, Lenin, Socialism, Communism and all the other terminology found in Soviet school books. The instructions were passed down from the new headmaster – an elderly teacher who was married to a Polish woman. We knew that be received his orders from a higher German authority, and to keep our jobs we had to obey him.

The family I stayed with treated me well. The landlady was humorous, and through the long winter nights she always made us laugh. She also told fortunes, and people came to her to be told of the fate of their husbands who were fighting on the Front Line. She always welcomed the villagers and gave them answers. In return, they would bring her bread or other food. There was plenty to eat there. One day, I asked her to tell me my fortune. She thought about it quietly, and approached me later, the following day:

'Oh, there is good fortune ahead for you!'

That was all she ever said, and the brevity of her answer puzzled me.

Her little boy was one of my pupils, and we sat together at the table to do our homework. He wrote his alphabet diligently and I prepared the lessons for the next day. In the evening, we would go outside and ski. Winter nights in the village were joyful. I liked my job; I helped my landlady with household tasks; I talked to the villagers. I had taken my first independent steps in life. Deep down, however, I was unhappy. I had not heard from my parents, and I missed them.

One Sunday, I asked somebody who was travelling to the market to take me with them. They agreed. Early in the morning our light sledge slid through the snow towards the town. The brilliant-white carpet was also decorated with rainbow-coloured stars as it reflected the sunlight. I watched the beauty of the passing scenery. There could be no other terrain in the whole, wide world as beautiful as Ukraine's.

I returned to our house by the stream and hugged my

mother. Nadiya and Auntie Chrystyna were there, but Anatoly was away with my father in Chepliyivka. He had been welcomed back to the parish. I was told that hundreds of people from surrounding villages had gone to the church and had prayed with tears in their eyes. It was the first service there in seven years. It was the day of Our Lady, so the whole village celebrated. There were dozens of weddings, christenings, special prayers for the living and the dead, and for those missing or fighting in the War. Mother was quietly concerned about the demands made of my Father:

'But,' she said, with some joy in her voice, 'he loves his work and he is fully dedicated.'

Mother explained that the church had to be re-consecrated as it had been used as a social club. Everything that was lost had to be found, and everything that was destroyed had to be rebuilt. The biggest loss was of prayer books and textbooks. There were none left, so Father had to borrow whatever he could from neighbouring parishes. He spent his nights copying out the prayers needed for his church services. Mother was worried about his health. She was thinking of joining him in the village, even though stories circulated of Communist partisans executing anyone in a position of authority under German rule. This included the priests. Rumours of atrocities continued to spread.

'I cannot leave your father alone,' Mother said. 'So, let it be God's will. I shall leave here and join him.' She made her final decision in front of me.

I loved my parents dearly, but the life they were about to go back to frightened me. I felt ill at ease. I was uncertain for them. For years, I had been frightened to admit who my father was. I had even blushed in the classroom when the word "priest" was mentioned. I had suffered scorn and had been deprived. At one school, I went unrewarded because my father was a clergyman. They even refused to give me sweets at the May Day parade because of him. They also sent me out of meetings. I had cried at those insults, and I longed to be just like my friends. Now, Father was a priest again – reinstated, honoured, respected and loved by hundreds of people, and I was being treated with special respect and attention, even here in the town. I was the daughter of a man who had overcome any fear of serving God, but I still felt uncertain.

Times were hard. Anatoly often went to the market with the villagers and brought some bread home. I then met friends in the town and discovered how difficult it was to get hold of any food. Mother and Natalya decided to go and join Father, so they went to find someone at the market to take them to him. Auntie Chrystyna was left to live alone in the house, and we all promised to help her to look after it. I then walked back to work in my village.

Christmas arrived. My landlady prepared the food, and early in the morning she took her family to church in a neighbouring village. I didn't go. I stayed alone in the house and couldn't sleep. I lay in my soft, feathered bed and thought about the recent changes in our lives. A small, gentle-blue light burned in front of the icons. The long shadows were like ghosts in the room. The white snow shone through the window. The same dark sky, the same stars and the same snow covered the earth, yet life had changed and everyone had been affected. Only one year ago, there had been no lamp in the East corner of this room. Now, icons could also be seen – decorated with embroidered cloth. Only one year ago, nobody had gone to church on Christmas Eve, yet everybody was there once again, ready to celebrate the arrival of Christmas Day. For several years in school, they had taught us that there was no God and no Christmas. Now, once more, these ordinary working people – peasants who had laboured on the collective farms – seemed to have regained everything. Above all, they had regained their faith in God, regained their Church and regained their Christian traditions. I lay there alone. It was quiet and peaceful, but somewhere outside there was a war in which two systems were fighting for supremacy of our beautiful country. I could not predict an outcome. I only knew that my people would always be there, and I belonged with them.

Christmas passed joyfully. It was 1942 and I was almost nineteen years of age. I was teaching children how to read and write, but I avoided the delicate subjects of religion and politics. Ironically, I was so much in need of further education myself. The Epiphany and my birthday were approaching, but I was now alone. I was far from my dearly-loved parents and family, and although I was doing my duty at the school, I remained amongst strangers. My heart was empty, and I longed for love and affection. I felt the pain of having cut myself off from my father. I had become stubborn and proud and would not go running back to him.

It was the day before my birthday. I sat at the table by the window reading "The Origin of Species" by Charles Darwin. Two of the landlady's children sat opposite me and did their homework. From time to time they looked at me with a smile, and made a small show of their obedience. I was unable to concentrate on Darwin's science. Instead, my thoughts quickly turned to my father's soft and gentle, brown eyes which had always looked at me with love and sincerity. Tears came to mine, so I closed the book and hid my face at the window. I could hear horses and a sledge approaching. The sledge stopped at the gate, and I saw my brother.

Anatoly had come to take me home, but I was determined not to go. I stood there, strong and unmoved as though ready for battle. A few minutes passed before my landlady opened the door allowing him inside. He was wearing a fur hat which he did not remove when he entered the room. Covered in snow, he held his horsewhip and just stood there. Without even saying hello, he gave a strong and determined command: 'Get ready!'

'Tolya,' I said to him, weakening suddenly. 'What's wrong? Why don't you come in properly and say hello, take your coat off, get warm, and rest from your journey?'

'There's no time,' he replied in a serious tone, and again he insisted: 'Get ready! We must be home before dark.'

'I'm not going,' I said, but my voice failed to sound as determined as his.

He caught my hesitancy and repeated: 'Get ready! I shall be feeding the horses.' He then went back outside.

'We're still on holiday,' the children said.

'Yes, they're right,' the landlady added. So why don't you go? You want to see your father and mother, don't you?'

I had never told her about my father, and I could not tell her now. Deep down I really longed to be at home, especially as it was my birthday on the following day.

Without a word I went to my room, dressed in a coat and scarf, took a change of clothes in my bag and said goodbye to the children and their mother. Anatoly looked at me, and I

117

noticed a faint smile on his face. He was spreading some hay on the sledge. He then covered the hay with a rug. He told me to take my place, sat at the front, waved goodbye to the family and whipped the horses. We departed.

I soon forgot about the recent past, and before long we were brother and sister again. We talked as though nothing had happened and we made remarks about the roads, the horses, the weather and our fear of partisans in the forest. Anatoly told me how anxious mother had been about me. She had wanted to come with him to beg me to come home – for my birthday, at least. She wanted to see how I was living. Father had tried comforting her but did not believe I would return as I was as firm in my convictions as he was in his. Father was also worried about Anatoly coming for me alone. Many partisans were roaming in the woods. He then blessed my brother and promised to pray for us both.

As I sat and listened, I imagined my father giving everything of himself to his chosen way of life. He worked with all of his heart and mind, and always tried to do as much as possible. He had no idea of knowing how long he would continue to do so, but I knew he was happy that way. The absence of material comforts mattered less to him than his duty and service to God.

The sun began to set and the snow appeared to turn pink and then red as we approached the village. It was a delightful sight. Field after field of snow, trees, houses, and a colourful sunset combined to form a magnificent panorama. I knelt in the sledge and looked from every turn in the road as we approached our destination. A young girl ran towards us. Her golden, plaited hair dangled down beneath her maroon scarf.

'Nadiya!' I called. Within seconds she jumped onto the sledge and sat by my side. She looked at me and kissed me:

'Oh, you've come back: you have come back! How worried we all were. Mother will be so happy!'

Everything in the village seemed to be exactly the same: the streets; the river; the weeping willows; the old watermill; the road leading to the church. Absolutely nothing had changed. Had I been asleep through all my teenage years? Had it all been a dream? I was home.

The horses stopped by the door and Mother ran out to greet me. She was warm and carried the sweet smell of her cooking. She put her arms round me, kissed me, hugged me and helped me down from the sledge:

'I'm so glad you have come home! Father will be happy, too. Come inside, you must be frozen after the journey. Were you all right Tolya?'

Without waiting for his answer, she led me inside. I felt like the prodigal son. I was emotionally overwhelmed. After months of loneliness, I gave myself up to the happiness of home again, no matter what sort of home it was. I felt love, care, comfort and warmth. I needed little else. I was speechless.

I listened to what Mother had to say. She took my semi-frozen coat and scarf and pulled my boots off. I did everything she told me to do and without a single word of protest. It was as though I was a little girl again. My speech returned after I had washed and changed:

'Where is Father?'

'He went to give Holy Communion to a sick man,' Mother replied with reverence, 'but he will be back soon.'

We were sitting by the stove when the door eventually opened and Father came back. He was taller than I thought. His back was very straight and his head was held high. He carried a chalice in his hands and placed it on the little table in the corner. He made the sign of the cross and then turned to us. His face was radiant and expressed his joy:

'You came, my dear.' Father put his arms round me and kissed my forehead. 'Thank you, my dear! We are all so happy to see you.'

Finally, I smiled again. Mother had already set the table for supper. It was the Holy Night before the Epiphany known as "Kutia". We ate meatless dishes and finished with stewed, mixed fruit. Father took a homemade drink and poured it into our little glasses. He lifted his glass and said joyfully:

'Thank you all for coming, and for supporting me in these troublesome times. We are all together again. Let us give thanks to God!'

We raised our glasses to good health: 'Na zdorovia!'

The past disappeared. We were one happy family again, living together in the present. We chatted, laughed and talked about everything on our minds. Our faces were radiant.

The Epiphany, and my birthday, arrived. Everybody

greeted me with hugs and kisses, but I received no presents as it was wartime. There was no money, there were no shops, and there were no goods. People were happy to be alive and to be with their loved ones as they struggled on. The love I received was sufficient, and I thanked my brother from my heart for having brought me home. I had no other home, and it was the only place in the world where I could be truly happy.

We went to church. The sun was only just rising, and we continued to talk and laugh on the way there, but we did not feel the cold, even though 1942 was said to be coldest Ukrainian winter of the century. The huge church was packed. It had come to life again. I marvelled at the enormous amount of work that Father had done. Everything had been restored, and it looked as though nothing had ever happened. The icons, the altars, the embroidery, the covers, candlesticks, tables, and even the flowers had been restored by the tireless efforts of the women and craftsmen. Everything was clean, polished, painted and decorated in the traditional Ukrainian manner. The people's dream had come true: the church had been returned to them.

A new altar had been built. I heard my father's sincere and pleasant voice, and the powerful chorus of the huge choir that answered him. The entire service was melodic, and the choir of young girls and boys from the village had somehow managed to learn all of the hymns in a short time. Mother also sang with them. She had a beautiful voice and knew all the tunes. They were sung directly from the music manuscripts. People prayed, and some cried. They raised their eyes towards heaven, whispered prayers and asked God to bless their dear ones who were fighting somewhere far from home. They could only find comfort in God and hope. When the service ended, the procession moved to the river, and finally, when the pigeons were let loose, the choir sang the Epiphany hymn:

You were baptised in the Jordan,
And the Holy Spirit called You the Beloved Son.

It was wonderful to return to a warm home. Father came in, radiant and happy. He greeted us, blessed us and blessed the house with Holy Water. He then drew little crosses with a white chalk on the ceiling by the icons and above every door. It was to protect us from evil. I had seen him do this many times in my childhood.

We ate sweet and sour borshch, roast potatoes, a chicken, and diced-apple compote. There was enough of everything to keep us satisfied. Father then found some drink and we drank to my health and happiness, for the years to come. Sadly, it was the last time we shared my birthday together. No treasure in the world, no gift of precious stones, could have replaced the riches I felt on that day. From my nineteenth birthday, the simple gift of love would guide me through the years ahead.

When I arrived back at the school, the following day, the headmaster announced that the Germans had ordered the District Council to close all the schools. We listened in silence. The children were playing outside. Their innocent voices could be clearly heard. I felt sorry for them and began to wonder what would become of them. The bell rang and they rushed inside. Red-faced and bright-eyed they sat keenly behind their desks, ready to start their new term. How was a teacher supposed to tell these ten-year-old boys and girls there would be no more school because of the Nazis? I had to tell them, somehow.

'Why? Why? Why?' They fired their questions at me.

'It is an order from the District Council,' was all I could say.

We continued with a normal school day and delivered our final lessons. We then assembled the children to say goodbye. We asked them to continue learning alone at home by using their textbooks. Downhearted, we all went home. I decided to return to Krolevets, so I packed my belongings and waited for a lift on a sledge. I said my goodbyes. I hoped my landlady would see her husband return from the War. I kissed her children, and the little boy said: 'You were a good teacher. I wish you wouldn't go. So who is going to teach us now?'

'You will have to teach yourselves,' I repeated as gently as I could. 'Play a game of "school" with your sister and your friends and teach each other.'

He smiled politely, but said nothing.

My landlady gave me some bread and a piece of kovbasa for the journey. Life in the town was going to be poor:

everyone knew that. When I found a man who was travelling to the market, I put my case on his sledge and waved a final goodbye to "my people", as I called them. It had been my first meaningful experience with other adults and children. I liked them and they liked me.

I had no idea what I would do next. The horses were slow and the driver only muttered a few words. It was cloudy and the air was softer. I thought about moving to Auntie Chrysyna's. My books were there, and my friends were there. Perhaps it would have been better for me to have gone to live with my parents. At the beginning of 1942, I had no idea of what was about to happen.

Auntie Chrystyna was pleased to see me return. We struggled through the winter months with little fuel, so we burned turf. Then, one day, Anatoly came to visit and brought us some bread, bacon and barley. The neighbours, and in particular the children, saw us unpack, and for the first time in my life I saw how I was envied. I had not known that feeling before. I gave them some bread and also for the first time, I was glad to be able to help them.

Chapter 17

I heard that a new music school had opened and teachers were giving private lessons there. I had always wanted to learn to play the piano but could never afford it. Nicholas had played since his early childhood, but he had been a "somebody" whereas I had been a "nobody". I was from the poorest and lowest class of Ukrainian society. There had been little sense of even dreaming about such lessons when my parents regularly struggled to buy food.

With some lingering unease, I went to the house of a teacher who gave private lessons and asked if he would teach me. He was a tall, elderly, well-dressed man. He looked at me attentively when he asked my name. When I replied, he smiled and agreed to give me lessons twice a week. He said he knew my father. It was strange to see how people's attitudes and mannerisms had changed. Beforehand, people had seemed to be encased in a shell. I had never heard of this man before, yet he had lived in the town all of his life. He, too, could now be himself.

When I sat at the piano for the very first time, I thought I was touching a sacred, holy instrument. I soon started to play and it came to life.

'You must play Chopin,' my teacher said. 'His music will suit your gentle touch.' I took this as positive encouragement and continued to play with a greater desire to progress.

Life in Krolevets, meanwhile, continued to change. Dances were organised and young girls dressed the same way as the girls in Lviv. They wore makeup and their hairstyles were modern. There were plenty of girls I had never seen before. Life was evolving. They wanted to look beautiful, they wanted to live, and love, and be loved. They were like blossoming flowers, but they were aware that their beauty would die someday. Like blossoming flowers they responded to the sun, warmth and gentility. Only love would truly fulfil them, yet the only young boys to be seen were Germans. They appeared as young, healthy and handsome soldiers with sophisticated and gentlemanly European manners. It was inevitable that some of the girls would fall for them. They believed in one thing: love would make them happy, now and forever. The soldiers were keen to impress them. They lied and promised the girls a world of happiness: naïvely, the girls believed them. I looked on as an outsider. As far as I was concerned, the Germans were strangers and I would not go near them. They were enemies. I watched silently. I avoided the dances and read instead.

By now, my lifetime's collection of books completely filled a metre-long shelf above my bed. The German solders who occupied the school had thrown out the school's collection, and passers-by picked them up and gave some to me. Thankfully, the books were not my only friends. Every so often, I saw my old school friend, Marusya. She, too, avoided the Germans. We wanted to live and to be like "our people" – we wanted to remain Ukrainian.

We were happy to learn of the Town Council's plans to celebrate the 9th of March – the birthday of Ukraine's national poet Taras Shevchenko. A choir was being formed and rehearsals were to be held in a large, white house in the centre of town. When I was at school it used to be the Communist Party's headquarters – a building dreaded by everybody. In my mother's time it had been a parsonage, and my grandmother Maria Vasylivna (who Nicholas's grandmother remembered) used to live there. When rehearsals started I entered her former home for the very first time. It was beautiful. Had things been different, it may well have become mine.

The choir grew with each rehearsal. We sang Shevchenko's "Testimony". His poetry, which was set to the music of famous Ukrainian composers, spoke to all of us. Everyone was now speaking in Ukrainian – even the elder members of the Town Council. Ukraine's national spirit was reviving.

Then one day, about this time, some of the girls told me that I should go to German language lectures because there was a remarkable teacher there. Perhaps the girls were trying to find a boyfriend for me. I had no desire to learn German. I knew enough from school and university, and I did not like the language, but the girls' talk about the teacher intrigued me. Who was he? They knew. He was a young man from our town who had been a student at Lviv University. He knew several languages and was very talented. The girls said he was a genius with a lovely personality: 'He's just your type!'

For curiosity's sake I went to the lecture. I arrived early and talked to my friends. When the door opened I heard Nicholas's voice. Unmistakably and clearly I could hear him talking, but when I saw where the voice was coming from, I learned to my surprise that it actually belonged to the teacher whom the girls had been talking about.

He was called Mr Lukash. He was of medium height, slim and with blonde hair. He also had blue eyes and a pleasant smile when he spoke. My first impression was that he was a very charming young man. I thought I already knew him from somewhere, but I was not sure. I looked at him more closely, and then I realised that he was the wounded man who had come into our yard during the first air raid on the town. This coincidence immediately attracted me to him: I started to attend his lectures.

Mr Lukash soon learned that I had studied at Lviv University and was interested in life there. We walked home together and talked until I had to turn into my street at the bridge. I liked his simple ways; his natural and friendly approach; his sense of humour and profound knowledge. In

124

fact, I grew infatuated with him. Mykola Lukash and I were equals. We came from the same social background. Even many years earlier, I had seen his stately-looking father who had a white beard and noble face and I had wondered who he was. We both wanted to learn and to continue with our studies, and we had no feelings of superiority over others. We looked at life from the same perspective. His conscious love of our country, and his ability to speak pure Ukrainian had a strong influence upon me. It made me think in more depth about the wrongs the occupying powers had been doing to our people in our homeland.

Mykola was preparing a speech for the festival and I had learned to recite some of Shevchenko's poetry which was beautiful and easy to learn, and I loved it dearly. We prepared our national costumes and talked endlessly about where to find embroidered blouses, beads, ribbons and garlands, or how to make a skirt and jacket. The idea of being dressed in national costume fascinated all of us, especially now that the choir had surpassed one hundred members. We felt fully Ukrainian again, and we felt we were reclaiming our own land: Ukraine.

The end of February was approaching, but winter refused to give way. Heavy, grey clouds hid the sun, and ferocious winds and gales lashed snow into our faces. Storms brewed continuously, so people stayed quietly in their homes, cold and hungry, waiting for calm to return.

It was announced that German language classes would be stopped and the choir had to be disbanded. We were told it was on German orders. In the town centre where the glorious church of St Nicholas once stood, and where a statue of Lenin was subsequently blown up by the Germans, a gallows had been erected. A man was hanged there and was left to dangle in the wind for days.

Fear ruled. And more terrifying news soon followed. All young people were going to be taken to Germany. It was a blow which came like the thunder itself. It was sudden, unexpected and frightening. All Jews were to be executed, and all former Communist Party members had to be registered. Most of the young people, meanwhile, were Comsomol members.

Father came from the village to see me and told me to

burn all of my documents, but I didn't do as I was told. Instead, I found a small, metal tobacco box which had once belonged to my grandfather. I wrapped all my documents in a small piece of linen, put them in the box and buried it in the garden under the bench where I used to do my homework. It is probably still buried there today together with the thoughts, feelings and ideas which filled me as I grew. I was frightened; my parents were frightened; all of my friends were frightened, too.

The execution of the Jews began and continued through March. Those who had possessions and money fled before the Germans came, but the poorer and unimportant Jews were left behind. They believed the Germans would do nothing to them. But the Nazis were ruthless: inhumane. Even the children from mixed marriages were snatched from their screaming parents and shot. Everyone was terrified. Atrocious acts such as these had never been seen here before. Hatred of the Germans quickly grew.

In particular, the girls were shocked by what they had witnessed and were far less frequently seen in the company of the soldiers. I went to visit my old school friend Valya. She was the granddaughter of a former clergyman and was one of the cleverest pupils from my class. She told me how some of the girls were now luring German soldiers to have them killed. The Germans became very cautious.

April then saw the first deportation of young Ukrainians to Germany. Rumours spread that they were only going for six months, and that a good life was waiting for them. Realistic people, however, said the Germans were deporting us to do the worst jobs, and anyone who went would become a slave.

That breath of freedom – Ukraine's rebirth; national revival – had been too short. It had been quickly extinguished and the story of our people continued to be sad. We had been so glad to be able to go to church again, to receive an education, to have private property and to trade freely. On one visit to the market I had been amazed at the selection of goods for sale. Where had it all come from? Although it was wartime, oranges, lemons and chocolate could be bought. I had walked and admired everything. Given freedom, I thought, people could work wonders, but that freedom was rapidly vanishing.

In the middle of all of the commotion, Father came to the town once again, but it was neither to protect me nor to visit his sister. He came to borrow prayer books for Lent's services. He borrowed one from a priest in town and then looked after it as though it was the greatest treasure he had ever possessed. The book was large, with old, yellowing pages and drops of candle wax. At night, Father drew the curtains, lit a candle and sat until the early hours copying the prayers and psalms. In his beautiful handwriting he copied page after page of Church Slavonic, which I could neither read nor write. I was amazed at his dedication, devotion and patience.

In a time of war and after years of forbidden religion, it was not clear to most people which prayers had to be said for Lent. Father was determined not to overlook a thing. He had made his own blue ink, and copied word after word onto sheets of white paper. Often, I woke up at night and asked if he needed anything, or if I could help him, but he always refused. He sat there alone, writing on and on. His face seemed to have been lit with an inner light of love. I lay there and thought what a contrast it now was to the life he had once led, and I reflected upon the wonderful expression of his whole personality in the vocation he now followed. How could I ever have wanted to stop him? To see him at work was to learn about who he really was. I realised I had someone to teach me about the faith, dedication and hard work necessary to fulfil my own goals in life.

Spring came slowly. The seven weeks of Lent passed quickly, and Easter arrived. If no church was available, services were held in a house. I went to one such service, and to my surprise I found Nicholas's mother praying there. I knew she was praying for Nicholas and I joined her, realising that I still had feelings for him, but I did have to sort through my emotions. I would not see Nicholas as he was away fighting the Germans and Mykola was at home after the Germans had closed his classes, so I would hardly see him either. Our friendship was vague and had not developed into a relationship with arranged dates or meetings. Although I wanted to see him, I had little chance of meeting him except casually in town, or formally at the Employment Centre where he worked and where we all had to register.

I was given a job there. I had to register everyone from one area of Krolevets for a general census. With a notepad and pen, I went from one house to the next, writing down the names of the people who lived there. I was not welcome. I told everyone that I had been sent from the Employment Centre, but they unwillingly gave me the information I needed. Meanwhile, the poverty I observed in the houses came as a shock to me. Our people were very, very poor. The houses that appeared to be lovely from the outside told another story on the inside. Peoples' faces were stern, grim and low-spirited. I was glad when the job ended. I was made to do it, and was not paid.

I knew Mykola was working in the Employment Centre because some of the girls had told me. Wanting a better job, I hoped I would find him, but he wasn't there. I was given work in a vegetable storage house.

I sat with dozens of other girls and women by a large heap of potatoes to sort the good ones from the bad. It was an easy job and did not require much concentration, so I soon found myself telling many stories about everything and anything. I never stopped and the others asked me to tell them more, and they always listened with great interest.

The job was temporary and soon ended, but I had quickly made many friends. They were plain, ordinary townsfolk whom I had never known. I liked them, and they liked me because of my stories. Whenever I bumped into them in town they were friendly and told me about their worries. I saw one young woman called Anita. Her beauty and unpretentious simplicity was a delight for anyone to see. She had been an orphan and was now a manual labourer. She never had the chance to go to school and never said a word about her background. Our friendship could not last as it had nowhere to go. It could not develop into a mutual understanding based on an exchange of thoughts, knowledge or ideas.

Marusya was still my best friend, and I often spent my days with her. We talked about the books we had read, about school and university, and were happy together. Marusya had been studying Chemistry when the War broke out in Ukraine and she was still modest, calm and very thoughtful. My next friend was Varya – a neighbourhood girl who lived with her sister Tanya by the bridge. They were orphaned when their parents were killed in a train crash. Varya was younger than me but she was from the same school, and being neighbours we became friends. She survived despite the shortage of food and other supplies. She was practical, she ran the household, and brought up her younger sister. Her house faced Nicholas's across the water.

Other girls gathered in Varya's house and we discussed our future there. We discussed our fear of having to go to Germany. The discussions became heated. Although some girls were attracted to the idea of a better life in Germany, others were sarcastic and remained convinced that we were needed only as slave labour.

When the gentler winds of spring finally began to arrive, they brought new hope. I started to repair the house. Auntie was elderly and my parents were away, so it was my duty to do that work. A new stove had to be built. Father sent me some money and I found some workers capable of helping. I was responsible and authoritative. The old stove was taken to pieces under my supervision, and a new one was built. I paid the workers, and they were happy.

I then painted the house. This job was customary for a woman to in Ukraine. They say if a girl can paint the house, she is ready to be married. My sister Nadiya came to stay with me, and we painted together, inside and out. It looked like new. The white, outer walls sparkled in the soft, spring sunlight.

The gardening also had to be done. I prepared the flower beds by planting flowers. I lined them with red bricks. We planted potatoes and prepared the soil for the other vegetables. I felt satisfied that my first efforts were successful. Those who saw my work actually did say I was ready to be married. Auntie could not praise me enough. She endlessly hinted about marriage, but marriage, in my mind, was far away.

Occasionally, I met Mykola. We were glad to see each other and our talks were friendly and sincere, but they never went any further. I often thought about him, but we were both rather shy and idealistic, and neither of us dared to make any advances, but our friendship was growing deeper.

In the evenings, young people made a habit of going into

the park until curfew. We linked arms, often in fours or more, and walked up and down the roads and alleys, and we talked about all the subjects we could think of. The boys started separately, and then later the girls would meet up with them to form larger groups. Mykola talked very sensibly and wisely, and everybody listened to what he had to say with great respect. We usually walked back together. We talked all of the way, and stopped on the bridge for a long time. After warmly saying good night to each other, I would turn into my street and he would continue straight ahead. Although we liked each other and felt equal in many ways, there was no romantic spark. There was no feeling like I had felt for Nicholas. Nonetheless, there was sincerity and affection, and I even hoped he would be friendlier towards me. I longed for more of his attention because the thought of marriage was indeed firmly at the back of my mind.

Meanwhile, we had to prepare for Ukraine's biggest festival: Easter. Anatoly came to see me on Palm Sunday.

'You must come home,' he demanded.

'But I can't,' I protested, 'how can I leave Auntie alone, and all of my friends?'

'You have to come,' he insisted. 'I will not go without you.'

But where was my home? In the town, where part of my heart was with a new friend? Was it in the house that I had repaired for the spring? Or was it at the home of my loving parents, brother and sister?

I wondered what it would be like to spend Easter in town, in Krolevets. Although some young people did occasionally attend church services, most had not yet learned about going to church. I would probably only stay at home with Auntie on Easter Night.

It would be the right choice to go home to my parents. Auntie and I had so little food that our Easter table would have been very poor, and my friends did not celebrate Easter Day in the way in which it was supposed to be celebrated. They merely thought of Easter as stories from their parents and grandparents. At school, they had been robbed of all of our beautiful traditions, customs and beliefs, so it was better for me to be with my parents and in the village which remained the source of our age-old Ukrainian traditions.

Chapter 18

Father thanked me for coming to spend Easter at home, and Mother was again overjoyed to see me. She thanked Anatoly for bringing me back, whilst Nadiya continued to help in the kitchen. I was home and happy to be in this circle of dear faces that looked at me with love and affection.

Holy Week was special for all Ukrainians, but never more so than in 1942. Eight years had passed since the closure of the church, and everyone remembered their personal suffering.

Father held daily services and Mother almost always followed him there. She would come home happy and made sure that everything was washed and clean. It did not matter that her home was now just a single room divided by screens.

On the Wednesday evening she gave me one of the pure wax candles she had made: 'This one's yours,' she said, 'you'll be going to church with us.'

Her words were half-statement and half-question, so I did not answer her. I was unable to sleep. I remembered the time when I tried to imagine what "normal life" and "change" meant. I myself was changing, but I was growing into a life somewhere aside from these people, and I felt lost. I decided that it could only be a good thing to go to church with my parents and be beside these people. I fell asleep.

It was a lovely spring evening. We dressed in our best clothes and went to mass with candles in hands. People flocked from every direction, and it was not long before the church was packed. I stood in the gallery where Mother sang in the choir. I watched Father in his black and silver robes holding his candle over an ancient Bible. I watched the hundreds of people around him, each with their light. Their faces were sincere. They prayed, and they knelt when they heard the descriptions of Christ's suffering. They stood together again when the choir sang the psalms. Father spread gentle, white clouds of scented smoke from the censer, and I watched my candle burn with its still, straight and peaceful light. Tears filled my eyes.

My father had really suffered. Nobody knew this as well as I did, and I had failed to help him. I had added to his suffering by starting to believe that there was no God – just as we were taught at school. My father had served these people; he had brought them together in the goodness of God, and yet I had not wanted him to do so. Although I had been frightened for our lives, our future and our safety, this moment was worth all the risks he had taken. He was living his life to the full, and it was a thousand times more worthwhile than hiding away in an unknown shelter to guard us from potential harm.

I was so sorry. I cried and prayed sincerely with everyone else who was there. I listened to the readings. They had crucified the Son of God who came to His people with goodness and love. They were wrong, and I was wrong too.

Good Friday arrived, and the next service began in the afternoon. A procession of hundreds of people walked solemnly round the church. At the front there were four distinguished men carrying the Holy Shroud – an embroidered cloth with the embossed image of Christ. Father walked beneath it with a censer and a cross. The scent from the shining copper container lingered in the cool spring air and the words of the huge choir echoed back from the ancient tall trees which surrounded the building. The church itself was huge, but the dome and bell tower had been destroyed. Only the trees survived unscathed and they stood aloft, witnessing the revival of the ageold traditions that had been abolished for almost a decade.

Of course, the people were the true witnesses to all that had been, and they joined the procession with tears in their eyes. The Holy Shroud symbolised the death of their spiritual life, the past years of the church's closure and the present troublesome time of war in our land. Nearly everyone had someone in their family fighting at war and facing the danger of being killed. Members of the congregation cried openly and sincerely: not only the women, but even the most masculine men, too.

After going round the church three times, the procession returned and everyone knelt before the Holy Shroud which was laid upon a table in the middle of the church. Everyone kissed the Bible and the cross which now lay on the embossed image of Christ. Every aspect of the service was sacred and holy. It touched me. The scent from the censer; the flowers; the light from the candles; the whole of Good

Friday's service moved me with such sympathy for the crucified Lord, and with such a love of justice and objection to the betrayal by Judas and the unjust judgment, that I felt as though I was living through the very sacrifice God had made for His people. I kissed the Holy Shroud as the symbol of justice, love and goodness. There is so much wisdom in the Good Friday service, and so much beauty in the worship of Christ who died for the sake of others, that to know and to understand it is to enrich one's soul and one's whole way of life.

On Easter Saturday, everybody in the village busily prepared for the night service. Baskets were filled with food to be blessed in the early hours of Easter Morning. In every house it was the first Easter following years of a faithless, drab and dark life that had been filled only with toil and misery.

Mother told us what to wear and put her best dress on. When dusk fell we heard the church bell ring. That was now no more than a piece of railing hanging from a tree and banged with an iron bar. Father said a prayer. He then turned to us and said loudly and very sincerely:

'Glory be to God! May the joy of Easter be with you!'

He then turned to the icons and adjusted the hanging lamp so that it filled the room with light. He began his pre-service prayers. As I watched him I realised this particular Easter was the high point of his life: the symbol of the resurrection was everything. In his work, he too, had suffered, almost died, but now lived again. His big, brown eyes were peaceful and full of expectation. Dressed in his dark-brown cassock, and with a large, silver cross, he then set off. It was only nine o'clock in the evening and the service was not due to start until eleven. I knew he could not rest or wait a minute longer. Tonight, of all nights, he wanted to be wholly at one with his congregation and with God.

Anatoly followed Father to the church and at around half past ten, Mother was ready to go. Quietly and happily we made our way. The church was already full, but we went to the gallery where Mother joined the choir. I stood and looked to see who was there. An elderly man read from the Bible, and in the half-light his reading sounded like a prayer on behalf of us all. The women were all dressed in colourful scarves, and the men wore dark coats. Everybody held a candle ready to be lit once the service began. It was almost midnight and the lamps around the altar were lit to signal the start.

Father was dressed in dark vestments and stepped forward from the altar with a censer. He went round the Holy Shroud in the middle of the church, spreading clouds of sacred incense behind him. The choir began to sing the Easter Vigil. Just before midnight the Holy Shroud was carried into the apse. Father placed it carefully on the altar and closed the doors to the chancel. Silence followed. It was a long expectant silence. It was midnight. A light appeared on the altar and the voice of my father started to sing:

> *The Resurrection of Thou, Our Saviour,*
> *The Angels do glorify in Heaven,*
> *So, with pure hearts,*
> *May we glorify Your Name on Earth.*

From solemn tranquillity, everything came to life. The doors of the chancel opened and my father appeared, dressed in a sparkling, silver and white chasuble. The large shining cross, the church banners, the icons and the large paska on an embroidered cloth were given to the elder men. Then, everyone began to move: the priest, the men, the choir and all the people formed a procession and left the church. They went outside to announce to the world that Christ had risen.

The singing procession went round the outside of the church three times, their souls as true and bright as the stars in the sky. After the third time, my father lifted his large, silver cross, pushed the church door open and announced: 'Christ has risen!' The choir sang joyful melodies, ancient and dear. To have lived until this time, and to hear them once more, brought us all great happiness. Everyone's eyes shone with joy, and repeatedly, the choir sang:

> *Christ has risen!*
> *He conquered death and gave us life!*

It was the miracle of the Resurrection. Everyone went back inside. We had left the church dark and unadorned but returned to embroidered covers, flowers, and masses of burning candles. In the middle stood a huge figure of Christ with a triumphant face and a flag of victory in his hand. Reassuring, confident and joyful, this was a local craftsman's creation of the Resurrection painted in blue, yellow, pink and white. The craftsman was a farmer, and a talented artist. He had given us the icon which we believed saved Father's life. Now the same man had created the Resurrection in the form of Jesus Christ to stand amongst us.

The wonderful Easter Night service began. High above in the gallery, the choir sang gloriously. The door through to the altar stood wide open and I could see my father preparing for the Liturgy, but first there would be Easter Matins – a beautiful, joyfully sung service, followed by an interval. After kissing the cross held by the priest and accepting his blessing everybody again greeted each other with 'Christ has risen!' and the answer 'Indeed He has risen!' I went to find Mother in the choir, and I kissed her, repeating the glorious Easter greeting. She held me for a second, and then whispered:

'Your old teachers are here.'

'Who? Where?' I was very surprised.

'Look, here they come. They must have seen us.' She smiled, and stretched her hand out to a tall, well-dressed lady. To my astonishment it was Nicholas's mother, and with her was our headmaster, my favourite teacher.

'Oh, you've come here?' I was hopeless at hiding my feeling of surprise.

'And why not here?' answered the headmaster. 'We heard about the Easter service and about the fabulous choir in your village, so we decided to come. There are not that many churches open in Krolevets.'

'It is wonderful to see you here.' I then lowered my voice and asked: 'Why did you try to teach us that there was no God? And now, you show your belief in God?'

He had a ready-made answer. 'What we taught was what we had been instructed to teach you. We had to do our job. God is not only present in spoken words. He is in many aspects of life. We taught you goodness, compassion and love for the righteous. Without naming God, we wanted you to understand that He was the perfection we aimed towards.'

Once again, he even sounded like my favourite teacher of

old. His blue eyes were partially obscured by his spectacles, and his blonde moustache was turning ginger on his slim and clever face. I looked at him and was speechless, just as I used to be in the classroom where his wise and enlightening lectures would fascinate me.

'My God,' I said, 'how everything has changed.'

'You will have to change,' he replied gently. 'We have always been just as we are today.' He looked with approval at Nicholas's mother. 'You are now the creators of new life, though you have a long road to travel.' And with a smile, he added joyfully: 'But today Christ has risen!' He turned to Nicholas's mother and said: 'We had better go. The interval will soon be over.'

Maria Ivanivna, however, did not want to go. She looked at me as if wanting to say something; to share something with me.

'Do you hear from Nicholas?' I asked.

She smiled and replied gladly: 'Yes, I get letters from him. He hates the War.'

'How is he?' I asked, trying to sound indifferent.

'I pray for his safety. You know what war is like. I live with the hope that he will come back. I can only live with that hope.' She sighed and wiped tears from her eyes.

'Oh, he'll live,' I said. 'Nicholas will come back. He's just the type to find his way back. Of that I'm sure.'
I knew that I was speaking from the heart. Faith itself seemed to be speaking.

'Thank you.' She smiled.

I then imagined Nicholas in the church. I imagined the proud and unapproachable Nicholas; the serious studious and clever Nicholas. Our prayers went out to him, and I wondered if he could see the light and wisdom of Easter as I could see it. Would he join with me in the knowledge of God? I imagined not, and in the newly-found light of my heart Nicholas quickly faded, as though I had never known him at all.

His mother remained friendly. Calmly, she told me of the cruelty with which the Germans were treating our people.
'Our people want to live their own lives,' the headmaster said, joining in the conversation. 'No matter who oppresses them, our people will survive.'

'Yes,' sighed Maria Ivanivna, 'but for the right to live, we have to pay a price. My Nicholas is fighting for that right.'

'Let us hope that righteousness will prevail in our land.' I said cheerfully. 'It is Easter today, and I am so glad to see you in church. Come and visit us, we live nearby.'

'Thank you,' replied Maria Ivanivna, 'but we have transport to take us home. There are others from Krolevets who have come here and they gave us a lift on their cart. Besides, my mother will be waiting for me to return with the blessed paska. After all these years we want to be together with our families on Easter Morning, to break the fast, and to enjoy Easter's food.' They shook my hand and we parted. I felt so at ease, that if I had wings I could have flown.

The choir began to sing the second part of the service. It was half past two in the morning. I remained below with the people. I was happy to be with them. The congregation moved and made way for the priest to reach the furthest corners of the church with his censer. As they moved I saw Father in all his splendour. 'Christ has risen!' he said to me, and to everyone. I answered sincerely and in unison with the others: 'Indeed, He has risen!'

My thoughts began to drift and I saw an image of Father bending down at the side of the road mending the pavements. People were ignoring him. He pulled his cap down over his forehead so as not to meet their stares. Then I saw him go with a horse and cart to fetch wood from the forest. He looked poor and belittled, yet he was happily singing the psalms to himself as he drove through the fields. From what he had told us of his work, I imagined him standing in a row, before a rude and scornful master, having to do the worst job that the master could find. He was called names, sneered at and ridiculed. Patiently my father endured it all. And now, he stood before me, the same person dressed in white, full of dignity, dedication and devotion, serving God.

At dawn, a procession formed and left the church. It was similar to the one at midnight. The choir sang throughout, and Father carried a candlestick with three large burning candles and a flower in one hand, and a censer in the other. He, too, was singing. In front of him, the elder men carried a cross, the Bible, an Icon of the Resurrection and the huge paska on an

137

embroidered cloth. Following them was the congregation of the hundreds of people.

They collected their baskets of Easter food from the grass around the church. Each one was covered with an embroidered cloth. Huge Easter breads, colourful eggs, cheeses, meat, kovbasa, moulded butter, salt, tallow, and the first green shoots of horseradish came into view. After the period of fasting, this food now looked wonderfully inviting.

After the procession had been round the church another three times, the food was finally blessed with the sprinkling of Holy Water. It was a fresh and clear morning. In the East, the sun began to rise. The sky became lighter – pink, then orange, then red. It was a wonderful sight. The sun changed colour as it moved, but it also appeared to move up and down.

'I never believed it,' someone said. 'I had heard about this from my grandmother, but I thought it was just a story. Now I can see it is true. The sun appears to be rejoicing too.' The phenomenon lasted for a few minutes before the sun rose higher in the sky.

After the blessing, everyone began to leave. The long-awaited time had come for families to sit together and enjoy their Easter breakfast. I waited for my father by the window of our house, and I watched as everyone made their way home. My mother and sister set the table and lit the candles.

Triumphant, peaceful and happy, Father returned. He blessed us and wished us a happy Easter once more with the words, 'Christ has risen!' Once more we answered him, 'Indeed He has risen!' Then I went up to him and said: 'Christ has risen, Papa.' He kissed me on the cheek and said quietly and very tenderly: 'Indeed He has risen, my dear!'

'Forgive me, Papa,' I said, looking down at the floor. 'I was wrong. I have learned and understood so much in these last few days, and especially at last night's Easter Service. You were wonderful, and you were right. Please forgive me.' I kissed him on his cheek.

'Thank you, my dear. Now my heart will be at peace.' He smiled joyfully at the rest of his family. 'Are we ready to break our fast? Good. Then let us start our Easter feast.'

Hand-in-hand with my father I went to the table and I noticed a contented smile on my mother's face.

'Sit here,' she said, allowing me to sit next to my father. It was a wonderful family reunion. We sat at the table and looked at each other joyfully, and put our past experiences behind us.

'How grown up you all are, my dearest, and how wonderful you all look,' Father said. 'Whatever lies ahead, we thank God for this special day. Thank you for not letting me down, and for being with me today.'

He lifted the paska and cut the cross, saving some pieces for the following year. Mother cut an Easter egg and Nadiya cut the homemade kovbasa, the joint of meat and the cheesecake, and handed everything around. Anatoly poured some samohon – homemade vodka, which he had brought from somewhere in the village. We all raised our glasses.

'Christ has risen!' Father said. 'God bless you all with health and happiness!'

'Indeed He has risen!' We answered. We sipped our drinks and began eating. We took a coloured egg and tapped it against each other's.

'Are you happy to have come home?' Anatoly asked me with a smile, wanting to break my egg.

'Yes I am.'

He tapped my egg and it broke.

'Yours is the egg, and yours is the truth, Tolya. Thank you for bringing me home.' I gave him my egg, and I looked into his big, brown eyes and smiled. 'You grasped the truth sooner than I did. You are so practical.'

'I'm not like you then: our scholar!' He teased me. 'You should be out and about a bit more often.'

'This Easter is so special,' exclaimed Nadiya, who was always quick with her words.

'We have had to wait a long time and suffered so much for it,' Mother added, but there was no regret in her voice as she now had her family together for Easter.

Then, Father spoke solemnly: 'All of this is in God's will. Let our future be with his will. For today, let us thank God for everything.'

His eyes looked towards Heaven and the light that shone in them seemed to reflect back upon us. His was a wonderful power of love and care, and his was a protection and faith above any I would ever know.

'Are you going to stay with us now?' Nadiya asked, turning to me with a yellow, painted egg in her hand.

I smiled into her lovely, blue eyes and replied without hesitation: 'Yes, I shall be with you always. Here or wherever I am, I will be with you, with everything in my heart.'

I knocked her egg with mine and found my egg whole. I took Nadiya's egg and added: 'That is a promise.'

She smiled her approving smile and said to all of us in a simple and matter of fact way: 'I'd like us all to stay together.'

The sun came out from behind the trees. It shone upon our little house and illuminated the table where we had sat through our bitter years of suffering and deprivation. What had happened to us? We were the same family supporting our father in his mission to serve God and His people, but Father's hair had now turned grey, and Mother's face had aged. We had grown up with our own personalities, ideas and goals in life, but what did the future hold for us? We did not think about it on that Easter Morning of 1942. We were still enjoying every aspect of our reunion.

From the corner of the room the Icons of Jesus and Our Lady seemed to look at us lovingly, as though saying: 'We will always be with you. We know everything, and we wish you happiness and peace.'

Chapter 19

I took a deep inner happiness back to Krolevets. I felt confident. Town life had given me a variety of friends and new interests. I felt the pulse of life itself and returned to live with Auntie Chrystyna. I also hoped to see Mykola again with the possibility of continuing our friendship.

I went to Krolevets town centre to meet my friends, but I was greeted by shocking news. More Jews had been shot and were buried in a ravine just outside of the town. There were rumours that all the young Comsomol members would be next. Fear spread, and the gallows which had remained standing on the former site of St Nicholas's Church now had the bodies of resistance fighters hanging there as a warning to everyone.

Fear and insecurity soon grew greater amongst us when

we learned about a second deportation of youths to Germany. At first, the Germans had quietly asked for volunteers. They had promised a good life in their country, and a safe return home after six months. Some believed them, and the first train left the district loaded with adventurous and hopeful volunteers. Since then, however, nobody else wanted to go, and so the second transportation would be made up of young people, forced to leave. Notices were sent to all households informing the occupants that one child from each family had to go to Germany. Rumours soon spread that Ukrainians were being used there as slaves. Every person then dreaded having to leave.

Despite the turmoil, spring's sunshine continued to warm the earth and the flowers began to blossom. The trees were green; the grass was soft and silky; and Whit Sunday was coming closer. I packed a few of my belongings and went back to my parents. It was going to be another beautiful, Ukrainian religious festival. Every house would be decorated with green branches, and fresh grass upon the floors. Each one would be like a miniature Garden of Eden.

It was brave of me – a girl of nineteen – to walk back alone through the fields, woodlands and villages in wartime, but it was the only way home. It was a twenty-five kilometre journey but I could manage it, perfectly well. I knew every road and path and walked thoughtfully, and without any anxieties. I admired nature's green fields and peaceful forests, and the lovely, white houses and their gardens. The day was warm and sunny, so I stopped at a farmhouse to ask a woman for a drink of water: it was a perfectly normal thing to do.

When I moved on again, I entered a wood where a gypsy woman suddenly appeared. She was carrying a baby wrapped in a shawl. She looked at me, but with a very piercing, dark look, and she said:

'Let me tell you your fortune.'

'No, thank you. I don't want you to.'

'Let me! Give me your hand!' She insisted. Her dark eyes were hypnotic, and her coloured beads and big shining earrings intrigued me. There was also something romantic about her; it was as though she had stepped out of a novel I had read.

I changed my mind: 'All right, go on then.'

'Let's sit over there,' she said, pointing to a patch of grass between the trees.

We sat down by a pine tree. The sun shone down through the branches, and the birds chirped merrily around us. Altogether, it was a lovely scene, and it amused me. Half-seriously and half for fun, I listened to what the woman had to say.

'You are thinking about a boy with blue eyes, but he will not be yours. You will live with a dark-eyed man who has come from the army.'

I laughed. 'Would that be my father? He's dark.'

'No,' replied the gypsy.

'Then it will be my brother. He has brown eyes. He's dark.'

'No. It will be another man,' she insisted confidently. After a brief pause, but still looking at my hand, she continued: 'Something bad is about to happen to you. If you give me your dress or some money, I will turn this misfortune away.'

'But I have no money,' I said, 'and I have only one dress to change into when I arrive at my parents' house. So, if that's my fate, then let it happen.'

'Just as you wish!' She stood up and lifted her sleeping child into her arms. 'Give me something,' she begged. I looked into my bag and gave her a scarf. Without another word she quickly disappeared back into the trees as though the whole episode had been a fantasy.

I went on my way feeling a little saddened. So, my teacher will never be mine, I thought. What will become of me? I thought about it for the rest of the journey, and when I arrived home I immediately spoke to my father without thinking about what I was saying. I even surprised myself:

'I've come back, maybe for the last time.'

Father had just returned from church. He was dressed in his dark cassock and looked at me modestly and quietly. He was perplexed: 'Why are you saying that?'

'They're taking young people to Germany. Two transportations have gone already. I could be on the next one.'

'Oh, no, God forbid it!' He sighed. 'Come, let's go inside. Mother will be glad to see you.' But when we went into the house the first thing he said was: 'Vera says she may have to go to Germany.'

'Oh, no!' cried my mother, embracing me and kissing me. 'My dear you must not go!'

'Perhaps I will not, Mama. Let's forget about it and celebrate Whitsuntide.' We stopped worrying about Germany and the future and soon began to celebrate the Festival of the Trinity, wholeheartedly. Mother cooked and baked, and I helped her.

I did not realise it would be my last farewell. I had moved from place to place for the nineteen years of my life, and Mother had always created a place we could call our home. The embroidered covers and cloths would always be placed exactly where they belonged. We had several icons, and each one had a special significance. A glass bottle with the scene of the Crucifixion inside it stood beneath them, and just to the side of that Father would leave his thick books. A wooden divan was always placed along the side wall, but the old family mirror which overlooked the table was now cracked. It had cracked just before the start of the War. Everything was so dear to me. The only things missing were my own books, which were now in our little house in the town. I planned to return there with Mother and Anatoly. Nadiya would stay behind in the village and look after Father.

Before leaving I went to him and said: 'Bless me, Papa! These times are so uncertain.'

With a trembling hand he gave me his blessing. There were tears in his eyes when he kissed me: we would never see each other again.

Mother, Anatoly and I walked back to the town. For many years to come I asked myself why we took that decision. I could have stayed in the village, protected by my father, but it was as though another external force had pulled me back to the town. It was where I wanted to live, but just a few short days later, I would lose everything and everyone I had ever loved.

When we arrived, a notice was brought to the house informing us that I would have to go to Germany in three days time. Mother cried. I stood in the middle of the room, as though frozen. The future now seemed very bleak. My love, my hopes, my studies, everything I had ever wanted to achieve, the sacrifices I had made – everything was about to vanish. I stood alone to face the unknown, armed only with my schooling. Mother's cries and my brother's worried look were of little comfort to me. I did not cry: instead, I was comforting them.

'They say it's only for six months,' I said, but we all seemed to know it was not true. God alone knew how long it would be for. It didn't seem to matter to me. The following day, Mother went to the administrative offices to plead with the officials not to send me to Germany. It was of no use. At the Employment Centre they even tried to encourage my mother to send me there. The Germans told her that their sons were fighting and all young people would have to go to Germany for as long as the War lasted. If I didn't go, my brother would have to go because one child from each family had to. Anatoly made the offer to leave instead of me, but I seemed to have decided my fate already.

'No.' I replied. 'You stay at home. I am the eldest, and I have been away already, so I'll go.'

Anatoly had a girlfriend with whom he was in love and I knew that deep down he wanted to stay, but if either of us had been wiser we should have known that for a young man to stay at home in wartime was much more dangerous than for a girl. Had he gone to Germany instead, he might still have been alive today. When the Red Army returned to our region he was mobilised and sent to the Front Line without any training. He was killed in battle from a wound to the head. It was just two years after I was sent to Germany. My parents found out after the War had ended: Anatoly would only live to nineteen years of age.

We had made our decision without even asking for our dear father's advice. There were no telephones and no postal service and it was impossible to communicate with him in the very little time which we had, and it was a decision I have regretted for my entire life.

I had not fully come to terms with my choice. Mother, meanwhile, continued to beg and plead in vain with the authorities to allow me to stay. We had suffered enough persecution as the family of a priest. There was only one other way for me to avoid deportation and that was by being married. If Mr Mykola Lukash would ask me to be his wife, and I agreed, I would not have to go. I now longed to see him. He was somewhere in the Employment Centre working as an interpreter.

I met him in one of the corridors of the large building. He greeted me kindly and asked: 'Will you be going?' It was the question on everyone's lips at the time.

'I have to go, Mykola,' I sighed, and I looked at him with hope and longing.

'Have you passed the medical?' he asked with concern.

'Yes, and they have not found anything wrong with me.'

He was silent, and I understood that he could do nothing. There were German soldiers walking along the corridor. They were tall and intimidating. What could we do or say in front of them? Any inner hopes I had quickly faded. I knew he was helpless and would not fight my cause.

'Goodbye,' I said. My voice was full of reproach. Perhaps the ideas about the man I would have liked to have loved were romantic, but I would have expected my man to stand by my side and defend me. I was now fully convinced that he would not have been the man for me, yet several months later, in Germany, I met a woman from Krolevets who asked me:

'Aren't you the girl that Mykola Lukash was in love with and wanted to marry, but you had to leave? Talk went around the town for a very long time after you left.'

I was shocked and amazed to hear it.

He had shaken my hand and had said goodbye to me quite casually, as though we would meet again, but he said nothing more. I was heartbroken and ran into the gardens where I burst into tears. It was the first time that I cried and cried. I hid myself away not wanting Mother to see me. I had to make her confident that I would be all right. I was her eldest child and had to be strong. Putting on a brave face I went to see my friends to say goodbye. I then stayed by my mother's side for as long as I could and packed the few things I was allowed to take.

Someone had sent Mother a message that one of her old acquaintances – an elderly teacher of the piano and foreign languages – wanted to see me before I departed. Mother gave me her address and told me to dress well, and she sent me to see the lady by myself. I found her house on the outskirts of the town. Everything was quiet and peaceful. Trees, trimmed shrubs and a vast variety of colourful flowers hid the small cottage from the outside world. It had antique furniture and old pictures on the inside, and there were heavy curtains over the doors and windows which created an atmosphere I had only ever read about but had never experienced before. The elderly grey-haired lady came out quietly to greet me and welcomed me into her study. She asked me to sit down and talked to me for a few minutes. Then, she spoke some very calming words to me:

'You will be all right. Wherever you go, you will be all right. Goodness will always be with you.'

I had no idea why she said that. She had never met me before, and had only spoken to me for a few minutes. She did not offer me any tea or presents, but only those words, which in fact made the best present I could have ever hoped for. Who she was or why she wanted me to come and see her, was never explained to me by my mother. The visit and the blessing of her words, however, stayed with me always.

Anatoly had found out about my feelings for Mykola. Maybe someone had read my diary in which I had poured my heart out. He offered to go and talk to him, but I told him not to bother, so he didn't. Other girls also asked me about him, but I had nothing to say and I did not see him again, no matter how much I longed to. Fate was now leading me away. Perhaps the gypsy woman was right after all.

I now went everywhere with Mother and said goodbye to my piano teacher – the tall and handsome man in his forties, who was very attentive. He shook my hand, smiled and predicted that I would marry a German, and would be happy in Germany. That made me angry.

'I will never marry a German,' I protested, 'and I will not stay in Germany!'

'Oh, you girls, you all say that, but I wish you all the best.'

'Thank you for the lessons,' I said, preparing to leave.

'Don't forget that whenever you play the piano, Chopin is for you. You have the required touch.'

'I will remember. Thank you for everything.'

We parted and I told Mother that I thought he was talking nonsense. She agreed, and took my hand and said quietly:

'You will come back home.'

'Of course I will,' I said with certainty. How could I, for a fraction of a second, have thought otherwise?

My friend Marusya came to see me and stayed a long time. She was the only daughter in her family and was not going yet. Her clear, grey eyes looked at me lovingly. She said how sorry she was that I had to go. She was so serious but gentle. I loved to be in her company. She was my best friend right to the end and promised to accompany me to the station, even though it would probably be at four o'clock in the morning.

On the day before my departure I had to have another medical check and take a shower at the town's baths. I undressed and Mother held my clothes. She looked at me all the time, never letting me out of her sight. She knew she was about to lose me. It was painful for her. She looked at me lovingly, dried me and helped me to dress again. She was trembling, and her eyes were full of tears. She didn't say a word, and neither did I, and the walls of the public baths echoed with nothing other than the splashing of water. It was our last moment alone together.

On the way home we met a lady who knew my mother from somewhere. She approached her and said:

'Don't cry. Let go of her now. I am sending my two daughters to Germany. Let them see a better life than what they have here. We have nothing to eat. That's a fact.'

'How can you say that?' Mother asked in astonishment. 'Are you not sorry to be parted from your daughters?'

'Why should I be sorry? They will surely have a better life than they have here. I would rather die alone than see them go hungry and be poor. They have not seen anything good here, and you can hardly expect any good to come their way, so let them try to find it elsewhere.' She was very excited and laughed: 'Don't worry! Your daughter will be all right.' She had appeared like a ghost, she spoke and vanished, and then Mother shook her head:

'She is in denial. Why do you think she talks like that? She is laughing instead of crying.' I then began to understand that a person can laugh from despair instead of crying. I had never heard anyone speak about the way we were living in such a manner. Nonetheless, there was so much truth in what she had said.

'I don't believe she is sending both her daughters to Germany,' Mother said. 'One child from the family is enough. She is crying in her heart for her daughter and imagining a good life in Germany. God knows what life will really be like for you over there. Dear God!' She sighed and began to cry again.

'Why do we have to go through all of this?' I asked. 'We want to live in Ukraine and be happy.' I saw Mother's tears and stopped. I realised I had to comfort her, and I should have known all of the answers already. I took her hand and said gently: 'Don't cry, Mama. I will be all right.'

'What will I tell your father after you have gone? How can I go back to him without you?'

'There is no other way.' I now spoke with authority. 'I have to go, and if I don't go they will take Anatoly. I have also heard that they will come and severely beat anyone who refuses to go.'

'I know, but it's all so sudden.' She could not finish. A spasm took her breath away. She looked at me, and from the depth of her heart she asked:

'Why did you not go and see your father? How will he take it? Dear God!' She continued to cry and put her arms round me.

'Don't worry Mama, don't cry. I will come back.' I tried my best to comfort her. 'You'll see. I will come back a baroness. I will be rich, and I will come back to you.' I don't know where I found those words from. Mother said nothing more, and our conversation ended there.

On that last night at home, I went outside and sat on the bench in the yard. The night was calm. The moon shone, and myriads of stars sparkled in the dark-blue sky. A nightingale sang somewhere nearby. I realised how much I loved the world, my country, my mother, father, family and friends, and yet I had to leave everything and leave at four o'clock in the morning. Tears came to my eyes. I leaned against the bare trunk of a nearby poplar tree and cried bitterly. The tears ran down my cheeks and onto the trunk of the tree. I felt sorry for myself, and for my family and friends. I could have cried all night.

Suddenly, the white curtain in the window moved, and in the bright moonlight I saw my mother's face. She was watching me. She was worried and was enduring her own grief. I hid my tears and went back indoors to comfort her, and then I went to bed.

We woke up with the cock's crowing. The early dawn was already sending the night on its way, and the birds were in full chorus by the time we were ready to leave. Anatoly was sad and quiet, Mother battled with her tears, and Auntie Chrystyna made the sign of the cross over me. She prayed with tears in her eyes. It was a serious moment in which I felt like a sacrificial offering to the unknown.

Hundreds of young people from the town and surrounding villages had now gathered at the school. They were all to be deported. Relatives and friends stood with them. Everyone carried small bundles of clothing, small bags or cases. The Germans had given an order that we were not to take anything else or it would be burned at the border. Germany was rich enough to supply us with everything we would need. We believed them and only took things that were necessary for the journey. We had no idea that it was all part of a German ploy to use us for propaganda purposes in front of their own people. They could then say: 'Look at them! That's how poor they are in Soviet Ukraine.'

We had no idea what awaited, and we were fuelled only by the consolation of being able to see something of the wider world. We would see Germany – the home of the mightiest power in Europe. Some believed we would acquire a western lifestyle and become more cultured. We would then bring that culture back with us and become better citizens in our own country. Many were sceptical, however, and predicted that we were simply going to become slaves of the German Reich.

At five o'clock, as the sun rose from behind the trees of the town's park, an order was given to us to form four rows. Surrounded by our weeping relatives, we were made to march through the streets to the railway station. Boys and girls – hundreds upon hundreds of healthy, strong and robust older teenagers – each with a bundle or small case and a heavy heart, began to make their way.

We were stopped at the turning into the main road. A loud noise could be heard coming closer. Columns of marching German soldiers appeared – polished, strong, organised, and disciplined. They were like toy soldiers wound up to parade in front of us. They looked foreign and inhuman. We stood and waited until they had passed. We were ordered to follow them. Forlorn, we continued to the station.

As usual, the station with its white building, trees and gardens appeared clean and beautiful, but the wide platforms were now crammed with thousands of people waiting for the train. The German soldiers paced up and down. They were stern and serious and looked ugly and unnatural in the beauty of Ukraine's early morning sun. They were armed with rifles, but they were so few in number and we were so many. Why did we not attempt to overpower them?

Everyone seemed to have submitted themselves to fate and nobody raised a voice of protest, nor did anyone try to escape. We wanted to be rid of them but could only hate them through a sense of powerlessness. They watched us as though we were a crowd of slaves, and we tolerated them as something ill and ugly that we had to live with.

Most people sat on the platform. Marusya and I walked around. We broke a small twig from a tree and held it between us as we talked. We spoke to others on the platform and met some friends, but the one person I would have loved to have seen – Mykola – was not there. I looked everywhere as I talked to Marusya, but he was nowhere to be seen. He had not come and my heartache only deepened.

We returned to where Mother was sitting by my bundle. Anatoly stood by her side and looked at me through his big, brown eyes. The sun was rising and a bright spring day was bursting into life. Why were we being so downtrodden?

'Don't walk about any more,' my mother begged, 'stay with us.'

'Yes, Mama. We'll stay.'

I moved closer to my dear mother. She had been grieving whilst I had been looking for a man who failed to appear instead of staying with her for our last minutes together. I then put my arms round her to comfort her to the end:

'I will be all right, Mama. Don't worry. I will come back. I will become a rich lady, you'll see. Don't worry Mamoushka, you'll see.'

Then, turning to my brother I said: 'Tolya, you will take good care of Mother, won't you?'

He looked at me tenderly and sighed. We hardly spoke.

150

There no longer seemed to be any need for words. Everything seemed to temporarily stand still, except for the morning which grew brighter and brighter.

Suddenly, we heard a shrill whistle. A train appeared from afar. It whistled like a wild live animal as it moved rapidly towards us. Everybody stood up. They lifted their bundles and grasped the hand of a loved one. The Germans, ever alert, came forward onto the platform with their rifles in their hands. A noisy, black locomotive ran into the station trailing rows of dark-red goods wagons behind it. The empty wagons rattled past before slowing down to a complete halt. The Germans then shouted a command for us to board the train.

The still morning air was filled with screams.

'Oh, God! Oh, my dearest child! Where are they taking you? Will I ever see you again?'

'Mother, Mother don't let me go! Daddy, Daddy, save me! Don't let them take me!'

'Almighty God! My darling daughter! I won't let you go! I won't see you again! Oh, God!'

The whole mass screamed, wept, exclaimed, hugged each other, kissed and cried. It was like a hysterical mass funeral with thousands of young girls and boys at the centre of the stage. The circle of love which had united so many families' hearts and minds was breaking, and the pain was enormous. It ripped through the morning air.

Again, I asked myself why we were not strong enough to overpower the dozen or so armed Germans who ordered us to board the train. Were people frightened of guns? Or was this perhaps a helplessness learned from the previous occupying regime?

'Will I ever see you again?' Mother asked, as she looked at me, full of despair. She had now gone beyond tears, and just looked fixedly, never letting me leave her sight for a second.

'Oh, Mama!' I put my arms round her and kissed her. Auntie Chrystyna was crying, praying and blessing me. Anatoly wrapped his arms round all of us. Marusya also cried. We stood in a circle unable to tear ourselves apart.

A soldier came running and shouting. He waved his gun:

'Herein! Schnell! Schnell!'

151

'Goodbye! Goodbye, my dearest!'

'Goodbye, Mama! Goodbye, Tolya! Goodbye, Auntie! Goodbye, Marusya!'

I tore myself from them and moved towards the train. I did not notice where I was going or what sort of wagon we would be travelling in. My eyes were fixed upon my mother, my brother and the tiny figures of Auntie and Marusya, and the thousands of people crying and lamenting together. I looked one final time in the vain hope of seeing Mykola, but there was no sign of him.

The soldier shouted again and pushed me towards the train. I climbed into a wagon and stood by the door. I cried and watched the thousands who wept with their arms stretched towards us. Chains were pulled over the door and a whistle sounded somewhere when Anatoly suddenly jumped onboard. He held onto the chain on the door, and looked at me. It seemed to last an eternity. In that instant we parted for ever: it was as though we both knew.

A German pulled him away. Mother stretched out an arm, and I touched her for the last time. Another whistle sounded, and more screams followed from the platform and the train. Mother's face and her outstretched arms; Anatoly's waving hands; Auntie's blessings; Marusya waving her white handkerchief; my poor lamenting countrymen: all began to gradually disappear from view.

Only our ancestors could have previously witnessed such a separation in the days of the Tartar invasions – days of slavery and the slaughter of innocents. That was in centuries past, but we now lived in twentieth century Ukraine. Had humanity made no progress at all? Almost every person who boarded that train would never return home.

Chapter 20

I found myself surrounded by girls who were screaming and crying, and they were all complete strangers to me. I also cried, but silently. I thought of my mother's shocked expression; my brother's look; my auntie's face; and beautiful Marusya's tears. I felt hurt beyond reason and was completely overwhelmed. The tears rolled down my cheeks.

The train gathered speed. The wagons rolled and their

wheels clattered, but above all the noise, the girls' voices brought me back to the present. They were in hysterics. A dark brunette, who was dressed in typical town clothing, cried aloud and beat her head against the side of the wagon. She screamed repeatedly: 'Mother! Mother!'

Another girl attempted to comfort her. A white scarf covered her thick, plaited hair. She was beautiful and calm – probably a village girl:

'Stop it!' she said. 'Stop it or you'll kill yourself!' She took the girl into her arms to comfort her.

A third girl lay in the corner of the filthy floor. She sobbed loudly, and her small and delicate body was shaking. Her thin blonde hair was tied with a pink ribbon. From the way she was dressed I knew she was from a village. The girl with the plaited hair then made her way to the sobbing blonde. She sat down on the floor beside her and took her in her arms, nursing her like a baby. She said something to her, comforted her, and persuaded her to go to sleep.

'She's only sixteen,' someone whispered. 'She's an only daughter, and her mother is a widow.'

'Poor Olya,' someone sighed.

I was amazed that the girls were able to put aside their own sorrows and tend to others, and I soon learned that a group of them were from the same village. One small girl in a white scarf took out a bottle of water from her bag.

'Here, give her this. It should make her feel better.'

'Thank you,' said the girl nursing Olya, 'but save some for later, it's all we have.'

I watched them all. The sobbing brunette began to calm down. She stood at the side of the wagon with her head buried in her hands. The occasional shaking of her shoulders showed she was still sobbing inside.

'Katya, stop it or you'll become poorly,' someone warned her.

The girl with the plaited hair was called Oksana. She went to Katya and again tried to comfort her:

'Try to calm yourself dear. Crying isn't going to help you.'

The wide wagon door remained ajar, but it had heavy chains, and two German soldiers were guarding it. They leaned upon the chains and looked out at our beautiful, blossoming land. I looked at the fields through the gap. There were green valleys and blue rivers, orchards, and children playing near to painted houses: our beautiful Ukraine. What right did they have to come here, and then take us away? I wished I could have pushed the soldiers straight out.

The countryside's beauty calmed me. I stopped crying and sat by the door, occasionally glancing at the girls as well. I remembered a song we had learned, earlier that spring, in which a man was being taken away from Ukraine. He was sad and homesick when he thought about his true love. She was stunningly beautiful, with gentle, blue eyes, and dark hair that fell to her shoulders. Her ruby-red lips sang a sad song as she looked at him. Everyone was aware that "she" was his beloved homeland – Ukraine. The song was called "At times I am sad," and I compared the words to the scenery I could see through the open door of the cattle wagon – our prison. It was sad how the song described Ukraine's sons and daughters being taken away. And there we were: the latest ones being taken away, locked up in a train bound for Germany.

The Cumans, Tatars, Turks, Poles and Russians had previously occupied and taken our people into slavery, selling them at markets and using them for slave labour. Were we not going to be just like them – slaves of the twentieth century? Why did we have to go to Germany? My mind became preoccupied.

The sun was still rising and the temperature in the wagon began to rise. Someone asked for a drink, but there was no water. Someone else wanted the toilet, but there was no toilet. There was just a wagon filled with crying girls, guarded by the two German soldiers.

'What are we going to do?' I heard someone ask.

There was no answer, only the clattering of the train's wheels.

'Will someone ask the Germans what we should do?'

When we tried, they only laughed. In the end, some of the girls began to roll on the floor, in pain, from not being able to pass water. They did not want to disgrace themselves.

It was almost midday when the train finally stopped in the middle of some open fields. Everybody was ordered out to relieve themselves – boys and girls together. It was impossible to run away or hide because the field was open and vast, and the soldiers surrounded us:

'That's culture for you!' one of them shouted.

'Your culture will stick in your gullets yet!' a brave young voice answered back. Others swore and cursed them, too.

After about ten minutes we were ordered back into the train.

At least with one trouble resolved, the girls soon became more cheerful. We were hungry and began to eat some of our food. I talked to two girls who were sitting beside me. We had been to school together. One of them was Natalya – the daughter of one of our teachers, and the other was Valya – who had been in my class. We used to call her the wonder girl. She was always self-confident and was very intelligent. She never worked hard, yet she always knew all of the answers. The girls were both very presentably dressed and were under the impression that they were going to Germany for a visit, therefore they should look and behave as well as they could. Valya was wearing a beautiful, blue hat. Having nowhere to sit, the girls stood by the open door and talked to the soldiers. At first, I was disgusted by this and did not want to join in, but as the journey progressed I found myself listening, especially when the girls began reciting Esenin's poems, which we had not studied at school:

Oh, my life, you have passed,
Like a fairytale on a white horse...

The poems were pessimistic but beautiful, and I asked the girls where they had learned them.

'There are many things which we did not learn at school,' Valya answered confidently. She held out an old notebook and showed it to me.

'Let me copy the poem, it's so beautiful,' I said. She gave me the notebook and I was amazed by how many poems she had written there, most of which I had never heard of. I copied some of them, though my hand was shaky because of the train's motion.

We formed a small group and continued to talk about poetry. I noticed that the other girls began to give us long sideways glances. I didn't like that as I had always liked to

155

mix and talk with people as much as possible. Esenin's poetry and related sentimental talk were out of place: the poems were sweet, but the dirty wagon was obnoxious. I let go of the subject and went to the other side of the wagon where there was another partially open door. Some girls sat with their legs dangling out. They spoke in Ukrainian and I gave them a warm smile and sat on the floor beside them. They took little notice of me as they were preoccupied with their own thoughts. They were soaking up the scenery. Some of them were seeing it for the very first time. They had never been so far from home.

'Oh, look!' shouted a slender girl. 'There are so many cows! Where could they be taking them all?'

'Don't you know?' replied Oksana. 'They're taking them to the slaughterhouse to make sausages for the Germans.'

'And then they'll leave the bones for our people. The pigs! Where will anyone get their milk from?' Katya continued angrily. She sat in the corner by the door. Her auburn curly hair was a mess, and her face was red from crying.

We waved to the people, especially to the children, and they waved back. How wonderful it would have been to have jumped out and joined them – but nobody jumped. The train was now travelling at full speed and did not stop. We passed straight through the bigger stations and travelled quickly to the West. The girls were no longer crying. They had huddled by the doors, and only Olya stayed away. She remained alone in a corner of the wagon. She had stopped crying but did not want to listen to anybody, so even Oksana now left her alone.

There was a deep sadness on the pale and neglected faces of all the girls. Only from time to time, when the scenery changed, were they reignited with a small spark of interest. The further we travelled, the further we were from our loved ones. Everyone began to realise that life now had to be faced alone – without the love of a mother, father, sister or brother. Those who had left their boyfriends seemed to feel it the most. The thought of loneliness made everything look bleaker, but basic human instincts soon began to overrule these emotions: hunger and thirst were now setting in. After looking in our bags for food, we ate a little, but there was no water. The temperature in the wagon, meanwhile, was still continuing to rise.

The girls were angry. Some lay helplessly on the floor and went to sleep, but others could no longer contain their anger. Our group split into two. One group gathered by the door where the soldiers stood. They were mostly town girls – Valya, Natalya, Katya, and a fat freckled girl with ginger hair called Clara who began to shamelessly flirt with the guards. The other group sat by the opposite door, and they were mostly village girls. I was somewhere between the two groups and spoke the same language as the town girls, but I was also sympathetic to the village girls and kept on very friendly terms with them. I simply went from one group to the other and felt at home with both. I listened to the way the village girls began to talk about the town girls. They were angry with Clara and made bitter remarks about her:

'Clara, you have so much powder on your neck, we could make pies from it!'

'Fancy that! She turns up here, the whore!'

'How did she get into our wagon? I wish she'd go elsewhere.'

'Clara, tell the Germans we need some water.'

Clara came from Krolevets, but I had never seen her before. I came from a select group of young people who went to the Grammar School and then to university. We did not associate with other groups of young people in the town. Of course, we knew there were many others in the 30,000 population, but we had never come across them and Clara came as a shock. She constantly flirted with the soldiers and made us all very angry. Valya talked to them too, but Valya was a serious and decent girl. She did not flirt and we could see the difference, but that would not stop the girls from despising her for what she was doing.

The train stopped again and we were allowed to get out. There were trees growing nearby and someone had the idea of decorating the wagon with green branches. The trees were hacked and branches brought on board so that every wagon was decorated as a last farewell to our native homeland. The Germans said nothing, so our wishes seemed like a small victory. We felt as though part of Ukraine was coming with us and it cheered us up. Somewhere, a song was sung, and soon, one wagon after another joined in. There was unity, but the mood of the songs soon changed. They were sad and desperate, and sung by slaves who were being carried away into the conqueror's land.

The train continued to take me further and further from my family and friends, and from the life I had planned to lead. My plans and everything that I had ever wanted were now dead. No wonder Olya remained in the corner of the wagon half-dead herself. I felt the same way, only I did not lie down. I coped by talking to the others in the carriage. When the singing stopped, the girls sat silently and began to cry again.

Towards evening, the train stopped at a big station. We were ordered to go outside and were marched in columns of four to an empty school. We were told that we would be staying there for the night. We settled on a large and bare school hall floor. We were given a piece of bread and some tea. Someone then brought us some kovbasa – our last supper in Ukraine.

The following morning, we were allowed into the school playground and were even allowed to go into the streets of Konotop. I found a market and thought about escaping to Grandma who lived nearby. But when I thought of what might happen to my family, I resisted the temptation. I even found some people who came from where she lived, so I asked them to give her a letter. I wrote to her from an empty stall and told her of my fate. I said goodbye to her as though knowing that I would never see her again.

To this very day, I regret not having made a bid for freedom. I could have asked for a lift. I could have stayed with her until the end of the War. I later found out that Grandma had suffered during the War. She became blind and died alone, but not before strangers stole everything she owned. Her possessions were to be left as my dowry – and this included her very special dinner service. I bless her soul and will love her always. I even cry for her now as I write these words, and wonder what fate would have had in store for us had I escaped to be with her that day.

Later in the afternoon we were packed into the wagons again. It was hot and dusty and the train waited at the station for a long time. An orchestra appeared and played and I cried bitterly. I knew it was a last goodbye to anything that could still be called home. The orchestra reminded me of Nicholas. Somehow, I knew I would never see him again and the tears began to burn my eyes: 'Goodbye, goodbye,' my heart whispered softly.

The train finally moved off and it was not long before the sun disappeared and left us with the evening's cool air. We rolled on into the night and stopped again when darkness fell. Straw was pushed into the wagon and we spread it across the floor.

Here's our new German bed, girls!' someone shouted.

'Damn them!' an angry voice answered bravely.

We were just settling down to sleep when the door opened and some loaves of bread were thrown in. There was one loaf for eight people. Someone had a knife and equal portions were cut for everyone.

'Be glad for a piece of dry bread, girls. The butter's been left at home.'

'We may not even get this much when we reach Germany. We're still in our wealthy Ukraine,' someone said.

Those who could eat ate the dry bread, but they were sad as they were thinking of suppers at home.

The train moved on, and we tried to settle down again. At a later stop, two soldiers jumped into the wagon again to be our guards. They took no notice of our wish to sleep and talked loudly. They lit a lantern and hung it above the door. Noisily, they opened their cases and took out some bottles of drink, sausages, white bread and butter. Then they started to eat. Suddenly, one of them laughed and called for Clara.

One of the girls then shouted from the corner: 'She's not here!'

'Mädchen, come to supper!' laughed the Germans. They turned their attention to Valya and then beckoned her instead. She was lying beside me and pretended to be asleep. She did not answer. Very quietly she whispered to me: 'Don't answer them at all.'

The soldiers laughed and sat by their cases. They continued to talk loudly, and laughed and joked. Soon, we were all pretending to be asleep, but we watched their every movement. We were all very frightened.

After midnight, the train stopped again and the soldiers jumped out. They locked the doors and left us in the dark.

159

The train rocked and continued heading westwards.

'So, they've locked us up!' someone exclaimed in the dark. 'What if something happens? What if one of us wants to get out? What then?'

'Let's go to sleep girls,' said Valya with the voice of calm authority. 'We can't help ourselves by worrying.'

Soon, all the girls fell silent, and settled down to sleep. They respected Valya and trusted her, despite her friendly banter with the soldiers. That was an advantage as most of us could not speak German. I pretended not to know the language, because I did not want to speak it on principle.

At dawn, the train stopped near to a station, and the rattle of the locks and chains broke the silence. The doors were pulled open and we were allowed to climb out for a few minutes. Clara appeared from out of the crowd.

'I have a bad leg so they let me sleep in a medical carriage,' she said, pretending to limp. The others laughed and gave her their disapproving looks. She came back into our wagon and, crawled into the corner and slept all morning. We ignored her.

Before evening, we crossed the border between Ukraine and Belarus. There were thick, endless forests, poor unpainted houses in the villages and the people were different in their appearance. We felt we were no longer at home and were struck with a cold sense of reality. Heavy clouds covered the sky, and a cold wind now blew into the wagon. We shivered. It was late, and we had not been given anything to eat or drink. Those who still had a little food left ate eagerly. We were all hungry and thirsty and felt miserable again. Some girls started to argue, some cried, and some swore. All the same, they cursed the Germans and wished them all the evil that the world could throw back at them.

At last, the train stopped at a station. After a long wait, some boys were called out of one of the wagons to distribute pieces of black bread. Everyone eagerly grabbed a piece. It was dry, and there was nothing else except some water. Those who had bottles filled them. Water had now become a precious commodity.

The train moved on again and gained momentum, but the longer we travelled, the colder it became. It soon started to rain, and a cold wind such as we never experienced in springtime blew the rain into the wagon. We were wet and the combination of cold, hunger and filth began to annoy us intensely. The girls squabbled and argued again, and searched for an excuse to release their anger. They shouted at each other and began to fight for places to sit. They were like school children. Minutes later they were friends again and sat by the door talking and singing together. They sang more of the same songs. Their young voices were loud and clear and overcame the noise of the train's clattering.

'How nicely they sing,' I said to Valya and Natalya, with whom I was still sitting.

'They're just simple people,' said Valya with an air of superiority in her voice.

'They're from a village and they're our people, Valya,' I said defensively.

'But who could possibly appreciate them?' she said scornfully. 'Nowadays a modern and universal woman is called for!' She spoke as if she knew what she was talking about.

'I think a woman should keep her national characteristics. I believe that all nations should contribute their culture and traditions to the world.' I said, calmly expressing my inner thoughts.

'Nonsense!' Valya replied. 'Nations will die and universal ideas will live. We are all going to be universal.'

'I don't agree with you. Can't you see how nice it would be if our women added embroidery to their already fashionable dresses. It would enrich the world and your universal women. Besides, what friendship can you form with a man from another country?'

'Well, you're supporting Nationalism and I'm not!' Valya stated with a laugh.

I was shocked. 'Am I supporting the Nationalism which is associated with those Germans? No! But I would still like something of my own, a touch of Ukraine in everything universal, and a boyfriend from our country,' I said, with sincerity. I was now becoming aware of the marked differences of opinion dividing our people.

In the morning we stopped at the large railway station of Bialystock, Poland. It was sunny. A lot of Jews were working close to the station. They were doing hard labour – cutting large trees, mending the railway lines, and digging trenches or some sort of ditches. They waved and smiled at us. We answered them with smiles but we could not hide our shocked looks. They were such fine people who looked at us with warmth and understanding in their eyes, yet they were being forced to do horrible jobs. Armed German soldiers stood guard over them. They then stopped the workers from even looking at us.

The train was stationed for a long time. It became hotter and hotter, and we were all locked inside. The straw they had given us was dirty and began to rot on the floor: it stank. We were exhausted, shocked and bewildered. Suddenly, it seemed that a whole army of Germans had come to the train. They began unlocking the chains and ordered us all to go outside with our possessions. We were made to stand in columns of four and were marched towards some buildings near to the station. On our way, we saw some Jewish women working. They were well-groomed ladies doing manual jobs such as washing clothes in large containers, cleaning the roads and sweeping the paths. Their dark hair fell over their pale-white faces which had been covered with sweat and dirt. They did not greet us with smiles as the men had done. They had been made to work hard and remained indifferent to us.

The sun soon began to burn our faces, and dust from the roads covered us with an additional sheet of dirt. We were hungry, thirsty and very, very tired. The door to a low concrete building was opened and we were ordered to go inside. It was a bathhouse – a huge hall made from cement and with a stone floor. It had hundreds of showers. Hundreds of naked girls were supervised by soldiers who laughed and joked at how shy and tearful they looked. I was shocked by what I saw. We were told to undress and hand over our clothes for disinfection. A row of attendants smeared our heads, armpits and groins with a yellow, smelly liquid soap. Then, they sent us into the showers. Soldiers with containers sprayed us with more soap.

The smell of the soap, the steam, the humiliation and the exhaustion all overpowered me. I fainted. I remembered how the girls had hid their faces with their hair, and how they hid behind each other, but I remembered nothing else. When I came to, I was wrapped in a white sheet and surrounded by women in white coats. They asked me my name and age and gave me a drink of water. A kind woman spoke to me in Polish. She shook her head in disgust saying: 'Terrible! You are too serious for your age!'

I cannot remember how they found my clothes and how I got dressed, but we were marched back to the train. The sun was baking hot, and our heads now smelled of disinfectant and soap. Our hair had not been rinsed properly. We were wet and sticky and attracted the dust from the roads. Again, we cursed the Germans.

Back at the station they told us to sit beside the railway line and wait for the train. Dropping our bundles and cases to the ground we sat under the scorching sun for a long time. Someone said that we could have some soup but we did not want to go for it. Our honour had been so offended, that we had no appetite. I thought of my piano teacher's prediction of marrying a German: I swore I would never even respect one.

Valya lost her faith in the Germans too. She asked me to go for a walk along the railway line, and confided in me. She told me how she had talked to some soldiers at home because she knew their language. They had promised her that she would be happy in their country.

'If only I had known they would treat us like this. Now I don't believe anything good awaits us.' She cried. The tears rolled down her cheeks, but she did not wipe them.

'This is only the beginning,' I said, sighing. 'As they say, if this is only the blossom, what will the berries be like?'

Trains passed us carrying German soldiers who stared at us. We were two sad and lost girls, walking along the track. They shouted: 'Schön! Hübsch! Hey, beautiful! Hey, pretty!'

Were we pretty? We did not know. We could not see ourselves, and anyhow we did not care what we looked like. The insults of the soldiers in the bathhouse looking at us and laughing at us had wounded our pride. The whole world now appeared to be dark, cruel, strange and hostile. We were filled only with our feelings of hurt and humiliation. Natalya cried quietly as she sat on the embankment. She was lonely and forlorn, and refused to join us on our walk. The girls sat around and were also sad and lost in their own thoughts. Many were crying again. Clara appeared, red-faced, but with a broad and dirty smile on her sunburned, freckled face.

163

'Why should I cry?' she said to us. 'It could have been worse.'

That statement made the girls lose their tempers.

'Just get lost!' they shouted at her. Taking some stones from the embankment, they threw them at her until she left in fear.

Night fell before we were packed into another train. This time there were fewer wagons. We were squashed together and had to stay standing, and we did not know where we were being taken to. It was raining and drops of water leaked through the ceiling. It was impossible to sleep, and we remained standing for the entire night, cold and wet.

'That's Germany for you, girls!' came a voice from the dark, and similar remarks were made all night.

We were glad to see daybreak. The train stopped and we were ordered out onto a platform. We sat beside the track and watched as more wagons were coupled to the end of the train. Eventually, in more spacious surrounds, I was glad to be reunited with the group of girls I had got to know. It had been five days, and we now felt like a family. When we left again, most of us lay down and tried to sleep. The train moved rapidly, and despite the noise and damp, sleep overcame us, and we slept all morning.

I awoke at midday and looked at the girls. Disturbed, they sighed and twitched in their sleep. They were so young and innocent, but now lost in life's wilderness. Even Valya had forgotten about her appearance. Her beautiful, blue hat now lay by her side, squashed and forgotten. Her permed hair was dishevelled, and her proud face was marked with tears. She must have cried herself to sleep. Olya lay in the far corner. Oksana had put a protective arm round her but I could not see her face. Her shoulders twitched from time to time. She was probably crying in her sleep. Sonia, the small girl in the white scarf, was the only other person awake. She was busy taking something out of her bundle. She looked so poor in her simple, grey skirt and homemade blouse.

I sighed and looked out through the chained door where I saw well-kept houses, small gardens and green fields. I still did not know where we were, or where we were being taken to. What do I have in common with this place, I asked myself, or with these strange, unfriendly people who speak a different language, and who treat us like animals locked in cages?

Tears rolled down my cheeks. I did not care what I looked like either, and nothing mattered to me.

I lost track of time. The train ran on, and on, and on. It would only ever stop for a few minutes for us to go out into the fields. At some stations they brought us cooked jacket potatoes or a loaf of bread. Sometimes they brought soup for anyone who had a container, but the soup was so tasteless that we threw it away despite our hunger.

It was cold. We did not have such cold weather in the middle of June in Ukraine where it would be sunny and warm. We had no blankets and we were only dressed in simple summer clothing. We were therefore forced to cling to each other at night to keep warm. We had no water to wash ourselves with, and only the lucky ones who had a bottle could take some extra drinking water at a station whenever the train stopped to refuel. We were all hungry and exhausted, and we no longer cared when or where our journey would end. Then finally one morning, the train stopped and someone outside shouted: 'Berlin!'

Through the narrow opening of the door I noticed the golden rays of the sun reflecting back from the helmets of a multitude of horrible policemen. There so many of them. Why were there so many? We were not criminals. We were just innocent young girls and boys, taken away from our homes and our parents. After a long wait the door of the wagon was finally unlocked and we were ordered out.

Chapter 21

We took our possessions and jumped down onto the platform which was wet from the previous night's rain. There were people everywhere, hundreds of them, though they were not all from Ukraine. The policemen towered over us, menacingly, and they laughed as they counted their spoils: we hated them immediately.

At first, we stood and watched as hundreds of our teenagers marched past. Nobody cared if we were hungry, thirsty, or unwell after the journey. We were just treated like furniture. Eventually, they moved us on: 'Los! Los! Hurry up!' We were marched away from the station, again in columns of four.

After a long walk we arrived at a camp. Wire mesh surrounded a large space in an open field in which there were endless rows of wooden huts. Hundreds of our people were now standing there. Some were sat on their bundles looking bewildered. An iron gate was opened by a policeman and we were ordered inside. We met boys and girls who had arrived before us and who were already more familiar with their surroundings.

'Where are you from?' was always the first question to be asked. Everyone was looking for somebody else from close to their home. It was an effort to connect back to what had been lost.

'How are you getting on here?' was the second question.

'You'll see when you've stayed here,' was the invariable answer.

'How long have you been here?'

'One week. We are waiting to be sent to work. This is a transit camp.'

Having just obtained this information we were promptly ordered into a hut where we were given a piece of bread and a bowl of tasteless turnip soup. Most of us couldn't eat it, so we threw it away.

'At home not even the pigs would eat this,' said a girl in a white scarf.

Some, however, were so hungry that they did eat it. We tried to chew the hard black bread, bit by bit, but we couldn't eat much.

Another command was given, and we had to march to another hut. This time it was the bathhouse. We had to hand over our possessions for disinfection; go through a medical check; have a shower; then wait for a long time to get our possessions back. Dozens of naked girls stood on the concrete floor, waiting, talking or else arguing. We were ashamed and angry with the Germans. At last our disinfected and damp clothes, which were still very smelly, were given back to us, and then we were marched to another hut where bunk beds were allocated to us. At last, we thought, blessed rest. But rest was not yet given to us. No sooner had we settled into a corner when a loud voice ordered us to go outside for registration, and then for photographs, and then for a roll call. We were marched from one place to another for the whole of the day and remained completely exhausted.

It was dark when we finally managed to lie down. It had been a week-long journey of sleepless nights, but even then our hopes of rest were in vain. A group of boys burst into the hut and started to make a noise. They had been in the camp for a week and were bored and now wanted to become acquainted with the new arrivals. We started to shout at them and told them to go away. A policeman appeared at the door and one by one the boys disappeared. Peace was restored and sleep finally carried us deep into a world of dreams.

What future could we possibly see? What wishes could that dark night over Germany gather in from the thousands of newly-arrived slaves? Many of us would soon fall ill, many would perish, but everyone would suffer. We would always long to go home, but most of us would never return. We were in the hands of strangers – Nazi conquerors who had brought us here, but we still had to be somewhere in God's hands. Whatever good we had done in our short lives deserved some form of goodness in kind: 'Dear God and all the Angels…' I wished I knew how to pray. I would have prayed on my knees all night for all of us.

Morning came early with the order to get up and hurry to the roll call. We joined a queue at the kitchen for a piece of bread and a bottle of black coffee. We then went through more medicals, registrations and roll calls. And so it continued all day. We hardly had a moment to ourselves. The weather was hot all day and the dust from the roads seemed to add to the scorching heat. We felt tired and were almost suffocating. Days passed with the same routine: early call; queues; coffee and bread; roll call; revision of names; standing in the sun for another lengthy registration; queues; a bowl of soup at midday; roll call again, and so on from morning until night. Amidst all of this we remembered that we were human and wanted to make friends with others.

The girls from our group in the train were all in one room now, and we felt closer to each other than to all the others in the camp. Valya's hopes for the future had been re-kindled. She washed her hair and set it in a new style, and after putting on a black dress, she looked lovely. She told us about an aunt who was living in Berlin. She spoke German so she went to the office to ask for permission to go and see her. The people in the office helped her, and one day she went away and did not return until late in the evening. All she had when she returned was some saccharine. She gave us a tablet each and explained how it would sweeten the coffee. She then told us, with some pride, that she might get a job as an interpreter and that she was altogether lucky in her life. She did not mention her aunt again but remained full of enthusiasm. In the evenings, I walked with her along the camp's roads. She was proud, and walked as though she was at home in the park: she wore her best white dress.

Clara had found some friends in the hut where the camp authorities worked: a commandant, interpreters and clerks. There was a constant flow of businessmen looking for workers for their factories, mines, households or other jobs where we could be used as cheap labour. Clara appeared to be friendly with all of them. Her fat arms, neck and face were now red from the sun, but her abundance of freckles still made her stand out. She still continued to be so provocative that the other girls avoided her and turned the other way whenever she appeared.

Oksana still comforted young Olya and they stayed together in the hut. They slept next to each other and went everywhere in the camp together. They were like two inseparable sisters, even though they looked completely different. Olya was tiny and blonde with sad, blue eyes, whereas Oksana was tall with dark, plaited hair pinned above her oblong face. Her wise, brown eyes looked carefully at the world around her. It was as though an innate ancestral wisdom was guarding her in this new and strange situation. Olya never smiled and her lower lip trembled as if she would cry every time she looked at anybody or whenever she tried to speak. Even to Oksana she spoke like a little child who had been wrongfully punished.

Some of the girls soon found boyfriends and wanted to go to the same place of work. To do that, they had to declare themselves husband and wife. A table with a white sheet was placed close to one of the huts where a marriage ceremony would be performed. How much legal value it had, I never found out. Human emotions had to be dealt with or else be displaced or replaced. Deeply hurt by having to part from their loved ones at home, these girls and boys found an escape in newly-felt love and friendship and did not look too deeply into past or the future.

Personally, I had no interest in marriage. My heart still ached from leaving Mykola behind, and the thought of replacing him never crossed my mind. I longed for the times when we were together and I regretted not speaking about how we felt. I knew that I would not have said anything unless he said something first, because that is how I was. I was shy, and I expected a man to make the first advances. Perhaps the gypsy woman was right, because fate never brought us together. I was wrapped up in my sorrows and shared them with the gloom of the others. There seemed to be thousands of us in the camp. I wondered how many more such camps there were all over Germany.

One day, after more than a week of waiting, we were ordered to leave the huts, with our belongings, and were told to go to the square where the camp authorities and employers met. It was early morning and the sun was rising in the East – "our home," as we then called it. It was a large and bright sun that morning and we were ordered to stand in its heat for the entire day. Thousands of us had been squashed into the open square without water or food. The dust, dirt, heat and perspiring bodies coupled with the endless waiting was soul destroying. By late afternoon we were crying from exhaustion and despair.

Finally, some finely-dressed gentlemen began to appear. They wore immaculate pale suits and matching hats, and held fine sticks in their hands. As they approached from the offices, they looked at us as though we were a mass of objects far below the heights of their human standards. We soon learned that they were the owners of factories and mines. A man in a white shirt appeared on the steps leading to the offices and began to call out numbers. We all had numbers. There were no family names – no brothers or sisters, mothers or children (although we knew of some). And there were no boyfriends or girlfriends: just numbers. Twenty or fifty numbers would be called and those people had to stand to one side. If the numbers did not come out together, relatives and friends were separated. The cries, screams, begging and pleading did not help. The German gentlemen would wave their sticks and groups of "numbers" would be led away from

169

the exhausted, crying crowd.

'Later, later!' they said indifferently to the separated mothers and daughters, friends and relatives, 'you will find each other later.'

Ignoring the scenes of separation the man in the white shirt appeared again on the steps of the office and called out some more numbers. My number was not called, but in the next twenty-five calls all of my friends from the train were led away. I said goodbye to them. They were the last links to my native town. I felt as if I had been left on an island and abandoned in an unknown world. Then the man reappeared on the steps and called out:

'Who can speak German?'

My first thought was to say nothing. I would never say I could speak German: never. Unfortunately, the girls who had travelled with me quickly singled me out: 'She can speak German,' they said.

'No!' I wanted to cry, but it was too late. My number was called and I was ordered into the office where I was introduced to a group of fine-looking German gentlemen. I was to be the interpreter for the girls from my home town and district, with whom I had travelled in the train. They were glad to have me, but I was furious.

'Why did you tell them I can speak German? I don't want to speak German. Never!'

'But you'll be able to help us,' replied Oksana.

'And we would like you to be with us,' said Lena, a pretty girl with black, curly hair and big, grey eyes. She smiled at me.

'Oh, Lena!' I sighed, 'I would love to be with you, but I do not want to speak German!'

There was no more time. A gentleman waved his stick and our group was led away.

'Goodbye, everyone!' We waved to the waiting crowd and were marched to the gate of the camp.

I was not used to speaking German. I had learned the language at school and a bit more at Lviv University. I knew some grammar and some poems by Schiller, but I had never spoken the language or used it in practice.

I was quickly introduced to a thin and nervous gentleman with a humped back and was told that he was the commandant of our new camp. He looked at me with his small, green eyes and twisted his face into a smile. He told me to tell the girls to hurry up. We marched through fields and entered the suburbs of Berlin where the houses were pretty and clean. With envy, I thought there was life behind those white lace curtains, where families and the love of normal human life could be found. We were exhausted, untidy and dirty, and well-dressed people came out to look at us.

Another two gentlemen walked with us. One was a tall grey-haired and blue-eyed man who was introduced as the manager. He had a kind look, so I was not at all frightened of him. The other was a larger brown-eyed man who said he was an engineer, and he looked at us with some sympathy. Neither of them said much to me and walked behind the column. The commandant, however, never left me alone. He talked constantly and repeatedly twisted his nervous face. He asked me questions and I had to dig deep into my knowledge of German to be able to understand him and then find some answers.

After an hour, we reached Berlin's subway. I was ordered to tell the girls to tidy themselves up as people were staring at us. The girls swore at him, and for the first time, I had to invent a polite answer when he asked me what they were saying. The sun was now setting and the busy station was bathed in golden rays of light. I watched the people from the platform as we waited. For the first time in my life I saw how German women looked. They were serious and modestly dressed, but in good taste and they were very proud. Older people looked at us with sympathy, but the others just ignored us.

When the subway train arrived we were told to get inside. The carriage was almost empty so we sat on the wooden benches. I looked at our girls as the train sped through Berlin. How indifferent they were. Their tired faces did not express any interest in the passing streets, buildings or crowded stations. Considering where they had come from, they should have been excited, but they were blind to everything going on. They could only see what they had left behind. What good was this huge and noisy city to them, even if it was the centre of the world's attention? Like me, they were homesick and lost in the life of Berlin: June 1942.

After another long walk from the station we arrived at the factory where we were destined to work. We were allowed to wash our hands and were led into a canteen, in a cellar, where we were each given a bowl of soup. We were then led to a hut and locked inside for the night. It was filled with bunk beds and I was pleased to have one by the window. There was also a washroom, so I finally managed to have a wash. Other girls were so exhausted that they just fell onto their beds and tried to sleep, but the talking, shouting and quarrelling soon started all over again. The rough, hard mattresses on the bunk beds made us think of our soft beds and feather pillows at home. Then, the tears came again.

It was still dark when the hammering of the camp's metal posts woke us. The commandant burst into the room shouting at us to get up: 'Aufstehen! Schnell! Schnell!'

'What's he saying?' one of the girls asked, sleepily.

'We have to get up.'

I went from bed to bed asking the girls to get up. We were told to hurry. The girls swore and complained of being woken so early. They were tired, but they all got up, combed their hair and got dressed. We washed as quickly as we could with the commandant shouting at us constantly. Finally, he led us out of the camp and into the factory.

In the canteen we were given a slice of bread and a cup of coffee. It was still dark outside and we had no means of telling the exact time. The commandant, who asked us to call him Herr Zell, appeared again. He shouted again, except this time we had to work.

The factory was a textile mill which printed woven fabrics. The dyes were prepared in one room where they were constantly boiled, and the steam and vapours filled the huge adjacent room where the printing took place. The smell was so strong that we began to sneeze, and tears quickly rolled down our cheeks.

'What a horrible smell!' the girls said, putting handkerchiefs to their noses. They were about to begin working there. Huge frames holding the patterns were filled with dye and moved from end to end of a long table upon which rolls of material were stretched. A long fine brush in the frame was controlled by the hands of two workers

172

standing opposite each other. I had to explain what the girls had to do, and so they began their seemingly difficult task.

Having finished my translation I was taken upstairs to the design room where the patterns were prepared. I was shown how to help the designer, and my job was to trace the patterns onto the canvas on the frames. The room was clean and had an open window. The designer was an efficient man, and he was kind, but we did not talk much. I was glad not to be in the printing department with the smell of boiling dyes, and my work was not so difficult either. At midday, we took a dinner break in the basement canteen where we each received a bowl of soup. The Germans ate in a separate canteen, so we had no idea what they ate. We worked from six in the morning until six at night. For our supper we were given a few small jacket potatoes, but every day when we arrived back at the camp, the girls complained of being tired and hungry.

The summer evenings were light, and after six o'clock I preferred to leave the dormitory and go outside into the yard. There were some trees, a patch of grass, and even some flowers in the flowerbeds as the camp had been built in the grounds of the manager's estate. There were big houses nearby, and Berlin's noisy streets. People continued to look at us from their windows and balconies whenever we were outside, but I took no notice of them. I walked round the garden. The trees, the patch of grass and the flowers were all I had left to remind me of how beautiful my beloved Ukraine was.

I felt great emotional pain – a terrible longing to be home. I did not yet know it, but this was the beginning of many long years of homesickness – an incurable ongoing illness which dampened my spirit and lessened my energy. It made me feel like I was an invalid in a foreign country. I walked to the gate. It was locked. We were all locked inside. I cried bitterly in the stillness of that beautiful summer evening. What had we done to deserve this? Clouds then came over and the evening sky quickly turned dark.

Back inside, the girls were arguing and shouting at each other again. Oksana came to me and asked: 'What can we do with Olya? She never stops crying. No matter what I say or do, she cries and cries, all of the time. She doesn't want to

173

talk to anybody, and she hardly touches her food. She'll be ill before long.'

Oksana looked at me. Although her eyes looked sad, she never lost her confidence. She was strong and would endure anything thrown at her. Even then, I felt comfortable with her.

I went to Olya's bed and found her turned to the wall, but no matter how gently I tried to persuade her to say something or to eat some food, she just lay there with her lips trembling. I asked the other girls to treat her kindly, and they all tried to console her, but it was of no use. She worked all day, and in the evenings she just lay there crying, never wanting to face up to anything new: her whole being was still at home.

Lena's bed was next to mine. Lena had lovely black hair, long eyelashes and fine thin eyebrows. Her cheeks were rosy and her round face radiated a friendly smile. She was from Krolevets, but I had not met her before. She was younger than me and was not so well-educated, but she was so perfectly natural in her attitude and behaviour that I couldn't help being friendlier with her than I was with any of the other girls.

'Poor Olya,' I said to Lena, 'how can we cheer her up?'

'Nobody can do it,' she replied simply, and sighed. 'She's crying for her mother. She's an only daughter and they broke them up.'

Lena was busy sewing something from tent canvas which we were allowed to take from the factory. Seeing her so calm and composed made me feel better.

Katya slept above Lena. She was a thin and tall girl who had a slim face and sharp, grey eyes. Her dark hair was always plaited and pinned to her small head giving her a lightly rounded look. She sat on her bed and joined in the conversation:

'You know, all the crying in the world won't help her. I'm telling you girls, we have to stay alive. I'll live and you won't find me crying.'

It was Katya who usually organised the girls. She forcefully put some makeup on my face. I had never used makeup before. Katya applied powder and rouge, lipstick and mascara and then, leading me to the mirror she said: 'Take a look at yourself! Isn't that better? Girls, see how nice Vera looks!'

I looked at myself and smiled: 'But I don't have any makeup,' I said.

'So, we'll get you some.' Katya was so sure of herself. It was as if the whole world belonged to her. 'We want you to look nice. For the time being you can use mine.' She started to draw lines over her thin eyebrows. Sitting on her bunk she held the little mirror high above her and almost touched the ceiling in the effort to make her plain face look more attractive.

'So, who are you meeting tonight?' asked Svitlana, a girl with golden hair who had joined us at the transit camp.

'Oh, I'll be meeting a millionaire.' Katya replied.

Svitlana's favourite occupation was looking in the mirror. She constantly combed her hair, setting and resetting it. Her round face was plain, and she also had slightly bulging, blue eyes and a large nose. Her lips were full and red, and her cheeks were always pink. Nonetheless, she thought she was beautiful.

'And who are you going to make happy? One would think you were going to meet a prince,' Katya said, from the top of her bunk bed. 'You play with that mirror as though you're preparing for a grand date.'

'And all in good time, just you wait and see,' laughed Svitlana in reply.

Little Sonia, the girl who had had a bottle of water in the train and who always wore a white scarf, was busy washing. She was always helping somebody quietly and obligingly. It was as though she took pleasure from her service to others.

'Sonia, bring me some water,' called Katya. Immediately, Sonia brought her some, without a word.

The other girls reproached Katya: 'Couldn't you get it yourself? Fancy you using her that way! Sonia, don't bring her any more!' But Sonia would always obey and would do anything anybody asked of her.

'It is strange how everyone is behaving so differently in this new life of ours,' I said to Lena.

'Well, people are different to begin with,' she answered simply. I knew she was capable of looking after herself. She could go through anything with the same quiet, composed smile. And she had it in her to send evil away and find goodness within. That's why I liked her. She gave me a very concerned look: 'Olya is really poorly. Can we not do anything for her?'

I replied: 'I can't do anything. We're locked in here and there's nobody around. I'll try speaking to Olya again. I am so very sorry for her, but I really don't know how to help her.'

Olya was still crying. Her young body was still facing the wall, and she was shaking.

'Olya, stop crying!' I said firmly. 'They'll take you away from us. Do you want that to happen? We all feel like you do, but we have to get on with life, and crying won't help.' I put my hand on her forehead. She was hot: 'You'll make yourself ill.' I spoke more calmly and she seemed quieter, but she still didn't answer me. After a while I left her. Oksana then sat beside her again.

From the corner of the room Anna appeared. She was a practical, down-to-earth girl from the same village as Olya. She was well-built, forward and abrupt, and spoke every word like a soldier giving commands.

'Leave her alone. You will only make her worse. Everybody has to nurse their own wound. Let her sleep.' I looked at Anna. She had big, brown eyes and suntanned skin. Her brown hair curled slightly and it suggested she was far gentler than the sharp way in which she spoke. I thought she must have been a brigadier on a collective farm.

'Maybe you are right, Anna,' I said. I went to my bed, to my own private corner by the window. I even had the luxury of a window sill on which I put some flowers and personal possessions.

We had to be up early again. The food was poor, and with the passing of each day we became increasingly hungry and tired. The girls protested and asked me to translate their grievances. Every time I complained to the commandant he became furious and shouted back at me. I took no notice. To me, he seemed insane and I had no respect for him. Neither did I fear him. Seeing him shout and twist his face was like watching a sick and crippled man.

Another problem was the locked gate. We longed to get out of the camp and walk in the streets to be amongst the people, to feel at least a little bit of freedom. We had received our first minute wage and so we had some spending money, but they would not let us out, not even at weekends.

Then one day, we made a spontaneous protest. It was a lovely Sunday evening. We had washed and cleaned the barrack and went out into the yard. The evening was warm and we wandered around not knowing what to do. We started talking, and some of us started to cry. At first we cried quietly alone, and then others joined in. Then, unrehearsed, we started to cry louder and louder, all of us together – thirty girls in a circle on the patch of grass. People in the surrounding houses came out onto their balconies and opened their windows. The whole block of houses watched us as we cried louder and louder. Suddenly Herr Zell came running towards us.

'Was ist los? What's the matter?' He shouted and waved his long thin arms. We did not stop crying. He started to run round us. He was helpless and rather comic. Finally, not being able to stop us, he called to me.

'Why are you crying?'

'We are homesick, and we want to be allowed out of the camp,' I stammered through my tears. 'Why do you lock us up? We want to go out.'

'Ha! Ha! Ha!' he burst out. 'You want to be free. Ha, ha, ha! You will never be free. You were brought here to work and you will stay here as long as we want. You will never get out of the camp. It's an order, do you understand? Stop crying! The whole street is looking at you. Do you want the police to come? Ha! Ha! Ha!' He left us with his horrible laughter and went to the gate.

I told the girls what he had said and they were very angry. They shouted back at him, calling him names with every swear word they could think of in Ukrainian, but he did not come back. With the anger we stopped crying. We sat on the grass until late at night: a few girls genuinely continued to cry quietly.

We went to work with headaches and long faces in the morning. Herr Zell tried to be nice, but we ignored him. Having suffered, we ignored all the Germans and refused to talk to them. Later on, I was called to the manager's office. It was luxurious, and he sat in a very comfortable chair. Tall and going grey, he glanced at me with a wise look in his eyes, and he spoke softly:

'I hear you organised a crying protest last night.'

'I didn't organise any protest. The girls happened to be crying, and I cried, too.' I answered calmly.

'Why?' he asked. 'Don't you know you could be arrested by the Gestapo?'

'What, for crying? No.' I said, unable to hide my first sign of fear. 'I didn't know that. We're homesick, and we'd just like to go out. Why do you lock us up in the camp?'

'It's an order and I can not do anything about it,' he said with a hint of sympathy in his voice.

'But it is a very cruel order,' I replied. 'We are not prisoners. We are young girls and we have not done anything wrong. We want our freedom.'

He looked at me with surprise: 'You are a very brave girl to even dare to talk like that.' Then, after a short pause, he added: 'You may go.'

I told the girls what the boss had said. They were cross and cursed the Germans. Oksana was concerned and came up to me:

'Be careful how you talk. They could take you away.'

'I was telling the truth,' I said.

'The truth is not always the best thing for you.'

The door suddenly opened and I was asked to go to the commandant. I was not frightened, but the girls begged me to be careful. At Herr Zell's office I was given some pieces of material on which the capital letters OST (EAST) were printed in white with blue borders.

'Cut them up and give them to all the girls,' he said with a sneer. 'Tell them to stitch them onto their clothing and to wear them all of the time.'

I could see a scornful laugh in his small, green eyes. We, the East European workers were going to have to wear a badge with the letters OST just as the Poles had P and the Jews had a yellow star. Without a word I went out of the office. Tears ran down my cheeks.

'The twentieth century...' I was talking to myself, '...the Germans are mad. It won't last long. It won't! Never! Never! Never! They are so inhumane and stupid, so very, very stupid!'

I took the strips of cloth to the camp and told the girls

that we had to wear them. I asked them to help me cut them up. I cried throughout, and seeing this, the girls sympathised and remained silent.

'Stupid German rules!' Katya exclaimed eventually as she looked at the material.

'They can pin their hackenkreuz to their ass!' Anna laughed from her top bunk.

'So! Now we are branded girls!' concluded Oksana.

I looked at her and felt a pang of pity and sorrow. It hurt me to see Oksana wearing OST on her breast. It looked disgraceful. It belittled her and robbed her of any dignity and respect. I sighed and said nothing.

Some of the girls stitched the emblem on neatly, but some just attached it to their blouse haphazardly: they hated it. We were all upset. It stuck out on our clothing and would be with us for the next three years. We were to become known as "Ostarbeiters" – workers from the East, and amongst ourselves we used the word "Ostowtsi". We would be different from others, but we would remain the equivalent of slaves. Bit by bit, it would destroy our personalities and it would turn us into a special class from which new personalities would emerge.

Katya sniffed: 'Fancy wearing these labels. Well, if they want me to wear one, I will, but it won't be for long. Do you know girls, I am proud to be from the East because I love the East!' She then pinned the badge to her grey dress.

Even then, as far as I could see, Katya was not Katya any longer. She was now marked, belittled and becoming a stranger, and she knew it, too. From that day on, we all began to change. We felt it, and we surrendered to it. The only way we could deal with it was by isolating ourselves. The rest of the free world on our doorstep continued to be hostile to us. Some of the girls became depressed, some cried, and some tried to act with a braver face, seeking their own means of escape. It was a reality which hit us harder than any other. The darkest side of Nazism had arrived. We were Ostarbeiters, we were being dehumanised, and some of us were about to be worked to death.

Other news soon came which spread like wildfire. A group of Ukrainian boys were being brought to work in our factory. They lived in another camp across the road, and at

179

work we could meet them every day and eat with them at meal times. We met them with our OST badges pinned to our blouses, and it was only then that my inner anger began to rise to the surface:

'Why didn't you defend us?' I shouted at them. 'Why did you let them take us to this country to be treated like lepers? You: the men, the warriors, the defenders! You could have stopped them!'

I resisted from expressing anything more. They were only teenagers. Other girls were much friendlier, and by the end of the day they knew each other's names and history.

'He's a schoolboy.' They pointed to a tall, dark boy with an oblong and handsome face. 'They call him Kolya. He was captured in his local market and deported. And that one is a tractor driver called Dmytro. They forced him to come to here even though he was unfit for the army.'

'Oh, he's nice-looking. I do like him,' Anna admitted bluntly.

'Well, let's see whether or not he likes you,' snapped Katya.

'So, who said I want a boyfriend here?' Anna replied in defence of her statement.

It was another new chapter for us. The boys had to wear the OST badges, too. They swore at the Germans, and the Germans asked me what they were saying. I usually answered and said they were tired and hungry. There was an older man with the boys and he made us laugh as he did not know any German words and refused to learn any. He spoke in Ukrainian to everyone, and even when it came to money he insisted on using our word "fedir" instead of the German "pfennig". He worked hard but seemed to get thinner with each passing day.

The majority of the Ukrainian boys were between sixteen and nineteen years of age. They were all very nice-looking and healthy. On Sundays, when we had more time to talk, they were allowed to come into our camp. The young schoolboy, Kolya, was kind and friendly to me. He had dark-brown hair, a long face and brown eyes. I liked him and we talked together like a brother and sister. Then there was Serhiy – a village boy with sparkling, dark eyes that always smiled. His wavy, brown hair always fell to one side of his

180

forehead. He, too, was friendly to me, but as with Kolya, it was impossible to imagine him being someone extra special for me. The girls were jealous however, and I noticed them watching.

'What does he see in her?' I heard Anna say of Serhiy. 'He never comes to talk to me.'

'There are girls like her who understand boys,' someone replied, but I could not see who it was.

'He likes to talk and finds things to say to her,' added Katya, 'that's the only secret.'

From then on, I began to avoid Serhiy, but he smiled at me and was always nice.

Then there was Boris. We all knew his type. He had been brought up in an orphanage and was probably the child of a family that had been ruined by the State. He had bold, blue eyes, blonde uncombed hair which stood up, and a cheeky face. He was always ready to fight and defend himself, but we knew that underneath the brave, young fighter there was a gentle weeping soul who responded to kindness like a flower to the sun. We all liked him and looked after him as we would a younger brother.

Once, at supper, when the women in the kitchen did not give us enough potatoes, the boys began to protest. They decided not to eat their supper and demanded to see the commandant. Herr Zell soon came running into the canteen. He was furious. Shouting and waving his long arms he seized the nearest chair. Then, holding it high above his head he came running towards us. He was ready to hit someone. What personal power I had, and what possessed me to respond, I do not know, but I stepped out of the crowd, took hold of his arm and said calmly:

'Herr Zell, they are hungry, that's all.'

To my surprise he lowered his arm and calmed down. He pulled his sleeves down, and straightened his shirt and tie. 'Who started this? Was it you?' He pointed at young Boris.

'No,' I said, 'we all started it. We are hungry.'

'You will get more potatoes, but he is going to spend the night in the cellar,' He then took hold of Boris and pushed him out of the canteen towards the cellar. The cook gave us extra potatoes but we could not eat them. Boris was our hero, and after the commandant had gone, we gathered by the cellar door and started to push some of the potatoes through the small opening in the window.

'How are you in there?' we asked sympathetically. We were ready to sacrifice anything to help set him free, and we wholeheartedly wished him a good night. He was released the following morning and walked out triumphantly.

One Sunday afternoon, some of the girls climbed over the fence and ran to the shops to buy some lemonade. They came back along the same route and were excited by their achievement. It marked the beginning of our adventures, but the start of trouble for me. That first time, the girls were lucky. Nobody noticed them. Then, they went again, and others followed their example. We discovered a park nearby, and more shops beyond the corner of our road. We could buy ice cream and lemonade and even some sweets. We had earned a little money and wanted to spend it. The summer's days were hot and the air was full of the fragrances of flowering lime trees, roses and shrubs. The magic of summer was overpowering – especially for the younger sixteen to eighteen-year-old girls. How could any of us live without our freedom? We could not follow the rules, so we began to break them.

We climbed over the fence and ran away from the camp. Most of that time was spent in the park. I learned later that it was called Wannsee Park. Its lake was surrounded by ancient trees, and music could be heard from the bandstand. People strolled and enjoyed their Sunday afternoons there. It was a heavenly feeling to be able to walk along a street like a normal human being. I felt that all the weight had been lifted from my shoulders. I felt so light that I wanted to fly away.

Herr Zell lived with his wife in a flat opposite the camp and, to begin with, did not notice our adventures. Neither did the police watchman who sat in his hut at the gate, but eventually somebody reported us. One Sunday afternoon, Herr Zell came running into the camp, shouting and screaming.

'How dare you go out of the camp?' Of course, I was the one held responsible and he shouted at me and threatened me by waving his arms. I stayed calm. Again, he appeared as a sick man to me, so I did not bother to argue with him. I stood in front of him and maintained my silence. Then finally, I spoke:

'Herr Zell, it is wrong to keep us locked up. The girls want to experience just a little bit from life. We are all young and we aren't doing anything wrong.'

'Donnerswetter!' He swore in German. 'You are not allowed out of the camp and that's that. Schluss – end of the story!' He then ran away like a dog that had been barking for a long time. We were left quiet and subdued.

The very next day, Herr Zell called to me after work and asked me to go to his flat. I was surprised. To my astonishment his wife – a plump and well-dressed lady – made me very welcome. Herr Zell was as sweet as sugar, and fussed over me, saying nice things. The table in the middle of the room was laid for tea. The fresh white, buttered rolls smelt delicious. I had not seen anything so homely for a very long time, but I was not asked to sit down. Instead, they asked me very sweetly if I would report to them the names of any girls who went out of the camp, in future. I was furious. So that was the reason for their polite approaches. With dismay, I understood that they wanted me to be an informer.

'No,' I said, 'I will not do it! I want to go out of the camp myself. It is wrong to keep us locked up as though we are prisoners. We haven't done anything wrong.'

They were amazed by my response and became very cross: 'You ungrateful girl!' They shouted. 'You could have had all this if you had helped us!' They were pointing at the food on the table.

'Please! Do you expect to buy me off?' I retorted in anger.

'There is no way! I will eat what the girls eat, and I will not betray them for anything in the world because they are right. They want what I want. We all want to be able to leave the camp, and you should not lock us up like prisoners.' My words were very firm, and clear, but I delivered them calmly and assuredly.

How naïve I was. I knew nothing of the German concentration camps, or of the Jewish holocaust which was happening at that time. Blessed are the ignorant, as they say. I learned of all that later on, but at the time it felt right to make my protest.

'You impudent girl!' They shouted again. 'How dare you

talk to us like that. Go! We do not want to see you any more!'

Herr Zell opened the door and I walked out, leaving the table untouched. I still wondered what they would do with so much good food left upon it. I wished that I had eaten at least one buttered roll. Then I smiled to myself. Never! I would never have taken it from them – the scoundrels.

I told the girls what had happened and they were amused.

'How stupid those Germans can be,' said Katya. 'I wish they would bring those rolls to us. That would at least make them seem wiser.'

'Let's sing a song,' suggested Anna, 'let them see that we are all together.' We went outside and sat on the grass singing one song after another until darkness fell, but my refusal to report the girls' camp exits cost me dearly: it changed my destiny.

The following morning, I was told to stop working in the design room and was sent to work in the worst section of the factory – close to where the dyes were prepared. Everybody who worked there sneezed constantly. Tears ran from their eyes, and their faces were red, as though sunburned. My companion was an elderly well-built woman, but I had never worked so physically hard in my life. The fumes from the boiling dyes, next door soon irritated my eyes and nose. Tears and sweat rolled down my cheeks and down my neck. I was hot and suffocating. In addition, the woman who worked with me was unkind, rough and often very nasty to me. I guessed she was Polish, but she was pretending to be German which meant having to be more German than the German women themselves. Her eyes bulged.

I knew it was my punishment and I persevered despite the hardship. Back at the camp, I was so tired that I just fell onto my bed and slept. Sleep was the only relief and consolation I could receive, but that was not the end of the matter. One week later, Herr Zell triumphantly brought in a new girl and announced that she was to be the new interpreter. He did not say another word to me. Showing his revenge, he simply walked past me and ignored me like an angry schoolboy who had been fighting with a rival. I smiled to myself and said nothing.

The new girl was called Helen. She was tall and well-built with a long nose and a very self-assured manner. She was well-dressed and from the way she laughed we knew that she was the same type of girl as Clara. She walked into the dormitory and put on an act: she ignored everybody. Finding an empty bed, she spread her belongings out. Everybody looked. She was not wanted in our newly-formed family.

From the day Helen walked in, life took a downhill turn. She swore, and before long, other girls started to swear, too. The next day at work, Helen was seen kissing a Czech man and the girls immediately seemed to lose their standards of knowing right from wrong. The rota I had organised for cleaning the washroom and barrack was ignored, and the place became dirty and neglected. Helen told the girls to stop going out of the camp and threatened to report those who dared to climb over the fence. Her German was poor, but each time Herr Zell or any of the other Germans talked to her, she laughed. She walked past me, as though she knew everything about me, and she held her head up high. I ignored and despised her, and was glad I did not have to interpret any longer, though I did feel sorry for the others. The boys whistled at her, but they would still come to me for help if they needed something from the Germans.

On Sundays, we were locked in again and did not dare to leave the camp. The girls walked around with long faces and even the boys, who were allowed to come into our barrack in the afternoon, could not cheer them up. Only a few weeks had passed since Helen's arrival, but now the girls were swearing and quarrelling again. Some of them came to me and quietly told me of their troubles. They explained that Helen had stirred up gossip which had caused them to fight and fall out with each other. They wished I was still in charge.

Maybe this was the reason why one lovely summer evening, after we had finished supper, some girls called me to the gate to meet a visitor. I was reluctant to go as Helen was in charge. After all, why should I answer all the questions that curious visitors were always asking? The girls insisted. Besides, Helen could not be found, so I went. To my surprise, I saw an unfamiliar but very handsome gentleman. He was tall and very elegant – he was dressed in a light-grey suit. In his hand he held a snow-white handkerchief with which he gently wiped his forehead. He held it like a valuable treasure and gently folded it away in his top pocket. Under his other arm he was holding a book.

The policeman at the gate allowed me to go outside and talk to him. The stranger held out his hand to greet me. His deep-blue eyes looked at me gently and sympathetically. He had thick, dark eyelashes and he was clean-shaven. His dark-brown hair was set in such a style that he looked like a prince. Quietly, and almost shyly, he told me that he was from the Russian Orthodox Church community in Berlin which wanted to help us. He had already had a long talk with the commandant to allow us to go to church on Sundays. He said that the commandant was unpleasant and had initially refused to give permission for us to leave the camp, but he then obtained it from the director of the factory on the condition that he would take full responsibility for bringing us all back to the camp. Meanwhile, he had brought me a book to read. It was "Resurrection" by Leo Tolstoy. I thanked him, sincerely.

Some of the other girls came out and talked to him through the wire fence. They asked him who he was and where he lived. I learned that he was the son of Russian emigrants who had left Russia after the Revolution, when he was a small boy. He had a sister who was a ballet dancer, and he lived with her in Berlin.

The news of being able to go to church on Sundays was greeted with great joy, and he promised to talk to the director again. The commandant then ran out, shouting at us to stop our conversation. He told the visitor that it was time for him to leave. The girls started to swear back at him, and he asked what they were saying. To protect the girls I said that they were glad to have a visitor and were cross because he had just ended their conversation. Our new friend smiled gently at me, approving of my translation. He then said goodbye to all of us.

With the book in my hand and still somewhat surprised by everything, I returned to the barrack where Helen was standing in front of a mirror putting rollers in her hair.

'Why didn't you call me?' she demanded in a superior tone.

'The girls asked me to go because they couldn't find you.'

She was now angry: 'So, what did he want?'

'He has permission to take us to church on Sunday,' I

said, 'and he's going to help us.'

'To church, huh?' sniffed Helen. 'Who wants to go there?'

'We want to go!' shouted the girls who had now gathered near her. 'You needn't come if you don't want to.'

'None of you are going!' She shouted. 'I am going to tell Herr Zell that you pushed me out and didn't let me talk to that man.'

'You had better keep your mouth shut,' Anna said calmly, but she said it with such authority that nobody would dare to challenge her. 'You can stay here with your Herr Zell, if you like, but we're all going, aren't we girls?'

'Yes! Yes!' answered the chorus of voices.

We did not know whether Helen ever said anything to Herr Zell or not, but on Saturday night we washed our hair and put paper rollers in. Early on Sunday morning we dressed in our clean clothes and were ready to go. Helen stayed behind.

At nine o'clock, our friend arrived. We had called him "our friend" since he first came to see us, even though we knew his name was Michael. His sister came with him and he introduced me to her as soon as we were out of the camp. She was tall, slim and very graceful. She was not very beautiful, but we really liked her. Her behaviour was straightforward and her conversation was simple, and she was so friendly in her greeting to each one of us that it seemed as if she had known us all her life. Her name was Nadiya, and I liked that as it was also my sister's name.

Herr Zell looked on nervously and told the girls not to run away. We smiled and felt relieved once we had gone as we could forget about him and walk freely along the street. I walked between Michael and his sister, and we talked like good friends. We went on the subway, walked beside the river, and finally we arrived at the church. There were many people standing outside as it was early and the service had not yet started.

Church had a special significance for me, and as soon as we entered the sacred building, everything else was forgotten. My dear father was with me in spirit. I seemed to hear his voice and see him at the altar. Mother, too, was near to me, as were my sister and brother: everyone that I loved. How I missed them. How I wanted to be with them. I prayed and cried throughout the service. The girls stood close to me. We kneeled and prayed when we were supposed to. It was a confessional mass and we all went to Holy Communion. I saw Michael glancing at me. I felt respect for him, but for the time being, my father and family occupied the space in my heart.

When the service over, we went outside and met the people. They were kind to us, asked us questions and looked at us with sympathy, all the more so when they saw OST stitched to our clothing. How nicely they dressed. I noticed one young girl who looked elegant and beautiful. She was wearing a navy-blue suit with a single brooch pinned to her lapel. I will dress like that one day, I thought. All I had was a brown, summer dress with a white, flowery pattern and a little, white hat. I had washed and ironed my dress, but it was getting old, and I felt far from adequate standing next to the Berliners.

'How do you like it here?' I asked one of the ladies who talked to me in a friendly manner.

'Well, we miss our country but we have to carry on. We can buy what we like and we have made our homes here.' She smiled at me and then signed: 'You have to get on with life, wherever you are.'

It was my first Sunday outside of the camp. I was not sure how I should behave, but I was sad as I continued to think of my parents and home. Tears filled my eyes once more.

I heard someone say: 'It was hard for us, too, when we first came, but then we got used to it. Time will heal you.'

A plump lady put an arm round me. Her kind eyes looked into mine. She was wearing a perfume that reminded me of my grandmother.

In a trembling voice I said: 'Never! I will never get used to it. Oh, how I miss my father and my mother. My father is a priest, and in the church it seemed as though I could see him.' Her arm tightened round my shoulders and she became even kinder to me.

Michael came across and asked me if we were ready to go.

'We will help you,' said the lady and she kissed me on

the cheek.

I did not notice how we got back to the camp. My thoughts were still with the church and the people I had just met for the first time. They were so well-behaved, modest, intelligent and very, very kind. I had not met people like that before. I had read about them in books, and imagined them, but I had never met them. Well, not many. I then remembered my uncle who had come to visit us when I was a little girl. He was just like these people were, but my parents could not live like they did. They had to work hard to bring us up. Almost all of the other people at home were the same. And there was always a shortage of everything in the shops. We had to queue, and sometimes we were lucky to be able to get anything at all, perhaps just a garment of some sort. Besides that, there was very little money in circulation. How could we dress well and develop a taste for clothes and fashion? I could see the difference immediately, and I liked their behaviour. They were so normal and friendly, with fine manners, elegant movements and quiet voices. Why hadn't we been brought up the same way? How I liked them. I would have loved to have been like they were. It was going to be my goal in life: I would become like they were. I sat in the train thinking these thoughts and noticed nothing until we arrived back at the camp. Michael said goodbye and promised to return on Saturday, and I thanked him.

We had a better dinner that Sunday after which Herr Zell told us we could go to the park. We rejoiced at the news. We ran along the streets and felt like birds out of cages. There was a kiosk at the corner where we bought lemonade and ice cream before making our way to the park's lake and trees. It felt as though we had come back to life.

From that Sunday onwards, we were allowed to go out of the camp in the afternoon, but only on the condition that we wore our OST badges and returned to the camp on time. But as soon as we left the camp we removed the labels in order to feel like human beings, and to be no different from the others. We pinned them back on when returning, and thus pretended to be obedient.

Soon after that, we were taken by Herr Zell and one of the engineers on a sightseeing trip to the centre of Berlin. For the first time, we ventured into the centre of the mighty Third

Reich. We saw the wide Unter den Linden Strasse, the monuments of King Wilhelm I and King Friedrich Wilhelm III, the Dom – a beautiful Lutheran cathedral, the bridges over the River Spree, the Opera House and the University which seemed higher than Heaven. We were also shown the Reichstag – perhaps the greatest symbol of Germany's power, where the changing of guards was being watched by hundreds of onlookers.

Many hundreds, perhaps thousands of well-dressed, happy people were walking freely through the wide streets of the capital city, but we were either looked down upon or ignored. We served as propaganda to show Germans how poor we were.

I would be wrong to say that all Germans were the same. There were elderly people who appeared to be normal and who had clearly not been indoctrinated by the Nazi regime. They were kind to us. We could see the sympathy in their eyes and they would sometimes give us a sandwich or an apple, and they would shake our hands warmly and sincerely. I would thus never lose my faith in humanity, no matter which government was in power. I love people and my love lives with me through all the wrongs and hardships that can be encountered.

I watched our boys. They looked powerless and helpless, but in their bright, young eyes I could see the protest and rebellion against everything around them. They looked at us and felt guilty of their inability to defend and protect us. They, too, were slaves who had been rounded up at the churches, cinemas and other public places in Ukraine. They, too, had been packed into cattle trucks and transported here for hard labour. If some of them were as helpless as children, then it was only because they were still children. We felt the awakening of our maternal instincts, and we spoke to them as though they were our brothers.

When Michael came, the following Saturday, he asked to see me. He told me that he had permission to take a few girls with him, and he wanted us to visit his house. I enquired to see who else wanted to go. To my surprise, Helen said that she did. Katya, Anna and Lena came, too. The five of us walked together and followed Michael to his home. Helen flirted with him, laughing and talking all the way.

When we arrived, we were met by his sister, Nadiya, who led us into the dining room. The table was set, and I thought it was just like our Easter table. There were all sorts of lovely sandwiches, sausages, salads, white rolls with butter, and cakes. We sat talking for a while and were then invited to take our places. Everything tasted so good, and it felt like being at home again. After we had finished eating, Nadiya asked me to come to her bedroom with her, where she asked me to sit down. Putting her arm round me she said in a soft and sincere voice:

'You are a really lovely girl. I want to give you one of my dresses.' She opened her wardrobe, and smiled gently: 'Come, choose any dress you like.'

I was astonished. The huge wardrobe was full of beautiful, expensive dresses. How could I choose one of these? I then thought about it. In my present situation, I should choose something that I could wear anywhere. Going through the whole wardrobe, I chose a simple black, crepe dress. It had long sleeves and a round collar.

'You have made a wise choice,' Nadiya said, and she kissed me. 'Come. Let's go back to the girls.'

Helen was now sitting next to Michael and crying. She was telling him her story. Her father had been arrested just before the War, and no one had seen him again. Everybody believed her and sympathised with her. I thought she was acting and seeking attention from Michael and the other guests who had now joined us. Just as soon as we entered, the conversation changed and Helen stopped crying. She began to talk and laugh loudly.

On the way home, each girl was given a blouse as a present, but Helen became very jealous when she discovered that I had been given a dress.

'Why didn't they give me one?' she asked bluntly.

'Maybe they didn't believe in your tears,' said Anna. 'Why did you have to tell your story to someone you'd never met before in your life?' She was not afraid of Helen, and to my surprise, Helen did not answer and said nothing more on the subject.

'They like you,' Lena said quietly, looking at me through her big smiling eyes. 'I'm so glad you were given the dress. After all, you do help us all the time.'

191

Helen must have heard her, because she shouted back: 'I'm your interpreter, not her.'

'Don't boast about it. We can ask help from whoever we want to.' It was Katya who replied defiantly from her top bunk bed. She put on her new blouse and said triumphantly:

'Look girls, isn't this a lovely blouse? Aha, now I'm rich, and I'm going to be richer still, just you wait and see!'

Michael and Nadiya had given us a bag of sweets, and biscuits to take to the rest of the girls. We had been asked to share them out. The girls liked them, except Helen who was still sulking.

A few weeks later, Michael and Nadiya brought us a big bundle of clothing. I opened it in front of everybody and we shared the contents. If someone did not have a certain garment we chose the most appropriate item for them. There was a lovely navy-blue cardigan. I would have loved to have owned it but the girls refused me to have it as I already owned a cardigan. Mine was red, and I didn't like it. I approached the girl who received the blue one and asked her to swap it with me. I told her that my cardigan had long sleeves and was much warmer. She agreed, and I now had what I wanted – a lovely little cardigan with glass buttons. It fitted me very nicely, and I felt well-dressed, but when winter came it would be the only additional piece of warm clothing I could wear, and it had short sleeves. I had made the mistake of putting beauty before comfort.

The following Sunday, I went out in my new cardigan and felt confident and sophisticated. Michael met us in the park. Helen flirted with him again, and to my surprise he seemed to be attracted to her. The way Helen acted disgusted me so much that I left them alone and went with some of the girls to another part of the park. In the evening, Michael came back to the camp and someone told me that he wanted to see me. He had brought me a book, and we talked by the gate. I no longer saw him as admirable, but I saw him as an ordinary man who could be attracted to girls like Helen. I talked to him as to a good friend, but I also remembered that men often lose respect for a girl who is too easy.

We met several times in the following weeks. When the other girls ventured through the park, Michael stayed with me. Walking in the shade of the huge trees, he told me about his life before the War, and how he and his friends would get together to have a good time. They used to meet in restaurants and had vodka and pickled herrings which were popular in Russia.

'Those were the days,' he sighed. I saw things differently, of course. I had grown up in a life of hardship, deprived of rights, food and clothing. He was a worldly man who was used to seeking pleasure. He was attractive, good, generous and polite. He was a gentleman, but I knew instinctively that he would not become my hero, and I would never choose him nor follow his ideals. I wanted the man of my choice to be someone active, romantic and with a purpose, but Michael did not have any of those characteristics.

Michael aligned himself with the monarchists who were aiming to restore the Tsarist regime in Russia. His father had been a minister before the Revolution and emigrated to Riga in Latvia. Michael grew up in Europe but had travelled to many countries of the world. In particular, he liked England, and he would have liked to have lived there. England was a free country with freedom of speech. He worked as an interpreter in the German army and took the chance to see Ukraine, Belarus and parts of Russia, but he did not enjoy his work and was sent home on the grounds of ill health. He came to live with his sister in Berlin after as she was left by her husband – a high-ranking German officer – now away in the War.

I listened to his story and imagined everything that had happened in his life. I understood why he was so well-behaved. He came from the aristocratic class that had been destroyed in Russia during the Revolution. I appreciated his friendship, and I liked to talk to him. He and his sister were good, kind, genuine people who had helped us, and I thanked God for having met them.

As we walked along the park's wide avenue listening to the distant music, the sun began to set and lit his pale suit with its orange beams. His shirt was immaculately clean and ironed, his white cuffs showing below his jacket sleeves. His whole personality breathed dignity and nobility. I was really proud to be talking to him and looked at him as someone from the past – a hero from a romantic novel of the nineteenth century. But he was someone who did not really fit in with this life and surroundings, and he did not fit in with mine either.

Seemingly able to read my thoughts, Michael looked at me gently, and said good-night. Slowly, he went on his way and I joined the girls for our walk back to the camp. I was unaware of them watching us and I promptly walked into a barrage of sarcastic remarks. The attacks continued for days and then weeks. I knew Helen was jealous, though I also knew she would never have and keep Michael. She could flirt with him, become friendlier with him, seduce him and receive gifts, but for the time being she twisted everything I said. She gossiped about me and told lies to the girls and to the commandant.

One day, we almost had a fight. It was in the evening when we were having our tea break. I was looking through the open window, enjoying a breath of fresh air when some finely-dressed ladies stopped by the window. They spoke to me and said they were immigrants who had left Kiev in Russia.

'Kyiv is not in Russia!' I said.

'Of course it's in Russia,' they replied.

'How can it be in Russia if it's the capital of Ukraine?' I replied with a smile, as though talking to children. We argued for quite a while until the Germans came back from their break and stopped us. They told me off for talking to outsiders.

'What does it matter if Kyiv is in Russia or Ukraine?' Helen said to me when we went back to the barrack. 'Could you not see that those ladies were rich? And if you agree with them they might return and give us more presents.'

'Oh, how can you say that!' I almost screamed at her. 'I would rather starve than say that Kyiv is in Russia.' I was furious.

'It's always the same!' Helen sniffed proudly, and left me perplexed and annoyed.

At that time, I knew relatively little of the ageold political struggles of Ukraine. I was like a child saying what I believed to be right, yet I was still unaware that hundreds of thousands had fought and died in order to express such rights. Did those ladies see me as a politically conscious adult Ukrainian, or did they see me as a child? Ukraine's struggle was continuing in that summer of 1942 with the Ukrainian Insurgent Army fighting both German and Russian invaders. They at least tried to defend our people from more suffering. I can smile now as I look back at my naïve but honest way of defending the truth: it became my whole way of life.

The atmosphere in the camp was becoming intolerable. The ladies returned and gave Helen some money. She promised to buy something for all of us but she was never seen giving anything to anyone. The girls learned that we had argued with the rich ladies, so they blamed me for being rude to them. Whether Helen had perhaps said something about me to some Germans in the office, or whether Herr Zell was perhaps eager to send me away from the camp, I do not know, but a day or so later he came into our barrack and announced that I had to go to another camp. Another six girls would go with me.

'Where are we going?' I asked calmly.

'You will see!' Herr Zell laughed nervously and showed his crooked, brown teeth, and twisted his high, bony shoulders. We had to be ready by early morning. I said goodbye to the girls.

'It's all Helen's fault. Why don't they take her?' said Anna. 'We were happy before she came.' Anna came over to shake my hand and wished me good luck. I parted with Lena. I was in tears. She was staying, as were Olya and Oksana. Katya was coming with me, and Sonia too, and four others. All the boys were staying behind except for brave Boris. Herr Zell again laughed sarcastically then handed us over to a big, fat commandant dressed in a black uniform.

He was from Berlin's huge Lichtenberg Camp of around two thousand people. We were taken there and were led to a barrack which was shared by more than fifty girls. It was dirty, noisy and dark with only one small window, opposite the door. I was given a bed and a thin blanket. There were no sheets or pillow cases. The camp held over two thousand people who all worked in the huge Knorr-Bremse metal plant, several miles away. I realised that transferring us to this camp was a form of punishment. Until then, I had lived in comparatively reasonable conditions. I now had to bravely face this new environment.

We would have to get up at four o'clock in the morning

and be ready by five. After roll call, and an hour-long walk in columns of four, we began work at six o'clock and finished at half past five in the evening. The night shift worked from six in the evening until six in the morning. We were not allowed to walk on the pavements or take a bus or tram. The three kilometre morning walk was particularly hard and degrading. We were a herd of twentieth century slaves – overworked, tired and ragged, and we were paraded through Berlin's glamorous streets. We were given a half-pint bottle of ersatz coffee and a half-pound piece of black bread. We had to work until twelve noon when we were given a bowl of vegetable soup – boiled without meat or fat, and that had to last us until seven in the evening when we returned to the camp in our regimented rows. Finally, we stood in another long queue to receive a second bowl of vegetable soup.

Life was hard, and hunger had a powerful grip. I had been a rounded, young girl with rosy, plump cheeks, but I soon began to grow thinner and thinner. My face became long and bony. I barely recognised myself in the mirror. I used to smile at the world, but now it had done this to me and to others around me.

Fortunately, my status at work improved. Whilst registering me for a job, the Germans asked me what I had done at home. On learning that I was a student and knew their language they gave me, and some of the other girls, a test in German. I was the only one who passed it, so they gave me a job as a clerk in the manager's office. I had my own desk and had to prepare the invoices, order forms and wages. I added a white collar to my navy-blue cardigan and was therefore dressed decently. I also cut my hair short and pinned it overnight so that it became wavy.

My status in the camp remained the same as everyone else's. I had to get up and walk at the same time, and the food was the same as for the others. I was tired but I was also becoming thinner and unwell. When the first cold morning arrived I had nothing other than my short-sleeved, navy-blue cardigan. It was too thin, and I had no proper shoes, either. A gardener in the previous camp had given me a pair of his wife's shoes in exchange for a pair of slippers which I had made from materials in the textile factory. Those shoes, however, had high heels and they were the only pair I had.

Walking and working in them, all day, nearly crippled me. The only possible alternative I had was to wear some wooden clogs which they handed out, but I had not been given any as I already had a pair of shoes of my own. Life was getting harder, but thankfully it was bearable because I had made some new friends.

There was Nina who was a tanned, brown-eyed girl from Donbas – the centre of East Ukraine's coal mining region. Direct with her words, but wise and beautiful, she seemed to adore me and asked me to come and share the corner of her barrack. She had a friend called Shura who had masses of ginger curls hanging over her thin, oval, freckled face. She was an orphan and had blue eyes, and liked everybody who was kind to her. Nina had already chosen Shura as her closest friend. Now I joined them, and the three of us could always be seen together. They had jackets from home, and with the cold weather setting in they took me between them, linking arms on the way to work. I felt warmer even in my short-sleeved cardigan. Their friendship warmed me too. We talked and joked, and cursed the Germans, calling them names whenever they shouted at us to hurry up.

Sometimes, we would burst into song and the whole column of two thousand young Slavs joined in. In the dark, early mornings our songs woke the Germans in the nearby houses and flats. They came out onto their balconies, sleepily watching us. We were their slaves, but the songs were ours. The guards were also helpless. They ran around and shouted at us to stop singing but we would feel so united that we took no notice and continued with one song after another. It made us feel better. Nina and Shura worked on the machines and we did not see each other all day, but after returning to the camp, we would be together again.

Katya occupied the top bunk bed opposite to me. She, too, was gradually getting thinner, but she was now learning to trade. On the way back from work she would slip into a shop and buy a turnip – the only food we were able buy without ration books. The guard at the gate checked to see that we did not bring anything in with us, but Katya seemed to be lucky and smuggled it through. After our meagre supper, she would wash and peel the precious vegetable, cut it into pieces, and then sit on top of her bunk bed from where

197

she would call:

'Is anybody hungry? Turnip! 30 Pfennigs a piece!'

At first, the girls were cross with her. We earned about three Marks a week and with that money we had to buy second-hand clothes and shoes in the camp, or whatever else we could find on Sunday afternoons when we were allowed out. All the same, hunger remained the master of all, and the girls would buy the pieces of turnip, slip back to their corners and chew them like mice in little holes.

Hunger and hardship frequently made the girls angry, so fights were commonplace. There was always a commotion in the room, and the dreary cold barrack was often like a hive full of angry bees. Some girls became ill. Little, lame Sonia now had an abscess under her arm. It was big and she was in pain, but she was sent to work just the same. In the evenings, she would dress it, and not being able to do it alone she asked for help, but nobody helped. The abscess was so horrible to look at that everybody was frightened to go near it. Little Sonia, who had always helped everyone else, was now ignored. Finally, I went over to help her, and she was so pleased that she would have done anything for me.

It became colder and I became ill. I had tonsillitis, and then tonsillitis, again. I had no medicine or rest, and I had to go to work for twelve hours a day, just as everybody else did. It must have been my strong constitution that saved me for I recovered both times and continued to work without any time off. Then, in October, my foot became painful. I went to the factory's First Aid point, but the male nurse said it was nothing and sent me back to work, but by the next day, my whole leg was so painful that I could not walk. Two policemen took me by the arms and led me to a tram. They watched over me like a criminal. I was put in the camp's sickroom. I was very hot and the male nurse who took my temperature whistled: it must have been very high. From that moment onwards, everything in my life changed once again.

Chapter 22

I was unaware of the camp's barrack for the sick. It was small, dark and dreary, just like every other barrack, and it stood opposite the guard's hut. It was on slightly higher ground with steps leading up to the front door. Inside, there was a small room where one male German nurse and a tall, well-built female Russian nurse sat at a table. Another room was used by the doctor to examine patients. He was rude and completely ignored their complaints. He was even known to have hit his patients in the face to tell them to go back to work. We did not know whether he was a qualified doctor or just an orderly. He was a German and we had to see him if we were ill.

I was brought up in front of this nasty man with the help of the two policemen who explained that I could not walk. I had already seen him once before – when my foot began to hurt, but he then sent me back to work. Now, he looked at my leg and took my temperature. I could only guess at what the thermometer showed him, but he looked at it and told the nurse to put me to bed. It was a dark October evening. I was tired, cold and ill, and sleep was all I wanted. To my dismay, I was led into a small, dirty room where there were about eight beds. The rough mattresses were made from sackcloth and filled with straw, as was the pillow. One thin blanket with black and yellow stripes was all that they gave to each patient, and there were no sheets or pillowcases. I was put on a bed to suffer the pains which were spreading across my body. I did not yet know it, but I had rheumatic fever.

In the corner of the room, enclosed by a wooden partition, was a large bucket which was used as the toilet. Its putrid smell filled the room, and the dirty floor and windows looked as though they had never been washed. The sick people around me moaned. Someone cried, and from another room I could hear some screaming. I learned that venereal diseases were being treated there. I was not brought any water or medicine, and there was no mention of food. Later that night, Sonia came to see me.

'Have you had anything to eat?' she asked. On hearing my reply she went to the kitchen and brought me a bowl of soup. I could only eat a few spoonfuls and then she went back to the barrack to bring me a piece of her own bread and some water. I was so grateful to her that tears streamed down my cheeks. A few hours later, the big, Russian nurse brought me two little white tablets. She forced them into my hand and told me to swallow them. When I asked for some water she swore and then brought me some in a metal mug. I then drank it and swallowed the tablets. After that I dried my eyes and went to sleep.

I stayed in that horrible sick room for a month. The doctor never came, and I received no further nursing care at all. We were left to suffer and fight for our lives. The nurses flirted and laughed with each other all day in the reception room but they never came anywhere near us. Dinners were often missed, and we waited for the girls to come back from work to bring us a bowl of soup. I could not walk: not even to the toilet. The pain I was suffering was excruciating, and I had to bite my lips so as not to scream. The girls who could walk helped me during the day, but at night I had to somehow manage by myself. In fact, I would crawl on my hands and knees across the room.

Some of the girls who were with me were ill with chest infections, and some had abdominal pains and abscesses, but at least they could walk. There were no washing facilities, but they could go somewhere else to clean themselves. I was left unattended with a temperature of up to 40 degrees, and with pains in my joints. I was given medicine only when the nurse remembered, but she usually forgot. The girls who came to visit me looked at me as if I was condemned to die. The German nurse looked at us with horror in his eyes, and quickly went away as though we were not worth looking after.

I was completely alone. I could not write to my mother or father and I had no one to support or encourage me. One night, Nina came to see me, but to my horror she did not come anywhere near me. Standing by the door, and with hostility in her voice, she said cruelly:

'So that's what you are: a priest's daughter! Ha! No wonder you are so soft and gentle. Intelligentsia! Here you are!' She then threw my diary at me, and left the room.

I had given the key of my locker to Sonia, and Nina must have rummaged through it, found my diary and read it. I had written about my feelings, my homesickness and my love for my family. I must have mentioned who my father was. So my secret was out. To be a priest's daughter was looked upon as a disgrace in Soviet society, and that society was still here amongst us, including my friends, and I knew I had now lost

200

them. I clutched my little book of memories and cried bitterly.

Nina had been cruel and heartless. She knew I was ill, unable to walk, and in great pain, and she did not show the slightest sympathy for me. Yet before that, she had said she loved me as her best friend. I knew she would not come to see me any more, neither would Shura – soft, smiling Shura, who was easily led by Nina. I was hurt, and the emotional pain I felt was as great as the pain in my body. In despair, I wrote a letter to Lena, who had been left behind in the first camp. She was my only friend now, and I knew she would not mind who my father was. For the first time in my life, I started to actively differentiate between my friends. Sonia posted my letter and I felt better. Although Lena would not be able to come and see me as no one was allowed into this camp, at least she would know of my fate.

The days passed and they were filled with constant pain, filth, and the smell of the toilet. I tossed and turned on the bare straw mattress. Other patients came and went. They had stomach troubles, headaches, chest infections, but they were soon sent back to work. I still could not walk and my temperature continued. A month had passed and it was near to the end of November. A doctor finally came to see me. He examined my limbs and said that I should be sent to a hospital. The male nurse carried me in his arms to a lorry which was used as the ambulance. They sat me on something hard and uncomfortable, and after about an hour's journey I was admitted to a camp hospital somewhere on the outskirts of Berlin.

It was Mahlow Hospital, and I calmly accepted my fate there. I learned that it was famous for the deaths and suffering of thousands of young people including intellectuals and famous personalities – all those who could not stand the harsh life inside the German camps. They usually had a history of chest complaints such as tuberculosis – which was then an incurable disease, and which was exacerbated by the lack of food and medicines. The doctors and nurses at this hospital were themselves prisoners of war who had been captured from the Red Army.

I was carried by a porter into a cold room where they registered me and then sent me to have a shower. The thought of water and of being able to wash myself immediately filled me with joy, but to my horror I was put onto a cold, stone floor and cold water from the shower was poured over my aching, feverish body. I could not stand it and fell to the floor and tried to crawl away. From a distance someone ordered me to wash myself. I longed to be washed, but to have a cold shower on a cold stone floor shocked me. Somehow, I managed to wash my hair, but in the end they had to put me on a stretcher and carry me into a ward.

I was put into a clean bed with blue, chequered sheets. It was a luxury. Dozens of girls watched me as I lay there only half-conscious and exhausted. A nurse took my temperature and asked me questions: another took a blood sample. At last, I knew I was being properly cared for. A third nurse came and brought me some cooked carrots in a bowl. I couldn't eat them, but to have some food brought to me was another luxury. My pains were still bad and I felt too hot, but I smiled at the girls around me before falling into a deep sleep.

I was woken by a group of doctors in white coats. To my surprise, they were Ukrainian prisoners of war who were sent to work in the hospital. They were attentive and kind and asked me many questions before examining me. When they tried to move my legs I cried out, but they insisted on moving all the joints and told me to exercise them in bed. It was simple, heaven-sent advice, and I was grateful to receive it.

The doctors moved on from one bed to another and I listened to the complaints of the other girls. Some were ill with pleurisy, abdominal troubles or permanent headaches, and some were recovering from operations. They were all young, like me. There were ten of us in this ward and we soon got to know each other. For the short duration of our stay we became friends, as people do when they are in trouble. They all recovered and were sent back to the camps to work. I outstayed them all. New girls came and went, but I was still very ill and unable to walk. The pains in my joints were so bad that the doctors wanted to give me an anaesthetic when they tried to straighten my limbs, but I refused and chose to suffer the pain instead. At night, I would lie awake, unable to sleep, but I kept quiet, and only groaned occasionally.

A single, blue lamp burned all night, and I watched the

girls as they slept and I listened to their groaning. A night nurse would come in every now and again. One night, a girl called Juliana got out of bed. She took a mirror from her handbag and started to comb her long, brown hair. She was lovely, but her eyes seemed strange. She combed her hair for a long time, and when she noticed that I had moved, she looked at me with a penetrating stare. Her long hair was hanging loose, and with the comb in her hand she came over to my bed and continued to stare at me for an uncomfortably long time. It was a frightening look that she gave me, but eventually she spoke to me, slowly and definitely:

'You are so young, and now you are dying.'

'I am not dying!' I exclaimed, 'I'm getting well and I'm going to live, thank you very much!'

'We will all die here!' She shook her head and moved away slowly. Shocked by her comment, I continued to watch her. Wearing her long, white nightdress and standing in the blue light of the lamp she resembled a ghost. She was beautiful, but she was losing her mind. I knew it from the look in her eyes. I was frightened. She settled down upon her bed and spread her long hair over her body. She then folded her hands on her chest – the same way in which Ukrainians lay a dead person in their coffin. She immediately appeared to be dead.

I could not sleep. A few hours later, a nurse came and covered her with a blanket. Thinking that she was asleep and feeling more secure, I fell asleep, too. Early in the morning, however, I was woken by noises. The strange girl, Juliana, was missing. Nurses looked for her everywhere, the police ran around the grounds of the camp, dogs barked and there was commotion all over the hospital: a patient had escaped. Yet it didn't seem to matter that the patient was sick or losing her mind.

Everyone in the ward was now awake, and the other girls were hoping she would not be found. One of them said: 'She told me that she would run away and go home to her mother and sister. When I asked her how she would find her way home she said that she would continue walking to the East, towards the sun, because that was where her mother was.'

'They'll put her in a concentration camp if they find her,' another girl said.

203

'More likely, they'll put her in a lunatic asylum,' a third girl added. 'Did you notice her eyes?'

I had seen many illnesses already and watched and listened to the girls' sufferings, but to see this beautiful girl losing her mind came as a shock. I thought again and again about how she had come to me in the middle of the night to tell me that I would die. From where did I get the strength, the faith and confidence to say that I would not die, in spite of my pain and immobility? I did not know, but it was as though some unknown power had said the words for me.

All morning the alarm sounded and the police, nurses and doctors continued to look for one sick girl who had dared to escape from the hospital. The search lasted until midday. Finally, they found her. She was on an empty bed in the TB barrack. She had covered herself with a blanket and had slept peacefully all morning. When they asked her what she was doing there she simply answered:

'I came here to die. Everybody in here is dying.'

They took her away and we never saw her again. Watching the sunrise, we always remembered her words: 'If I go to where the sun is rising I will find my home.'

One day an older lady was admitted to the ward. She had a thin face and wise, blue eyes. Without taking any notice of any of us, she opened a book and began to read. We all liked to talk to a new patient, so I asked her what she was reading:

'It's none of your business,' she answered bluntly.

'I am sorry,' I said. 'It's only because I love books.' She did not say anything more but continued to read for quite some time. Then suddenly turning to me she asked:

'Why are you in here?'

I answered quietly: 'I have rheumatic fever.'

Her eyes widened and her voice was suddenly and surprisingly full of sympathy. 'What are they doing for it?'

I liked her kind soft voice, her concern and her sympathy. I actually liked her from the very beginning and I told her the whole story – the way I had started to become ill; the month spent in the sick room; and the tablets that I was now receiving for my pain. For the first time in a month, I felt I could talk to someone who was like a close friend.

Her name was Tatyana, and she soon became the heart of our ward – she was a substitute mother, teacher and nurse.

She had been a medical student in Krakow, and she now had asthma so her stay would be a long one – which we welcomed, for the right reasons. We soon heard the fantastic story of her life, and many other stories which she told us at night. As soon as they locked us up, we gathered by the burning stove in the middle of the ward. At first, I could not get out of bed, so I stayed where I was and listened attentively. She led us through the adventures of the mafia, American gamblers and robbers, the English underground and the Count of Monte Cristo's power. In every story, good triumphed over evil, and the hero freed those who were wrongly imprisoned, or rescued loved ones, or helped captives. Of course, we saw ourselves as imprisoned, enslaved and captured, and our vivid, young imaginations gave us the hope of one day being rescued and returned to our loved ones in Ukraine.

Tatyana had a big problem of her own. Her only joy and happiness was her son who had been captured in Krakow. He had been taken away to Germany and she had tried to find him, but had failed. His name was Modest – a rare name in Ukraine, and she asked everyone who came to the ward if they had heard of him, but nobody had, and so her search continued in the same manner.

One night, Tatyana told us the wonderful story of her life. She came from a large but poor family that lived in St Petersburg, and when she was young she had black, plaited hair. Everybody said that she was beautiful, but she did not yet know it herself, and when she was sixteen her father arranged for her to work in a big store. One day, a gentleman came to buy something and never took his eyes off her. He bought her the most expensive presents and her parents protested, but he came to their poor, little house and asked them to allow their daughter to go out with him. They allowed it, but only on the condition that her brother would always accompany her.

So, their turbulent courtship started. He was a diplomat and belonged to the aristocracy. In order to take her into his circle of friends he had to buy her the most elaborate outfits and jewellery. She looked so lovely that everyone admired her at every ball, and all the men always wanted to dance with her. However, when she was introduced to his family they rejected her, but this did not stop the couple from marrying. When her parents began to worry about her dowry, he said that he did not want anything but her, and on the wedding day he sent food and drink to their house so that all their friends and neighbours could feast. When the bride and groom came to the reception in his family's house, however, she felt that they were still rejecting her and would not accept her as their daughter-in-law. In her innocence and naïvety she ran away from the reception and locked herself in a bedroom. No matter how much they tried to persuade her to come out, she refused. In the end, the bridegroom had to tell the guests that his bride had developed toothache. Her account was wonderfully graphic and included the rest of their first night of passion together.

She eventually found great happiness. His family rejected her only until she became pregnant, after which they surrounded her with all the comfort and luxuries they could think of. When she was in labour, she lost so much blood that she needed to have a transfusion. His sister was of the same blood group and offered her blood. From that time on, she was related by blood and the whole aristocratic family finally accepted her. Her boy was called Modest. He was a joy to everybody, but not for long.

Revolution came to Russia and Tatyana's husband sent her and the baby away to the summer resort of Yalta. He travelled as a diplomat until one day he returned home, sick with typhoid. She nursed him and did everything she could in that time of war, but she could not save him, and he died. Then when the family dog was found hanging from a door handle she began to lose her mind. The little boy was taken into custody and their property was confiscated, and then looted. She was eventually allowed to return after her condition improved, but there was nothing left. Penniless, sick and homeless, she did not know which orphanage the boy had been taken to, but she was determined to find him, so she went from orphanage to orphanage asking for a boy called Modest.

She finally found him, and quite by chance. A group of orphans happened to be walking along a street when one of them ran away. The supervisor called after him:

'Modest, come back!' She knew it was her son.

Tatyana then went on to work in a hospital and trained to be a nurse. She never married again, but lived with her son in Krakow until the War broke out. The Germans took him away – her one remaining love. She could not bear to lose him a second time, so she followed him by volunteering to go to Germany herself. She did not care about the conditions in which she travelled, or worked, or lived. All she wanted was to find her son, but the Germans would not help her. Desperately, she asked everyone she met if they had heard of him, but nobody ever had.

In the semi-darkness of the ward, by the burning stove, we momentarily lived the wonderful but tragic life that Tatyana had led. We could see her beautiful, blue eyes and dark, greying hair falling upon her face, and we could imagine her beauty when she was younger. The more we knew about her, the more we loved her. The following day, we were all as kind as we could be to her. How much better we could love each other if we knew just that little bit more about each other. It's true what they say: "to know is to understand and to love".

One morning, a former Red Army prisoner of war called Tosya came to take my temperature and commented casually about the nearby TB barrack:

'Oh, that dreadful Tuberculosis Ward! People are dying there one after another. Fifteen died yesterday, and every day it's the same. Now there's a young girl dying. She is so lovely. She's blonde with big, blue eyes.'

'What's she called?' I asked.

'Olya,' Tosya said, softly.

'Olya!' I exclaimed. 'I know her. Where is she from?'

'What is the matter with you?' Tosya said firmly. 'Don't get excited. You are ill yourself. I think she is from the Sumy district.'

'Oh, no!' I cried. 'It is her. I know her. We travelled together, and were in a camp together. Let me see her. Please, let me go to see her!'

But the nurse again replied firmly: 'You cannot see her.'

'Oh, but I must!' I cried. 'She has nobody.' And I suddenly remembered that Olya had had her fingers caught in a machine. 'She has some fingers missing, doesn't she?'

'Yes, that's right' said the nurse, 'she had an accident in

the factory.'

'It is her! I exclaimed again. 'Oh, please, do let me see her!'

Seeing my anxiety, Tosya said: 'Look, you cannot walk yet. I will have to get a wheel chair to take you there. I'll come back later.'

I lay there quietly thinking about Olya; how she had cried from the very beginning; how we had tried to help her and cheer her up; how sad and pale she had looked the last time I saw her. She had to wear a black glove over her injured hand and was ashamed of it. Her lips had trembled when I spoke to her. How on earth were we supposed to have saved her? I always wished I could do something for her.

I could not eat anything that morning, and I could not rest. I was so sorry for Olya, and for all of us. Would we all die here? For the first time, the thought really struck me, and I felt as though I was somewhere outside, looking in.

Tosya came back to the ward later that morning. She was silent and sad.

'How is she?' I asked impatiently but quietly.

'She died this morning at nine o'clock.' Tosya shed a tear from her long, black eyelashes.

'No!' I cried.

'Tsh, be quiet!' she replied. 'Don't cry and don't say anything to anybody. I should not have told you. You just look after yourself and get better.' She then quickly left the ward.

The girls asked me why I was crying, and I told them the whole story of Olya. That day, the whole ward was quiet. Even Tatyana's stories and her efforts to cheer us up could not change how we felt for the young girl.

The days passed and patients continued to come and go. I stayed on fighting my pain and was still unable to walk. Tatyana stayed too. She consoled me and told me to stop taking massive doses of aspirin as it would damage my heart. She taught me how to make compresses for my legs and applied them. Every night, I worked hard to rub my swollen joints. I was so tired after doing one leg that I had to rest before starting on the other. Sometimes, Tatyana watched me and would get out of her bed and bandage my legs professionally. I was very grateful to her. She was the dearest person to me at that time, and our affection was mutual. One day she said to me:

'I wish you could be my daughter-in-law.' I had never seen her son Modest, but from what she had told us, and from her great love of him, I was flattered and wished for her to find him.

The weeks went by and Berlin, meanwhile, was being bombed. Every night at eight o'clock, the alarm sounded. The lights would go out, and the staff would then run down to the cellar. We remained locked inside our wards. Anxiously, we listened to the sound of the approaching planes, and then all hell would break loose. The bombs seemed to be falling all around us, lighting up the thin walls of the barracks. The ground shook, the windows clattered, and we were so terrified that some of us cried hysterically. We crawled under the beds and covered ourselves with pillows and blankets. We expected our lives to end there and then. When the bombing stopped and a siren finally sounded the "all clear", we came out from under our beds. We were pale, and wet with tears, perspiration and urine. After some time, a nurse would come in to ask if we were all right. We would ask her:

'Why don't you let us go to the shelters?'

'Such are the rules,' came her unhelpful answer.

Every night of that winter, we dreaded eight o'clock and prepared for the hellish bombing to be repeated again and again.

It was nearly the 25th of December: Christmas. Through the iron-barred windows we could see a white carpet of snow. We were glad because it looked just like Ukrainian Christmas does on the 7th of January. It was our first Christmas away from home. A tall German nurse came into the ward to give each of us a piece of cake. It tasted wonderful. When New Year's Eve came, Tatyana told us to wish for a dream. I dreamt about watches that night, so she predicted changes in my life.

On the morning of New Year's Day, a young girl called Ludmilla was admitted to the ward. She was a beautiful blonde girl. Her mouth was blue, and she was unconscious from having tried to poison herself with ink. She worked for a rich German household, but she could no longer stand the cruelty of her mistress. The doctors tried to save her life, but at eleven o'clock she was pronounced dead. It was pathetic to see her beautiful young body on the bed, motionless and with no further sign of life. Even the doctor – Tamara Pavlova wiped her tears, and the nurses cried openly: we all did.

The 19th of January came. It was my twentieth birthday, and I wanted to treat the girls to a sparkling drink. I eventually managed to buy some lemonade from the camp shop. The girls wished me many happy years with our traditional Ukrainian birthday song, and when evening came we all became quiet again as we waited for the alarm to sound. I prayed: 'Oh, God! Please don't let there be another raid today. Please!' Already trembling, I waited for eight o'clock. Time seemed to move much more slowly, and each minute was like an eternity. Finally, somewhere in the distance, eight o'clock was struck, and a minute passed: two, three, four, five. Everything was quiet. Was it possible? I believed it more and more. There was no alarm at all. I thanked God for such an unforgettable present. It was like a small miracle. All the girls felt equally relieved to be able to spend just one peaceful night together.

The following evening, the alarm sounded again, and the bombings continued throughout January. I had no idea how many bombs fell on Berlin in total, but through the windows we could see flames and smoke all across the city, yet not a single bomb fell on us. I like to think that perhaps the pilots were aware of the position of the Mahlow Camp Hospital and its foreign patients.

The nightly bombings still affected us. Many of the girls were left with trembling hands and staring eyes. It was Tatyana who again came to our rescue. She told us new stories. They were so frightful and hair-raising that we soon began to forget about the raids. She knew so many stories about ghosts, apparitions and heroes like Robin Hood who helped the poor. We loved her tales and imagined ourselves taking the places of those heroes.

Tatyana's asthma was gradually getting better, and at the beginning of February she was discharged and sent back to her camp. She had not heard anything about her son. Parting with me, she said:

'I will find him, and then you can meet him. He's a fine boy.' She kissed me goodbye. I never saw her again, and I do not know whether she ever found her beloved son.

I was now getting better myself. Later in February, I got out of bed. It was strange to be able to stand on my feet again. The world seemed to judder, but I held onto the bed and then walked to the next, and then to another. I was then allowed to have a bath. The water wrapped me in warmth for the first time in months. I sank into it and then fainted. One of the nurses heard the splash and came to rescue me. Nonetheless, I was slowly making progress. My legs strengthened with each passing day, and slowly, I learned to walk again.

The patients changed. Gone were the long-term girls to whom I had become attached. New girls came in, but time spent in the camps had already spoiled them. They had learned to swear and tell smutty jokes. I did not like the atmosphere they were creating and so I withdrew. Then, one day I decided to tell them some stories. I thought that instead of listening to their smut I would tell them something more refined. They liked what they heard and asked for more, and that pleased me.

One day, as I lay on my bed, I wanted to sing. Remembering all the songs I knew, I sang and sang. I found joy, and took no notice of anybody else around me. I was alone in the world: I had no one. I was no longer shy, proud or reserved. I wanted to live for others. Going from bed to bed I started to help the sick. I passed them water. I talked to them and cheered them up. They rewarded me with their loving looks, kind words or with little gifts. One girl gave me a lovely pink scarf, and I treasured it for a long time thereafter as a token of our friendship.

The doctors would not discharge me, but I was getting better and I knew that I would soon have to face up to harsh realities again. We were not allowed any visitors, but then one day some of the girls from the first camp came to see me. They could not come in, but a nurse brought me a small, linen bag full of rusks from their daily rations of dry bread. They must have been collecting them for some time. I was so overjoyed that I wrapped myself in a blanket and went out of the barrack to wave to them. It was a sunny day. The snow glistened and barbed wire separated us, but how glad I was to see them. Wrapped in the blanket, and in my blue and white, striped pyjamas, I must have looked a sight. All I could think about was seeing my friends, to be able to wave to them, and to thank them for thinking of me. I had only known them for a few months and they were my only link to my home. I thought it best not to write to my parents about my illness.

My appetite was returning, but I was not given enough to eat, so I started to earn food by letting one of the night nurses use my bed to sleep in at night. For this, she would bring me her pot of soup. I would eat it and was satisfied. Doctor Tamara then brought me some of her stockings to darn in exchange for some pieces of bread.

One day, Nina came to see me again. For some reason, they allowed her in. It was a Sunday, and most of the staff had gone away. She came up to me shyly and smiled. She apologised for her past behaviour.

'I don't know what you have in you, but I can't help liking you. So, I've come back and brought you something.' She gave me a small bowl of margarine and some bread. 'I now know the cook.' She had anger in her voice: 'He's a devil, but at least I have enough to eat.'

'Tell me about life in the camp,' I begged her.

'What is there to tell you? It is cold and dirty. The girls shout and scream and there is always someone quarrelling in one place or another. It's the usual hell. Are you better?' she asked. 'When will you be back?'

'I don't know,' I replied, 'but I am learning to walk again.'

'You had better learn well,' she laughed, 'you'll have a long way to go yet.' She kissed me goodbye, and said she hoped I would be better soon, and out of hospital. I appreciated her visit, though I was worried about how she would treat me when I returned. At least her visit reassured me that I would be all right with the girls, in spite of everything.'

I had not yet been discharged. Girls came and went, and the hospital was becoming as familiar to me as my own home. As soon as I had learned to walk again I entered other wards. In one of them, I found a boy called Horokh who was from near Krolevets. Because of the connection, I went to visit him every day. He was very ill with kidney disease, and there was little hope for him. He seemed to know it, and was sad and pale. He was also very hungry, so I started to share my rusks with him. One day, he asked me to tell his mother about him, when I returned home. I promised to do so, God bless him. He died before I left the hospital.

The number of TB patients began to increase. They could not all be accommodated in the special wards, so some were brought to our barrack. There were some young and handsome boys. Desperate and sad, they begged for a cigarette or some money. All they did was play cards all day, as though the game was the only consolation for their vanishing lives. I was so sorry for them. They seemed to be cool, distant and withdrawn. They were living in another world. It was cruel that they should die so young, and without their loved ones knowing how they were.

I continued to feel completely alone in a world which was somewhere between life and death. I remained unwell and could only walk with difficulty. My future was unknown, but from out of the darkness, I did see some light. It was as though someone was near to me, watching me, reassuring me, and re-kindling my spirit. There is a God I thought, and I felt a spark of power inside me. I continued to fight for my life and health. I continued with the exercises, I bandaged my legs, and I did everything the doctors and nurses had told me to do.

I lay in bed and quietly sang to the girls, and they liked it. They wanted me to sing more, and to tell them stories. This was my favourite activity now. I lived in the present, I was happy, and I welcomed my gradual return to health.

'We are going to discharge you,' said Doctor Tamara, smiling at me with her lovely, blue eyes.

'But you will have to go back to your camp,' said one of the male doctors.

A German nurse who was real leader amongst them wrote something on a piece of paper: 'You will go back to the camp tomorrow.'

Doctor Tamara came to me and took my hand and said quietly in Ukrainian: 'You are better. You must stay alive. Promise me you will look after yourself. We're unable to do any more for you.'

'Thank you,' I said, 'I will never forget you. Thank you, for everything.'

She squeezed my hand and said lovingly: 'All the best to

you. Remember, stay alive and look after yourself! All right?'

I smiled and whispered: 'Thank you, I promise you I will.'

She smiled and joined the other doctors. My bed was near to the door and she smiled at me once more. There was so much warmth and genuine concern in her smile that I felt fully reassured. I smiled back, and after the door was finally closed, I never saw her again.

Chapter 23

I was taken back to the camp by ambulance and after a checkup, I was re-registered at the commandant's office. The camp was full of dozens of grey and decaying, dirty barracks. Muddy, trodden paths lay between them. It was midday, so everyone was still at work. I returned to where I had previously stayed and was disgusted when I opened the door. The air was stale and heavy from the smell of unwashed people, and the floor, table and benches were covered in a sea of filth. It was like an old battleship, abandoned by its warriors. And the people here were like warriors, I thought. Whilst I was in hospital, they too, had continued to fight for their lives through the harsh winter, but they had done so without sufficient clothing or food. They had continued to leave and return in an ongoing cycle. I sensed their struggle; their screams and shouts; their pain and anger; their hunger, thirst and frustrations. I was now a newcomer, and although my body was weak, I felt strong in soul and I was ready to face the next battle to survive.

A camp guard who was on duty pointed to an upper bunk where I would have to sleep. A metal cupboard was still mine, and I found my diaries there. Nina had put them back. A few of my other personal belongings were also still there. I took a blanket from the guard's room, together with my weekly ration book. I was then left by myself for the rest of the day.

At seven o'clock in the evening, the girls returned. When the door burst open, they went straight to their lockers, grabbed their little red bowls and ran to the front of the queue for supper. They were all thin, dirty and extremely hungry. I sat and watched them from my bed, and someone who noticed me asked casually:

'Are you back? We thought you'd never come back.'

'How clean you are! You're so clean and white!'

'Not like you,' said Nina. 'You haven't washed for a week.'

'And what am I to wash myself with when there is no water around here?' Replied Anna angrily. She, who had been the strong "brigadier" girl, had changed. Her lovely face was now much thinner and darker. Her curly hair was uncombed, and her clothes were dirty and torn.

'I washed myself with some of my coffee,' said Sonia. She was still wearing a white scarf and looked tidy, but her shoulders were now visibly hunched.

'I bring water nearly every night because you're too lazy to go for it yourself. It isn't my fault that someone used it all, and there was no time to go for more. You should have gone to get it!' Sonia's voice was sharp and she seemed to be cross which was far from typical of her. A quarrel started. There was shouting, and then screaming.

Nina came across to me and smiled: 'I'm glad you're back. Don't take any notice of them. They've all lost their minds.'

Nina's friend Shura slept in the bed below me. She came in with a boyfriend, smiled at me and said simply: 'Please, don't mind us,' and they began to cuddle on the bed.

I watched as life continued around me. I must have looked frail but clean compared to all the others. At the time, I was not sure exactly how I looked as there was no mirror in the barrack, but the boys soon came up to me. They asked me questions, and I answered them calmly, but they continued to search for answers.

A boy called Andriy stayed longer than the others. His round face had been burned. He told me that he had fallen asleep from exhaustion and fell onto the stove. In the middle of each barrack there was an iron stove with pipes that heated the room for about fifty people. To get warm, you had to be near to the stove which was red-hot in the evenings. I felt sorry for him. He told me he had been a sailor and loved the sea. He also liked singing, and to prove it he burst into song in the middle of our conversation. I was surprised. He was a tenor and his voice was clear and soft. Maybe because of his

215

singing and his clear, blue eyes, I paid more attention to him than to the others. He was shabby and dirty, and so visually impoverished that I wondered how I could even have begun to like someone in such a condition. I had grown up to appreciate that love was something beautiful, pure and clean. My mind drifted off as he sang, but I told myself, not for the first time, that I would not love anyone until this war was over.

It was now the middle of February 1943, and we had no idea of how the War was going. Our war was about daily survival. The cold weather persisted, and I had neither a pair of shoes nor a coat. I did not know how I would make the journey to work – which I was due to start in two days time. I worried, and did not know what to do or who to turn to.

I told Andriy about my situation, and he said: 'If you have some money, I'll get you a pair of shoes.'

'But I don't have any,' I replied.

He said nothing, and returned to the stove. The girls and boys sat there and talked. Andriy then started a song and everyone joined in. Forgetting about their hunger and quarrels, they sang one song after another and I joined in, too, from the top of my bunk. My youthful optimism was stronger than the concern for my penniless state.

The following day, I went to the commandant and told him that I had no shoes or coat to go to work in. He said he could give me neither. Big and fat, and with a red face and large spectacles, he looked frightening. The green uniform, which clung to his huge frame, made him look even bigger.

'Go to work! Work girl!' He shouted at me. 'Go to the doctor and then to work! All right? Now go!'

I left with tears in my eyes and immediately went to the sickroom which had vastly improved since I was there last. I found an elderly doctor there. He examined my legs, which were still painful, and said I was able to resume work. However, he also said he would write a note to say that I should walk at the back of the column on account of my pains.

'But I have no shoes,' I said, through my tears.

'I cannot give you any shoes.' He looked at me as kindly as he could. 'Buy yourself a raffle ticket. You may even win a pair. They're raffling a few items.'

'But I don't even have any money for a raffle ticket,' I said, and I turned to leave.

'Wait,' said the doctor, 'I will buy you a raffle ticket. If you are lucky you will win yourself a pair of shoes or a coat.' He then took out his purse and bought a raffle ticket from the male nurse who was standing nearby. I thanked him and took it with me.

My number came up, but I won a blouse, not shoes. It was made from grey wool and had a low cut neck, and short bulky sleeves.

'You can always wear a scarf round your neck,' said the girls, who examined my prize. 'You're lucky. It suits you.'

In my new blouse, I went to see the doctor to show him what I had won with his ticket. He seemed to know about it already, and did not want to make any further comment. Instead, he gave me a parcel containing a pair of shoes and told me not to say a word about it to anybody.

These are my wife's. I hope they fit you,' He closed a door which led to another room.

Thank you very much,' I said, 'they will save my life.'

'Here, try this,' he said. He handed me another parcel. When I opened it there was a black coat inside. It was warm but much too long for me. 'Take it to the sewing room and they will shorten it for you.'

I had no idea there was now a sewing room in the camp. I thanked the doctor sincerely and went there. They took the coat and promised to alter it for me.

The coat was not ready in time for work. It was still cold and frosty, and my short-sleeved cardigan offered little protection. The girls told me to take a blanket, but that was not allowed and I did not want to get into trouble. I still had my silky, pink scarf and was grateful to even have that. It was half past four in the morning. We were counted and led away for the walk to work. I could not keep up and was shouted at and pushed by the police guards: my letter from the doctor was useless.

When we finally arrived, I decided to see the commandant. I wanted to tell him about the letter and complain about the way I had been treated. I went to the office and was sure of my rights, but I was again being naïve. The office was overcrowded with men in green uniforms who were also wearing swastika armbands. They were smoking, talking and laughing. I must have looked pathetic, standing in the doorway with OST clearly visible on my cardigan, but I had now gone beyond the stage of being frightened. Bravely, I went to the commandant, and in my best German language I said:

'I have just come out of hospital. I cannot walk quickly, and I have a letter from the doctor telling me not to walk with the column. The guards, however, have pushed me all the way to the factory.'

I showed him the letter. The commandant of our two thousand-strong slave camp casually took my letter, narrowed his eyes and blew smoke through his nose. Disinterested, he said:

'All right, girl. Go to work.'

'But my letter? Can I have it back?'

'You will get it back in the camp.' He was about to shout. 'Now go!'

I left. My complaint was ineffective, but I had to fight for myself. There were no rights here, and nobody else would stand up for me.

My secretarial job was over. They had decided that I could not walk from one department to another with paper. Instead, I was sent to a section where I could sit and measure machine parts. I would check to see that their sizes were correct. It was a monotonous and boring job. The parts were oily and my hands were always dirty. I was nearly always hungry – and I could never forget it.

The days passed, and there was still no sign of my coat. Every night, I went to the sewing room, but it was never ready. Then, someone whispered to me: 'Get some methylated spirits from the factory, and they'll soon finish it for you.'

Methylated spirit was used to clean the factory's machines, but I soon learned that people in the sewing room were drinking it. I therefore asked an elderly German, who was always good to me, to try and find me a bottle. It was risky to ask for it and to smuggle it back into the camp, but I had no other option. I was lucky, and took the bottle to the sewing room that same night. By the following morning, my coat was ready and it fitted me well. It looked lovely, it was warm, and it made me feel very happy. In fact, all the riches in the world could not have made me feel happier, and the girls were happy for me too: 'You do look good with it,' they said, knowing what I had just been through. And they were not in the least bit jealous.

Winter dragged on, and March finally arrived. My personal fight to survive continued, and apart from sore throats and colds, I concentrated on my fitness and was able to walk more comfortably with each passing day. I then saw myself in a mirror: I looked thin and very stern.

I started to go out of the camp on Sunday afternoons. At first, I went to visit my friends back at the first camp, near the park. They were glad to see me and I thanked them for the parcel of rusks they had sent me. I told them about Olya's death and they sighed. They had all changed. From delicate, dainty girls they had been transformed into hardened, dark-skinned, female slaves, and their smiles seemed to have died with their youth. Their eyes were stern and sharp, and their words were short and abrupt. The clothes they wore were drab and dirty, and their hair was unkempt: they no longer cared about anything.

Helen was away somewhere, so I did not see her.

'I wish you were still here with us,' Lena said to me. 'We can't stand Helen. She makes us all quarrel. She is really bad.'

Lena's rosy cheeks had faded, but in her grey-green eyes I found a friendly light of joy. We arranged to meet on Sundays to go out together: we were still allowed to leave the camps.

The following Sunday, I visited Nadiya and Michael. They were surprised to see me and apologised for not coming to see me in at Mahlow Hospital. They had been told that visitors were not allowed. I felt hurt, but I said nothing except to explain that my friends had brought me the rusks from their daily rations. They were embarrassed. I wanted to tell them that I had real friends, but by saying this I would be reproaching them. They were glad to know I felt better. At the end of my visit, a young girl dressed in a beautiful, pink blouse came in, and from the way she greeted Michael I knew she was his girlfriend. I remembered what his sister had once said to me:

219

'I would like Michael to marry a girl who has had no hardship in her life.'

Where could he possibly have found her in these troubled times? My smile was bitter. They asked me to come again, but I made no promise. I went back to the camp. I knew I belonged there with the girls with the way of life which had bound us together. I was happy to be with them again. That night, I went to each of them in turn and tried to say something nice.

My time spent in Mahlow Hospital had protected me from the filth and neglect which now surrounded me, but I might have died there just as easily: many others did. Thankfully, I survived and I had learned to look after myself. I always washed – at least once a day, and I looked after my hair and kept my clothes tidy and clean.

Boys took notice of me, and at work, Frenchmen blew me their kisses. Dutchmen spoke to me politely, and a tall and handsome Czech man sent me a message to say that he was madly in love with me. I just smiled. None of them touched my heart, and I never felt the need to be attached.

Then, one day, Nina introduced me to a tall and quiet boy called Paul:

'He's the one for you,' she said, smiling at me through her shining, dark eyes. We sat and talked for a long time.

Paul then began to call to see me every night, and the girls thought we were a pair, but I felt nothing for him. What is love? I asked myself. Why does everyone sing and write about love? Paul is good, he's a friend, but I don't feel anything for him. Perhaps love is just the invention of poets and musicians. I talked to him, and Nina approved of our friendship, and Shura sent me happy glances whenever her boyfriend was present with her.

One evening, Paul stayed longer than usual and told me his foot was hurting, and he couldn't walk.

'No, I don't think so,' I said, 'you should go back to your barrack.'

He began to make advances which frightened me.

'No, Paul! Never!' I said very firmly. He did not dare to touch me. He knew that if he did, I would scream. So, he just bowed his head and walked out of the barrack. I could not sleep that night, and the next day, he was sulking.

'So, you refused him,' snapped Nina. 'Who is it exactly that you're waiting for?'

I said nothing. Paul tried to talk to me and apologise, but I could not face him. I was cool and aloof and felt upset. He went away soon afterwards and left me alone. I was glad, but I was not left alone for long.

Andriy, the sailor, started to tell me his stories. The wound on his face had not yet healed, and he was still unwashed and wearing drab clothing. No matter how good his stories were, even when he tried to sing to me, my liking of him could grow no further. At least Paul was always clean, I thought. I then remembered someone trying to say that love and death should both be clean.

Nina became increasingly sarcastic. She liked Paul and wanted me to fall for someone, just as she herself had done.

Who are you saving yourself for?' She repeated. She then laughed bitterly. 'Are you planning to become a nun? Do you think you're better than everyone else?' She continued with her nagging every time she came near to me.

'Leave her alone!' Shura stood up in my defence. She gave me a friendly smile and said: 'Take no notice of her.'

I looked at her tender, blue eyes and pale freckled face which was surrounded by her mass of ginger hair. She now had dark rings under her eyes, but she was happy with her Peter, and I was glad for her. I smiled at her and said nothing. How could I explain to her that I did not really know what love was, or that I felt nothing for Paul or Andriy?

Winter began to recede. The days became longer, and we could see everything around us in the morning and at night. The Berliners were living a life of their own, undisturbed by the sight of thousands of slaves marching through their city streets. I watched as well-dressed women walked freely, locked arm-in-arm with elegant men: lovers, sweethearts, or friends. Was it just? At least my thoughts were my own; thoughts which nobody could ever take away from me.

Paul came up beside me. He wanted to protect me from the police who were still pushing me along. He told the guard to stop it because I had not fully recovered. To my horror, the policeman hit him with his truncheon and told him to go back to his place. Paul became angry. He had been humiliated in front of me and the other girls, and I was just as angry, but we could do nothing about it. He went back to his place swearing loudly, and I started to cry. Deliberately, I slowed my pace, and that made the guard angrier. He was small and jumped around on his crooked legs like a duck. I hated him. I could have smashed him, cursed him, and wiped him from the face of the earth. Hatred stopped me from crying any longer. I wanted to do some mischief, just to show this ugly "guard dog", as we called him, that I was not a mindless slave, but a human being.

'Girls,' I raised my voice, 'let's sing! Let's show this "guard dog" that we are people, and not just numbers. Shura, sing something!'

The girls lifted their heads and looked at me in surprise. Shura's started to sing. Another voice joined in, and then another. Within a minute the whole column had burst into a loud and powerful song. The guards ran around, ineffectively shouting at us. They ordered us to stop singing, but we took no notice. We sang one song after another and the bewildered Berliners had to look and listen. Windows opened and the locals looked out.

We returned to the camp that evening feeling uplifted. We had not been punished for our singing because the police did not know who to punish. Paul came to see me. He still felt ashamed for having been hit. I understood and tried to be friendly, and I could not help telling him how angry I was. I told him I had started the singing, which he was pleased to learn. He was tall and clean and was now more like a brother or a friend to me. We talked until late into the night. Meanwhile, Andrew sat by the stove talking to some of the girls. From time to time he burst into song, and cast sideways glances at me, perhaps looking to see if I was listening.

At work, the following day, I went to my locker to fetch my ration book for supper. It was missing. I searched everywhere and turned everything upside down, but there was no sign of it. It had been stolen. I saw scratches on the lock. Someone had broken in. I told the other girls, but they were too concerned with their own hunger and laughed at me.

'You should be more careful!' One of them shouted.

'Try and catch a bird in the sky!' Another girl answered sarcastically.

I went to see the commandant, but he refused to give me

a replacement coupon for supper. He told me to return the following day, but I would only be given one dinner a day until the end of the week, and that would be without bread and margarine.

I became desperate. I fell onto my bed. Maybe I should finish it. There would be no need to get up tomorrow at four o'clock. There would be no need to walk the endless road, or be beaten by the police. There would be no need to have to work twelve hours a day, and no more pain. Yes, finish it, but how? I thought for a while: medicine. There was some medicine in the top of my locker. If I drank it all, everything would finally be over. I looked for the bottle and found it. I removed the cork and put it to my mouth, but the bottle was empty. The medicine had dried out. I threw the bottle away and fell on the bed again and covered my head with the blanket to cry.

Someone then tugged at the blanket and touched me. I opened my eyes to see lame Sonia standing there with a piece of raw turnip in her hand. With her brown eyes, and with one of them now squinting, she smiled at me and whispered:

'Here, it's for you. Eat it. You haven't eaten tonight.'

I took the piece of turnip from her with my trembling hand, thinking she was the most beautiful girl in the room.

'Thank you,' I said, 'I will repay you one day.'

'Eat it, and don't be so silly!' She turned and went away in the most casual and normal manner.

Raw turnip was still the only luxury anyone could have. I looked at that precious piece and measured it with my eyes. I understood exactly how hungry I was. I ate it carefully, slowly, bit by bit, and after finishing it, I lay down to sleep. I then had the most wonderful dream. The sun shone, and I was at home with my mother and father. I did not want to wake up, but at four o'clock it stated all over again: 'Aufstehen!'

The sky was lighter and appeared to be a pale-green colour in the East. Everything would have been quiet except for the sound of the thousands of trampling feet – mostly in clogs. The slaves were on their way, again, to twelve hours of labour in a dirty and noisy metal plant where the only light came from light bulbs, and where the noise of the drilling and screeching metal forced them to scream and shout to be heard. I was hungry and I had not received my ration of bread

223

and had to make do with just a little coffee. The walk made me hungrier. Life was hell itself.

I told Sonia about the dream and she smiled at me and explained: 'To dream of the sun means to love, and to dream of your mother means something new will come into your life.'

When we arrived I was sent to the manager's glass-fronted office. I was surprised to learn that I would be changing to the night shift. I was shown to a new table with different mechanical parts. Dozens of eyes in the room were watching me.

'Who's in charge here?' I asked abruptly, without a greeting or a smile. I did not care what people thought of me, or who they were, or how I looked. I wanted nothing to do with them. I noticed the window and the rays of the rising sun breaking into the room. They shone upon a man who now came towards me. I could clearly see his blue overalls, white face, and blonde hair which fell across his forehead. His deep-blue eyes were looking back at me. They were like two clear lakes, and for a split second I wanted to drown. I wanted to die. Regaining my grip on sanity, I said to him:

'I have been sent here, and I want some work.'

'Don't be in such a hurry, Barishnia,' he said, addressing me with the Russian word for Miss. It annoyed me so much that I could have struck him. I said nothing, but asked him to show me to my place. He looked saddened for some reason, and eyed me from top to toe. Without a word, he then limped and led the way and I followed. He sat me down with a box of machine parts, and I was left to check them over.

I began my work, but from time to time I felt the long looks from his deep-blue eyes. I ignored him. There were French, Dutch and Belgian men and women working around me. They all smiled at me when I looked at them, and I tried to be polite to them. After a while, the supervisor returned to check my work. Holding an instrument, he asked me my name, where I was from, and what I did at home. When I told him the name of my home town he smiled and said:

'I've been there. I was wounded there.' After that, he left me and went back to his seat. At lunch time, when everybody else went to eat, I put my head on the table and tried to sleep.

'Why don't you go for your dinner?' the supervisor

asked.

'My ration book has been stolen,' I replied, regretting to have to admit the mischief of my people. Not wanting to continue the conversation, I put my head on the table again. The French and Belgian women had some sandwiches. They started to talk loudly. Suddenly, someone touched me gently, and when I lifted my head I saw an old Belgian man offering me a piece of bread. I was hungry, but to take a piece of bread was to be like a beggar. I was proud and I refused to accept it. No matter how much they tried to persuade me, I would not take it. I was not a beggar. Something inside me refused to let me accept it. I noticed that the supervisor was quietly watching my whole performance:

'Why don't you want to take the bread?' he asked.

'Because you are not allowed to give us anything,' I replied boldly.

He then said nothing more, but as he left for home he placed a sandwich to the side of me. It was wrapped in crisp, white paper, but the sight of it made me angry. I wanted to throw it away, or to throw it back at him, but he had already gone. One by one, the German workers departed and then the foreigners, but I did not finish until six o'clock. Hunger continued to eat away at me. Finally, I ate the sandwich, but I hated myself for doing so.

After arriving back at the camp, I went to see the commandant but I was only able to obtain my ration books for soup. I ate my soup, and then went outside to be alone. The evening was warm, and the spring air was gentle and fresh. I spread my blanket on a patch of grass and looked up at the sky. The first stars were beginning to appear and I realised that I had not seen the sky for months. There was still beauty up above.

I was dreading the night shift. It meant twelve hours of work, and the same one hour walk each way, but I began to feel alive again, and in tune with the universe. I regained my will to live.

I went back inside. As usual, the girls were quarrelling with each other. The room, which only had two small windows on each side, was dark and stuffy. I wondered why they never went outside, and I walked past them wanting to go straight to bed.

225

'Where have you been?' asked Sonia, smiling at me. 'Out with a boyfriend, perhaps?'

I smiled back at her and said: 'I found a patch of grass behind the barrack and stayed there. It was lovely.'

'What, all by yourself?' She asked inquisitively.

'No. With my thoughts,' I replied. I covered my head with a blanket and said good night. I knew that if I only sat on my bed, Andriy or Paul would come to talk to me. I wanted to be alone. I seemed to have found some inner peace and quickly fell asleep.

In the morning, I borrowed two Marks from Katya, who was trading turnips, and I bought a portion of bread from one of the girls who worked on the night shift. I drank my black coffee and ate half of my bread and began to feel better.

The workers at my table greeted me cheerfully. A Frenchman called Joe blew me a kiss. He had brown eyes and displayed two full rows of white teeth when he smiled. The old Belgian man still wondered why I had refused his bread, and between them sat Desilia – a large and jolly French girl. None of them spoke in German.

'Bonjour! Bonjour!' They greeted me.

Herr Blanke was a lame, grey-haired German with gentle, blue eyes. He sat at the end of the table, and as I approached him he stretched out his large hand to shake mine. It was the normal German way to greet someone, and he greeted me warmly and asked how I was. On the other side of the table sat Herr Shultz – a former sportsman who was recovering from a heart attack. He was now only able to do some light work. At the top of the table sat our supervisor. He watched me shake hands with Herr Blanke, and I looked back, worried about what he might say or do as we were not allowed to talk to Germans. Desilia caught my worried look, smiled at me and said:

'Herr Margraff is a good man,' and she smiled at him, too.

I said remained silent, and began my work. I tidied and cleaned my workspace and then built pyramids from the parts I had checked. The supervisor soon came over and checked my work. Everything was correct:

'Don't hurry so much,' he said, 'you work very hard.'

'What else am I to do?' I asked.

'Did you get your rations at the camp?'

'Only some soup,' I replied, 'I'm not allowed bread or margarine.' I sounded indifferent.

'How long will that be for?'

'One week.'

'So, how will you survive without bread?' He continued.

I blushed: 'I'll manage,' I replied, and bent over my work so that he could not see my face.

'And what did you do at home?'

'I have told you, I was a student.' I did not stop working and continued to answer his questions.

'Ah yes, a student,' he tried to be pleasant, 'and what did you study?'

'I was a student of Ukrainian Philology,' I answered proudly.

'You speak German very well.'

'Thank you.' I then lifted my head and reminded him of the irony: 'We're not allowed to talk to you. Isn't that correct?'

'Nonsense!' He exclaimed. 'I don't believe in all that. They go too far!'

I became sarcastic: 'It's your country which gives the orders.'

'But it's not my fault,' he said, defending himself.

'But you fought for it!' I knew I was now going too far, but I was trying to be frank with him.

'I have had to follow orders,' he said sadly, 'and I have had my share of troubles. I was wounded when I was fighting in Ukraine.'

'I am so sorry,' I said. He may have been annoyed with me, but at least I was not afraid of him. I smiled and felt better for speaking truthfully. After all, he was a German. Herr Blanke and Herr Shultz could not hear our conversation from where they were sitting. The others clearly did not understand German and added nothing to our conversation. Somehow, I felt that the supervisor would not persecute me for my frankness.

I sat and worked and started to sing one song after another. I wanted to express my inner feelings, but these people did not know who Ukrainians were. And what did they know of the gentler side of the soul that could give so much? I felt very emotional.

227

'Good, very good!' said Desilia loudly.

'Keep singing!' smiled the Frenchman.

The supervisor then came over and started to check my work. I stopped singing and sat quietly. After a while, he asked: 'Do you like singing?'

'Birds in a cage don't stop singing,' I replied. I looked at him, wondering if that would make him angry.

'So you think you are in a cage?' He was being serious.

'It's worse than that!' I reminded him bluntly. 'Birds in a cage are fed and looked after: we're not!'

'We are building a new Germany. After the War, life will be better,' he answered thoughtfully.

'So why don't you build Germany on German soil?' I asked him boldly.

My frankness amazed both of us. He looked at me and said defencelessly: 'It's not my fault.'

One of the directors appeared and made his way towards us. I noticed his slow and dignified walk. The supervisor was in no hurry to run away from what he should not have been doing in the first place – talking to an Ostarbeiter. I smiled to myself and wondered how important or dangerous I was if others were not allowed to talk to me.

A flood of memories then came back to me. I was at home again with my parents who cared for me and loved me. My thoughts were with them and with my sister, brother, grandma, auntie and friends: if only they knew where I was. Now what was happening? Who were all these strangers around me? It was wrong to have taken me away from the life I knew, and to make me work in this hell when all I wanted was to learn and study, and discover new dimensions of thought and art, and the achievements of the human race. Now, I was not even allowed to talk to others. How wrong it all was. I stopped singing and continued with my work which was dull and uninteresting. I wanted to find some sort of inner peace.

I was still terrified at the prospect of having to work at night, but when Monday came I no longer had to get up so early. I did not have to rush for coffee or stand in the dark, cold yard waiting to be counted. I was glad. After a good morning's sleep, I had the whole day alone without the continuous background noise, commotion and quarrelling in the overcrowded barrack. I thought it was heavenly. May's sun was bright and warm, and I felt full of energy. I cleaned the barrack, washed the windows, changed the straw in my mattress, and still had some time to myself. Before returning to work, I even managed to look into a mirror, comb my hair and put some makeup on. I wore my grey, chequered blouse, and the pink, silky scarf tied in a bow. I looked young and was still full of life. I was glad to be alive and breathed the fresh, spring air.

The factory now seemed closer. I then ran up the stairs to the fourth floor and said 'good evening' to everyone working at our table. They looked at me in surprise and smiled – but only as if to say 'wait until you get to the end of the night.' On that bright evening in May, the setting sun shone through the window over our table. My locker was nearby and I hurried to fetch my tools, but the locker wouldn't open. I tried and tried again by twisting the key one way and then the other, but with no success. It was time to start work. Hopelessly, I turned to the supervisor and told him of my problem. He tried it, but he couldn't open it either. Without a word, he then fetched a spare bunch of keys, but that didn't help either.

'What a lock!' He exclaimed. In the end, he broke it: 'And you are very hard to unlock, too,' he said jokingly. His face was so close to mine that I could see into his eyes, but I looked at his olive-coloured skin and red lips. For a fraction of a second, I forgot about the whole episode. The whole world seemed to be in him, but it was only for a fraction of a second. I walked away and noticed that everyone was gazing at us.

'I'm late,' I said.

'Why? Do you always want to work and be on time?' His voice was soft and sincere.

'You'll punish me if I don't,' I replied with a smile. I returned to my place.

Desilia started talking to me, and I was happy to answer her. Joe smiled at me. He touched his big, red lips and blew me another kiss. The old Belgian man murmured his way through a song and looked at me from time to time. I returned a polite smile.

Downstairs, the machines stopped and the dusty

workshop became quiet. On one of the tables, where the day staff worked, I noticed a bunch of lilacs which a German woman must have brought from her garden. I picked up the vase and placed it on our table. The fragrance was lovely. Someone then gave me some fruit powder to make lemonade. I fetched some water and filled the coffee bottles. We joked and laughed as we drank either the red or green drinks. To me, it seemed like we were having a toast, but a toast to what? It was just a lovely, simple moment.

The hours passed unnoticeably, and the sky darkened. Blinds were pulled over the windows. The table was lit by hanging lamps, and we were like an island of light in a sea of darkness. As midnight approached, we became tired and sleepy. I noticed Desilia close and open her eyes, and the old Belgian nodded over his instruments. Joe's head dropped from time to time, and he gestured to me as if to say I was keeping him awake. I put the lilacs closer to where I was sitting and enjoyed the fragrance.

Midnight passed and the supervisor came to check my work.

'Tired? He asked.

'No,' I replied.

'Do you have your ration card?' He looked at me sympathetically.

'Just for the soup,' I did not want to say any more. After all, why should I explain my feelings to him? He was a German and it was the Germans who had brought me here.

As though reading my thoughts he said: 'Do you have any friends in Berlin who could help you?'

'No, but I'll manage,' I said. Not wanting to talk to him, I pushed my work away and stood up and went to where our girls were gathered in the ladies room. It was our place of escape from the monotony of work and the foreign people. We spoke in Ukrainian there and we could say what we wanted. We would stay there for as long as possible. I talked to the girls for a long time, perhaps for too long, because when I returned I found the supervisor sitting in my place and doing my work. Another box had to be fetched and he came with me to show me where it was. Then, to my surprise, he helped me to carry it to the table. I thanked him, and he handed me the documentation.

230

'But there are two notes,' I said, and suddenly I stopped breathing. The first piece of paper was the usual signed order, but on the second there was a drawing of a window with the sun shining in the sky, my locker, and the figure of a girl standing between the window and the locker. Underneath it, in neat handwritten French, were the words "I love you, little stranger". I stood there, motionless, for about a minute, and then I crushed the paper in my hand and threw it away.

'You have thrown it away.' His voice was surprised and sincere, and resonated in my ears. His eyes looked at me gently and enquiringly.

'Yes,' I replied, as though nothing had happened, 'we have to work.' I sat down in my place.

He went away. It seemed as though nothing had happened, but I sat there in wonderment. The feeling completely filled my body, my mind and my senses. I had never felt it before. What a wonderful powerful feeling. It changed everything around me. Even this workshop now seemed to be like a palace, and the table was like a banqueting table. The beautiful lilacs blossomed and the lemonade seemed to sparkle like wine. I felt numb. It was a strange feeling. Thoughts began to enter my mind. Is this the love they write and sing songs about? Then suddenly, an alarm sounded in the distance.

We were all hurried along the corridors and down the stairs to the basement. Desilia carried her yellow teapot in her hands. The old Belgian limped behind her, and the supervisor walked calmly behind all of us. I caught him looking at me, but he was being protective and considerate.

The basement was full of people. Thick pipes for oil and water ran across the ceiling. There were some shower cubicles for the Germans which we had never seen before and everything had been kept clean and tidy. People walked about or stood waiting for the end of the air raid. Ukrainians gathered together. No one appeared to be frightened. When the bombs started to fall the boys said they would hit the Germans really hard. I found a bench in one of the corners and lay down. I was tired and needed more sleep. Some of our boys looked at me and said:

'Look at the doll over there!'

'She's one of ours,' added another one. I did not open my

231

eyes to see who they were, but it felt nice to be called a "doll" by "one of ours".

When the air raid ended, we were sent back upstairs. Desilia looked tired and sleepy. Joe was already at the table and he smiled at me. The supervisor was the last to return.

'Is everyone all right?' He asked, looking around.

'Have they dropped some bombs?' Desilia asked.

'I believe so,' he said with a sigh.

'Then, we were lucky,' she added.

In French, Joe asked me if I had slept. Desilia translated, and I smiled at him.

'Yes Joe, I have slept a little.' Joe put his hand under his head and pointed at me, meaning he wanted to sleep with me. Everybody laughed, and I replied jokingly:

'Then let's go under the table, Joe!' Desilia translated again, and Joe waved his hand.

'No! No! Not enough room!' We all laughed. The alarm had interrupted the night's routine, and nobody wanted to continue.

The supervisor came over to me and checked my work again and then talked to me openly for the first time. He told me that he had been a student before the War and wanted to be an engineer, but the War had put an end to his ambitions. He had fought in France and had been to Poland. When the War with the Soviet Union started, he was sent to the Eastern Front. He said it was terrible there. He was wounded in Ukraine, near Kharkiv. Now, he had been given light work in the factory.

'Has your wound healed?' I asked, daring to look deep into his eyes.

'No,' he said modestly. 'It won't heal for a long time.' I dared not ask anything else. He started to talk about Berlin. He was a Berliner and loved the city and wanted me to see more of it. He wished I could see a different Germany, not the one I was seeing in the camps and the factory. There are some beautiful places: the opera house, the concert halls and the museums.

'But we're not allowed to go to there.' I said. 'You Germans have made slaves of us and we're not even allowed to talk to you. Don't you think it's all really stupid?' I stood up, wanting to go away, but I was too easily caught by his eyes.

'You need a new box of parts,' he said with authority. 'Come. I will help you find one.'

Reluctantly, I packed the box I had finished, and wrote the invoice for him to sign. Then, we went together to fetch another box. It was heavy, and he cringed as he lifted it.

'Oh, your wound,' I said with concern.

'It's all right,' he said quietly, before going back to his place. He appeared to be in pain. I sat down and worked quietly, though I was slightly confused and upset.

When morning came, I had to take my tools to the reception window in the next department. As I walked through the semi-darken workshop, the supervisor came along with the bunch of keys he had borrowed earlier in the evening. We arrived at the reception window. It was closed, so we knocked. As we waited, the sun came up. Wonderful, fresh, pink rays shone upon us, and we smiled. The window in front of us finally opened and the sleepy face of the watchman appeared. We handed in the tools and the keys, and our hands touched. I felt so young and wonderfully light-headed. We laughed at the watchman's face. He looked puzzled when he looked back at us.

I smiled at Desilia and said: 'What a lovely morning!'

'Is it spring in your country too?' she asked.

'Oh, yes, it is springtime now.' With those words my thoughts immediately raced home.

Our shift ended, and the day workers started to arrive. The Ukrainian girls were the first. Tired and angry, they came through the workshop door then smiled and waved at me. We were still one people, and I knew I belonged with them.

'Have a good sleep.' I heard the supervisor say as he stood by my side. His eyes met mine again. He was on his way home and had already changed. He looked handsome. In the full sunlight he appeared to be much older, and was not just a boy ready to play games. Older and more mature, he was a warrior who knew what he wanted and was ready to fight for it. Although I knew the extent of his power, I also knew that I would never want him.

What a feeling, I thought. More thoughts flashed through my mind like lightning. I should never insult this feeling. I replied as though I was talking to a little boy: 'You have a good sleep too, Herr Margraff.'

He was surprised, and was caught out and disarmed by my official-sounding tone: 'Auf Wiedersehen,' he replied. His eyes closed like shutters to shield them from the light. I noticed his pale and saddened face. He did not look at me again and went on his way.

'Auf Wiedersehen!' shouted Desilia with a broad smile.

'Good! Good!' repeated the old Belgian.

But Joe shook his head: 'No good! No good! German!'

Herr Blanke gave Joe a sharp look: 'Do you think all Germans are bad?'

'No. Yes.' stammered Joe. 'The Germans came and took me from my home, too.'

Herr Blanke looked sad and said nothing. Then he looked at me with his kind, blue eyes and smiled. He bowed his head like a gentleman: 'Auf Wiedersehen, Fräulein!'

The room became quiet, and revealed a thick cloud of dust on the sun's rays. We worked on, but once Herr Blanke had gone we began to feel more relaxed. Desilia packed her bag, Joe went off somewhere else, and the old Belgian stopped working. I realised how everyone was silently conscious of the Germans.

The night shift lasted for a week and continued on alternate weeks. I soon got used to it, though I became paler. I was shocked whenever I saw myself in a mirror. I had Monday's free, and some free time on Fridays, and I liked nights better than days. My mixed feeling towards the supervisor, Herr Margraff, changed me: it nourished me and hurt me, but it also enlivened me. I continued to look after my clothes and my appearance. I wanted to be presentable next to those with whom I worked with. When I went to bed, I put rollers in my hair. I wanted to be better, alert, and part of the life around me, but it was war. How could anyone really be happy when there was a war going on?

I surrendered myself to the endless long marches and the weary days and nights of work, and the hunger and filth of life in the camp. Amidst it all, I began to find peace within myself and enjoy my existence. I found confidence and smiled, but I was also hurt because I had a longing which I knew would never be fulfilled. I started to read German books, and I wanted to see more of German life, but I also wanted to do some mischief – something out of the ordinary.

The opportunity came the following week. When I went onto the night shift, Herr Margraff came to my locker and asked me if I would like to go to an opera. I was startled. Did he want me to go out with him? As though reading my thoughts he smiled and said gently:

'I have a friend at the Opera House and he has given me two tickets. You could go with one of your friends.'

'Oh,' I said relieved, 'Thank you,' and I took the two long, white tickets from his hand.

'I want you to see a different Germany,' he said.

I asked myself how I could possibly go to the Opera, but I would be determined. None of our girls wanted to go with me, so I found a Dutch girl called Ursula who was eager to join me in my adventure. There was only one problem: I had to get there and back undetected.

As we made our return journey one evening, I disappeared into a side street and waited until the column had passed. I then walked to the nearest subway station and met Ursula in the centre of Berlin as arranged, and we completed the journey to the Opera House. The wide Unter den Linden was full of cars, trams, traffic lights, and masses of people. It overwhelmed me. Who could have imagined that just a few stations away there was suffering in the many camps full of slaves for the mighty Reich.

I had stolen a taste of freedom and I had to make the most of it. I had changed into a black dress given to me by Nadiya, and I decorated it with a string of silvery beads.

We entered the Opera House and joined the crowd. Our seats were on the balcony, and I had a view of the whole auditorium. It was a splendid place, and unbelievable to be there. It had large candelabras, velvet seats and masses of elegantly dressed people who were taking their places. Was it my eager look that drew the attention of some inquisitive eyes, or perhaps the simple way in which I was dressed? Ursula was wearing a simple suit with a white blouse. She was tall and blonde with an open, healthy face and brown eyes. She just ignored everyone else, and I joined her in pretending that we had an equal right to be there.

We were watching "Madame Butterfly" and it was the first opera I had been to in my life. When the performance started, I was captivated. I read the booklet explaining the plot, and was thrilled by the beautiful singing and acting.

When the opera finished, I parted with Ursula and made my own way back to the camp. Overwhelmed by the evening's experience, I had not yet thought about getting back inside. I felt full of my right to do as I should be allowed to do. It was foolish. So, instead of looking for a secret entrance in the fence, or instead of going through a neighbouring Belgian camp, I went straight to the main entrance and rang the bell at the gate. A policeman came out. He roared at me:

'Where on earth have you been?'

'To the opera,' I replied calmly.

'What? He roared. I showed him the ticket stub.

'And who gave you those tickets?' he screamed.

'A German I work with.'

'Donnerswetter!' He swore. 'Come. I am taking you to see the commandant!' He led me to the commandant's room. Everyone there looked at my ticket and swore, but no matter how much they wanted to know who had given it to me, I refused to tell them.

'Someone wanted me to see a better Germany,' I said simply.

'Get out!' shouted the commandant, and the policeman took me out and pushed me hard in the back. I almost fell down. I cried and went into the barrack distressed and angry.

All the girls were now asleep except for Sonia. She asked me where I had been, but I did not tell her the truth. I felt as though I had stolen a piece of pleasure from my crude surroundings, so I did not want to say a word to anyone about it.

After covering my face with a dark blanket, I could again vividly see the splendour and magnificence of Berlin's Opera House, and the wonderful performance there. I loved it deeply. I had seen a beautiful side of a life which did not belong to me. At least now I had experienced it, I felt richer and happier.

Chapter 24

One Sunday afternoon, at the end of the summer of 1943, I met the man who would change my destiny. I had spent most of the day with Lena at Tiergarten Zoo. It was a beautiful park where the smaller animals were allowed to roam freely. On the way back we went to see the Brandenburg Gate and finally returned via the nearest subway station. We were looking at a map, when a Ukrainian voice behind us asked: 'What are you girls looking for?'

We turned around to see a tall, dark man with bushy eyebrows and curly, black hair smiling at us. His eyes were friendly, but his face was pale and rather grey, and he was poorly dressed. He talked to us politely and explained the directions we needed to take. We were heading for Gesundbrunnen – on the same route as his, or so he claimed. On the way back, he spoke all of the time. What a talkative person, I thought. I was glad to remain silent as I was naturally shy. He switched from one subject to another but spoke Ukrainian beautifully, and by the end of the journey, I was completely overwhelmed by his personality. Just before parting, he asked me if I would be going out on the following Sunday. I said that I knew of a Ukrainian Orthodox church in Berlin and wanted to go there.

'I will see you in church then,' he said gladly, and he shook my hand as though he had known me for a long time.

The week passed, and I had almost forgotten about our meeting. My plan was to purposefully go to the Ukrainian Orthodox church, rather than to the Russian one which I used to go to until then. I left the camp with a group of workers, and hid in a side street. After removing my label, I immediately headed for the nearest subway station. I arrived at the church far too early, so I decided to go for a walk by the canal. It was a bright, sunny morning.

I thought of home and tears filled my eyes. I felt lost and alone, and sorry for myself, and for the other girls, and for all the wrongs that had been done to us. When I noticed people entering the church I wiped my eyes and followed them in. Even then, when I remembered my dear father once again, the tears rolled down my cheeks. Standing to the side of me was a tall, dark gentleman. He was praying with sincerity, and he knew when to stand and when to kneel. I glanced at him and wondered if he was the man I was supposed to be meeting after the service. I was not sure. I stopped crying and began to think about all the men I had known in my life. What exactly was I looking for? What kind of emotional condition was I really in? Who would I live and share my life with? Nobody seemed to be trustworthy enough to stand by my side, and that included the latest person I had been infatuated with – a German.

The priest stepped forward with the chalice and blessed the congregation. I glanced at the tall, dark man who had quietly made his impression upon me. Just for a moment, I believed that I could go to the altar with somebody just like him. When the service ended, I went outside and he came towards me. Stretching out his hand, he greeted me simply and said:

'Good day! Let's go for some dinner.'

It was him.

He led me away from the crowd to another street, and when he found a restaurant, he invited me inside. I was embarrassed. Why should he buy me dinner? I told him I had a sandwich with me and that embarrassed him. He then asked the waitress to bring us a plate and a knife.

'Camp bread, is it?'

'Lichtenberg's very best,' I replied, 'but it is a special sandwich. It's made with salo – Ukraine's finest. My mother sent it to me.' I took a neatly wrapped packet containing the pork fat sandwich from my bag, and put it on the plate.

He tasted my precious gift and asked me to pour some of the steaming soup which the waitress had already brought. I was glad to be the lady at the table and immediately began to feel more secure. He bought the dinner using his ration card. It was simply wonderful to sit in a restaurant and to be able to dine as everyone else did. He talked all the time, so I didn't worry about leading the conversation. Then, after eating, we spent the whole afternoon together in the park.

His name was Ivan. He was a true Ukrainian counter-revolutionary who wanted to promote the Ukrainian cause. Ukraine was struggling for independence – trapped between the two superpower enemies of Communist Russia and Fascist Germany. He was the son of an architect who was

238

active during the First World War when Ukraine saw better times as an independent country, and it seemed clear that he had inherited all of his father's ideas. He was brought up in Southwest Ukraine – Transcarpathia – a territory which had proclaimed independence in 1939, and he then went on to study Law at Prague University. After that, he became a criminologist and lawyer in his home town of Uzhhorod. He now combined and shaped his entire knowledge to form one single goal – Ukrainian liberation.

As he told me about it, I wondered if he had any interest in me or whether he was just trying to lure me into political Ukrainian activities. I had never met anybody wanting to see an independent Ukraine, so I listened to him with great interest. A new page in my life's studies was being turned. We walked along the avenue by Tiergarten Zoo where everything began to look different because of the new political horizons which were opening up in my mind. I was fascinated, enchanted and captivated by everything I was being told. Although Ivan had his habit of jumping from one subject to another, it was forgivable. Finally, after accompanying me back to the camp, he shook my hand and we made arrangements to meet again on the following Sunday.

Inside the camp, I told the girls about the new friend I had made.

'At least he's one of us,' Nina said.

'Be careful with those political ideas of his,' said Shura. 'Stalin would punish him. What does he look like?'

I smiled and said: 'Oh, he's tall, with very dark, curly hair, but his face is thin and pale.'

'So, who isn't thin and pale these days?' added Katya.

'You're lucky. I wish you a very happy friendship,' smiled little Sonia.

At our subsequent meetings, Ivan brought me books and I read them and I passed them on to my friends to read. I told them all about his ideas and talked about him endlessly, but I still could not determine whether he was more interested in me or the promotion of his Ukrainian political ideas.

Then, one day, he failed to turn up. We had arranged to meet at Grunewald subway station. I arrived in time and waited there. I waited for a whole hour but there was still no sign of him. Naturally, I was very upset and returned to the camp downhearted and confused, but the following day I received a letter from him. He asked why I had not gone to Gesundbrunnen station where we should have met. I realised that I had mixed up the names of the stations. Inside the letter, however, there was also a card. It was beautiful and showed a warrior on a horse about to jump from a cliff. Above him, in the sky, Our Lady appears to save his life. Having listened to Ivan's counter-revolutionary ideas for the past few weeks, I imagined that he was the warrior and I was the one who was saving his life. It was very easy for a girl to have such thoughts. On the back of the card he wrote the words: "The one who is thinking of you". That made me happy. I was also very pleased because he had contacted me so quickly. I kissed the card and put it in a special place.

I wrote back to Ivan and explained my error, but this time I named the station where we should meet. Rich in the knowledge of his ideas and of his personal attention to me, I went to meet him that Sunday with greater confidence. I wanted to look smart, but I had nothing to wear except my grey blouse and a skirt. I therefore went to see Sonia who was going out with a singer. I knew she had a lovely, blue dress, patterned with flowers. I asked if she would lend it to me just for that day, and gladly she agreed. We were both the same size, so it fitted perfectly. I put on some makeup and went to meet Ivan feeling more suitably dressed.

He greeted me with surprise, looked at me and said casually: 'You look very lovely today. Where shall we go?'

'Let's go to church, I said without hesitation. It was early in the morning, and Sunday was always a special day for me.

'There's no service at the Ukrianian Orthodox church today, but we can go to the Ukrainian Catholic church, if you like.'

'Oh! I don't know anything about that church,' I said. So on the way there he explained that since 1596 the Ukrainian Greek Catholic Church had existed in Galicia in West Ukraine, and I would find the church very crowded.

Indeed, the large church, where the service had already started, was full of independent Ukrainians who now lived in Berlin. Their passports were stamped to say that they were Polish citizens. They could live in private houses or rent rooms or flats. They were all well-dressed and spoke in Ukrainian, and they did not look any different from the other Berliners.

The service was slightly different to the Ukrainian Orthodox service. There was no choir, and the congregation sang together. They knelt at different times during the service, and almost everyone went to Holy Communion. The priest also delivered a very wise sermon. Outside the church, Ivan greeted many of his acquaintances and spoke to them as though he had known them all his life. He introduced me as his friend and many of them looked at me inquisitively, but with friendly smiles. I listened to everything and observed everyone, but I said little. I was like a sponge soaking up everything around me, and it would be a whole week before I could meet Ivan and do this again.

Ivan's story was romantic and very different from that of Michael – the Russian émigré whose ideal was to live in high society with vodka and zakusky – hors d'oeuvres. I had never known about Transcarpathia – a mountainous Ukrainian region covered with forests, and I had never been taught or told about the fight for independence there. In my eyes Ivan was a hero, a true warrior, and a man with ideals and purpose in his life. I liked him more and more each time we met.

He had been in Berlin since 1939 and had Czechoslovakian papers because he came from the area of Ukraine previously belonging to Czechoslovakia. He had fought for the independence of Transcarpathia against the occupying Hungarians and Romanians who were then allied to Germany. The Carpathian Mountains were the pride of all West Ukrainians. Serving as an army officer, Ivan and his unit were stationed there, but they found themselves surrounded in combat. For weeks, the men went without proper food and ate buds from the trees and drank water melted from mountain snow. After finally breaking out, many of them fell, but most were captured by the Romanians. They were called "rebel bandits" – wanted men, who were then shot dead. Despite being captured, Ivan escaped but he was wounded in an eye and a leg.

Ivan then described the scene of an execution to me which he had witnessed just yards in front of him. He watched as his friends turned pale before being shot. The rest of his men were saved by a miracle. Moments after the execution began, a lady of nobility was passing by on horseback. She asked who the people were and why they were being executed. On hearing the answer she intervened, and with the help of some ministers who were of Ukrainian origin, she halted the proceedings. The survivors were taken to hospital and given small sips of milk as they could no longer digest anything properly after several weeks of starvation. Ivan had an eye operation and a bullet was removed from his skull. His vision was saved, though he was bandaged and left without sight for many weeks. On recovering, he was sent with others to Berlin where he became a labourer digging canals. With him, there were many intellectuals and prominent Ukrainians of whom he loved to talk.

When summer turned to autumn, we met twice a week. I began to run away on Wednesdays, either finding my way back through a neighbouring Dutch camp, or else through an opening in the fence. Our meetings gave me a more meaningful life, and I looked forward to them. Ivan never brought me any food or presents other than books. We never talked about food. From the way he looked, I knew that he was always short of something to eat, even though he rented a room and was entitled to a foreigner's ration book. Those who had a book were allowed to eat in restaurants and they could often receive soup without a ration card.

One day, he took me to the Marienplatz where the Ukrainian Relief Committee had its offices. He introduced me to some of his friends and talked about making new documents for me because he planned to rescue me from the camp. He talked about this possibility, though it would be very dangerous for both of us. If we were caught, we would both end up in concentration camps. I listened to everything he said, and I spoke little. To leave the camp, and the girls, would mean giving up my chance of ever going home. I would have to stay in the West, and I did not know of his plans for me. He had not said anything so far. So, for the time being, I remained silent, too.

Meanwhile, news spread from the Eastern Front where the battle was being waged between the Russian and German armies. Inside the camp, we heard of the retreat of the

German army and how Stalin had liberated Ukrainian towns. I heard that our district was now under Russian occupation. Painfully, I began to realise how cut off I was from my parents. I feared for my father because the Communist system was being re-established. Surely he would be killed or persecuted together with the rest of my family, and what would become of me, a priest's daughter, should I try to return home? These thoughts tormented me and kept me awake at night. What was I to do? Should I try to escape from the camp, as Ivan suggested, and try to stay in the West? That would mean never seeing my parents or my country again. And what did the future hold? I did not even know Ivan that well. Who was he? Was he an adventurer who was also out to conquer me? Or was he a thoroughly honest and sincere man? I could not say.

Then, one day, we were caught in the rain. We were in the park so we ran to a shelter. It was a quiet place, and Ivan put his coat over me. As we stood close to each other, he drew me closer to him and kissed me. Then, he casually asked: 'Will you be my wife?'

I stood there still clinging to him and said nothing. He did not press the issue, but from then on he introduced me to all of his friends as his future wife. I was amazed and was also rather annoyed. Why was he so sure of himself? I had not given him my answer, and I had not consented to his proposal, despite not having said anything to deny it. We continued to meet throughout the autumn.

On the 2nd of October it was Ivan's birthday and he told me he wanted to have a small party and invite some of his friends. It was a Saturday and I managed to leave the camp in the afternoon. I wore my best black dress and my string of silvery beads, and I tidied my hair as well as I could. He met me at the station, as usual, and he looked at me inquisitively. I could see he was feeling rather uneasy. His method of dealing with his nervousness was to talk, and he never stopped talking on the subway. Eventually, he led me to a house I had never seen before.

I was led into a large room where a table had been laid. A lady was making coffee in the kitchen. As we waited for Ivan's friends to arrive, he put his arms round me, and seeing us both in a large mirror on the wall, he said with a happy

243

smile: 'I am going to have a lovely wife.'

I smiled back at him in the mirror and said nothing, but I submitted to his firm embrace. We had a lovely party and drank a toast to the future. He then announced our engagement officially to his friends. There was no ring as we could not afford one, but the announcement had been made and I was now being drawn into a new and enchanting life, not really knowing what I was letting myself in for.

We knew it was very difficult for foreigners to get married in Germany as the rules were very strict at that time. You had to have a certificate showing who your parents were, and you then had to undergo various interviews and formalities which we would never be able to pass. Ivan wrote a letter to his brother at home and told him of his intention to marry me. That gave me the confidence to know that he was being sincere. From that moment on, I believed that he was my only friend in a world which was slowly starting to crumble around me. The War was coming ever closer to us, and it was impossible to be sure of what would happen next. At least I now had a good friend, and I treasured him.

Ivan talked to me about the possibility of a proper escape from Lichtenberg. He advised me to write to Lviv University to ask them to send a certificate to prove that I had studied and lived there. On the evidence of that certificate, we would be able to get new documents stating that I was a recent evacuee from Lviv, after which I should be able to obtain an Ausweis – a small, green identity certificate issued to West Ukrainians who had lived under Polish rule. I would be entitled to a ration book, accommodation in Berlin and a new job. I wrote to Lviv, and after a few weeks I received the statement to say I had lived and studied at the University there. Ivan then applied for my new documents.

Christmas came. I had heard nothing more about the application, so I began to lose hope, but we did at least have a little Christmas tree which a policeman gave us. I broke away from the column and ran risks just to buy some decorations and candles to make it look more attractive. When we lit the candles, I burst into tears. I remembered home and my parents. Somehow I knew I would never see them again. I lifted my head and watched the flames flicker. I had to be strong and I told myself that I would live to conquer all – no matter how hard life would ever be.

The girls gathered by the tree and we sang all the carols and songs we knew. We celebrated by holding hands, and we danced with joy. In the ongoing poverty of Lichtenberg Camp, the Christmas tree now provided the only spark of hope for our future.

Chapter 25

It was the 19th of January 1944, my twenty-first birthday. I thought of what had happened in the past year, and what had happened in the hospital. I had not heard anything more of Tatyana, but I remembered her prediction about a change in my life. I treated the girls to some lemonade and sweets, and they all wished me a happy birthday with many more to follow.

A few days later, I went to meet Ivan and he brought me the best possible present: it was the little, green certificate which would be the passport to my future. How I treasured it. It would take me to an unknown new life and future with him, but it also meant a separation from the girls, and any thoughts of returning home. I was overwhelmed. I thanked Ivan and he begged me to hide it. I could not show it to anyone. At our subsequent meeting, he began to make the arrangements for my escape. He reassured me with his dynamic will and certainty. I, meanwhile, remained doubtful.

The girls began to talk about the German atrocities that could yet ensue. As the Front came closer, rumours began to spread that we would all be executed by firing squad, or perhaps by gas. They'd heard one German policeman saying to a beautiful girl: 'What a pity your lovely head shall have to roll.' It was psychologically very menacing, and fear gripped us. The bombing also went on and on, and one evening one of them hit our factory. Many Italian workers died there in the basement which was flooded with hot oil from the pipes.

I went in search of Lena to tell her of my intent to escape and I told her about Ivan's proposal. She listened to my news with her usual smile and asked me quietly: 'Do you love him?'

I was surprised and smiled at her: 'What is love, Lena? There is infatuation, fascination, even falling in love, but all

245

of that is just part of growing up for a girl. I told you how the former German soldier charmed me and wrote a note saying that he was in love with me, but what could he offer me amongst countrymen who are my enemies? How can I forgive them for what they've done to us?

I'm seeing Ivan in the church where I first thought I could marry him. It's strange, but it's true. I like him very much, and I admire his ideas and his dedication to Ukraine. He is an honest and serious man, and I shall share my life with him. Yes, I love him. Seriously, I do.'

I had said more than I realised, but by talking to Lena I had made my feelings, and my decision, known. I said goodbye to her, and asked her to keep my diaries which I did not want to take with me as I tried to escape. Maybe one day, when I was free, I would be able to fetch them from her. That, unfortunately, never happened: they were all burned when a bomb later fell on Lena's barrack.

I told my secret to just one other person. She was a beautiful girl called Ksenia who nearly lost her life when taking aspirin to terminate her pregnancy after a Czechoslovakian had raped her. I knew she would keep my secret and would help me. To my surprise, she told me that she, too, once had a similar offer but refused it because she did not love the man making the proposition. Nonetheless, she was very happy for me and promised to keep the secret. She said she would gladly help me to escape.

I went to work as usual, but work stopped at night during the summer. I had not seen the supervisor for a long time and was told that he had been taken ill. Then, one day, I noticed him going into the manager's office. My heart leapt. I waited for him to reappear and met him in the passage. His face was pale and his eyes were half-closed. He did not smile, and neither did I.

'How are you?' he asked.

'I'm fine, and how are you?' I asked with concern. 'You're ill. Is it because of your wounds?'

'I've not been well for a long time,' but he smiled gently and continued. 'How is your life?'

'Oh,' I suddenly wanted to be honest with him, 'I've met some friends, and I'm going to escape from the camp.' Somehow I knew I could trust him and I wanted to express my trust. I could see that he appreciated it.

He looked at me and asked: 'Just one friend, perhaps?'

'Just one friend, and many friends,' I replied. 'Our people in Berlin are helping me. I've found a big, Ukrainian community here.'

'I wish you luck,' he said. 'Did you know they used to call you God's Darling? Here, take this book as a small present.' He handed me a wrapped book and went on his way, out of my life forever.

Somehow, I thanked him and stood there in the passage. I was stunned, and again for a fraction of a second I forgot where I was. I opened the book to see Schiller's poetry, which I loved, and the first poem I could see was "Star at Night". How poignant, I thought.

I returned to the table where a recent transfer to Lichtenberg called Anna, asked politely: 'What did the German say to you?' She looked at the book.

'He said goodbye to me because he is ill from his wounds, and he will not be coming back.'

'He was a good supervisor,' she added, 'and a very handsome man.'

I said nothing and went back to my work. I was deep in thought all afternoon. An inner voice seemed to say: 'That was a beam of light in the darkness of your life. It saved you from despair. It woke you up.' It was indeed a light in the darkness, just like Schiller's poem.

I smiled to myself and began talking to the other girls. I exchanged a joke with Joe and spoke to Desilia, and I then went to speak to Herr Blanke. I was glad to see his friendly face. I told nobody else of my plans.

A week later, Ivan made arrangements for me to visit the Employment Centre and the transit camp where I could obtain the Ausweis document needed by evacuees to obtain work in Berlin. He suggested I should try to find a job in a restaurant where I would be able to feed myself as I was very undernourished. The plan was to break from the column in the morning, meet him at the station, and from there he would take me to the offices.

It was the 2nd of February 1944. Nervously, I went through the perils of obtaining the papers. It was very difficult for me to tell lies and to pretend that I had just arrived from Lviv, but Ivan told me to do it, and so I did. The scariest moment was at a camp outside Berlin where I needed to have a medical examination. The doctors were Ukrainian prisoners of war, and it was even harder to lie to them than to the Germans. I passed their tests, registered in the necessary offices, and by the end of the day I had the papers. Ivan advised me not to take them to the camp, so he kept them.

We went to a nearby coffee house and had a drink, waiting for the column to make its way back to the camp. I told Ivan that I would never forget the girls. I felt guilty about having to leave them behind and even had some pieces of paper on which I had written my promises to them. Ivan was shocked to learn that I had carried them with me all that day. He was not convinced by my dedication to my fellow countrymen. Instead, he talked about the practical ways in which a good wife could help in the home.

I merged back into the marching column. Nobody noticed me, so I thought I would return safely, but at the gatehouse, where the police were stationed, I was suddenly grabbed by a strong hand. I was pulled aside and shouted at by a guard:

'Where have you been? You haven't been to work today!'

I was shocked and frightened, but replied calmly: 'I have been to the doctor, a private doctor.'

He swore and shouted at me, and said that I would be called to see the commandant. He pushed and let go of me. That night I was very frightened. I spoke to all my friends and hoped the commandant would not want to see me. When I returned to my barrack it was very late. Everybody was asleep, except for little Sonia. She said nothing, and when I asked if anyone had been looking for me she said no.

I was glad when the night was over and wondered if anything would be said in the morning, but the whole day passed quietly. Desilia asked me if I had been poorly and I said yes, but I added that I was now feeling better. I knew the threat had passed, and I began to grow in confidence. For the first time, I believed it was worth taking the risk.

The escape had to happen soon, in case the police detected something wrong with my paperwork. We chose Tuesday the 12th of February. I was to go to work as normal. Then, when the call for evening soup was made, I was to take my belongings to a hole in the fence from where Ivan would take them. The risk was enormous. I did not want to leave my clothes behind as we could not afford to buy any new ones. I should stay in the camp for the night and slip away from the column on the way to work, and hide in a side street until it was safe. I had already done this before. I should then make my way to the nearest subway station where I would meet Ivan.

I worked normally, all day that Tuesday. My secret was shared with Ksenia and she helped me to maintain my confidence. After returning from work, I felt tense and guilty, but who could see my feelings? Everyone only cared about themselves after a hard day's labour. The evening sky was calm and night began to fall. The banging of a piece of railing signalled the time for supper. Everyone hurried from the barracks with their little red bowls, and pushed into the queue. The police were relaxed in their hut knowing that everyone was only interested in eating. A few of them looked on at the queue, but hardly any guarded the fence. We chose that moment.

Dark clouds were floating across the sky. Somewhere, a church bell rang out as I ran with Ksenia towards the hole. On the other side, we could see Ivan walking up and down the quiet street. Scared and breathless we pushed my case through. We said nothing and quickly ran back. It was only when we were in the barrack that we allowed ourselves to take a deep breath and smile.

'Success, thank God!'

'Thank you,' I said to Ksenia. 'You are the only one I can trust.' Ksenia appreciated my faith in her and gave me a sweet smile.

'It was risky,' she said, 'and we would all have been in trouble if they'd caught us. I hope nobody catches Ivan.'

I had thought of that, but said nothing as fate was now leading the way. Deep down, I seemed to know that everything would be all right. We took our bowls and joined the queue for some soup.

That night, I made sure I went to see all my friends in the camp. I was sorry to leave them to endure more suffering. I thought of home and how Stalin would not forgive us for living in the West, no matter what. We would probably be

249

sent to Siberia, and in my state of health I could not possibly face it. It would be the end of me. My youth kept me going and all I wanted was to lead a full and meaningful life, and to do so many more things. I felt the powerful desire to be free.

Ivan had given me some cards and on each of them I wrote a message with a warm goodbye and best wishes. Before leaving each of my friends I pushed a card under their pillow. I knew that when they came to make their beds I would be gone. The most touching parting was with Shura. She was nursing a baby boy now, and was worried about feeding him. The baby had ginger hair, like his mother, and was called Kolya. She let me hold him and I was glad to nurse this tiny, precious life in my arms. The only treasured possession from home that I had managed to keep was a small, feather pillow. I gave it to Shura and told her to nurse the baby on it. She was very grateful as all she had was a mattress and pillow made of straw. We talked for a while and when she turned away, I pushed a card under the pillow. It was one of the best ones I had with a picture of a crucified woman symbolising Ukraine. Little children in national costume cried at her feet whilst two eagles, marked with a swastika and a red star, attacked her. Desperately, she looked to heaven, praying for help. I wanted Shura to understand our homeland as well as my aim to take up the struggle for liberation. So, on the back of the card I wrote:

'I am going away, Shura, with those who want Ukraine to be free. Goodbye. And good luck to you and to your family. I shall always remember you.'

I said goodbye to Nina without leaving her a card. I knew she could not be trusted.

I arrived back late at my barrack. Sonia was still awake, so I sat on her bed and put my arm round her shoulders and said:

'Sonia, I am going away tomorrow. I will not come back. Don't say anything to anybody. Thank you for all you have done for me. I wish you...'

Tears came to my eyes. I wished for her to arrive home, safe and happy. The thought of her going home, and of not knowing when, gripped my heart. The thought of what was probably awaiting her made me feel even worse. Tears rolled down my cheeks, and I only managed to add: '...I wish you well.'

'You're escaping,' she smiled, and her eyes shone with sincere joy, 'I'm so glad for you. Good luck!'

'Thank you Sonia. I trust you won't say anything.'

'Of course, not! Do you have a friend? Someone to help you?'

'Yes Sonia. I told you about my friend. We are going to be married.' I had not realised how certain I was. Something stronger than hesitation was now rooted in me.

'How very nice,' she said. I wish you luck. Come and see us when you're free.'

I will,' I replied confidently, as though free already. 'I promise you.'

'You are lucky. I do hope everything is going to be all right for you. I shall miss you.' She started to cry and wiped her tears with her hand: 'We may perish here, you know,' she stammered, 'but I am glad you're going. Don't forget us. Tell them all; tell the whole world about us and our suffering. Tell them what they've been doing here.'

We were both crying now and I took a towel from under her pillow to wipe her tears.

'I promise you, Sonia. Tell the girls, later, that I promised to tell the world about your suffering. I will live to do just that, and I will never forget you.'

Ksenia came over to us and we sat whispering for a long time. I gave Ksenia my favourite pink scarf and gave Sonia everything else which I could not take with me; it included a woollen rug that I had brought from home.

'Look after your legs. They are poorly,' I said with sympathy.

'Thank you. My legs are always painful, but what about you? You'll need it.'

'No, you keep it Sonia. You need it more than I do,' I then wrapped my rug round her crooked thin legs. We then kissed each other goodbye.

I hardly slept a wink that night, anticipating what was about to happen. Again and again, I continued to wonder if I had made the right decision. When the rail was banged at four o'clock I was the first to get up. I packed what few things I had left, cleared my locker, made the bed and said my prayers quietly without anyone noticing. I often prayed under my

251

blanket so the girls would not laugh at me. No one else prayed, and anything religious was frowned upon or even mocked. I stood nervously in the column waiting for the roll call. The sky was dark and the lanterns made it appear even darker and more frightening. Where would I be going? Fate could still lead me to work and return me to the camp, but I would not allow it. Come what may, I had to go.

As soon as we had left, I looked for a side street and watched the police guards. It was getting lighter and I had to be quick. The girls around me were half-asleep, and took little notice of what was happening. Sonia walked behind me, and I told her to say that I was sick should anyone notice my disappearance.

The opportunity finally came when someone at the front of the column fell to the ground. The guards ran past us and everyone stopped for a few minutes. I slipped into a side street, leant against a wall, and waited until everyone had passed. It seemed to take an eternity. Finally, when the noise of the clattering feet died down, I took a deep breath.

I wanted to shout out and say I was free, but I ran and ran, not quite knowing where I was going. Eventually, I found my way to the subway. I talked to myself and cried. I tore the OST label from my coat and threw it away. I then dried my tears, wiped my face and bravely asked for a ticket to Gesunbrunnen where I had arranged to meet Ivan.

It was almost six o'clock in the morning and workers were now hurrying to work. Nobody took any notice of a girl in a black coat and knitted white cap travelling on her own. I sat in the train and looked at the other passengers. They were all preoccupied with their own problems. I was aware that each of us was an island, unique, and with undisclosed secrets.

I stepped onto the platform at Gesunbrunnen station, free and confident. I greeted Ivan with a smile, and we immediately went to find a job at the Employment Centre. We asked for work in a kitchen, and I was given a job at a small restaurant with full board. They knew I was a registered refugee. We fetched my case from Ivan's apartment and then found the restaurant which was in a block of large houses in Berlin's Wiesensee district. An elderly couple greeted us warmly and showed me a room on the first floor. On hearing that I was a student they apologised for not having something better, and tried to please me – as though I was someone of superior status. As soon as the door closed and I was alone, I laughed: God, me a student! After two years of slavery, how far from the truth that seemed. At least I had a room, and a room of my own. It was long and clean and furnished. After two years of camp life this was a luxury. I had wonderful dreams that night as I slept in a soft and clean bed.

In the morning, I began my work. I had to pretend to be a lady who did not quite know how to work, and to eat as little as possible. I worked hard, and I was very hungry. I pretended not to eat much at the table, but as soon as the landlady was out of the kitchen I grabbed the potatoes and then ate them behind the door. The cook was called Frau Lange, and she cooked well. I helped her with everything. She was polite and friendly, and her husband was also kind to me. I enjoyed my freedom, which also meant I could go out in the evening. I ran and ran, saying to myself: 'I'm free.'

There was one remaining problem, however. Once a week, my employers liked to go out for a drinking session with their friends, and they would not leave me by myself in the flat. I had to go with them, but I could not drink and was unable to share in their laughter and gaiety. They were all in their fifties and I was a young girl, and I had a studious mind. I was also full of sorrow and sadness from my past years of experience. I had little in common with them. No matter how friendly they were, or how sincerely they invited me to join them, I couldn't do it. I sat at the other end of the hall and watched them drinking. They talked and told jokes, and enjoyed themselves until long after midnight.

I became increasingly angry with my employers for making me go with them. They seemed to be good, hard-working people. They were decent and kind, yet this behaviour belittled them in my eyes. One morning, they were quiet and seemed to be ashamed of themselves, yet they still would not agree to leave me alone in my room. I had nowhere else to go as Ivan worked at night, and we could only meet briefly at eight o'clock in the evening.

Towards the spring of 1944, the bombing of Berlin increased and the air raid sirens sounded more frequently. We had to leave work and run down to the cellar at the end of a long corridor. I was no longer frightened. On one of those days, just after we had finished serving dinner, the alarm sounded again. I was finishing the washing-up and decided to tidy everything, and this included washing the floor. I thought that by the time the bombing started, I would be finished. I continued calmly and was in the middle of washing the corridor when my boss, Herr Lange, appeared in the doorway:

'Come on girl. Stop working and run to the cellar. Hurry up!'

I wanted to protest, but he refused to let me stay. He told me to run, and so reluctantly I did so. We had just reached the cellar door when we heard the airplanes. I was making my way down the steps in front of Herr Lange when suddenly there was a massive explosion. A bomb fell on the house – on the very spot where I had just been standing. It had become a heap of rubble from the three storeys that had collapsed upon it.

We had all fallen down. It was dark everywhere and there was a lot of moaning and crying from the others already in the cellar. Someone shone a torch, and I could see I was bleeding. Frau Lange was crawling on the floor and her husband was sitting on the steps, stunned and only half-conscious. Someone tried to help us. My leg was hurting and I realised that blood was pouring from my calf. I had a large cut and someone applied a dressing to stop the bleeding. A man said that the door in front of us had been blown out from the power of the blast and its splinters had wounded some of the people. A brick had fallen on my boss and he was concussed. Frau Lange was shocked but unhurt. Meanwhile, a rabbit that lived in a cage in the cellar had gone mad. Everybody was in shock. The women cried and trembled.

When the raid was over, we managed to scramble our way out and saw how the houses had been reduced to heaps of rubble. If it had not been for Herr Lange ordering me to go downstairs, I would have been dead. I was grateful to him for the rest of my life.

The pipes beneath the floor had burst and water flooded the cellar. The Lange's apartment was ruined. The bomb had fallen directly on the kitchen and corridor, and their rooms had fallen through into the basement. All the glass and crockery was broken, the fine furniture was ruined, and the linen and clothing were now drenched. To everybody's surprise, my room was the only one in the house to survive the blast. Nothing had moved, and you would never have guessed that a bomb had just exploded in the same building.

We were all asked to go to the nearest school where we were given coffee and sandwiches. Those who needed help were given First Aid by the doctors and nurses in attendance. Herr Lange seemed to have recovered. He was pale but active, and asked if anyone else needed help. Frau Lange was calm. I shall never forget the moment when she went back into her ruined kitchen and pulled an alarm clock out from the rubble where the stove used to be. She put it to her ear, and said with a smile: 'It's still going, you know – just like life is still going on!'

To Frau Lange, the clock was one small part of the interwoven tapestry of life. She did not cry or panic, but simply carried on and tried to salvage her linen. She made me find a long stick with which we tried to pull each piece from the water. She was fully preoccupied with the task, and was pleased each time she salvaged something.

As we sat together in the school hall she ate her sandwiches, and said how good the coffee was.

'We are going back,' she said resolutely. 'We shall sleep in your room. We are not spending the night in here.' She looked around and remained composed. She looked at the distressed people knowing she was fully capable of coping with life under any circumstance. We went back to the ruined apartment and continued to salvage whatever we could. When night came, we settled down to sleep in my room. Frau Lange slept in my bed with me, and Herr Lange slept in a chair.

The next day, my employers found somewhere else to stay and we moved from the ruins of their once beautiful restaurant. The new apartment was on the second floor. I was given a lovely room, even better than the one I had before. It did not have a restaurant, so I was told to work as a household servant. It was easier than working in the kitchen, but inside I continued to protest: 'I'm not a servant. I will not remain a servant,' but for the time being, I had no choice.

I had to continue working hard. Frau Lange was pleased with me, and Herr Lange also calmly accepted me, but only as someone he owned. I knew they had recovered from the disaster because their drinking sessions began again. Once more, they would not allow me to stay alone in the apartment and made me go with them. They went to the other remaining restaurants in Berlin where they would drink, sing and laugh as though nothing had happened. Usually, I took a book with me and read in a corner of the room, but their laughter and loud voices disturbed me. I decided I had to start going out on my own.

One day, I went to see the girls in the camp. I walked near to the wire fence until some of them finally noticed me and came to talk to me. I wore a floral skirt which my Russian friends had given to me for Easter, and a white blouse. Nina came out, as did Shura with her baby boy in her arms. She smiled with her usual big smile. Little, lame Sonia was also overjoyed to see me: 'You look really nice,' she said, 'how are you?'

'I'm working hard,' I replied, 'but I was nearly killed by a bomb. It fell on the house where I was working.'

'You're so lucky, then. You look different. Don't forget about us. It is terrible here. Bombs are also falling on the factory...' She was unable to finish. A policeman was making his way down the street and one of the girls warned me. I turned and recognised him. It was too late to run, so I stood there calmly. When he reached me he looked at me and I looked at him. For a fraction of a second we recognised each other. It was a second upon which my life depended. Then, he lowered his eyes and continued on his way. Frightened, I said goodbye to the girls and went in the opposite direction. I never went back to the camp again.

Ivan was shocked when he learned about what I had done.

'You were very lucky,' he said angrily. 'You could have ended up in a concentration camp.'

Bless that policeman, I thought to myself. Not all Germans are bad.

Then one night, when my bosses went to their drinking session and promised to be back by ten o'clock, I went to the cinema and returned after ten, but there was still no sign of them. I stood in the passageway, walked round the house, came back to the door – there was nobody there. It was a cold night. I was tired, cold and hungry. I stood waiting for ages. When they finally returned – drunk and jolly, I protested:

'I am not made of wood! It is after midnight, and I have stood here since ten o'clock. I'm cold and I'm not going to do it again.' I was furious with them.

Frau Lange said she was sorry, but Herr Lange was equally angry:

'If you don't want to stay with us, you can go.'

'Very well then, I will,' I said. 'I would like to work in a restaurant again. You treat me as a servant, so why don't you let me stay at home when you go out?'

'Nobody stays alone in our apartment,' he snapped. 'If you don't like it, tomorrow we will go to the Employment Centre and we will find you something else.'

'Very well!' I replied.

Frau Lange pleaded with me not to leave them. She told me about her only son who was coming home soon on leave, and she wanted me to meet him, and she would need my help. She asked me to say sorry to her husband and make up for our argument, but I refused. Her pleading with him did not help, either. We went to bed, still disagreeing.

In the morning, we were all gloomy and silent. Neither of us apologised. Herr Lange sternly told me to get ready to go. I packed my belongings and said goodbye to Frau Lange, who cried. I was sorry to part from her. I liked both of them but because of their habit, I wanted to leave.

At the busy Employment Centre, Erich Lange recommended me to a friend – an owner of a big restaurant, but warned him, cautiously:

'You will have a good worker, but you will have no peace with her.'

A broad, stout gentleman with a rough face and glasses looked at me sternly and asked me to register at the counter: his name was Kurt Wittsack.

Chapter 26

I was taken immediately to the centre of Berlin, near to the Alexanderplatz, to where the words Wittsack Restaurant were written in large letters above a glass door. The door opened into a huge dining room, beyond which there was a steamy kitchen. Cooks were busily working there. I was introduced to the person in charge – an elderly, grey-haired lady called Elsa, who was Herr Wittsack's sister-in-law. Her first look was far from friendly. Two waitresses were standing by the door. One was a lively and pretty blonde called Annie and the other was a dark and beautiful girl called Lottie. They took no notice of me and continued with their conversation. Another young girl with mousy-brown hair stood by the sink. She was introduced to me as Herr Wittsack's daughter, Daisy. She looked down at me, though she manage to smile, but that was because I was about to replace her.

Herr Wittsack's wife, Frau Emma, appeared from behind the bar. We were introduced. She was a stout lady with a double chin and little, grey eyes which were set deep inside her face. She hardly murmured a word when she greeted me, and appeared to be busy but she was also unhappy. I was then led to a little room in which there was a bed, wardrobe, table and chair. This would be my home for the next nine months.

It was late in the spring of 1944. It was warm outside and the trees were already fully in leaf. My duties would start at six o'clock in the morning by opening the door for the staff and then taking the dog, Mampa, for a walk. Walking through the streets of Berlin with a big dog took some getting used to. That was because in Ukraine, dogs either roamed freely or were tied to their kennels. After returning, I had to clean the restaurant, including the bar, doors and windows, and then the ladies' and gents' cloakrooms. I hated it. It was a huge restaurant. I wasn't used to doing such work, either. My life had been about books and learning, during which time my mother had deliberately protected me from doing too much housework. Now, all the cleaning was mine to do. I worked hard, and everything had to be done by ten o'clock when, puffing and moaning, the boss would come down from his bedroom still dressed in his pyjamas and dressing gown. He was almost always angry. He would inspect my work and always find faults. He would then shout at me at the top of his voice. On one occasion, when I hadn't found the floor cloth, I remember him yelling:

'Get your knickers then girl, and make sure you wash them, too!'

I had already washed my knickers, but I didn't dare to

mention it. When he'd finished shouting, Herr Wittsack would go to the bar and have a long drink. His moody and silent wife would usually follow him over. Eventually, she would snap at him and he would snap back at her, and only then would they both get washed and get dressed. Usually, by eleven o'clock, I'd be really hungry. Herr Wittsack, his family, the cook and waitresses would take their places at a table in the corner of the restaurant, but I had to sit alone at another. By then, I felt so hungry that it did not matter where I sat. All I wanted was a cup of coffee and my ration of two rolls.

After breakfast, I made the Wittsack's bed, cleaned their room, and returned to the kitchen. The restaurant would already be open for dinner, and the waitresses would bring the dirty plates and cutlery for me to wash. The stove and the floor had to be washed, too, so it would be ages before I could have some dinner. If the boss had shouted at me in the morning, he sometimes felt guilty and would then give me a little extra to eat. Sometimes he brought the food himself. It was as though he wanted to apologise for his earlier behaviour. At times, I loathed Herr Wittsack and his family. The head cook, Elsa, was the only friendly person there and she would offer me a piece of bread and butter at an opportune time. I would never have dared to take it myself for fear that someone would notice it go missing. Elsa often smiled and told me not to worry about Herr Wittsack's temper:

'We have a saying. If a German man is not cross in the morning, he will be worse in the afternoon.'

As time passed, the waitresses became friendlier. They sympathised with me as they, too, had all been shouted at by the boss at some time or another. Annie told me that she was Polish by nationality but had lived in Germany for a long time. She was married to a German political prisoner: I then saw her going out with a German SS officer. The hackenkreuz on the sleeve of his yellow uniform was clear for all to see.

Lottie was simple and friendly. I often wondered where she had come from as she had a very dark complexion, but she never said a word about her background. She was married, and her husband was fighting somewhere at the

Front. After a while, Daisy, too, became friendlier. She emphasised that her name was English and that one day she would go to England. At that time, England may just as well have been a distant planet to me: I was not interested in discovering anything about it. I only thought about returning to Ukraine – a place increasingly more like Heaven on Earth.

The days passed, and the weeks and months followed. I only had a few free hours in the afternoons and couldn't go out much with Ivan, though sometimes I would take the dog out just to meet him in the square. Occasionally, I had a free half-day on Sundays, but that was only ever in the afternoons so I couldn't go to church either. I persevered. There was nothing else I could do, and my complaints about Herr Wittsack's behaviour would only ever fall upon deaf ears.

'Do they give you enough to eat?' Ivan asked. I said I was not complaining about it. He then added: 'You should be glad to receive any food now. Germany is falling, the army is retreating and people are beginning to speak of hard times ahead.'

I had lived in the present and thought little about the future. The Germans were still continuing to believe in their Third Reich and their leader – Adolf Hitler.

It was the summer of 1944, after the unsuccessful attempt on Hitler's life. The conspirators had been arrested and executed, and this prompted a comment from Lottie:

'Just think. For generations and generations the children of those conspirators will be condemned for what their fathers attempted. It is unthinkable that anyone should make an attempt on the Führer's life.'

I remembered her words a year later when Hitler finally committed suicide, taking the Third Reich with him. What would she have made of that?

The bombings started again. We usually had to leave everything and run quickly to the basement of a neighbouring chemical factory, together with the other residents in the street. One sunny morning at breakfast, Frau Wittsack shouted that someone had broken one of the china cups from her tea service which was laid out on a table, covered by an immaculately clean, white tablecloth. The siren then sounded so everyone started to run. Outside, the ground beneath our feet was already shaking from bombs exploding nearby. I was frightened.

I made my way down into the chemical factory's basement and leant back against some cushions in the corner of the room. I thought that if anything further happened, I would at least have something soft to protect me. Another bomb fell, and the whole building rumbled above us. The lights went out, and there was silence. Children began to cry, and then word quickly spread that we had been buried inside. The entrance was blocked and there was indeed no way out, so we waited until someone came to rescue us. From somewhere beyond, a voice shouted to say that there was an old oven built somewhere in the wall, and if we opened the oven door we would all be able to get out. Some of the men began to search for it, and when they found it they began hammering. An opening was eventually made and it led to a narrow and dirty passage. We made our way out, just as soon as we knew the bombing had stopped.

I had, by now, lost all track of time. Outside, it looked like hell on earth. The bright sunny morning had turned into an artificial night. Everything around us was burning. Heavy smoke and flames filled the street, and clouds of ash fell through the air like snow. It was a terrifying sight. And though we failed to realise it at the time, we were all black and filthy as well.

The bombing had ruined Herr Wittsack's restaurant. The fine bone china cups, of which his wife was so proud, lay on the floor in tiny, jagged pieces, and the white buttered rolls which had never yet been offered to me, were now covered with a sheet of thick, grey dust. The bar was ruined. The Wittsack's bedroom was also ruined, but to my surprise, once again, my room remained untouched, only this time there was dust, and water from the firemen's hoses. My belongings were all there, except for a piece of material my friend had given to me for my birthday. I had hidden it under the mattress. It was a lovely piece of chequered, silk cloth that I planned to turn into a blouse, but it had now gone. Perhaps a fireman had taken it. I thought nothing more of it. I was simply glad to be alive.

I gathered my possessions and packed them into my suitcase, but I did not know exactly what to do next. The buildings were ruined and the fires continued to burn. There were shouts, noises and flashes from the fire engines, and I felt that I could not possibly stay there. Herr Wittsack came into my room. He looked sad and subdued and said I would have to go and stay with Annie, the waitress. She had agreed to take me until the building was repaired. Herr Wittsack was already making plans to reopen the restaurant.

I moved to another part of Berlin – to a large apartment where Annie lived by herself, and I was given a large bedroom with a high, soft bed. The window opened out onto a garden and I enjoyed the peaceful, natural scenery which I had not seen for such a long time.

That night, after having a bath, I climbed into bed wanting to catch up on my sleep, but my hopes were in vain. Annie came home with her boyfriend, the SS officer. They had supper, and I heard glasses tinkle, but then they started to argue. I could not bear to think of what they were shouting about, and I could not sleep.

Annie had shown me a large crucifix hanging behind one of the doors where she had made the sign of the cross saying: 'This is what protects my house.' I had wondered why it was behind the door, but said nothing. Now, lying in bed and unable to sleep, I thought about the crucifix and prayed that everything would be all right. I hoped her Nazi friend would do nothing to Annie or to me. I was frightened. What if he knew who I really was? The thought terrified me. Bravely, I lay awake and was ready to face anything. The arguing continued all night.

In the morning the officer had gone and Annie came out silent and red-faced from crying. She said nothing about the quarrel, and otherwise treated me like a member of her family. We ate together, cleaned and washed, and went to work. We tried to get the restaurant back to a standard fit to serve dinners again.

Ration books with the word "Stamm" written on the front were being used, but there was one dish available also called "Stamm". It was a thick nourishing soup that anyone could buy without needing the ration book. My boss was pleased to be cooking it himself in a very large saucepan and he gave generous portions to the hungry public. Many people now had no homes, but they were all prepared to pay the asking price of the soup. Herr Wittsack was satisfied, and I could see it in his reddened face. Now was the time for him to make the most profit, and he wanted us to hurry to get the restaurant fully restored. It took over a month. My room was repaired, so I could return. Herr Wittsack's room had also been repaired, so he and Frau Emma could return from their daughter's home where they had stayed.

I wondered why they had bothered to reopen the half-ruined restaurant as the bombing continued to go on. We were in the centre of Berlin with the Front drawing closer each day. Surely Herr Wittsack had enough money, a family to think of, and his safety to consider. Maybe he genuinely cared about others, or maybe he simply wanted to make a profit, or both. He re-employed his staff, and his daughter had to work with me because there was too much for me to do. The number of saucepans of soup doubled, and then trebled as people arrived in endless queues. Often, it was completely sold out.

Another of Herr Wittsack's daughters, Charlotte, appeared with her small daughter, Yuta. Charlotte was a happily married, beautiful young lady who was not used to working, or serving others. Her husband was fighting at the Front and her father decided that she should work in the kitchen to help the starving people of Berlin, but not before they had all argued.

'You don't know what work is,' shouted Herr Wittsack. 'Look at that girl.' He pointed at me. 'Learn from her! She knows how to work!' I was surprised to hear this, and kept quiet.

White-faced and very pretty, Charlotte moved around the kitchen with grace, but whether she liked it or not, she had to work. Little Yuta was with her, and we all liked her and played with her whenever it was possible. Then one day, Charlotte's husband came back on leave. He was a young, weather-beaten soldier. There was much whispering and quiet talk. Herr Wittsack sighed and his wife wiped her tears. They did not say anything to me, but I realised that they were talking about the tragic situation at the Front.

Charlotte and her husband slept in the Wittsack's apartment. I had to clean it and wake them up in the mornings, and I often found them in bed. They were a happily married couple. Charlotte's body was so beautiful and her husband was so handsome that the picture of their happy marriage in their bedroom stayed with me as a symbol of love and beauty. Their little daughter, Yuta, became attached to me. I like children, and always found a way of getting on with them. Playing with Yuta was an absolute joy. Perhaps because of that, my boss was kinder to me. The shouting ceased and more attention was given to my well-being.

Meanwhile, I continued to meet Ivan on Sunday afternoons, and we talked about the future, not knowing what would happen once the advancing Russian army arrived. He hinted that we would have to head west because he would not return home to a Communist occupation of our country. My heart ached as I longed to see my parents. I tried to persuade him, promising to share everything with him, even if we had to go to Siberia, but he was adamant. He knew much more than I did and called me naïve.

Those times were very uncertain, and with every minute of every day we were grateful to be alive. The future was intangible and could never be as important as the present. Every time there was a raid I always wondered if Ivan had survived, and I tried to phone him. Panic struck me whenever I imagined what might happen if I was to be left alone. How would I make my way back, even with my new documents? What would happen if the Communists ruled Berlin? I knew that Herr Wittsack wanted me to stay with them because he thought I worked well, and to have a cheap servant would be ideal for him, but what future would that leave me? None. Where was my future? If I was at home again, what would I encounter? Persecution. I could not go there. So, my only way forward was with Ivan. Frantically, I rang him until I received some news. When I knew he was alive my mind would return to normal.

It was late in the summer and Herr Wittsack organised an outing to the river. We all went including his family, little Yuta, the waitresses, and even Elsa – the head cook. We travelled on the subway, and in the freedom offered by Berlin's public transport system everyone's true personality began to blossom. Herr Wittsack made us laugh. He thought up jokes, posed and pulled so many funny faces that we could not stop laughing all the way there.

We had a picnic of sandwiches, rolls, cakes and coffee,

and I soon made my way to the water as I loved swimming. I had a swimming costume, so I changed in the bushes, and then swam along the river. It was not so warm, but I loved being in the water. It made me feel free and in control. I returned, pale from the cold, but I was happy. Everyone admired my ability to swim, and I began to feel like a different person. Herr Wittsack made everyone laugh again, and I joined in and had a hearty laugh, too. In fact, I could not remember the last time I had laughed so much. We continued, all the way back, and in the subway people looked at us with surprise, and at times with suspicion. After all, half of Berlin was now standing in ruins, and every minute brought the threat of more air raids, but the German mindset also had to try and appreciate the present and live it to the full.

We returned home and were happy. I was sent to fetch some ice cream and brought a whole bowl, with jam, for each person. It was an enjoyable and fitting end to a lovely day – the only free day we ever had together.

They say that after laughter the crying will come, and so it was on the following day when I fell ill. My swimming had caused some inflammation and I was in terrible pain. But that was not all. Just before dinner, the police arrived and told us we all had to go to the Gestapo Headquarters in the Alexanderplatz.

'Why? What have we done?' demanded Frau Wittsack.

'You will see, madam,' replied the policeman sternly.

Herr Wittsack was worried. His sense of humour had now gone, and he was subdued and quiet. He murmured: 'Is it because of my accounts? I wonder. Huh? The Gestapo?'

I was frightened. What would become of me if they found out that I had escaped from the camp and that Herr Wittsack had employed me? Would all of us be punished? They say that fear has big eyes. I noticed how frightened everybody was.

The Gestapo Headquarters was a huge building with many floors and with prison cells at the top. We were led into a large room and left to sit on wooden benches. Officers walked up and down and were dressed in their horrible uniforms. Frau Wittsack looked subdued, Lottie was quiet but Annie was at the point of panicking. Daisy, however, was more like a little cockerel – foolish and proud, though even in

265

her beady eyes I detected a hint of fear. We sat there for a long time, because that is how the German police tormented people.

Herr Wittsack grew angry and muttered loudly enough for the Gestapo to hear him: 'We feed the starving population, now dinner won't be ready in time'.

Finally, after many hours, we were told to go into another room. An officer in full uniform sat at a desk. He looked at us with piercing eyes and we looked at him – a horrible-looking, stern man. He asked the name of my boss and then stood up and began to shout:

'You know that Germany is bleeding and fighting for her survival, and you, a pure German, dare to laugh. Why were you and your staff laughing in the subway yesterday? Why were you rejoicing when everyone else was crying? Are you glad that Germany is falling? Where were you going yesterday?'

Herr Wittsack would not have been more surprised if lightning had struck him. Relief and calm returned to his face.

'My restaurant feeds people, and we are going to be late serving dinner. As for the laughter, we took a day off by the river, and I made my staff laugh. It is my fault, Herr Inspector. I am rather a humorous person. I work hard, but when I am off duty I let off steam.' He then raised his hand to point at me and continued: 'Normally, I shout, and that girl will tell you so, otherwise, I argue.' And he pointed at his wife. 'But I can make them all laugh when I am free from worry, and we do have many worries, Herr Inspector. My restaurant was bombed recently. We have repaired it and we are now serving the public again.'

The Gestapo officer paced from left to right, behind his desk.

'Don't you know what is happening at the Front? Don't you have a son in the army? You made the whole carriage laugh? Damn you, you fool! I could have you put in a concentration camp! I could have you executed! You, a humorous person! To hell with your humour! Be glad that you are alive, idiot! Go, and don't let me hear again about your fits of laughter! It is your job that has saved you! Go! All of you!'

The door was opened by a policeman and we were

escorted back to the street. We breathed a sigh of relief.

'Donnerswetter!' Herr Wittsack swore. He wiped his forehead. Sweat was pouring down his big, round face: 'You can't even laugh nowadays! Fancy that! Huh! The Gestapo! Damn them!' He was talking to himself, but we could hear him quite clearly.

Everyone had fears of their own, but nobody knew of mine, or of the relief I was feeling. The hard work at the Wittsacks now seemed like work at a holiday camp after a visit to the Gestapo's Headquarters. Had they found out who I was, I would have been imprisoned, sent to a concentration camp, or worse. Fear aside, I was ill and had to see a doctor. I was allowed to go after we had finished dinner. A female doctor examined me and gave me some medicine. I was in pain, but I had to continue working, and put up with it quietly.

Over several days, my condition improved. We continued to work hard and the number of customers increased, but the bombings continued, too, and the Berliners became gloomier. Rumours spread that the Front was now on German soil and moving closer. Some people resigned themselves to the inevitable fate of being occupied by the Russians and even said that the Russians were not so bad. Some even admitted that they had a red flag hidden away somewhere. I listened to one woman who had only just recently praised the Nazi regime and Hitler. It was odd to see how the instinct for survival began to change her attitude. I listened quietly to several such conversations and never said a word. I had to think of what I was going to do.

Mobilisation was announced and Herr Wittsack was called up to go to the Front. His protests and arguments about the importance of his job were now of no use at all: every able-bodied man had to go. His wife packed a small case for him and his family tearfully said goodbye. We all wished him good luck and promised to keep the restaurant going.

It was strange to see how differently everything was done when Herr Wittsack was no longer there to shout or make remarks. I worked peacefully and noticed how the quality of my work improved. My nerves were calm, and I could even afford to smile at the others. The head cook joked, and the waitresses smiled, too. Even Frau Wittsack seemed more relaxed and began to treat everybody with more respect. We all worked hard and the kitchen was able to keep up with the public's demands.

There were more air raids and the bombs continued to fall. The radio and the electricity supply would normally be cut off, and we would have to guess at what was happening. During the raids, we hid in the cellar next door, and on coming out we would look at the clouds of smoke rising over Berlin. We were not hit again, and life continued with more queues of hungry people. The saucepans of soup would quickly empty. I washed them, and I washed them thoroughly. Daisy was amazed at the way I did this because the saucepans were so big I could have easily sat inside them.

One day, news spread that the Gestapo Headquarters had been bombed, and the prisoners on the top floor had been killed in their cells. Again, I dreaded to think what would have happened to me had they known who I was. Again, I thanked God that I had not been detained there, and I continued with my work.

Then, one night, I heard a knock at my window which looked out onto the yard. I pulled back the curtain and jumped suddenly. It was the terrified face of Herr Wittsack.

'Tell my wife I am here,' he said in a trembling voice.

I went to the back of the building and woke Frau Wittsack. She jumped out of bed and opened the apartment door. I shall never forget the sight: Herr Wittsack was now a broken man – thin and dirty. His head fell to his wife's shoulder and he wept.

'Oh, Emma, Emma. What has happened to us? We are finished... Everybody is dead... So many have died... I escaped... We cannot fight any longer... Everything has collapsed...' He continued to cry like a small boy.

'Now, now, come into the bedroom,' Frau Wittsack replied.

She led him into the bedroom and he slept for days before he recovered and returned to work. He never stopped telling us stories about the battle in Frankfurt. The whole army had been obliterated and most of his friends had been killed or wounded – left without legs or arms, or else they were blinded or burnt.

'We are finished,' he said. 'The Front will be here in no

time and we have no way of escape. The Russians will come, and that's for certain. We will be occupied.' Everybody fell silent. The waitresses no longer smiled at the customers.

'What will happen to us?' everyone asked.

'I see a bleak future,' said Lottie.

At my next meeting with Ivan, I told him everything I knew, and he said that we would have to escape from Berlin.

'We have to go. I will not stay under Russian occupation.'

I was heartbroken. Day after day I went on with my job, wondering what was going to happen. Herr Wittsack was being good to me now. He had changed completely since his return, and I no longer felt like his slave. He didn't shout at me. On the contrary, he started to talk to me as if I was a member of his family. He surprised me when he asked about my shoe size because he was going to buy me a pair of boots.

'You can stay with us, just like one of our daughters,' he said simply.

His offer now shocked me. That's why he wanted to buy me some boots. He wanted me to stay. After all, when the Russians came I would be his shield to defend him, and he would want me to work in his kitchen forever. Oh, no, Herr Wittsack, I thought. No. This is not why I am here. I will not stay with you and I don't want any boots from you. Sensibly, I kept my thoughts to myself.

One afternoon, after finishing work Elsa, the head cook, invited me to her home. I agreed to go with her. She was very friendly and told me that she always carried all her jewellery and money in a little case should her house be bombed when she was at work. She trusted me to carry it for her. As we sat inside the bus, we never stopped talking. She told me her whole life story, and I was so deep in conversation that when we had to change buses I forgot her precious case on the seat. We only realised after the bus had gone. Panic struck us both, but she did not reproach me. Patiently, she found a policeman who arranged for the bus to be stopped: the case was later picked up from the transport office.

I was sorry for what had happened, and I was grateful that the evening worked out so well. We slept peacefully that night, and the following morning, we returned to work together. We had grown closer. In the mornings, Elsa made sure I had a large piece of bread before I started. I never went hungry before eleven o'clock again.

Time passed. Autumn soon gave way to winter. Snow fell, and then Christmas came. The buildings around us were in ruin, but everybody celebrated. The restaurant was clean and polished. A Christmas tree was delivered by some of Herr Wittsack's friends and we decorated it, placing it in the middle of the dining room. The restaurant looked festive and bright.

The Germans organised a party and gave their presents to each other on Christmas Eve. Little Yuta was there with her mother, as were other relatives and friends of the Wittsacks. The waitresses wore their best clothes and everybody was in festive mood. I wore my best, black dress with the silvery string of beads and joined in the festivities. When everyone sang, I sang too. Annie noticed that I was a soprano and asked me to sing a song for them:

'Sing one of your songs,' she said. 'Sing the one you like best. Sing a Ukrainian song!'

I hesitated, but then they all began to request it. Overcoming my hesitancy I began to sing. They applauded me and asked for more. Smiling, I sang one song after another. I felt self-assured, even though I was surrounded by strangers, but I noticed that Annie was crying.

'Why are you crying, Annie?'

'Oh, you have reminded me of my home life.'

'Are you from Ukraine?' I asked sympathetically.

'My parents were, and I lived there.'

Finally, I started to understand something about the real Annie – why she had been so friendly to me since shortly after my arrival, and why she had almost panicked at the Gestapo Headquarters. Nobody else knew who she really was either. She was thirty and must have come to Germany before the War, but deep down inside it was now clear that she was one of ours, and my song had awoken all that was dear in her heart from her childhood and youth. After that evening, I looked at her in a different light. I was rather sorry for her, and was friendlier than before. She reminded me that I should never want to forget my homeland as she had done, and she now smiled at me with a mixture of warmth and sadness.

Christmas Eve was jolly and happy. We all held hands

and sang together. We danced in a circle, and when twelve o'clock came, we exchanged our presents. To my surprise, Frau Wittsack gave me a set of lovely, warm underwear. I treasured it for many years to come. Daisy gave me perfume, and little Yuta gave me her photograph and some handkerchiefs. For that one festive Christmas night of 1945 we forgot there was a war on. The Front was moving closer, and the future was bleak and uncertain, but we celebrated the birth of Christ – the greatest event in the history of mankind – as one whole Christian family. Christmas made life beautiful again and brought light into some of the greyest days of hardship we had ever known. By the New Year, the paths of our lives would lead us away in different directions, and each of us would meet with a different fate. Some of us would live and some of us would die, but that Christmas Eve would live in our memories forever.

Chapter 27

Christmas came and went, and the bombings resumed. We worked hard between the air raids and were always happy to have survived. Whenever we met, Ivan talked incessantly about escaping from Berlin.

'We will perish here,' he said. 'Once the War is over we can decide what to do, but first of all we have to escape from here. Nobody is allowed to leave the city, but the Ukrainian Relief Committee is preparing to evacuate and we can go with them. You must get ready.'

When I told Herr Wittsack that I wanted to leave with my boyfriend he was furious. He shouted at me, and the others were shocked by my plans, too.

'How dare you go away? I will report you to the Gestapo!' He shouted furiously, at the top of his voice. He then sneered at me, sarcastically: 'With your boyfriend, huh? How well do you know him? He is a stranger to you. He will cheat on you and leave you, and then what? You are going nowhere, I am telling you.' He then spoke to his wife, came back, and demanded that I give him my passport.

Patiently, I withstood his outburst, and despite my silence I became more and more determined to make my plans to leave. I fetched the passport from my room and I gave it to him. I cried all that afternoon and said nothing to anyone.

The next time I met Ivan, I told him what had happened. He was sad and thoughtful: 'You will have to leave them secretly,' he said, simply.

'But what about my passport?' I asked.

'We will have to think of what to do. We may be able to get some form of temporary document. Or, you can say you were bombed and you lost it.' He was always so positive and confident in his plan to take me with him that I could not possibly doubt that his intentions were honourable. 'In any case, don't worry,' he added with a smile, 'there's time yet.'

The days passed quickly and we had to come up with a plan for my next escape. I worked hard without saying a word to anyone. In fact, I then had another idea. I started to tell everybody that I would not go away, and that I didn't know my friend well enough to do so. I pretended to be happy doing my work. Two weeks passed, and the matter seemed to have been completely forgotten. I continued to work hard – without a single break, but I continued to meet Ivan early each morning when taking Mampa for a walk.

We met in a small square not far from the restaurant. Mampa was happy to run around, sniffing at the bushes. Ivan told me that the Ukrainian Relief Committee was almost ready to leave Berlin. We had to attempt the escape on the following day.

I would have to get up early in the morning, when it was still dark, and open my window. Ivan would then take my case away. Then, I had to continue working as normal until dinner, after which I would ask for the afternoon off. I would then have to try and ask for my passport back because no one was allowed to walk through Berlin without one.

We did exactly as planned. I had a sleepless night, waiting for dawn and a scratching sound on the windowpane. I opened the window and handed over my suitcase. I felt like a burglar, even though the possessions were my own. It was a risk. Someone could have seen me from one of the hundreds of windows overlooking the yard. There could have been a postman doing the early morning round, but we were lucky. Quietly, I closed the window and went back to bed. I did not hear any commotion so I knew that Ivan had gone away safely.

I locked the wardrobe and kept the key in my pocket just in case anyone looked inside and found it empty. I dressed in my best underwear, and left some old clothes in the drawer. I then went to work as though nothing had happened. Mampa jumped up at me, excitedly. It was a busy morning, and we all worked as hard as usual. By three o'clock in the afternoon, even Herr Wittsack had noticed how hard I had worked and said:

'You can finish, girl! You have worked hard.'

'May I have the rest of the afternoon off please?' I asked casually. 'I haven't had a break for almost two weeks.'

'Yes, you can go out for a short while,' he said kindly.

'Thank you.'

I went to my room, washed and changed and wrote a letter to Herr and Frau Wittsack. I thanked them for having me and expressed my regrets for having to leave them in this way. There was no alternative for me as my destiny was not to be with them, and I had to follow my own path in life. At the end of the letter, I said goodbye and wished them well. I put the letter under the tablecloth on a little table which stood by the door of my room. I knew they would find it there, but not until after I had gone.

Ready to leave, I saw Herr Wittsack sitting with his family at the round table in the restaurant area. They were having afternoon coffee and talked loudly. From time to time, they burst into laughter. It was a sign that they were in a good mood. I went over to him and asked politely:

'May I have my passport, please?'

Everyone looked at each other, but they knew I was not allowed to go out without it. Herr Wittsack stood up, therefore, went to his room and brought it back.

'Here you are. Don't be long.'

Frau Wittsack looked at me suspiciously, but said nothing. Her husband was the boss and everybody obeyed him.

'Where are you going?' Daisy asked eagerly.

'I am going to see my friends,' I said honestly.

'That's good. You go,' Herr Wittsack said, and he turned back to face his family. He ignored me, as though I had been interfering.

'Goodbye,' I said quietly and normally.

273

I went to the door. Of course, I thought they would stop me there and then. I could not believe that I would be out of their power. With my passport in my bag, I was free once again. It was only when I reached the subway that my heart stopped pounding.

I went to Ivan's place of work and found him waiting for me. Everything had been packed and nobody else was there. There were only bare tables and cupboards, and some papers on the floor.

'We shall leave tomorrow morning because they will be looking for you tonight. It is best if you sleep here. Nobody will look for you at this address,' he said confidently, 'but I'm afraid you'll have to sleep on one of the tables.'

'Will I be here alone?' I asked anxiously.

'No. I shall be around, finishing the packing.'

It was very strange. On my first night of my freedom I slept on a bare table. It was hard, and my bones ached but I was glad to be on a road to somewhere new. I knew I was taking big risks – to trust Ivan; to escape from my workplace; to escape from Berlin. However, I stepped into this new adventure with confidence. I could not see any other way. Berlin was burning and the Soviet Army was about to take over. I tried not to think of what might happen if I was caught with papers deemed to be "false".

In the morning, we boarded a train to West Germany. We reached Wasserleben, a village near to the Harz Mountains. We had to say we were Berliners and had to speak with a Berlin accent. I could do that, but the way the Germans spoke to us was very difficult to understand.

Ivan had been working with the Ukrainian Relief Committee in Berlin. It was an organisation which had helped Ukrainian prisoners of war, and Ukrainian Ostarbeiters, with Germany's laws. With the approach of the Soviet Army, they had been given permission to leave Berlin with all of their paperwork, their library, and food – which had been prepared for distribution. I knew very little about this work as Ivan had never talked about it. Now, I began to meet well-educated West Ukrainians who knew that I had escaped from an Ostarbeiter camp. They looked down at me, and despite my perfect Ukrainian and German pronunciations, they remained unapproachable. Because of that, I treated them like they

274

treated me. Ivan was indifferent to them. He ignored them and began to spend as much time with me as he could.

We had to split up. I was taken to a farmer's house where I was given some supper. There was a friendly old lady there with her daughter – a woman of about my age. There was also another young woman, her daughter-in-law. She had taken over the running the household. She was brisk and efficient, but she looked upon me as an unwelcome intruder.

Ivan, meanwhile, hid away in another farmhouse and worked in the local school hall using everything the Ukrainian Relief Committee had brought with them.

It was February, and the weather was very cold. I was fed at the farmhouse, but the young woman, whose husband was away fighting at the Front, was mean, and she cooked very meagre dinners. I was hungry and befriended the older woman. She was tall and well-built but she had to obey her daughter-in-law. I noticed that she was frightened of her. Sometimes when the younger of the two was out of the kitchen, the elder would hide a thick slice of bread under her apron and bring it to me. I was very grateful to her.

The daughter-in-law was about my age, and one day she saw me reading a book and said:

'I have never read a book in my life.'

I was astonished: 'Why ever not?' I replied.

'My mother won't let me read. She says books are dirty, and unless she has read one herself she will not allow me to read one. She never has the time to read any, so I never will either.'

'How strange,' I said, 'books are my best friends.' She lowered her eyes and said nothing else.

I passed the time by reading, knitting and sewing. I learned new German words and began writing German in old Gothic script. After all the work I had done in my life, I was suddenly left with nothing to do, but I could not just sit there without any work. I had a piece of grey, woollen material in my case and I decided to make a pleated skirt. I had never learned to sew but I painstakingly cut it out, tacked it, and then sat by the window for hours. I sewed, carefully making very fine and accurate stitches. I was amazed at how well I could do.

The skirt turned out wonderfully and my farm friends

could not believe that I had done it by hand. They knew I was a former student, and a refugee from Berlin, so they did not expect me to do their farming. Nonetheless, I became familiar with the farmyard and knew where everything was. This served me well as one sunny afternoon, when I went out of the house, I saw the old lady go into the shed where the cows were. I did not know what she was doing. Maybe she was shifting the hay or clearing the floor, but then suddenly I heard her scream and shout for help. There was no one about so I ran into the shed and saw a cow moving towards her with its horns lowered. In a split second, I took hold of a pitchfork and pointed it at the cow. My sudden reaction worked. The cow backed away and stood still and we both left the shed, sighing with relief.

'You saved my life, girl,' she said.

'I don't know how I did it,' I replied.

'You were very brave. That's how. Thank you.'

'I am glad I was there for you.' I smiled at her, and we both knew that we would never forget the incident.

February turned to March, and bad news began to spread through the village. The bombings continued and we could see the smoke and red skies above Halberstadt, Braunschweig and other towns which were burning in the distance. I was very frightened. My nerves began to completely shatter just as soon as I could hear the sound of a plane. I would run into a field because there were no shelters in the village. I ran, and ran, until I found a ditch and fell in. I then covered my head with my hands to drown the sound. I don't know how long I would lie there, but only when everything was quiet again would I lift my head, get up, and walk back slowly to the farm. The village was never bombed, but many soldiers would pass through. They were mostly Germans who did not want to fight any longer.

'We have lost the War. There is no point in fighting. My home is occupied by the Americans so I'm going back there,' one of them said.

I remembered the day when the Germans had marched into our home town of Krolevets. They were fierce, frightening and seemingly invincible. Finally, they had been conquered. How weak they appeared to be now.

I had been in Germany for three years, but it seemed like

an eternity. So much had happened, and I had suffered many changes. My homesickness returned, and I asked myself what I was doing there. I wanted to be at home, but I also had to think of what would happen to me if I was home. I struggled with my thoughts and was sad. I preferred to be left alone. It was only when Ivan came to see me that I recognised the reality of the situation, and then I would feel alive once more.

As usual, Ivan was cheerful and very talkative. He did not seem to have any doubts or regrets about his chosen path. He was adamant that he would never return to live under a Communist regime in Ukraine. He lived in the present and made plans for the future, but he was always careful not to say "our future" as he knew how I continued to suffer. He felt that I had hesitated over our relationship, despite his help. Only once, when we were in a tram heading out of Berlin, he said: 'Now you are mine,' but I didn't answer him. He seemed to know that I had to choose between my parents and country, or exile with him for the rest of our lives. He knew that it was a big decision for me to have to take, and he did not make the decision for me or beg me to stay with him. I knew that he was always giving me the freedom of choice, and for that I was always grateful.

Meanwhile, Ivan had made some new friends – Ostarbeiters in the village farms. His old friends ignored and avoided them, but Ivan made sure he talked to everybody. Soon, they started to come to my room where they would tell us about their lives and their work on the farms. They were all from Ukraine, mostly from East Ukraine. They wanted to know about the Front which was rapidly approaching, and they guessed that the Americans or the English would soon be taking over. They talked about their future. The girls all longed for home, but they were frightened of Stalin's persecutions. I knew they were as hesitant as I was about the future.

Spring approached. The pastures and meadows turned green. Deep down, I longed to live at home, in my country, with my parents, and with my people. Perhaps they worried about me too, and longed to see me. Perhaps they also prayed that I would return to them. Yet here I was, despite such prayers, choosing to turn away from them and losing all hope of ever seeing them again. The pain made me withdraw from the real world. I sat by the window for hours and looked across the fields and green meadows. It was as though I was in a hollow body with no soul. I was living in a divided world. Cruelty and tyranny existed out there and the sense of injustice prevailed. My thoughts protested. I would never lose hope of returning home: not now, not ever. That hope would live in me until the end of my days, no matter how far my journey would take me.

In Ivan I had a good friend. He was humorous, optimistic, kind and true to me. He was an understanding man. He was also mature in his future outlook. The spring days became warmer and we went for walks together. On one side of the village we found a beautiful meadow with a quiet river meandering through the trees. It became our favourite place and we spent many hours there, walking and talking amidst the natural beauty. Ivan had such a wide range of experience and knew so many stories that he was always himself and talked endlessly, jumping from one subject to another. Tall and strong and very handsome with his black, curly hair, thick eyebrows and slim, oblong face, he was a miracle in my life and I clung to him with all my being. Our friendship grew, as did my trust and faith in him. It came to the point where I could not imagine life without him.

It was almost Easter, and I loved Easter wherever I was, and I had to have an Easter cake and prepare all our traditional food. I talked to Ivan about it. He promised to ask others for some help. In Easter week he brought some flour, a few eggs, some butter and milk. Everything was so precious that I was frightened of spoiling everything. Perhaps my Easter cake would not turn out right. I had never baked in my life, so I decided to have a trial run. I mixed a small quantity of pastry and yeast, remembering how my mother had done it. I lit the stove in my room and baked it in a small, metal beaker. The smell from my secret baking wafted across the room, and not wanting the landlady to know about my experiment, I opened the window. Passers-by remarked on the lovely smell, but they could not tell where it was coming from. The minute, golden paska came out of the stove having risen beautifully. It tasted really good, too. I became more confident.

I thought of my mother constantly and the way in which

278

she used to bake. I imagined her standing there. Tears rolled down my cheeks. My baking was a success. The German ladies admired it, and they asked me what I had used to glaze the cake to make it so golden and shiny.

On Easter Saturday, I made hand-painted Easter eggs. Ivan bought a rabbit from a village boy, which I then roasted. I took a piece of white cloth from my case and covered the table. I then added some freshly cut flowers, the paska, eggs and the rabbit. We even had some salami. Ivan invited two new friends he had made in Berlin. They were single men and when they came into my room and saw the table they were amazed.

'Look at that,' one of them said, 'you would not believe that she had lived under a Communist regime for twenty years. Everything is just like it was at home.' We sat down and enjoyed the traditional feast which all our people enjoyed after fasting for the six weeks of Lent.

News of my Easter preparations quickly reached the people who had come with us from Berlin. Until then, they had ignored me. One of the ladies had bought a cake from the bakery, and in the afternoon we were invited to a party in the school hall which was used as an office. I put on the new skirt I had made, and my pink blouse. I was greeted very warmly, though I was not convinced of their sincerity. I behaved in a dignified manner. Their Easter cake was poor compared to mine, and the women had only managed to make some sandwiches. We drank lemonade and I tried to join in the conversation. One of them spoke some English, and I wanted to know the English word for Easter. It was the first English word I learned, and after this "Easter party", I was accepted into their company. It was not that Ivan and I were eager to join them, but at least I knew I had some new friends if ever I needed them.

Then, something so tremendously wonderful happened that everything else seemed to pale into insignificance. It was the second day of Easter. We did not have radios or newspapers, but somehow on that bright spring morning, when the Church was celebrating the Feast of Our Lady, news spread through the village that the War had ended. A treaty had been signed and war in Europe was over. I took a very deep breath. There would be no more bombing, no more shooting, and no more fighting. I ran straight into Ivan's arms and laughed, and cried, with joy.

'The War is over,' I repeated again and again.

'Yes,' he said sadly, already one step ahead of me, 'it has ended, but Ukraine is still occupied.'

'But there will be no more fighting,' I said. 'I don't think I can take any more.'

'Vera, we will have to fight for our rights for the rest of our lives,' he added. I did not fully take in what he had said, but I realised later that he was right.

It was not long before the village was occupied by American troops. We were free: free to think; free to build our future; free to live without fear of losing our lives. It was a wonderful feeling, and strolling along the river and across the green meadows, we were truly happy. We were two devoted friends who had come through the War and were spared to live and continue with our lives. We thanked God that we were alive and well. It was the 8th of May 1945. There were no celebrations in the village, and no fireworks, but life and peace were finally together again.

Spring was becoming warmer and warmer and he had to face some realities. The workers in the village were planning to return home, and they often held discussions in my room. They asked what the Russians would do to those who returned.

'We are not free,' Ivan repeated, over and over again. 'Our war is not over. Ukraine is still enslaved, and until our country is free and independent, you will not see me returning home.' I understood him. I loved him, and yet the love for my parents and my country continued to torment my soul.

Ivan's co-workers from the Ukrainian Relief Committee had all decided to stay in the West. They had no doubts and Ivan made sure I mixed with them. With the end of the War, I was no longer simply seen as an Ostarbeiter who had made her escape. I was a Ukrainian girl from the East, and they soon wanted to know more about me.

There was a swimming pool in the village where we all went swimming. I knew that I would have to face Ivan's colleagues and be equal to them, and the best place for this was in the water. I swam like a fish, but they merely splashed themselves before sitting down again on rugs by the pool. To overcome my shyness, I would knit or sew something as we talked. I would soon have a part to play in Ivan's community of West Ukrainians. I had lived under Russian rule, and they had lived under Polish and Czechoslovakian rule, but I could see this was going to be my new social group for the future.

We heard about the Yalta conference. Germany was soon to be divided between the American, Russian and English powers. Our village was situated in the Russian zone. Panic struck, and people fled westwards. Those workers who decided to return home made banners with slogans to greet the Soviet Army and started to praise Stalin. Ivan's committee prepared to evacuate, ready to head to the nearest town in the English zone.

Ivan came to me early in the morning to ask what I would do. The worst part about his question was that he didn't tell me what I should do. He didn't tell me to join him or say we were going. He simply asked if I was going with them. He knew of my hesitation, my divided love and my uncertain feelings, but the decision was mine. He did not plead with me, either. He just wanted me to be free to make my own choice. That made matters difficult for me. I was split in two and could not decide, but I had to be quick because the van with his fellow workers would be leaving shortly. I had seconds in which to direct my whole future one way or another. I hesitated, and again I begged him to return home but he said no, and said I could do what I liked. I was still free. I knew this would now be my final decision. If I went with him, that was it, I would never be able to return home. I would never see my parents and my country again.

I hesitated until the very last moment, and finally packed my belongings. Forlorn and in a daze, I followed Ivan to the waiting van. I was grateful to him for not making a single comment about my hesitancy.

We headed westwards, and the tale in the van was of the Soviet Army's rapid approach. They were taking one village after another. The great powers at Yalta had decided the fate of millions. Masses of refugees were following us in cars, and on foot. They were all fleeing from the Communists.

By midday, we arrived at a town called Goslar, in the Harz Mountains. It was the first time in my life that I had seen mountains. They were almost as high as the clouds, and

I longed to climb up and explore them. I wanted to climb to the very top. We were to settle there. The town was full of refugees, and there was no accommodation left except for a large school hall. We all settled on the floor and were glad for a small space. Young and old were mixed together: professors, teachers, writers, scholars, labourers, farm workers and children.

I felt better being with so many others who had also fled from the Russians. I was young, and the love I had felt for my parents was so powerful that it had outweighed reason. The hundreds of people around me knew better than I did. I submitted to my fate, and prepared to share it with them: they had suffered, too.

Ivan continued to be cheerful. He enjoyed being in a crowd and again talked to others endlessly. I could hear his voice from one end of the hall to the other, but I knew he cared for me. He soon returned with some bread.

The following day, Ivan went through the town to look for a room and found a small attic. I moved in. It was in a terraced house on the outskirts of Goslar. It was on the third floor and had one dormer window, a bed, a table and two chairs. There was a small stove for heating and cooking, a bowl for washing and one saucepan for cooking. It was small and simple yet I was very happy to be on my own after sleeping on the school's floor. Ivan found himself another room, somewhere on the other side of Goslar. I never saw what it looked. The life we shared revolved around my room.

After settling in and unpacking my things, we went for a walk. There was plenty of beautiful scenery just behind the house. The short street led to green meadows and valleys that rose slowly up towards the mountains which were covered with thick forests. I had missed nature so much those last few years that I ran like a child and headed straight towards them, but they were not as close as I thought. I returned breathlessly to Ivan who was walking with dignity along the road. From the look in his eyes I knew that he wanted me to be dignified too, but I laughed like a child and this time I chatted away, happy to be free to enjoy nature's beauty. Cows grazed in the pastures, shepherds blew their horns, and other couples walked along the road. The sun shone brightly and illuminated the mountain tops and valleys. It was beautiful, and I did not mind staying in a small and simple attic if I could also spend time out here.

Goslar was a town to which many hospitals had evacuated their patients during the War, and it had not been bombed. There were no ruins like there were in the other towns we had travelled through, but there were hundreds upon hundreds of refugees. Each nationality gathered together in different parts of the town. Ivan soon found a group of Ukrainians and somehow they found a large meeting room. There was a very learned couple amongst them who organised the meetings, of whom the wife prepared a bulletin of the latest world news. There were discussions and lively conversations, and I soaked everything up. My mind began to reawaken after the years of work camp life.

My body and soul had been battered, and I still did not know what was happening, or what might happen next. It would take a long time to fully get used to this freedom. The only blessing I had was Ivan, and I clung to him more and more. Our friendship deepened and grew more and more sincere. He would come to my room and tell me the latest news. We scraped food together and I cooked soup from whatever we could find. It was a desperate situation. There was no money in circulation and there was nothing left to buy in the town. People simply exchanged what they owned for food in the villages, so the struggle to survive continued. Finally, UNRA – The United Nations Relief and Rehabilitation Administration – came to our help. A shop opened in which we could exchange newly-allocated ration tickets for parcels of food.

It was a great joy to receive the first food parcel: it had proper food. I went to my room, locked the door, and having real, white bread and real butter, I started to eat. I loved it and did not want anybody to disturb me. I ate, and I ate to my heart's content. There was also some coffee, cigarettes, tins of meat, fish and jars of jam and jelly. It was all so precious, after years of hunger and malnutrition. We blessed UNRA and all who had organised their wonderful help.

Everyone became more cheerful and eagerly awaited news of our future. There were rumours that the West would fight the East and America would fight Communism whilst it was still weak. Everybody believed that Communism would

283

not last. We believed that sooner or later Ukraine would be free, which would allow us to return home. We were the displaced people of Europe, and we never knew where events would lead us to next. In fact, we were actually aware of more conferences of world powers, more negotiations, and the division of Europe, but there was no sign of war on Communism. It meant exile, but where? As the weeks and months passed we wanted to settle properly.

A priest came into our community, and we hired a beautiful large church in the middle of Goslar. Sunday services started, and hundreds of people attended and found consolation in their prayers. There was a choir, and we both joined the group of voluntary singers. There were even some professional opera singers, and an elderly choirmaster. People from all walks of life joined in. Someone even started publishing books and a small newsletter, but there were also the gossipers and a crowd of idle listeners.

My marriage was on the agenda, but Ivan kept silent. Every man appreciates his freedom and does not want to part with it easily. Some of his colleagues had already married and teased him. I began to wonder if we would be married at all. My doubts grew, but I did not show it and I kept our friendship sincere, without any selfish tricks or needless flirtations. But my heart continued to be full of mixed emotions: homesickness on the one hand, and my feelings for Ivan on the other. As the weeks passed, homesickness caused many people to return home. News spread of one person after another returning to Soviet repatriation camps. Soviet propaganda had called upon them to return, promising mercy and a good life. Then, a conference agreement was reached between the superpowers calling for all Soviet citizens to return home, but if necessary, they would be forcibly repatriated. Panic struck everyone who did not want to return. The church was filled with people praying for guidance and a safe future.

In the house where I lived, there was an elderly gentleman, his daughter and two grandchildren. A Ukrainian lady worked for them as a servant. The gentleman was a widower and treated the servant as his new wife. They were not married, and everyone knew of their relationship. They were kind and friendly people, and they told us that if we

284

wanted to use their ground floor accommodation, which had a large hall and kitchen, we would always be welcome. They liked Ivan and he and the elderly man often talked late into the night. Shura, the Ukrainian lady, served coffee and I talked to her in another corner of the room, or else outside in their beautiful garden. It was summer and the sweet peas were in bloom. They had a wonderful scent which reminded me of home. Shura noticed my sad face.

'Are you crying?' she asked quietly.

'I'm longing to be at home. How I would love to be at home,' I explained

'Your home is where you heart is. There is no life at home for those such as us. Stalin won't forgive any of us for having lived in Germany.'

'Oh, Shura,' I signed, 'all the Stalins in the world can't stop my heart from aching. I love my home, my parents and Ukraine so much.'

'Are you going to get married?' she asked. 'We all feel the same way, but we have to get on with our lives and you have a good friend.'

She was right, but my heart still ached. I was sad and quiet when we returned upstairs. Ivan was cheerful. He was always cheerful after having a long conversation with someone. Suddenly, he put his arms round me and asked me quietly and gently:

'Will you be my wife? Shall we get married?'

I looked into his lively, hazel eyes and I saw his hesitation, his anxious face and his uncertain voice. I realised how foolish I had been. I had doubted him all the time. I smiled gently, and he kissed me. At the same time, we both decided that there was no other way than to bind our lives together, forever.

Chapter 28

I was certain. No matter what else the future had in store, we would be married.

'We shall have a fabulous wedding,' I said.

'But how can we do it? We have no money, no food and no clothes,' Ivan replied.

'I can do it!' I replied with such an assurance that I even

surprised myself.

We already had a circle of friends in the town. We had the choir, friends who came with us from Berlin, and several other new friends we had made along the way. So, we wrote a list of guests and it numbered more than thirty.

'I shall hire a dress. Shura will tell me where I can find one, and I shall go to the exchange shop with the cigarettes and buy a pair of shoes – but they must be white or silvery.'

'What about the food?' asked Ivan asked looking worried, 'and what about the room?'

'Shura said that we can use the sitting room and kitchen, and as for the food, I will go to the village and get some by exchanging our coffee and cigarettes.'

'I am not going to let you do that,' replied Ivan. 'You are going to be my wife, and that means I will not let you go out there and trade.'

'Oh, yes I will! Anyway, what's wrong with that? We need the food, and we have the goods to exchange with people who have exactly what we need. I don't see anything wrong with that.' It was almost a quarrel, but I won quite comfortably and had my way.

We went to the registry office and to the priest to book a date. The registry office could fit us in on the 18th of July, but the priest was not free until the 28th.

'Then it looks as if we shall have to have two weddings,' said Ivan humorously.

'No, we shall have our proper wedding day on the 28th when we can be married in church,' I said, again with certainty. Having been shy, timid and uncertain about my situation, my surroundings, and my future for such a long time, I now discovered a new stronger self, alive inside of me.

It was the end of June and we had enough time to prepare. Thanks to Shura, I hired a beautiful wedding dress and veil. It was a straight dress made of pure, white satin and was covered with masses of transparent lace. The square-cut neckline was adorned with satin bells. It was a necessity and a dress worthy of the occasion. Although I had never worn anything so beautiful, I was not particularly overjoyed. Although the dress was not really mine, I had first dreamt of having this great occasion at home.

In the exchange shop I found a lovely pair of shoes. They were silver with a sling-back, and they fitted me perfectly. Then, the question of the wedding rings came. As there was no money in circulation, jewellery was only available in exchange for gold or silver. We had a silver teaspoon. So, we cleaned it, wrapped it carefully in white paper, and took it to the jeweller's shop. An old gentleman greeted us politely, and after listening to our problem he promised to make it into two rings.

'If there is any silver left I shall make you a locket,' he added with a smile. He seemed to be glad to help us, and was pleased to have some trade.

Having solved the problem of the dress and the rings, I began to plan the reception. I knew of an elderly lady and asked her to come and visit us. I asked if she would be the Lady of Honour. For the Father of Honour I chose our choirmaster, and then two girls from the choir to be my bridesmaids. Ivan chose two of his friends to be the best men, and they discussed where they could go to find some meat.

'Don't worry,' said Stefan, 'we'll get some from a farmer.'

'And I'll get some potatoes and vegetables,' said Vasyl.

On the 18th of July we went to the registry office with Stefan and Vasyl as the only witnesses of our civil marriage. I wore a navy-blue satin dress with a little white collar. A dressmaker made it from material which Ivan had given me in Berlin. We asked our best men to dinner and drank vodka to toast our official wedding. I made some varennyky – our traditional pasta dish with potatoes and cheese inside, served with sour cream. They went down well. The men praised my cooking and told Ivan what a good wife he had chosen. It was only the second time in my life that I had been under the influence of alcohol. I became gay and very witty, and soon forgot about everything other than the fact that I felt happy.

When our best men went home, we were left alone. We were both happy. We felt settled and had each other, and we were glad to have sealed a decision that both of us had been putting off. We were comfortable in the knowledge that we were now bound together for life. We were man and wife, but as we still needed the Church's blessing, I sent my official and lawfully married husband back to his apartment to wait for another two weeks.

And those two weeks proved to be very busy. Early one morning, I set off on foot and walked to the nearest village. The sky was blue, the birds were singing, and the fields were a very pretty sight in their green and blossoming glory. I had to get some food from the farmers, but I had no idea how they would treat me. I was, after all, a foreigner. Would they send me away from the village and ignore my attempts to exchange goods with them? I had never done anything like this before.

Bravely, I knocked at the door of one of the farmhouses. A man opened it, and I told him that I wanted to exchange some coffee for some eggs, butter and flour. He looked at me, and for some reason, which took me by surprise, he asked how old I was.

'You look very young,' he added, and asked me into the house. As soon as I showed his family a jar of coffee they produced some eggs and butter.

My first effort had been successful, and it made me braver. I began to knock at the best houses and asked the farmers for flour, bacon, eggs and butter in exchange for the coffee and cigarettes. Coffee was precious for the Germans. It was very expensive and very difficult to get hold of, but we had an ample supply in our UNRA parcels. I returned home triumphantly, and when Ivan came to my room that evening I showed him all the treasures I had obtained. I went to the village several more times, and by the end of the two weeks we had accumulated a very healthy store of food. I even managed to find two cotton sheets as we had no bedding with which to start our married life together.

On the eve of our wedding, I woke up early and worked all day preparing the tables in the sitting room. I helped in the kitchen where my lady of honour and the two bridesmaids were busy cooking and baking. Everything was perfectly done. The roast beef, vegetables and potatoes were prepared, ready to be cooked the following day. Two wonderful gateaux were also made with butter cream, and they were prominently displayed on the wedding table.

There was just one more thing. The flowers had not yet been delivered, and the shops were just about to close. Ivan, meanwhile, was nowhere to be seen. Knowing that I would be busy, he had gone to a choir rehearsal. Perhaps this would be the way of things to come. Although I was proud and happy to be able to do most myself, I still wanted Ivan to fetch the flowers. Luckily, he returned just in time, but for the first time ever I gave him a telling off. Obediently, he went for the flowers, but came back with a large spray of white gladioli.

'And what are those supposed to be?' I nagged. 'They were supposed to send us roses!'

'They had no roses, so I chose some gladioli. What difference does it make? They're flowers, aren't they?'

That night, I went to bed late: very late. There were still so many little things to be seen to, that I regretted having been alone. I had no sister to help me, and no mother. I felt as if I was in a dream – as though everything wasn't real – and as though I was acting out a part in a play about my life.

Our wedding day finally arrived, and it was bright and sunny. Apart from the absence of my family, the whole day was like a miracle. Early in the morning, my two bridesmaids came and dressed me, and for the whole day I was made to feel like a queen. They did not allow me to do anything except to give orders to those in the kitchen preparing the feast. There was borshch bubbling in a large pan, fried meat and vegetables in a casserole, puddings and cakes, and the two large wedding cakes which were smothered with buttercream and decorated with cherries.

My dear friend and fiancé, Ivan, arrived at half past ten with his best men – Stefan and Vasyl. All three of them wore dark suits with a white flower and ribbon pinned to their lapels. They looked smart, and my bridesmaids equalled them by wearing beautiful, pink dresses. One of them was called Natalya. She was tall and blonde with big, blue eyes and a tanned face. She was the daughter of an artist and she was lovelier than any picture that he could ever have painted. The other was Hanya. She was dark, with thick, black hair and smiling, brown eyes. They and the men added beauty to our wedding. Stefan had his smiling eyes, and the serious-looking, tall, blonde Vasyl, graced us with his kindness.

We walked to the church forming a full procession through the streets of Goslar. It must have been a lovely sight on that bright Saturday morning, the 28th of July 1945.

People came out from their houses to look at us, and British soldiers stood to attention as we passed them. It was warm as we entered the church and it was packed with our guests. There were also others there who were waiting for their weddings to be held, later that day.

Our ceremony was traditionally long and reverent. The priest bound our hands with a scarf and crowned us with glittering, gold crowns. He led us round the altar three times, and the choir sang the wonderful wedding hymn "Hosanna, rejoice!" We exchanged our wedding rings, and finally were pronounced husband and wife. We felt great joy with the blessing, the congratulations, the photographs and finally, the journey back together, arm-in-arm. Our bridesmaids, the best men and our guests walked behind us. Onlookers waved to us and wished us good luck. The soldiers saluted. We smiled and smiled again. We were very happy and kept looking at each other along the way.

The wedding reception was equally wonderful. Our Father of Honour had arranged everything perfectly. After the guests had taken their places and grace had been said, the bridesmaids served dinner. Our spoons were tied together and the guests laughed as they watched us eat our borshch from the same plate – a symbol of our togetherness. The dinner was tasty and plentiful. There were drinks, and everybody was soon very gay and happy. German children peeped in through the open windows. Later, I handed them some pieces of cake and sweets.

Someone had brought an accordion, and so the music played and we danced, but Ivan would not join in. Everybody begged him to, and I pleaded with him, but he just waved his long arms, not wanting to take that first step. I never really understood his reasons, but I suspected that a gypsy had once told him his fortune and said that he should never dance. Of course, I knew he was far less superstitious than he was stubborn, and it didn't stop me from dancing. I love dancing, and on my wedding day I danced with everybody else who was there, and the celebrations lasted late into the night.

Occasionally, when I was seated, I thought of everyone who could not be with me on my special day. I knew that I was entering into a new chapter of my life and saying farewell to all that I had previously loved. It saddened me, and tears fell from my eyes. I wiped them away and made sure I smiled at Ivan and the guests. I tried to be positive. After all, didn't every bride leave everything she had ever loved to start a new life with others?

Parting is sad, but I did not even know if my parents were still alive, and for sure, they knew nothing about me. There was no post now, and everyone was afraid to try to make contact with their loved ones because of Stalin. I relied on fate. I knew my parents would have wished me well, and they would have blessed my husband, too. After all, he had saved my life and helped me to escape from the camp and from Berlin. I prayed and asked God to bless both of them.

Finally, Ivan and I were alone together, fully wedded. We had spent years alone wandering in fear and hesitation; uncertainty and danger; poverty and homelessness. We were still just as poor, but we were happy despite everything we had been through. Just as all other young couples, we didn't worry about the future. We lived in my little attic bedroom. We used our new bedding, and we continued to use it for many years to come.

'You're my wife,' my husband said again and again on our wedding night. 'You really are. You know, I didn't think you would stay with me. I thought you would go home. I know how much you love your home, but now you are my wife.'

'Yes, I am yours now,' I whispered into his ear as I clung to him tightly. We were both very happy.

Our honeymoon was spent in the mountains. Not having any fuel with which to cook our food, we went out the next day and collected wood. It was a wonderful outing. We climbed high and soon found ourselves up above the clouds. We sang songs, and we called to each other, and we made the echoes ring far and wide. There were hardly any others around and we felt like the mountain belonged only to us. The sun shone down from above, but the rain fell from the thick, grey clouds below. It was a wonderful experience. We were free and very happy together.

We climbed down, collected some dry wood and brought two bundles home. I lit the stove and cooked some soup. I opened some of the remaining tins from the food parcels. It was now my duty to feed us and concoct as many dishes as possible from what little we had left. I did my best. I never made a dinner without soup as my mother had always taught us to eat something cooked in the middle of the day. We also had a small ration of meat each week which I would treasure like gold.

There was a tomcat which came to our room, and I always welcomed and fed it, but one day it stole our meat ration. How it managed to find its way into the cupboard I shall never know, but I found it finishing off the meat in the corridor. I was so cross that I smacked him with my hand, and shouted. He went out and never returned, but I was the one who felt I had been taught a lesson. I was sorry to lose our furry friend, but we laughed and lived the rest of the week as vegetarians.

We took an active interest in the life of our small, Ukrainian community in Goslar. There was a family living near to us, the Troyans. They were older people who had emigrated after the Russian Revolution. We referred to them as "the first emigrants". They were well-educated. The husband was an engineer and his wife was a teacher, and they had a thirteen-year-old boy. The two small rooms they rented became the centre of community information, news and gossip. They not only knew of the news from our community, but they knew the world news, too. If we wanted to know when the next church service or important gathering was to be held, we could rely on them. We loved going to see them and were always welcomed. Mrs Troyan was a dressmaker and her table was usually covered with cloth and threads, and a large sewing machine. When visitors came, however, she pushed her sewing away, set the table and entertained the guests with whatever she had stored away in the corner of the room. She cooked very tasty meals and was like a mother to us all.

One day, we heard that two girls, who had wanted to return to Ukraine, had escaped from the Russian repatriation camp and had arrived back in Goslar. They came to ask the Troyan family for shelter. One of the girls, called Maria, was Vasyl's lost love. They met each other during the War and had fallen in love, but she would not leave her parents in Ukraine for an unknown future. She had left Vasyl heartbroken. Now, she and Anna had returned to Goslar and told their story. The camp commandant and his policemen had tried to rape them. The girls in the camp had all been made to cut their hair and had reason to believe they would be sent to Siberia. Fearing the worst, Maria and Anna decided to escape having witnessed what was happening there.

I listened and trembled inside. How naïve and trusting I would have been of Soviet authority, and how glad I was that I had not made the same mistake. The girls' story convinced us that we were right to stay where we were. The wounds and pain of parting from our loved ones at home were now finally beginning to heal.

At first, Vasyl stood back and greeted Maria coolly, but they soon forgave each other and were radiant in their newly-found happiness together. Their wedding was announced and Maria soon became pregnant. Everybody rejoiced again at the happy news. I was so happy for them that I started to write a play, but there was also some serious work to be done.

Ivan was a Ukrainian political activist, and he and his friends talked about politics, endlessly. I listened passively, but when there was something to be done I was keen to help. We had a typewriter from Berlin and I was asked to type news bulletins. I did this willingly, believing that I was helping the freedom fighters, who in my imagination were always romantic.

I had finished played my part by morning. Boys would then stand below our window at pre-arranged times, and we would throw rolled-up bundles of typed papers to them. The boys caught them and waved to us with a smile. I did not take too much interest in everything that was wrapped in those papers but I was glad to help my husband and his friends. I was taking part in the counter-revolutionary work through which the most prominent Ukrainians hoped to overthrow the Russian occupants. After everything, by helping to establish an independent Ukraine, I would perhaps find my only hope of ever returning there.

The summer months were sunny and warm, and we did not have any paid work. We continued to go to the mountains and walked through the long valleys. We admired the greenery, the shepherds with their flocks of sheep, and the colourful dresses of the local girls. We longed to be alone together and climbed the highest mountain, walking through the pine trees on the way. We sang loudly and laughed with joy when we finally reached the top. Again, we stood above the clouds, and the forest, and everything on earth: our honeymoon continued.

On our return we collected berries and mushrooms as well as wood. At the UNRA shop they were still handing out food parcels, and if we needed eggs, bacon or barley I could go to the village and continue exchanging the coffee and cigarettes. However, when the parcels from UNRA suddenly stopped, we had to provide for ourselves.

I gathered nettles and sorrel leaves to make soup. My memories of the famine returned to haunt me. Life was hard again, and we were very hungry. By Whit Sunday, the shelves of our attic room were completely bare. On the Saturday we went for a walk in the mountains and foraged for our Sunday dinner. Ivan walked by my side, but as soon as we reached the forest he ventured along a path where shrubs and small trees grew in the hope of finding something there. Suddenly, he called to me and when I finally caught up with him, I saw a bag full of tins. He had tins of meat, sardines, milk and other edible goods.

'What a surprise!' I exclaimed. 'But whose is it?'

'It must be a soldier's bag prepared for a weekend picnic with his girlfriend,' replied Ivan.

'Should we take it?' I asked, believing him.

Ivan looked round and started to pack the tins into our bag. We turned around and headed for home.

'Someone must be praying for us,' I said as I started to open some of the tins.

'And someone will be very disappointed,' Ivan replied, 'but he is sure to have more than what we have right now.'

We had a wonderful and plentiful Whit Sunday, but it came at a cost. We discovered that our savings of approximately 100 Marks had disappeared from our room. No matter how hard we looked, we never found them. Someone must have stolen them. Although money was not being used at the time, it would soon be back in circulation. Now however, we had absolutely nothing. It seemed to be our punishment, and it taught me a lesson for the rest of my life.

We had friends at church and in the choir. The priest, his wife and their little girl came to visit us, as did his sister-in-law and her handsome husband. We formed a circle of friends. Together we went to the valleys and forests and had long conversations. We laughed and told stories and enjoyed the sunny summer days of 1945. Life was powerful and we were young. The sun shone and the scenery of the Harz Mountains was so beautiful that it was easy to feel happy. We were able to speak our own language, we could pray in our own church, and we could sing in our own choir, but we also learned that none of this was possible back at home.

Chapter 29

The forced repatriation of Soviet citizens was confirmed, and I was one of those classed as Soviet. And although Ivan had Czechoslovakian documents, there would be no way in which Stalin would tolerate marriage to foreigners. If we returned home together we would be forced to separate, and we would both be punished in the process. The stories which continued to spread through the community were like clouds of poisonous smoke, and they filled us with excessive anxiety. We were ordered to leave our accommodation and were moved into camps on the edge of the town. There were two such camps: ours was Oker, just over a mile from the centre of Goslar.

When the time arrived, we packed what little we had and said goodbye to Shura and our landlord. They had been kind to us, and we thanked them for everything they had done. They wished us well.

To reach the camp we had to walk across open fields. The harvest was over and the sandy earth already felt cold. It took us nearly an hour to get there. The camp was situated in the fields and was surrounded by a wire fence. A watchman stood at the gate. For once, the watchman was a Ukrainian. He wore a national, blue and yellow armband on his sleeve. After looking at our papers, he led us into the commandant's office. A tall, blonde man greeted us politely and examined the papers again. We were shown an empty room in one of the barracks. These were the married quarters. We were very pleased to be given a room of our own. There was a bed, a table, a few chairs, and in the corner of the room there was an electric stove with one ring.

I tidied up as well as I could. I put our marriage icons in the corner above the bed, together with a simple embroidered cloth that Mrs Troyan had given to us as a wedding present. I covered the table with a piece of linen that I had kept from the textile factory in Berlin. And now, for the first time, we had a proper room. I tried to make it as homely as possible.

The camp was large. It had its own church, a choir, a school and a dramatic society. Everyone there was Ukrainian, including the administrators, and the only exception was an English supervisor. We received our ration of food and began to lead a Ukrainian community life which was complete. My husband and I both sang in the choir. I was also asked to teach, and I took charge of an elementary class of about twenty eager young children.

More than anything else, I had a secret wish to be given a good part and perform on stage in the dramatic society. I was a newcomer, however, so I was not known to the director – an elderly actor from home. The other members of this well-trained group were also eager to act and used all the tricks they knew to be given a part to play. It was as if a place in a professional theatre was at stake. At first, they only asked me to be the prompter. I was disappointed, but I worked keenly and dutifully satisfied the director and the actors. Work on the second play began. It was a comedy and I was given the part of a lady. I was happy, I learned my lines, and when the day of the first performance came, I put my whole heart into it and did so well that everybody praised me. I had no idea that acting could be so exhausting. So, by the time I had finished I could do nothing other than go back to our room and fall onto the bed and sleep. I was then given parts in the other plays, and soon I was given leading roles.

In a way, Oker camp was like living in a mini republic with a Ukrainian Greek Catholic church. We all loved it. The priest there was young, tall and very kind. We cleaned and decorated the church and then sang with all our hearts every Sunday and every feast day.

My life was now busy with the school, the choir and the dramatic society. For these activities I was given a ration book as a working member of the camp. Ivan, meanwhile, had a job in the camp's administration. We knew little of what was happening in the world outside. We feared the

Russians and dreaded the thought of repatriation, which was being enforced at other camps. There were rumours of suicides, escapes, and the splitting up of families. Little did we know that one and a half million people were sent home from the German prison and labour camps.

Winter came. Food rations were cut and the bread changed to corn bread. It was yellow and tasteless. There was a shortage of everything, but we were young, newly married and happy, and laughter still filled our room. It was very cold so Ivan found me some gloves. They had a warming device inside them. We laughed, but it worked. We marvelled at this German invention, and never saw anything similar to it again.

Ukrainian Nationalist politics spread through the camp and soon came to everyone's attention. The followers of Stepan Bandera began to overrule the others and heated discussions and clashes soon started. My husband did not belong to that group. In fact, he opposed them because he belonged to the original Organisation of Ukrainian Nationalists who followed the leadership of Colonel Andriy Melnyk – a fighter from the First World War and the time of Ukrainian independence. Melnyk had not collaborated with the Germans and his members had worked underground, but many were arrested, tortured and killed. A new organisation was formed and was made up of young people eager to fight Communism under the new leader, Bandera. There were many, but they too were killed by Germans, especially when the Ukrainian Insurgent Army was formed to resist both the Russians and Germans, equally.

Most of the men from West Ukraine had fought in the Ukrainian Insurgent Army, and they had been through the prisoner of war and labour camps in Germany. Others came from the Soviet Army, but not many of them knew the historic facts however. Oral propaganda spread through the continuing political discussions and activities. The administrators of the camp were followers of Bandera, and my husband was working with them, but it cost him his job.

Money was back in circulation and we could not live without an income. Thankfully, Ivan still had many friends in the town and found a job in a Ukrainian arts and crafts shop. Many people were employed in carving and made Ukrainian caskets, ornaments, and musical instruments – especially the bandura, Ukraine's national instrument. Ivan had to get up early to walk into town. I never missed him setting off. I got up when he did. I made his breakfast, prepared his sandwiches and saw him off with a kiss. He came home in the evening and was happy to find me waiting for him. I spent my days in the school and talked to many interesting people, and I continued to listen to their stories.

There was an elderly couple whom I liked most of all: the Pidshany family. They lived in another barrack and I would often go to visit them. They told me how they had owned a large farm and had worked hard all their lives. Then collectivisation came – the period of rural change that had helped to create the famine Ukraine. Everything was taken from them and they were turned out by the Communists in the middle of the night. It was winter, snow fell heavily, and their children were little. They walked through the fields to the next village where an aunt lived. Most locals were frightened to let them in or help them as they had been classed as "Enemies of the State", but the aunt sheltered them for one night and then moved them on to the Donbas region where the husband found a job. One of the children died on the way and another was sick.

'But God saved us,' the old lady said. 'Our son was taken to Germany, and we followed him over before the Soviet Army arrived. We don't know where he is but we will continue looking for him.' She wiped her eyes with the end of her apron. And then, as if none of this tragic history had ever happened, she showed me how to make pancakes.

'Will you help us to write some letters?' her husband asked me. 'We have to write in German, and we know where he used to work.'

I agreed and began to write letters which were sent to many places in search of Sergei – their son. We never found him, but his poor parents never gave up hope.

One day, the camp was shaken by the news that someone had escaped from the transit camp near the port of Stettin, and the stories he told were terrible. Girls had had their heads shaved before being sent to Siberia to work in the coal mines for five years: the boys were being sent for ten. They were simply ordered to leave their belongings in a heap and made to leave.

298

We been torn away from our roots and transferred to this cruel way of life. And it was a similar story for countless thousands of us. We received neither letters, nor news, and we had absolutely no contact with home. We did not dare to write, not even for many years to come. We were frightened, isolated and removed, and none of us was in a position to say what the future would have in store. We could not even imagine where we would settle. Only when Ivan returned home from work could I settle in myself and feel free from the insecurity, which would silently eat away at me.

Chapter 30

The harsh winter of 1946-47 gradually came to an end, but life in the camp went on. I continued to teach the children and I was given more lead roles to play in the dramatic society. In one play, I was given the part of a flirt and dressed in nineteenth century costume. I was taught how to behave like a lady and used a fan as one of my props. I put my whole heart into it, and when the performance ended the audience would not stop applauding.

'You played the lady so well. I shall never forget it,' said one man.

I also wrote a play for Mother's Day which the school children performed admirably. The headmistress suggested a plot, and I wrote the words. A backdrop of forest scenery was painted by an artist and the children dressed in national Ukrainian costume. I was happy with my achievements, and the headmistress grew fonder of me. She even came to visit us in our room. She would teach her young daughter how to behave – how to stand, sit and eat like a lady. Nobody had ever taught me such manners as they belonged to high society, and I did not. I listened attentively.

For Easter, we cleaned the church and adorned it with embroidery and flowers. Everybody went to confession, and I felt I had to go even though it was the Catholic Church. As a teacher, I had to set an example to others. Ivan bought some food, and I prepared it for the Easter blessing.

Everybody arrived at the church at dawn and stood outside in rows. The priest came out, dressed in golden robes, and the choir followed him. The first rays of the rising sun broke through, and the food was blessed. We kissed and gave each other our traditional Easter greeting: 'Christ has risen!' In the afternoon, we held a party in the camp's hall. The choir sang again, and the children recited poetry. They also danced in national costume. Easter 1947 was happy for all of us. Uncertainty, though, continued to hang over our future. Where could we make our home?

After Easter, a group of Quakers arrived from England. They were young ladies dressed in uniform and they smiled at us in a friendly and polite manner. They brought us food and showed us much kindness. We showed them our church, the school, the concert hall and the rooms where we lived. They said they would help us.

Soon afterwards, English language classes were organised so Ivan and I went along. Ivan's friend, a Doctor of Economics from Ukraine, lived in the town but came to the camp to teach us. I liked English from the beginning. There were no complicated declensions and conjugations of nouns and verbs as there were in German or Ukrainian. We found the spellings difficult but persevered and made notes of all the rules. Our exercise books were quickly filled, and we did plenty of revision in our room. I had read many German books by this time, having borrowed them from the town's library. My German was so good by then that English seemed to be easy.

We prepared a concert for the Quakers who were helping us. The choir learned new songs and dressed in national costumes made from any pieces of material that could be found. On the night, a small number of officials came, including a representative from UNRA. They sat with the Quakers in the front row. The concert was a success and the choir was duly praised. Group photographs were taken of us in our costumes, together with the Quakers. They brought peace with them, and we liked them very much.

It was said that we would be given the chance to go to England, or to Canada, or possibly to Australia or America. Screening started. We all had to go before a commission and answer many questions. Those of us who had Soviet citizenship were frightened to admit the truth for fear of being forcibly repatriated. People therefore invented their place of birth and usually declared themselves as Polish citizens. As

300

my husband was Czechoslovakian, I declared myself likewise. We lived as if on the edge of a precipice. After the screening, we may have been evacuated or repatriated. It all depended upon the commission's decision, but then the commission disappeared and everything went very quiet.

New rumours started to spread, and there was talk of going to England or Canada. I discussed it with Ivan. Deep down, we did not want to leave Europe, or travel far from Ukraine. We still nurtured the hope that something would happen to make our return possible. We therefore decided that England would be the best option. We also thought that our stay would be temporary. Canada, America and Australia would have been much too far away.

We had been married for one year. Normally, young people gather new possessions, settle down and start a family, but our first year was a year of waiting. It was a year of struggle in which we had survived a camp life marked by a shortage of food and few normal, everyday facilities. Yet we had lived as a Ukrainian community. Ivan had made many friends and had acquired authority, and I was a successful teacher. I was friendly and had earned the respect of others in the camp, but it was only a temporary period of transition.

A new commission came to the camp and asked us who wanted to go to England. Our decision had already been made, so we signed up to go. Many others were going with us, but they chose England simply because it was the first place on offer and it meant they could quickly leave camp life behind. There had been a severe shortage of food. For several weeks, we had not had any bread except for a ration of tasteless corn bread, and there was hardly anything to cook with. Everybody wanted to settle down properly. We were now worn out from being shunted around from one place to another, and of being uncertain. We had lost our "normal life" five years earlier. So, the majority signed up for England. Not everybody went, however. The sick were rejected, and pregnant women were not allowed, either. Women who had children also had to stay behind. Their husbands went ahead of them and had to earn enough money before their families could follow them over. We were told that we were going to work in factories.

So that was to be my new future. After a grammar school

301

and university education in Ukraine; after becoming a secretary and a dishwasher under the Nazi regime; and then a teacher, actress and singer in a German displaced person's camp, I would become a factory worker in England. Of course, I was not quite sure exactly what to expect. I went to town to buy a black pinafore with white buttons and imagined life in an English factory. After that, we started to pack.

A few more days passed before we finally departed, and there were many tearful scenes. The women with the children screamed for their husbands. Theirs was the most painful separation. We were all sorry to part. Although we had lived a camp life, it was a Ukrainian life in which part of our country and culture had survived. Now, we appeared to be losing it all over again. We all cried.

The children brought me so many flowers that I could not hold them in my arms. Parents thanked me for my efforts and many also added that they would never forget me playing the flirtatious lady. Friends kissed me, their faces awash with tears. Finally, we climbed into the waiting military vans and waved goodbye. The image of that parting still brings those tears back to me today.

Chapter 31

We left on the 28th of May 1947, and for another three weeks or so we went through more camps and screenings until finally we were allowed to board a ship. It was huge and also carried hundreds of English soldiers. It was the first time in my life that I had seen the sea.

I could see that the vast expanse of water was going to divide me from my loved ones, but as the waves began to grow in power, I began to draw courage from them: 'I really would like to live in England,' I thought.

The crossing was very rough and disturbing. I was sick and thought I would never see land again. Apparently, wonderful dinners were being served in the ship's dining room. Naturally, Ivan enjoyed the food, but I on the other hand could not eat a thing. The journey lasted for the whole night. We tried to sleep in our cabin, but I was much too ill to rest. Exhausted and pale, I finally went up onto the deck at the break of dawn. In the distance I could see the dark outline of England's coast. The soldiers were already preparing to disembark. They were excited and very happy to be returning home: I, meanwhile, could not believe I would be back on dry land.

It was the 17th of June 1947. We arrived in Hull and were taken by bus to an old military camp called Full Sutton, near York. After registration, I was led away to the women's side of the camp and Ivan was led to the men's side. There were fifteen other girls sharing the room, and I chose a bed by the window. I was happy to have a place where I could rest and sleep safely.

The camp was large and had many hundreds of refugees. We were the displaced persons of Europe, known simply as DP's. We were of many different nationalities and from various social classes, but the majority of us were young and healthy – our many medical checks had shown us that. There was a canteen in the middle of the camp where we were given breakfast, dinner and supper. The food was better than it had been in the German camps, but we still felt hungry and undernourished. Each of us was given a half-crown (that's two shillings and sixpence, or 12½ pence in today's decimal money) and we used it as our weekly pocket money. That's how our life in England began.

We had not seen anything yet of the real England. The camp was surrounded by fields and woodlands, and when I went for a walk with Ivan, clouds of midges followed us everywhere. The soil was wet and marshy, so we had nowhere to sit to have a picnic, read or just talk.

'What a strange country,' I said, 'with all these flies, boggy ground and woodland undergrowth. It's so different to ours.'

'Well, we have to live here, now, dearest,' replied my husband. 'You can't do anything about it.'

'I wonder what English people are like?'

'I'm sure we'll meet some soon.' Ivan was now becoming impatient with the flies, so we turned back to go to the camp.

'And I wonder how long we will have to stay in this camp?'

'Only until they take us away to work somewhere.' He then told me he had been offered a job sweeping the camp but had refused it.

In my free time I studied English. I sat by my bed and was rarely seen parted from my books. I wrote exercises, learned new words and revised the grammar from the lessons we received in Germany. The girls in the barrack laughed and giggled. They talked about boys and teased me for always studying instead of joining them.

'You'll dry your head out,' they said. I took no notice.

'You were lucky to be married so young,' they added. 'That's when girls are not so mature. But now we're older and wiser it's hard for us to find a husband.'

'You'll find one,' I said, feeling proud and secure with my status.

As the weeks passed, we were able to save some money and wanted to buy something. We learned that the City of York was not far away. It was possible to walk there and buy bread without a ration card. York was huge and was full of shops and people. We bought a whole loaf of white bread, which was so soft and white it was like cotton. We also bought some kippers, and on our way back we had a simple picnic. We had such an appetite that we almost ate the whole loaf. We could not cook in the camp and had no hot water, so we rinsed the kippers in cold water and ate them raw. We loved them so much that we went back for more the following day, and we ate them for years to come – always uncooked.

The Ukrainian community began to regroup and formed a choir and a dance group. Before long, we were giving a concert to our English hosts. It was very difficult to get hold of our national costumes, so we had to make them. The concert was a huge success and people of other nationalities praised us for our initiative and inventiveness:

'No matter where you find Ukrainians, they always have a way of creating a song and dance,' they would say. We were very proud to hear that statement.

A full month passed before anyone was taken to work, and it was on the 17th of July when Ivan and I were called from our barracks and put on a bus with ten other families. We did not know where we were heading to. I looked at the countryside through the window not knowing the names of any of the villages. Eventually, the bus stopped and we were told to step down. We were in a big city with dozens of factory chimneys and sandstone houses in narrow, cobbled streets.

'This is Bradford,' said a gentleman, 'and I will take you to a hostel.' We took our luggage and followed him. We were a group of married couples of different nationalities – Ukrainians, Estonians, Latvians and Poles, and we did not know each other.

We were on Shearbridge Road, and the hostel was a partitioned room on the first floor of a warehouse. Within each partition there was one bed, one chair and a small table. The partitions had no ceilings so couples could hear each other talking. In the corridor there was a cooker and a sink. We were told that we would be given work in a textile factory. It felt strange to be left alone in a strange city, in a strange building and with strange people. We still had some pocket money and were able to buy some food. We then went to sleep.

The following day, we were taken to the factory. We walked along the narrow, dark, cobblestoned streets, overshadowed by tall buildings. All around us everything was made of sandstone, and it was all black. Finally, we arrived at a small and noisy textile factory in City Road. We were taken through the various sections where I could not believe how much noise was being made by the weaving looms and spinning machines. I could not imagine myself working there and felt slightly frightened. Then, they took us into a large, well-lit room with dozens of tables where women were sewing. It was the mending department and I was told I would start working there.

I was glad. It was relatively peaceful and fairly clean and I was soon put to work with an elderly woman called Emmy. She showed me how to check the long pieces of material. I had to find faults in the weaving, underline them with chalk, or mend them.

Emmy was kind and patient. She was tall and well-built with grey hair and rosy cheeks, and her grey eyes seemed to love and understand me from the start. It was not long before she told me her life's story, and about her work in her church. She had a husband and three children in their teens and cried because she had fallen in love with the choirmaster.

'You know,' she said, 'to love in your youth is not too bad even if it's impossible, but to fall in love at my age is terribly painful. You know it's your last chance of true happiness, and you know it's impossible when he also has a wife and family.'

I was surprised that she had told me her most intimate secret, but I listened silently. Only my eyes expressed my sympathy. Emmy then told me more and more as though we had known each other all of our lives. She insisted on being called Emmy, though I was not used to calling an older woman by her first name. I therefore resorted to calling her Mrs Emmy, and did so for a long time, and she never reproached me whenever I did something wrong.

Such was my first proper meeting with an English woman. I liked Emmy, and to my surprise I liked my work. I wore the black pinafore with white buttons. I was given my own table, and I mastered the art of mending cloth. It was not so easy. Often, the patterns were very complicated and it was difficult to match them, but Emmy always came to my rescue. Sometimes, I would burst into tears for not being able to fix something well.

The supervisor, Tilly, would also come over to me. She was small and plump, and was also very active and kind. She, too, would show me what to do. Her little head was covered with thick, black curly hair and it would shake, but I never heard a single harsh word from her lips. I liked her, too. There was something motherly about her. She supervised over one hundred workers at a time. Nobody had any grievances with her and she walked between the tables as everyone's friend. It was so different to Germany where everyone lived in an atmosphere of fear.

It was all new to me. Here, everybody called each other by their first names. I remembered the proud and arrogant German women. We never knew their names at all, and they never shared anything with us on special occasions. In fact, many of them had been really nasty to us, even chasing us out of the factory at break times. Here in England, the women were calm, kind and good-natured. For the first time, since the end of the War, I felt at peace, and it was as though I had come home, and as though there had been no war.

An elderly lady called Edna worked at another table. She

was a widow with one son. Her round face and grey eyes reminded me of my mother. Whenever she looked at me she smiled and spoke kindly. She was a real treasure to know at that time. I was still lost and homesick, doing a job which was just a job and which had nothing to do with my real aims in life. Edna reminded me of home, of peace and tranquillity. Later, she let me use her address to write to my mother, and I stayed in touch with her until she passed away. It seemed strange that she would eventually die in the same year as my mother.

I learned to sew very quickly and did my "picks" faster than the others. I would sing quietly as I did the burling – checking the material, unpicking the knots and marking the faults. Whenever I needed anything I would not hesitate to turn to Emmy or Edna who became my good, reliable friends.

Ivan, meanwhile, was sent to work in the warping department. He soon learned to master his machine and worked without complaint. He had never been the sentimental type, and no matter what life would throw at him he never made a fuss. Before the War, he had worked as a lawyer, but that seemed to have died in him forever. He was here, earning his living, and doing what seemed to be his only way forward in life.

At the end of the week we received our first wage packets. Ivan earned 3 pounds and I made 2 pounds and 10 shillings. For the first week, we ate our dinners in the canteen free of charge. Then, we took our ration books and began to buy our own food. There were plenty of oranges in the shops which we could buy without the books. In the German hospital they had given me just the one orange at Christmas. I had never eaten an orange before that and I thought it tasted heavenly. Now, I could eat as many as I could afford. Perhaps my body needed the precious vitamins and minerals that oranges supply. They were my first luxury in England. And we had never seen bananas before. Stalin considered them an unnecessary luxury and so did not import them. So, when we saw bananas in the shops for the first time, we did not even know what they were. But we tasted them, and we liked them.

Our rations were also unusual. We had never been given cornflakes before, so we did not know what to do with them.

The bacon was also cut in thin strips. Why was it cut like that? At home our bacon was stored and sold in thick pieces, but the thin rashers we were given here were a puzzle to us. We tried to eat it raw, but it was hard and tasteless. We did not have a frying pan so we could only boil the bacon in soup. The bread was white and soft, so we were not used to that either. In Ukraine, such bread was only used at teatime, like teacakes, and could not satisfy a healthy appetite.

Now that we had wages, the factory canteen charged us for our dinners. It was not expensive, but because we tried to save on a low wage, it was difficult. Many of the other workers simply ate sandwiches prepared at home, but Ivan insisted that we must go to dinner. I then remembered my mother's rule that we should try to eat something cooked in the middle of the day, so I went with him. It was the only time we saw each other during the day, and I particularly enjoyed eating the steam puddings with treacle and custard. We were still somewhat hungry and wished the lady who served us the dinners would give us more, but we never dared to ask. Nobody else did, so we didn't either. Today, whenever I think of people slimming and who struggle to keep their figures in shape, I think of the time when I worked and was hungry. It is a terrible feeling, and I have appreciated every available scrap of food I have eaten, all of my life.

We made some friends in the hostel. There was a young couple in the next partition – a hard-working Ukrainian man and his young Polish wife. They both worked in the weaving department and complained of the noise which had made them half-deaf. They shouted to each other: 'Andrew, come and wash your feet!' His wife called him every night, and we always remembered her by that call.

Another couple was an elderly man and a beautiful divorced woman. She was illiterate as her father had taken her away from her school in Stalin's time. Now her husband was teaching her to read and write. After work he taught her the alphabet, but only after her many arguments and protests.

There was also an Estonian couple – a beautiful blonde we had seen in the camp, and an ex-diplomat – a thin and pale gentleman with a bald head and large spectacles. The woman was proud and pretended to be a lady, but one day when a doctor came to see her she continued to be full of herself. He asked her if she played Chopin at home, but she did not even know who Chopin was. She was put to work in the same room as me, but I could never make friends with her as I never felt drawn to anybody who pretended to be better than they really were. It was not long before she left her husband to live with another man, and then another one after that, and who knows how many more.

When Sundays came we did not know what to do. There was nowhere to go to and there was no one we knew in Bradford. After breakfast, Ivan and I went for a walk. There was a church not too far away. We could see its high spire standing out between the black chimneys, so we went there. The inscription on the board by the door said St Andrew's Anglican Church. There were not many people inside. There were no icons or candles and the grey, stone walls were bare. The congregation was singing psalms and we stood at the back. We were strangers, but at the end of the service the minister shook our hands and smiled at us as if he had known us all of his life. I liked that.

It was still early and we wandered aimlessly along the street. Some people came towards us and we could tell they were Ukrainian. We greeted them and shook their hands with great pleasure. We could speak freely in our own language again, and the torrent of words flowed and flowed. We told them who we were and discovered everything about them. They had arrived in Bradford at the same time as we had. They, too, were working in a textile mill, but they had found a church – something similar to ours in Ukraine. They invited us to come with them. We followed them along the dark, stone streets. The church was full. Icons decorated the walls and incense filled the air. Candles were burning and a priest in a golden robe served Mass. We liked it. After many years of camp life and a make-do hut for a church, it felt much better. We were in St Patrick's Roman Catholic Church and met more of our people outside, after the service. We were pleased to learn that we were not the only Ukrainian settlers in the city.

We went to St Patrick's every Sunday. Ukrainians gathered outside the church and with every passing week the gathering grew bigger and bigger. Then, one Sunday after Mass, a priest came out and asked us who we were and why we had remained in our gathering outside. I was the only one who understood English, so I told him that we were new settlers in Bradford and we liked their church, so we had gathered there to talk to each other. He was sympathetic and offered us the use of the church hall. The large building nearby had a hall with a stage, a basement and spacious rooms. We could use the hall on Sunday afternoons and on Tuesday nights.

St Patrick's offered us a new direction and probably did not realise how much they were giving to us. We soon filled the building. First, we organised a library by collecting and exchanging books. I was appointed to be a librarian and sat at a little table by the door where I asked people's names and addresses and whether they wanted to borrow or lend a book. I found it interesting because I was getting to know more and more of our people. Some were very intelligent – former leaders of societies, and others were artists, actors, singers or musicians. There were families with small children and people from all walks of life. Then, knowing that I could speak English, I was asked to start English classes at weekends and was soon teaching dozens of men, women and children.

A dramatic society was also formed, and an elderly gentleman who used to be a teacher at home promptly decided that Mykola Lysenko's famous operetta, "Natalka Poltavka", would be suitable for performance in Bradford. There was a musician who played the piano and a young boy who sang really well. However, there was no suitable girl to play the lead role. The grey-haired and noble producer, Mr Avakum Puras, thought about it for a few days and then approached me and said: 'You are going to play the part of Natalka.' I was stunned. I had never once sung a solo on stage before. I was rather shy and did not believe in my vocal ability, but no matter how much I refused, he insisted: 'You will play the part.'

Rehearsals started, and with them came a whole new experience. Every Tuesday night I hurried to the church hall. A piano provided the accompaniment and we learned to sing arias, duets, quartets and choral pieces. It took us a long time, but I noticed how my voice began to develop: the more I sang the better I sounded. Everyone praised me. You can't imagine the change it made in me – to be able to come to rehearsals and meet fellow Ukrainians, to be able to talk and sing after the weeks of uninteresting work, and the poor life we were leading in a hostel where we could only sit by one cooker and one water tap.

It took several weeks for a welfare officer to find us a proper room of our own. It was in the house of an elderly widow who lived with her son. We were glad to be able to move away and she welcomed us kindly, but she accepted us only on the condition that she would do the cooking. The house was small and had a front room, a kitchen, two bedrooms and an attic. We were given one of the bedrooms and the landlady slept in the other. Her son had the attic. The kitchen served as the dining room, and we hardly ever went into the sitting room. The rooms were small, the staircase was very steep, and the toilet was outside the house. Our room had a huge double bed, a sideboard, a wardrobe and a chair, but we were glad to have it. The one window had a view overlooking the blackened houses, walls and narrow streets, but it was conveniently close to the factory where we worked. The landlady took our ration books and started to cook. We still had lunch in the canteen, but when we came home a warm and tasty dinner was always waiting for us. We also had a cooked English breakfast every day. The landlady had previously worked in a wealthy household as a kitchen maid and taught me how to cook English dinners. We paid her a total of three pounds and ten shillings a week.

I was happy to accept the kindness on offer, but as the weeks turned to months I gradually became depressed. The monotony of the work and the dark surroundings, and the strangeness of everything else around me left me feeling homesick and helpless. I could only find relief in our social life which was the only way of connecting back to everything I had loved, but which I also knew I would never regain.

I still managed to learn more about myself. I discovered new abilities and hidden talents in the sharing of my knowledge with other Ukrainians. I made new friends and had discussions and even arguments with them, but at least I felt I could express myself and be genuine. And it was also a strange feeling to be a foreigner in someone else's country, where I could never fully be myself. It was only by being in my own community, being among my own people that I could feel wholly at one and act naturally, and be happy. I therefore became more and more involved in Bradford's Ukrainian community life.

A few months later, a Ukrainian Catholic priest came to Bradford and I translated for him. I asked Canon Curran at St Patrick's Church if we could hold Ukrainian Mass there. Permission was granted and Ukrainian Greek Catholic Mass was served in St Patrick's Church for the very first time. It was at the end of 1947. People came from all over Bradford, and within those walls, the church harboured the sorrows of a generation – lost and severed from their loved ones in Ukraine. They cried as they prayed for their families once more. Many years have passed since then, and Ukrainians have their own churches in the city, but the first tears shed by the refugees were at St Patrick's which stood as the bedrock for Christianity in the hearts and minds of many Ukrainians.

Not all British people were kind or friendly to us, however. There were those who swore at us and called us foreigners. Others completely ignored us. They simply had no idea of what we had been through. We trusted those who were kind to us and who showed us warmth and friendliness. We were people from religious roots and we had an inner, spiritual world. And once our concerns about feeding ourselves were finally over, we embarked upon enriching our Ukrainian spiritual life. We worked and lived for the evenings and weekends when we could meet and be together again.

Artists began to prepare the scenery for our operetta. Mr Petro Petrenko, a talented engineer, painted the canvas which some of the women had stitched together. It was a village scene with meadows from Ukraine's national landscape. We were nearing the time of our first performance, and Anna (the wife of Fedir Zinchenko – one of the few professional actors amongst us) had made me some beautiful costumes. She made me feel like a star. Everybody tried to help me. My singing partner, the very highly talented tenor Volodymyr Luciv, also looked at me with genuine admiration. When it was time for the dress rehearsals, I was nervous but I sang well, and the audience of selected people praised me and declared the operetta ready to be performed. We hired the

Southgate Hall, which used to stand behind Sunwin House. It was a big and beautiful hall with engravings on the walls. It was frequently used by amateur operatic groups, and the stage there was large and adequately spacious.

On the day of the performance I tried to push everything from my mind in order to concentrate on the part I had to play. Concentration and single-minded attention would help to guarantee success. I did not consciously know this at the time, but I succeeded. I sang my first solo and completely forgot about everything else. Hundreds of admiring eyes looked up at me, but I also caught the strict looks of the producer standing in the wings. I was Natalka, longing for my lover to come back to me. I sang and acted with confidence. Even one of the hall's stagehands wanted to know who I was. Everyone congratulated me and also gave praise to the whole of the Ukrainian Dramatic Society. Volodymyr and I were both on a high from starring in front of a capacity audience. We enjoyed the moment and remained good friends for many years to come.

The following weekend, we repeated the operetta in Halifax where another large, Ukrainian community had formed. This was followed a few weeks later by a third performance in Rochdale, which was the best so far. We had hired a bus, and talked and sang all the way back home. We were living our Ukrainian life, and temporarily forgot that early in the morning, we would be back at work in our English life.

Somehow, I failed to tell the ladies at work about my Ukrainian achievements. It all seemed so far removed from the life of the burling and mending department. Perhaps I was frightened that they would fail to appreciate the things which were most dear to me. We talked about cooking and housework and I continued to listen eagerly to the stories of their lives, which were told quietly and sincerely.

My dual life continued, but I was bored. Once I had mastered the mending of complicated patterns there was nothing more to learn. My mind became idle. I was, of course, craving more knowledge, but I was far from furthering my education.

'Have you worked here all your life?' I asked Emmy one day.

'Yes, why do you ask?' She was surprised by my question. I looked into her beautiful, grey eyes and her lovely, softly-wrinkled face and wondered how she could bury herself in this work for a lifetime.

'Don't you feel bored?' I asked.

'My dear, you have to earn a living, and it's a good job. Why? Don't you like it?'

'Oh, it's all right, I suppose, but it is a bit boring.'

I turned to my work and thought yes, indeed, I do have to earn my living. We would not have enough money coming in with only one wage, and we owned very little. All we had brought with us were the two white bed sheets and a pillowcase. We had to start our life, build it, and buy things. I thought of home, and the pain was so sickening that the tears rolled down my checks. I tried not to show them.

Knowing that I had no alternative other than to work, I started writing and reading poetry which I kept under the material draped across my knees. I would bring a book or some paper to work with me and snatch a few minutes when no one was looking. To read was like a drink of fresh water in a desert, my mind was that thirsty. In my circumstances, I would never be able to go to university again. The only way forward for me was to go to an evening class, so in the autumn, I joined Belle Vue Grammar School.

Sitting at a desk once again, and listening to an elderly professor I was caught out by a sudden rush of emotional pain. Memories flooded back through my mind, and the feeling that my life had been completely lost now gripped me. I could not return to Ukraine to continue my studies. I thought I had freedom of choice here, but it was an illusion. I was also married and marriage was a sacred union, and though Ivan was not a sentimentalist and never complained of his work or changes in his life, I knew there would probably be no more changes in mine. I had no proper choices.

I thought about it as I sat there at the lectures which followed. What subjects had I not taken: English Literature? General Knowledge? Psychology? In the years to come I would study many courses, perhaps one or two each year. One year I even tried to pass 'A' Level English, Russian and History. I went three times a week to those classes after a day spent at work, and then a quick dash through the housework.

In the end, it became too taxing on my health. It felt impossible to work full-time, to be a housewife and attend evening classes three times a week. Ivan didn't mind, just as long as I managed to go to work and do the housework, but my health was not as strong as it might have been after the rheumatic fever I had suffered in Germany. I constantly suffered from pain in one part of my body or another. Then sciatica set in and I was bedridden for weeks. My back had been giving me trouble from the moment we first arrived in England. I went to visit a doctor regularly, and he supplied me with hundreds of tablets which numbed the pain, but I was never cured. My body failed to keep up with my mind. Once and for all, I gave up hope of ever returning to university, but I carried on with our Ukrainian social life. At the end of the day, it provided me with a spiritual life in which I could heal, and it offered me further opportunities to grow and develop intellectually.

Chapter 32

One day, an elderly gentleman came to our house and very politely asked me if I could teach his three children to read and write in Ukrainian: 'Please save my children,' he pleaded rather dramatically, after I hesitated. 'I want them to be Ukrainians and to know their own language. Please help me.'

I was touched by the sincerity of his request and his faith in me, so I eventually agreed. Then, as the weeks passed, more and more parents expressed the very same interest, and before long, I started a Saturday school.

Naturally, I had to make changes. On Saturday mornings, I had to neglect my housework and hurry to the church hall where dozens of eager young faces would be waiting for me. I loved the children and loved teaching them, but I found it difficult. They were of different ages, and different backgrounds and had different standards of ability. Some came willingly, but others were forced to go there by their parents. Somehow, I coped under those demanding circumstances and taught them everything I could. We sang songs, played games at break, and in good weather we went for picnics in the park or in Heaton Woods. For special occasions we prepared more songs. Some of the children recited poems, and we performed plays on Mother's Day and Christmas. The community loved it. With tears in their eyes, they were happy to see their children doing so well, and thanked me for my efforts. Many of the parents gave me lovely gifts as a mark of their gratitude and respect.

In the spring of 1948, a Ukrainian Orthodox priest came to visit Bradford and we were given our first ever Ukrainian Orthodox service. This could not have happened at St Patrick's as that was a Roman Catholic Church. By this time, Ivan had been elected President of the Federation of Ukrainians in Bradford and the task fell upon us to find an Anglican church in which a Ukrainian Orthodox service could be held. We hired St Mary Magdalene Church. Not long afterwards, we were given a permanent priest – Reverend Opoka. He was then followed by Reverend Lev Skakalsky – a dedicated Orthodox monk. He was always very friendly with his congregation. I was elected to sit on a new church committee, and we formed a choir in which I sang. We held our services after the Anglicans had finished theirs, and it gave everyone enough time to arrive from neighbouring towns.

The church was close to where we lived. Like St Patrick's, it also had a hall with a stage and some small rooms where I could teach the children. Once the number of children began to increase, other community members offered to help me. We formed a teacher's committee and included more of the parents. St Mary Magdalene Church Hall came alive with activities. We were young and healthy, and we wanted to dress well, and look clean, and modern. We held choir practices, drama rehearsals and commemorated events from our national history. The hall would be packed with our people and it echoed with the words of Ukrainian songs, classical plays, lively conversations, opinions, arguments, but most of all – plenty of laughter.

It became my responsibility to look after the community's children. Not having any of my own, I gave all my attention and love to them, and over the years, many dozens came through the school. Some were well-behaved and talented whilst others were naughty or ignorant and altogether too lazy to learn. Through the years of their childhood development I could see the making of the adult:

those who did well at our school also did well in later life. Some of them are now doctors, teachers and nurses; others are craftsmen, builders and labourers. Most of them have done well for themselves.

My activities never stopped me longing to know how my dear parents were. Such was the nature of the unfolding Cold War that I wrote letters home under different names and I asked my English friends if I could use their addresses. I never received a reply. Correspondence with someone in the West was a punishable offence during Stalin's rule in the Soviet Union. Anyone who attempted to reply to letters would be placed under immediate suspicion, imprisoned and deprived of their human rights. It was an inevitable certainty that they would lose their work and status in life. Finally, Stalin died in 1953.

A new era began under Nikita Khrushchev, and after 1964 the true horrors of Communism were exposed. Thousands of prisoners were released from the camps and prisons of the Northern Soviet Union and Siberia and now described their horrific experiences. They had suffered prolonged tortures and had been forced to do hard labour in the mines and woodlands where they had also witnessed thousands perish around them. After having heard announcements on the radio, and seeing many press reports, we understood that Soviet policy was changing and decided to write to our parents more openly. Nonetheless, even by the late-1960s, we still lived in fear for their wellbeing.

I was now working at Salt's Mill, burling and mending in a large room under a glass roof. Many rows of girls sat at the tables there, mending the endless rolls of material. One of them was my friend – Pat Doherty. She was a lovely, blue-eyed, blonde girl who always looked at me innocently and sincerely. I thought how good it was for her and other English girls never to have experienced invasion, oppression or slavery, and how wonderful it was to live in her own country and have her parents and the freedom to do almost anything. I asked Pat for permission to write to my parents using her name and address and she agreed to my plan. It soon looked rather silly.

A few weeks later, letters began to arrive from my parents and then from my sister, who boldly wrote: 'Why do you hide and pretend to be Vera's friend? We all know it's you, and we're glad to have found you, and to know that you are alive.'

With the reply came the very sad news that Anatoly was dead. After the Soviet Army returned, he was sent to the Front with sixty other boys from the village. Only two of them made it back alive – one without a leg, and the other also seriously wounded. Ivan was not at home when I read the news. I knelt by the fireplace and cried so bitterly that I thought I would never stop. I felt guilty for leaving my family. It was as though I had betrayed their love for me, but there was nothing I could have done. I had chosen marriage and Ivan was a good and honest man doing his best for both of us. I could never leave him now and return home, regardless of how much my parents begged me to come back to them. I knew they understood, so when Ivan came back that night I dried my tears and greeted him with a sad but loving smile and then told him everything.

We soon learned that Polish transport firms were opening up all over England thereby allowing the opportunity to send parcels to neighbouring Ukraine. It was very expensive. Not only did we have to buy the food and clothing, but we had to pay almost 100% export duty on them. The parcels came as a great help to our relatives, and as I learned later, they were the best way of advertising "the Capitalist world" to them. We sent parcels to my family and to Ivan's for many years, but to do this we had to save and we sacrificed our own luxuries and household improvements.

In 1954, our seventh year in England, our landlady told us of her plan to move into a smaller Council house as her son was going into the army. It meant we had to leave. It was the middle of winter and Ivan was furious. He looked after our money and told me about our savings. He wanted us to have a small house of our own, instead of living in other peoples' rooms. I did not share his view because I was still clinging to the hope of returning to Ukraine, but I kept my feelings to myself as I also knew that the situation was realistically hopeless. Ivan put an offer in for a house but failed. Quietly, I was glad. He soon found another, however, and took me to see it. It was a small, black, terraced house facing the large walls of Lister's Mill.

'No!' I protested afterwards. 'I'm not going to live in a house facing the black walls of a huge mill such as that one.' So he went out to look for another one and found a cottage for a reasonable price. It had been neglected and had no electricity: only gas. He would have to borrow some more money which I agreed to, and we bought it.

After looking at houses in the wet and slushy February weather, Ivan caught a cold and also developed an abscess on his knee. His leg was in plaster when the time came to move, but that was no great problem as we owned no furniture. I packed everything we owned into one suitcase and hired a taxi to take us to our new home where we ate our first meal on the window sill.

We bought a table from the second-hand shop and I chose one that reminded me of my grandmother's table – solid, black wood with round carved legs. We also bought four chairs and a new bed. I painted the tiny kitchen at the top of the staircase as Ivan rested his leg. It was dark and cold, but I sang aloud because I was glad to be in a home we could call our own. Ivan soon recovered and worked very hard with his friends to make the house orderly. We made many alterations and improvements over the years. Electricity was installed, the floors were replaced, the fireplace changed, and a kitchen and bathroom were built in the cellar. Ukrainian craftsmen helped us, and after putting down the carpets we were extremely proud and extremely satisfied: a home of our own was something we had been deprived of since childhood.

We had not wanted children soon after the War as we did not have the means with which to start a family. Now, children would not come. Visits to a gynaecologist failed to help, so we resigned ourselves to fate and to God's will.

It was 1958 and I was still working in the burling and mending department at Salt's Mill, but I was becoming increasingly bored and started to suffer from backache. When I went to see the doctor, I was advised to change my job. My work involved sitting in a bent over position, most of the time. I also had to carry large rolls of cloth. Changing jobs was now permissible, so I asked the doctor for his opinion. He was young and sympathetic, and immediately suggested that I should go and work in a shop.

'Oh, no,' I replied, 'I don't really want to work in a shop.

I'd prefer to go into nursing or something like that.' I then suddenly remembered my father's wish for me to work in the medical profession. I had loathed the idea at the time.

'Nursing is hard work,' the doctor replied, but I was miles away.

'I have made up my mind,' I said, very sure of myself. 'I'll be able to cope with that.' Yes, I thought, life had brought me to the point where I could not work anywhere else but the medical profession. I was also aware that you could work in a British hospital and receive a wage whilst still training.

The doctor said nothing more, and when he wrote my medical report he did not mention any of my ailments. After many questions about my past and my education, my application was accepted at the labour exchange. I was then sent to train at the Ear, Nose and Throat Hospital of Bradford's Royal Infirmary.

Going to work in a hospital and becoming a nurse seemed to be like going into a convent and becoming a nun. I bought some black stockings and went to Dr Scholl's shop where they measured my feet and fitted me with a good pair of black leather shoes. I announced to my Ukrainian friends that I was going into the nursing profession. Ironically, as fate would have it, I had to start on the 24th of June – the day on which my brother Anatoly had been reported dead.

The hospital in Hallfield Road was a homely and beautiful place. It had a large hall with antique furniture, and above the staircase there was a huge oblong, stained glass window depicting an angel in clouds of rain, but with the sun shining above the clouds. There was a children's ward downstairs, and an outpatient ward with treatment rooms and a dispensary. Wide stairs led to the first floor where the operating theatre was situated, and there were wards with a matron's office between them. That was where I went first and where I was greeted by a sweet and gentle lady called Miss H – the matron. I was given my uniform, some crisp, white aprons, a white hat and a belt. Rows of lockers stood in the corridor, and one of those was given to me. I put my clothes inside and was taught how to wear my white hat. I was proud of how I looked and went on duty at half past seven in the morning in Lady Behren's Ward.

I had worked for ten years in factories and had become friendly with kind, working class, English women – charming girls who had laboured all their lives. Now, in the hospital I began to meet all the classes of English society, from the lowest paid porters to the highest paid doctors and surgeons. I was overwhelmed, not only with these people, but with the new vocabulary, too. Sister W was in charge of the ward. She was an elderly, strict and official lady, feared by everybody. She was a senior sister, and at meals (which we all ate in the same room) she began by saying grace. Then, if we ever wanted to leave the table, we had to ask for her permission.

By the end of the first day, I was exhausted and arrived home in tears. My feet were aching and I was spiritually numb. Ivan humoured me by saying that he had felt the same way on his first day in the army, but then he got used to it. After a while, his feet stopped hurting. So I persevered. I would not accept defeat in my new profession, but not before hiding in the toilet where I cried bitterly.

Classroom training started after a few weeks of practical nursing. I was sent to St Luke's Hospital where the tutor, who had to be addressed as Sister Tutor, taught the nurses. Although English was still a foreign language to me, and although many of the professional terms were still unknown to me, I worked through them all and received praise: 'Good material!' she joked with me regularly. Eventually, I passed my exams and became a State Enrolled Nurse. Sister Tutor advised me to train further, but knowing how busy my life already was, I did not want to proceed. Instead, I went back to my evening classes. I was hungry for more knowledge, and always looked for something new, interesting and inspiring. I always read and discussed everything with my husband who had received a full university education, so he was very knowledgeable in many subject areas. Our house was now full of books and papers which were in Ukrainian and English languages.

I continued with my career as a nurse and worked on every ward in the Ear, Nose and Throat Hospital, including outpatient wards and night duty. I was sent to work in the Fever Hospital on Leeds Road, then to St Luke's Hospital, and later on to the Duke of York operating theatre. The place I enjoyed the most was the Eye Hospital which was private and situated in the grounds of the Ear, Nose and Throat Hospital. It was carpeted and luxurious, and had a large portrait of Her Majesty Queen Elizabeth II above the staircase. I was put in charge on night duty there and the patients I met were all very interesting. I often talked to them for a long time, after my duties had finished. They were wealthy people and had paid large sums of money to be there. They were all intelligent and kind and were ready to talk about a wide variety of subjects. However, my work in the hospitals remained separate from that of the Ukrainian community, and I never talked to anyone from one side of my life about the events or people in the other.

Later in 1958, using donated and borrowed money, our Ukrainian community bought a large, detached house with a garden which had once belonged to a doctor. With great enthusiasm our men, including my husband, made many alterations to the house and transformed it into a social club with a hall and bar. There were several vacant rooms on the first floor which were made into an office, reception room and a school. The Saturday school relocated there immediately. It had a spacious garden and lovely rooms in which I and the other teachers could continue with our work. We organised Ukrainian concerts where the children sang to the delight of their parents. We also held regular dances at weekends.

By 1964 the Ukrainian Orthodox Church in Bradford bought its own church, Our Lady the Protectoress, in Eccleshill. It had been a Methodist church and had a large hall with many adjoining rooms. Again our people were keen to renovate it, but the conversion of a plain Methodist church to a traditional Ukrainian Orthodox church was a difficult task. Yet, like a miracle, the joiners and craftsmen appeared from out of the congregation. Nearly everybody involved was working in the textile mills and engineering plants at that time, and they made a wonderful job of it. An altar was built with a beautiful screen and doors, and an artist was found to paint icons. Every family donated money, and one family after another donated candelabras, banners, crosses and other articles – either specially ordered from Greece or brought by those who had been to Athens or the Holy Land. One family offered a carpet. Ladies brought embroidered covers and

322

tablecloths and other materials for the altar and the tables in the church hall. Over the years it became more and more beautiful. It became a real Ukrainian church to the delight of everybody who attended mass there.

A stage was built in the church hall with beautiful velvet, maroon curtains which were made by one of the women. The Saturday school was then opened there by a former pupil, and the children were fully able to keep up with our national Ukrainian traditions. At Christmas we held more nativity plays and sang carols. Father Christmas even appeared ceremoniously with presents, much to the delight of the children on the stage and the audience seated in the hall. We held dances there, parties, and meetings which included the whole Ukrainian Orthodox community of Great Britain because our hall in Bradford was large, bright and very comfortable.

The church choir continued to play an important part in my life. With the craftsmen and joiners, other talented men also appeared. Some of them learned to conduct the choir. Of those, some emigrated to America and Canada and went on to form choirs there. One young man brought booklets and sheets of Ukrainian music and we started to learn new songs. We sang spiritual music written by famous Ukrainian composers such as Dmytro Bortniansky, Kyryllo Stetsenko and Oleksander Koshits, and we sang native secular songs, too. We all loved the choir and the choirmasters. The frequent rehearsals, the singing in church and at concerts meant I was able to continue being with my own people. It was a privilege to belong.

Chapter 33

Summer holiday camps had been held in France for the Federation of Ukrainian Youth, and in the summer of 1968 I was asked to take a group of our children from England to holiday there. Our aim was to encourage them to speak in Ukrainian. As you can imagine, the children from France spoke little or no English and our children spoke little or no French, so they would all have to communicate in Ukrainian, or at least that's what we expected. I took charge of a group of fourteen and fifteen-year-olds from Yorkshire and

Lancashire, arranged their passports, visas and tickets, and then met them before the journey. I was to teach Ukrainian culture to the older children, and Ukrainian language to the younger. I had prepared a syllabus, between my work and household duties, and had made special notes on Ukrainian history and the essentials of Ukrainian grammar.

We travelled to London by bus, and then continued by train and by boat. From Ostend we took an express train to Paris where our contacts had booked a hotel for the night. The children were thrilled, and very lively. They giggled all the way, and on the train the girls even flirted with travelling soldiers.

An elderly Ukrainian lady called Nina Kovalenko, who was known to me from Germany, took us on a sightseeing tour of Paris. We went to most of the historic places, which included the Ukrainian churches, a library and the grave of our famous leader Symon Petliura who was assassinated in Paris in 1926 by a Communist agent. We took flowers with us. Paris was wonderful, but it was a hot summer's day and the children were not used to the continental heat which had no breeze. The girls could not sleep and continued giggled through the night. We spent one more day in Paris, and the experience was described by most as fantastic. The children were delighted to say they had seen the Cathedral of Notre Dame, the wide and powerful Seine with its huge bridges, and the beautiful square in front of the parliament buildings.

The following morning we continued on our journey by taking a train to the South of France. We arrived at a small station and then continued by bus to a village where we were given a vacant house for the younger children. The older children slept outdoors in tents. Meals were served outside in a big yard surrounded by trees.

The house had no running water or electricity and there were no locks on the doors. The beds were clean: we had brought our own linen. Boys aged 12 to 13 slept on the ground floor and the girls slept on the first. To begin with, nobody liked it there. They had to pump water from the well in the garden and wash themselves outside with cold water. They were not used to it. There were all sorts of creatures in the garden including worms, and the girls screamed every time they saw one. As the days passed, however, they began to love everything about the natural environment. They enjoyed seeing the sunrise, breathing the fresh and warm continental air, and simply watching the birds and insects.

In the crowded kitchen area, Ukrainian ladies prepared traditional Ukrainian dishes with some French cuisine, too. The children learned to dance and sing and had lessons in Ukrainian history and culture from the various tutors. At the start and end of each day, we gathered round our national flag to sing a few short hymns. We often continued into the evenings with a dance or a party. French summer evenings were warm and gentle, just like in Ukraine, but this generation could never have known it. They had long walks, and the boys went on their own runs. Friendships were formed. The boys fell in love with the girls, and girls fell in love with the boys. As teachers, we watched over them and tried to make their stay as pleasant as possible. We had a priest and church services. The priest acted as our choirmaster. He was a very friendly old gentleman, and his wife acted like a mother to everyone.

The teachers formed friendships of their own and met together for black, French coffee and long conversations. It was very enjoyable and I felt well: I was a teacher in the company of other teachers.

At the end of the three weeks, we held a concert, a party and a dance. That night, nobody slept a wink, and the bonds of Ukrainian friendship and togetherness were so strong that nobody wanted to go home. Parting at the station was painful. Everybody put their arms round somebody else and cried. It aroused many emotions and memories in the adults who stood by and watched.

The journey back was happy, but London now seemed to be a strange and cold place for the girls: Paris had won their hearts. When we finally returned to Bradford one of them sobbed when her mother came to greet her. It was as though something awful had happened. All the girl could say was: 'I don't want to go home.' It made us laugh, and I was happy that our holiday in France had been a success. I had also earned more respect from the parents. With a sigh of relief, I thanked God that everything had gone so well.

The camp in France gave us the idea of organising something similar in Great Britain, so the following year we booked a site in Scotland. Mr Fedir Kutsai, a gentleman from Oldham, took charge, and in the summer of 1969 we held our first Federation of Ukrainian Youth summer camp at West Linton near Edinburgh. We went there by train on what seemed like a long and slow journey. Looking after the children was not an easy task. We arrived in Edinburgh tired but happy, and the great city with its castle and places of historic interest did not fail to impress us.

We then went to West Linton by bus. The camp was nearby. It was situated in meadows and woods, close to a river and farmland. Everyone quickly settled into the wooden dormitories with their rows of bunk beds, and then immediately went out to explore the terrain. The children were delighted. We hoisted our flag, read out the rules and the programme for the camp, and started our two week break. A priest came from Edinburgh to serve Ukrainian mass, and wished us all a happy holiday in Scotland.

The children were between eleven and eighteen years of age. In the mornings, they had lessons in Ukrainian language, history, culture and traditions, and in the afternoons they had singing and dancing lessons. The boys also played football, and the girls learned to embroider. We made sure that plenty of food was provided in the canteen.

There were some incidents of misbehaviour: some of the boys went exploring and got lost, some raced rabbits, and some fell into the river. This was all harmless enough and made life in the camp seem all the more interesting and exciting. By the end of our two weeks, we held a concert which included a short play – which I translated into English for local guests and a group of French tourists who were staying in another part of the camp. The girls made national costumes and danced on stage to massive applause. The choir sang in Ukrainian. Then, the youngsters danced until late into night. It was another great success.

We returned home safely and everyone was happy. Mothers again thanked me for teaching their daughters how to sing, and all the more so as they could hear them singing regularly in the bathroom. The girls also talked endlessly of their experiences, and continued to embroider. The camp was repeated for several more years, and then at St Mary's camp in Folkestone, I was happy to be put in charge of everything.

Chapter 34

Just after returning home from a camp in Scotland in 1972, I received a letter from home informing me that my father had died. It came as a severe blow. I had always hoped to see him again. I loved him so much that I felt his soul was always in me, it was a bond which my words will always fail to describe. Now he had gone. I knew be had been ill, but I believed that he would live until we met again. I had been so busy with the children that I had no time to think about him, or even to pray for him. I could not even think of going home. Although it was strictly possible to do so, it was also strictly taboo in our Ukrainian community. Those who went home were counted as Communists or traitors. They were ostracised and avoided by everybody. I was now heartbroken. Nothing in the world mattered to me anymore.

Earlier that year, a friend of mine, Mrs Carson from St Mary Magdalene's Church, came up to me and asked if I would like to go on a pilgrimage to the Holy Land at the end of the summer. The price was reasonable, and so I agreed and paid the deposit. September was approaching, but I no longer wanted to go. I felt the world could no longer give me anything, but the money had already been paid, and Ivan insisted that I should therefore make the effort. Reluctantly, I packed my case and took everything necessary for three weeks in Israel.

We went by bus to London and flew to Tel Aviv from Heathrow Airport. It was the first time I had been to the airport and was impressed by its size and splendour. I realised that flying had become the modern way of travelling with an emphasis on speed, luxury and comfort. It was my first flight so I was naturally a bit apprehensive. I sat next to a Jewish lady who had come to London to do some shopping. She was confident and very talkative, so the time passed very quickly. We arrived in Tel Aviv late in the evening. Police in short-sleeved, khaki shirts boarded the plane and conducted a lengthy security check. Outside, it was wonderfully warm, and I felt as though my whole body was being wrapped in a soft and cosy blanket.

'Isn't it beautifully warm?' I said to one of the women in the bus which was taking us to a hotel in Tiberias. 'It's just like in my country.'

'It's funny you should say that. I was thinking the same myself. I used to live in Spain and it was very similar there,' she replied. 'I love this warm air. Where are you from?'

'I'm from Ukraine,' I said. 'Such a warm summer evening reminds me of home – especially with the dust in the air.'

The woman smiled at me, and we continued our journey in lively conversation. We were allocated rooms to share in the Scots Hotel. My new companion there was called Mary – a slim, elderly lady, who always read the Bible before going to sleep.

I woke up at dawn. It was warm and I felt I had slept long enough, so I quietly left the room. From the hallway a door led out onto a balcony. I could see a beautiful garden full of tropical trees and flowers, and the birds were already in full song. In the distance the sea was calm and peacefully reflected the blue sky. I was charmed by the beauty, warmth and serenity. The sun soon came up from beyond the sea's horizon adding sparkle to the surface. Huge, round, warm and powerful, it touched me. There were tables on the balcony, so I fetched my diary. I began to write about everything I saw in the Holy Land.

We went to different places beyond Tiberias, and they included Nazareth, Capernaum, Haifa, and Hebron. We also went across the Sea of Galilee where I met monks and pilgrims from the Russian Orthodox Church. They told me about the churches in Jerusalem and invited me to visit their monasteries.

After spending the most wonderful ten days in Tiberias, we went on to see the historic sights of Jerusalem. A vicar, who accompanied us, provided narrative from the New Testament, and mentioned the places that my father had read out to us on so many occasions. I was amazed to see how well preserved everything was, and saw where Jesus taught, prophesied and performed His miracles – the places where He turned water into wine, multiplied the bread to feed the five thousand and where He sent the evil spirit into the herd of pigs that were driven into the sea. There was also Bethlehem – His birthplace; the grave of Rachel who cried for her children, and the grave of David where people still light their candles and pray. It had all been kept spotlessly clean.

I took a map of Jerusalem and went to see as many places as I could. I found all of the Russian Orthodox churches and monasteries, too. The priests were dressed in their splendid robes and reminded me of my childhood, my father, and all the other priests I had once known but who had now passed away. I cried, and I prayed for my father. I felt he was still somewhere by my side.

Mrs Carson expressed a wish to visit the Russian Orthodox Church of St Mary Magdalene on the Mount of Olives. We went there one evening, and she was amazed at how wonderfully picturesque it was.

'Our churches are so plain by comparison,' she said.

'Beauty attracts people. They see beauty as part of God's creation. I wish you could see how beautiful our churches were. Mind you, most of them are now in ruins,' I explained sadly.

'I don't understand the language,' she said, 'it's all strange to me.'

'I know,' I replied. We continued to pray together.

I made friends with a small group of Ukrainian nuns from the church there. We then corresponded for many years to come. One of them was an artist. She painted icons and I helped her with parcels and small donations of money in later years. She sent me a beautiful picture of St Nicholas – my father's favourite Saint, and of St Peter drowning in the sea with Jesus appearing in the darkness. I have kept those pictures. I have also kept the wonderful memories of an unforgettable journey – a pilgrimage to the Holy Land which returned to me, a positive outlook on life.

Chapter 35

I knew my depression had lifted. I had a greater appreciation of my late father's vocation. He had been a true and dedicated servant of Christ, and had lived until almost ninety years of age. I now accepted his death, and knew I would always treasure my memories of him.

I asked for the usual memorial prayers to be said for him at our church, and arranged the customary memorial service for the fortieth day after his death. I did the same at the end of one year, and I continued to do this for several years. It is our national custom, and I would not let his work slip from living memory. I wrote long articles about the Holy Land and everything I had experienced there, and these were published in many issues of the Ukrainian Orthodox "Church News" magazine in London. The articles were also published in France and Canada.

I tried to be a good practicing Christian. Every Sunday I went to church, not only to sing in the choir, but to try and help people wherever and whenever I could, but my life was hard. I had to be up at six in the morning to prepare Ivan's breakfast and sandwiches before hurrying to my own work as a full-time nurse. On Saturdays, I ran the Ukrainian School. I was also a member of the dramatic society in which I was still asked to play leading roles (and I was easily persuaded as they were usually the roles of romantic heroines). So, I subsequently had to attend long rehearsals. I also kept up with my further education classes run by Leeds University at Belle Vue and then the Carlton Institute at Mornington Villas. Despite life being so demanding, I loved it.

In my spare time, if I could ever find it, I worked on a book dedicated to my father, in which I attempted to describe his suffering and persecution, and the faith of Ukrainians. I included the reopening of the churches after the fall of Communism. The book was called "Resurrection". I poured my love and homesickness into it and found consolation in writing about everything I had witnessed. I read the texts to my educated friends, and they made comments. I then wrote and rewrote them, again and again. To publish it would have cost me thousands of pounds, which I could not afford, but I continued to work on it. Finally, I found a religious publishing company in Canada, run by the Ukrainian Catholic Church who published it in instalments in their monthly magazine called "The Light", and in 1970 it was made into a book called "Christ Has Risen!" I received a copy, but it was not quite as I had planned – with a beautiful front cover, illustrated by one of our artists. Rather, they chose to use one of their own artists and the picture was far from what I had in mind. At least my first book had been published and it had been dedicated to my dear father. Unfortunately, I was unable to send any copies of the book to my family or others at home for fear of persecution by the, still powerful, Communist regime. However, I was able to hand some copies to my friends in England.

I had to move on, so I then decided to write a book dedicated to my friends in the camps of Germany. I had given them my promise. I still had a small number of diaries salvaged from Berlin. They had turned yellow and were torn, but I typed them out again in Ukrainian and put them in chronological order. I called the book "In German Captivity" and worked away at it, seemingly for years.

At work meanwhile, I had gone onto night duty and was put in charge of the newly-opened Ward 18 of the Eye and Ear Unit of Bradford's Royal Infirmary. I worked for five nights and had the weekend off, and that suited me. I spent nine years there, and during that time I befriended a wonderful person, Sister D. She was a Scottish lady who was married to the manager of a building society, and she taught me how to invest my money which, until then, had been managed solely by my husband who only had a small account at the Post Office. So, we began to invest our money in a building society.

We were told that our house was to be demolished and started to look for somewhere else to live. I had almost saved enough for the deposit, but we still had to take out a mortgage. Ivan, meanwhile, was now past the age of qualifying for a mortgage, and women were not allowed to borrow money at that time. We were in great difficulty, but only until a word from Sister D opened all of the necessary doors for us. I was allowed to take out a mortgage on a house and made the arrangements to pay it back before my retirement (which I managed to do). It was 1974 and we moved to a lovely, large, terraced house near Lister Park. When I stopped working nights and went back to work in the operating theatres Sister D would say: 'Each time you go I feel as though I've lost a finger from my hand.' In fact, some people, like Sister D, were like great treasures in life.

I realised that life is short and full of limitations, no matter how we live and love. And with my father gone, I had painfully learned that hoping and waiting could not be relied upon to bring two persons back together again. I now really wanted to see my dear mother, but our world was still divided by the Iron Curtain.

As far as I knew, returning to Ukraine would mean I would endanger myself and my family. And, no matter how much I wanted to go, I would need the right documents and money. When I made enquiries about how much it would cost, I had a shock. We could not raise such a huge sum, and Ivan would never agree to borrow it. I remember walking through the park feeling gloomy and depressed, but the idea of going home remained very much alive in me. I realised that the first thing I had to do was obtain British citizenship and a British passport. Whether I would go or not, I still needed to secure my legal rights, so I applied for British citizenship in 1975.

It was a long and painstaking procedure. First of all, I was visited by British intelligence services personnel. I then had to make an announcement in our local paper. I then went through lengthy interviews, and had to be represented by two English friends who knew me well – they were two senior Sisters from work. Many of my Ukrainian friends were interviewed and asked about my character and behaviour. Finally, in 1977 I received a positive reply from the Home Office which described me as a "god-fearing person". I received all of the necessary certificates and completed my application for the passport.

Around this time, I learned from a Polish Agency in Bradford that I could go to Ukraine by train. It would cost me a great deal less than going by plane, but there was another hurdle. If I wanted to visit my mother I would need a visa which would take a whole year to process. It was ironic given that hardly anyone travelled to the Soviet Union and the queue was therefore very short. It was dependant upon my activities in England, the conditions in which my mother and sister lived, and other unknown bureaucratic procedures.

I took the plunge and the first steps were fearless and decisive, despite the vast political differences between East and West. Nothing from the Cold War would stop me. I was a simple human being who only wanted to see her mother again, and it felt like a very long year waiting for that visa. Anything could have happened. My mother was nearing her seventy-fifth birthday, and I was worried about her ailing health. I had heard about trips to the Soviet Union by plane, and made enquiries. There was a package trip available which went to Kyiv, Yalta, Leningrad and Moscow. The price seemed reasonable, so I booked it. Ivan did not prevent me. He knew I had chosen him over my parents and he wanted me to be happy. We took the money from our savings.

I planned to make the journey at the end of May and knew I was taking a big risk. I listened to the Easter hymns played on the radio as I packed my suitcase. I then sang ours with joy. To fulfil my wish to return to Ukraine and meet my mother, and my sister and her children (albeit in a hotel), would be like a resurrection for me. I rejoiced despite the fear which was beginning to seep into my consciousness. I told myself that I would be all right.

I went to London by train and then to Luton airport. I joined the queue, handed in my luggage and went to the waiting room where I was greeted by the guide. Hardly anyone I spoke to was aware that "Kiev" was Ukraine's capital, but everything went smoothly. We landed at dusk, and I was expecting my mother to meet me there, but there was nobody. I found out later that my letter had not been delivered in time, but knowing that I was coming on that day, my mother and sister, and Ivan's brother and niece had come by train and were waiting for me at the railway station. They had waited all night, and even my aunt who was now ninety years old and who had never travelled anywhere in her whole life was with them, too. After enquiring about them at the airport and making an announcement over the public address system, I let go of my fears and thought about why they were not there. After more waiting and enquiring, I was taken to a hotel and given a room with an English lady called Ida. I spent my first night there. I was very happy with the surrounds, but extremely disappointed not to see my mother.

I woke up at four o'clock in the morning. Bright sunlight began to fill the room. Noise from a machine, cleaning the streets, prevented me from further sleep, but I was really excited to be in Ukraine once more. I washed and dressed and then, from the balcony of my room, I watched as Kyiv came to life.

At around eleven o'clock my niece found me after enquiring at all the tourist hotels. She then went back to the station to fetch everyone. I was at the top of the hotel stairs as they arrived and cast my eyes down upon my dear mother and the others. I had gone through so much suffering, so many perils, and here they all were. They seemed to be so small. I ran down the stairs and my mother ran towards me. It had been thirty-five years. I was just a girl. I held my mother in my arms until we could no longer keep our balance. We sat down on the staircase. My niece was crying and my aunt joined in. Finally, my brother-in-law helped us up and led us to the hotel waiting room. We could freely and openly be together there – a family filled with the overwhelming emotion of love and joy. Was anybody watching us? I really did not know, and I did not care. The Cold War and all of its artificial trappings paled into temporary insignificance.

My room companion, Ida, was very moved by what she saw and left us alone to spend some time together. I handed out presents as the others described their night at the railway station. We spent two precious days in the hotel, for which I had to pay extra. We went to Kyiv's currency shop called "Kashtany", and left my auntie behind because she was frightened of the elevators, lifts and the rushing traffic. I bought a fur hat for my brother-in-law, scarves and more small presents for the others. My mother wore a navy-blue dress which I had brought from England. We had dinner in a restaurant on Khreshchatic – the main street in Kyiv's centre. The days were sunny, and we talked and laughed. We were so happy to be back in each other's company. Nobody strange approached us, nor did anyone ask any questions or spoil our time together.

Late in the evening of the second day, we had to part company. We went to the railway station and waited for the train which would take my family home. It was yet another tearful separation, but I promised that I would come to visit them again next year, just as soon as I had another visa. The train slowly took them away. I was left to stand on the platform with my brother-in-law, Mykhailo. He was a big, strong gentleman who resembled Ivan, and with him was my dark-eyed niece, Maria, who was loveable at first sight. Gone were my sister's daughter – a beautiful young girl, and her son – a sporty and handsome young man, both of whom I had just seen for the first time ever. My auntie, who was once a local beauty, had kept repeating the words: 'I have seen Vera again, now I can die.' My mother had stayed as composed and as loving as she had ever been, and she never took her eyes off me for the whole time I was with her.

Our meeting in Kyiv was an experience never to be forgotten. I thanked God that I had managed to fulfil my greatest remaining wish, and the tourists with whom I travelled were moved by my story.

We travelled to Yalta by plane and the experience was far less emotional. It consisted of the beauty and splendour of palaces, Ukraine's Black Sea coast, and the grand "Yalta Hotel" – which was still under construction by a Yugoslavian firm. The weather was sunny and warm; the food was tasty and plentiful, and the tourists were falling in love with the region. One young boy exclaimed excitedly: 'This will become the best holiday resort in Europe!'

After a few days, the tour moved on to Leningrad where it was cold and damp, and it rained for the three day duration. We had to wear our warmest clothes and stayed in the "Leningrad Hotel" on the shore of the Neva River. We went to the Tsar's palaces, museums, and to a concert, but tickets for the opera were unavailable.

I also went to the wonderful St Jacob's Cathedral. The huge picture of Christ which hung over the altar, and a glass window, impressed me. It was now a museum, but it was difficult to know when it was open. No matter how my friends in the group wanted to go there after my recommendations, no one gained entry. It was the same story at most of the other churches and chapels. They were always closed, but they always had an attendant to give the same reply: 'We have no attendants to attend here, so we're closed.' It seemed that they were frightened to speak the truth and show the hidden beauty of God's Houses. It had been the same story in Yalta.

The Piskarev Cemetery, where thousands of citizens had died and were buried during the siege of Leningrad, was particularly impressive. Mass graves filled the grounds in front of a huge monument of a woman and the eternal flame. The rain continued to come down upon Russia's old capital. It was as though sunshine, warmth and love had forever left that famous city.

Our next destination was Moscow. Up until now, I had

335

had no trouble with the police or with any other authorities, but upon arrival in Moscow I felt frightened. I imagined that at any moment a hand would grab me from behind, arrest me, and ask me to come with them. We stayed in the "Hotel Ukraine" and I registered with the attendant. When she asked me my name I trembled.

'What a distinctly aromatic name you have,' she replied smiling.

My surname translates as "pine tree", and I felt more at ease. I had spent so much time needlessly imagining and worrying about things that would never happen.

Moscow was also wet and miserable. The hotel was plush and of a high standard, but the food was poor. My friends began to grumble and complain. There was no Ukrainian borshch, or fried potatoes with meat which we had enjoyed in Kyiv and Yalta. There were no puddings such as the wonderful gateaux that were served as Kyiv's speciality dish. And there was no warm or friendly hospitality as we had experienced in Ukraine.

We were taken on excursions to museums, and to the famous GUM department store – which I thought was like our old market, except everybody in Moscow was particularly proud of it. We went to a concert, and saw some churches which had been turned into museums or factories. However, I could see no functioning church anywhere. There was a monument to our great Ukrainian national poet, Taras Shevchenko, close to the "Hotel Ukraine". People appeared to be unfriendly and gruff when we approached them. They were not at all like the people of Leningrad who were much more polite, intelligent and friendly. On the whole, my companions were not particularly impressed by either Moscow or Leningrad. The boy who just a few days earlier had praised Yalta said: 'Goodbye, Russia. I hope I never see you again.'

My only encounter with the authorities was with an official at the check-in point at Moscow airport. He measured me up with a stare so hard and cold that I shall never forget it. He said nothing and let me board the plane. I returned to Luton, and then went home by bus. Ivan, meanwhile, had been filling his mind with all sorts of unnecessary thoughts during my time away.

I was to have trouble with my friends and colleagues in Bradford. My poor husband had already been confronted with all manner of questions from the community, but mostly "where has she gone?" On learning that I had flown to the Soviet Union there was endless gossip, suspicion, and more gossip. I bore everything patiently and faced everyone bravely, sincerely and innocently with my answers. I had to face aggressive accusations for having seen my mother. It seemed to matter little to them that I had lost my brother, and my father, and that my mother could soon be next. All they could see was that I had the audacity to go to the Soviet Union.

Despite the highly loaded feelings and attitudes I encountered in the community, I was determined to do everything to obtain another visa to visit my mother properly the following year. I had to have the documents and applications ready, and I would have to book the journey with a Polish firm. I learned to be quick, organised and decisive in everything I did.

Chapter 36

It took almost a whole year for the visa to finally arrive, but this time it allowed me to go straight to my mother and stay with her for a month. I planned the journey, and started to buy presents for everyone.

'You must be mad,' my husband said, 'six cases and a bag. Six cases! How can you take all of them?'

Somehow I did, and I was very lucky.

On the bus to London I met a posh couple who were going to visit a relative in Poland. They helped me with everything. We travelled by train, by boat, and then by train again all the way to Warsaw. They were met there by their family. As my next train was not leaving until eleven o'clock in the evening these kind people took me to their car and asked me if I wanted a tour of the city. I spent a wonderful day with them seeing all the places of interest. We had dinner together in a cafe and talked and laughed like life-long friends. I left the Polish capital that evening and took a very favourable impression with me.

The next train had a variety of passengers. When the

police came to check our documents I heard the conductress say: 'I have all sorts of nationalities plus one Capitalist on board.' She pointed at me, and I burst out laughing.

'You're calling me a Capitalist?' I asked. 'I've worked all my life! Exactly what sort of a Capitalist do you think I am?'

'We call you a Capitalist because you live in a Capitalist country,' she replied.

There was no laughter when we arrived in Bialystock where my entire luggage was checked.

'How can I open everything?' I asked of a demanding inspector. He summoned a porter who loaded a trolley and led me away. It was almost dawn and still dark. The train remained motionless in the station. I was the only traveller to be escorted to the luggage office. Even then, I had to wait a long time before three Polish policemen came out and ordered me to empty everything onto the counter. I had to do what they said. I opened my handbag which contained my documents and money, and left it on display. I was then ushered to a separate room, but I looked back to where my belongings were spread out. The thought of losing everything crossed my mind, especially if I was to die there. I told myself to stay calm and faced a couple of policewomen who were waiting for me.

'I don't have anything illegal,' I said, with a faint smile. Not believing me, they conducted a body search and found nothing.

The sun had already started rising by the time I returned to the train. I thought it may have gone without me, but it was still there, just as I had left it. The passengers looked at me from behind the windows. The porter then loaded everything back into the carriage.

The Customs officials had confiscated several scarves, materials, jumpers and gifts, saying that I had brought too much with me. I would also have to pay 200 pounds in tax. I said I only had 200 pounds on me and could not possibly pay them. They promised to return my goods on my return journey, but no matter how, or where, I enquired I never saw the items again. In the train, a guard changed 35 pounds for 35 roubles, saying what a lovely present I would be bringing to my mother, but at the customs checkpoint in Kyiv that money was then confiscated because I had no receipt from a bank. I had travelled a trail of economic corruption and there was no way to complain.

My sister was waiting at Kyiv railway station and I was glad to see her, but instead of taking me directly to Mother's she led me to a hotel. A young man in civilian clothing appeared and welcomed me to Kyiv and said I should stay for the night. In the morning, he would take me in his car and show me the city, and then I could travel on to see my mother. I was both surprised and disappointed. My sister was subdued and silent, and I was worried as I did not fully understand the situation. I had taken other risks, but I had to follow my journey through to the end, no matter what happened. I had a bath and then went to bed. Nadiya stayed with me in the same room. She told me how she had been approached by a lady who worked in her laboratory. She'd said she had a brother in Kyiv who would help us. It was a most unlikely story and could only have been a welcome to the web of the KGB.

The following morning after breakfast, the young official appeared and asked us what we would like to see in Kyiv. Bravely, I replied: 'I would like to see Saint Sophia's Cathedral, and Babyn Yar where the Ukrainian Nationalists and Jews were slaughtered by the Germans in the War.'

I also mentioned St Volodymyr's Hill and Monument, and the Dnipro River. It was no sooner said than done. He took me wherever I wanted to go and he talked to me politely. He told me how Kyiv had been ruined during the War and how Khreshchatic had been rebuilt. It looked magnificent now. My sister left us in the afternoon as she wanted to do some shopping, so we arranged to meet again at the railway station. I spent the rest of the day with the official who remained polite. As we sat on a bench by the famous monument of St Volodymyr, I asked him frankly and bluntly:

'Why do you put dissidents in prisons and camps?'

Without any hesitation he replied: 'They are interfering with our plans to build Socialism.'

On the way back to the railway station he took me to a cafe, bought me a coffee, and when an old Ukrainian woman walked in with a basket of fresh strawberries, he called her over and bought me a plateful. We finally arrived back at the station where Nadiya was waiting anxiously. She was worried because the train was already standing at the platform. The young man brought my cases and loaded them onto the train. Any lingering worries soon lifted when we travelled home through the night.

It was dawn when the West Ukrainian conductress called to say we had arrived. My sister was embarrassed to have to handle so many cases and promptly reminded me not to tell anyone that I had come from England: 'Just say you're from Lviv and then no one will trouble us,' she added.

We went to Nadiya's flat in town, and the plan was to go to Mother's home in the village later that day, but the authorities summoned my sister. She had to take me to the regional passport office and register my arrival. It took all morning. Crowds of people were waiting and there was a long list of questions to be answered. I asked if I could visit Krolevets where I had been to school, and if I could visit my husband's home and his relatives in Southwest Ukraine. They told me to write and ask for an application and they would consider giving me a permit. It would take a few days. It was a formal and cold welcome for me, and I was made to feel like an intruder.

'It's like being a broken-off twig,' I kept saying to Nadiya. 'I feel as though I don't belong here any more.'

She tried to console me and said she would not leave me alone for a single minute in the street. She was frightened that someone might cause trouble and snatch me away. Finally, she found a friend with a car, and late in the afternoon we set off for the village. Unbeknown to us, Mother had travelled by bus to meet us in the town, but luckily she recognised us in the car. It was such a great joy to see her again. I held my arms round her for the whole journey home.

It was dark. Auntie Chrystyna was waiting for me with tears in her eyes. Mother switched on an electric kettle to make some tea, but suddenly the circuits fused and we were left in total darkness. We lit a candle and ate some uncooked food with water. I then started to unpack my six cases because I was eager to hand out the presents. I had been to all of the main stores in Bradford buying everything I thought would be best for my dearest ones. There was a musical angel for my mother which played Christmas carols. Nadiya took the angel in her hands and sat on a chair by the table and looked at me very strangely. She played with it and wound it up endlessly, until finally it broke.

In a cool voice she then asked me: 'Why did you bring all these things?'

'They're for you,' I replied, 'they're my presents.'

'But we don't need any of them,' she snapped, 'we're quite happy as we are. What will other people say?' Mother tried to say something to comfort me. Auntie thanked me for her blouse and scarf, but my sister just sat there without saying another word.

I went to bed in tears. There was a large icon of St Nicholas in the corner above the bed, and silently through my tears I prayed. How eager and sincere I had been. I had lovingly sacrificed my hard-earned money for presents for my loved ones, and now I faced such a reaction from my sister. I tried to understand her. I understood that our lives had been completely different. Nadiya had been indoctrinated. She had gone through the War and German occupation when she was only sixteen years of age. She had seen the mass graves which the Germans had left behind. She had not even started her studies when she had to scrape dry blood and brains from the walls of her college where victims had been tortured and executed. Then, during college, she saw yet more famine in 1946-47. She had told me how hungry they had all been, and how hard it was to walk the 30 kilometres to the village to keep our parents from starving yet again. She lived in a military town where she worked as a manageress in a chemical laboratory and had to be a good example to all the employees, but she did not tell me she was a member of the Party. I did not want to confront her, but I expected that to be the truth. We were now in the village where Father had been a priest for forty years and where Mother had formed a choir that sang at funerals and memorial services, but it was in our home where they gathered for prayer. My sister was nervous about it and complained to me. She asked me to tell Mother to stop holding religious services or she would be in trouble, and she came out with her concerns right from the start of my visit.

Nadiya's son, Oleksander, was already in the army, and her daughter, Vera, was at school. She was a beautiful blonde nineteen-year-old girl who already had a life and friends of

341

her own.

So, who was I in all of this? Yes, I had gone through the War, the camps, illness and the dangers of Berlin, but now I came from a "Capitalist" country which the Communists were planning to overpower and destroy. Nadiya's factory was preparing gunpowder and ammunition for the next war, and here I was, from the West, well-dressed and with a heap of treasures from a world where peace had been the norm for the past forty years. I was a witness from that world with something to say – a representative, yet she did not like that. Maybe if I had returned to them as a pauper – ill, and with nothing to show or give, she would have liked me more. But I was an intruder – an unwanted person, and my loving feelings, sacrifices and risks had all been in vain. I had always loved my family truly, and had endured a homesickness that had never left me, despite the peace and happiness I had found with Ivan. I cried myself to sleep, downhearted and full of regret.

The following morning, as I awoke, Nadiya came to me and apologised. She lay down beside me and kissed me. She cried and spoke as gently as she could: 'I am so sorry. Please forgive me!' I put my arms round her slim body and kissed her, saying: 'It's all right. I understand. I understand.'

We got up together. Mother was used to waking up at sunrise and had already cooked breakfast and set the table in the kitchen. The sun shone in through the small window as we sat down. It looked more like a banquet than a breakfast. We ate, and talked, and laughed as though nothing had happened the previous evening.

Our joyful reunion, however, did not last for long. A boy came from the Village Council to tell Nadiya that there was a message from her District Council to say we must go there together. Nervously, we hurried to the bus and made our way back to the town. When we arrived, we were told that only Nadiya was needed for an interview: alone.

'You go,' I said, 'I'll wait in the garden.'

'No,' she said, 'it's not a good idea.' I could see how concerned she was for my safety. She took me to the house of a friend and spoke to her very quietly before leaving me in her company. Nadiya's friend had a grandson who was an unfriendly young man. He was particularly rude and unkind

342

to his grandmother, and demanded his breakfast, even though I was present. I thought of how youth was now growing up in Ukraine. Eventually, he left and my hostess turned her attention to me. She made me a cup of cocoa and we talked until Nadiya returned.

'Damn them,' she said, 'they won't leave us in peace. You have to go back there tomorrow. We had better stay at my place tonight.'

I asked her what they wanted but she only waved her hand and said nothing.

The following morning, we returned to the Council buildings, but we were separated. I was taken into a room and then locked inside, on my own. I felt uneasy – especially when I could hear the key being turned to lock me in. Eventually, a fat official came in to announce that he was from the Regional Council. He looked at me and began to seek answers to a list of questions:

'Who are you?'

'What do you do in England?'

'Why did you not return home after the War?'

I looked at him without showing any fear, and calmly answered his questions. I told him that I worked as a nurse and had married a man whose citizenship was different to mine. The Soviets would not permit me to do that at the time, so I stayed in the West. I also told him that I was teaching Ukrainian children, that we had our own church, and that I liked to sing in the choir. He asked if I knew of any other locals now living in England, but as there was nobody from our district I replied: 'No, I do not know of anyone.' When he mentioned politics I said that I did not mix with political people. He then seemed to be at a loss for more questions. He finally stood up, opened the door and said that I could go. Not believing my ears, I went out and immediately found my anxious and worried sister.

'Are you all right?' she asked with deep concern.

'Yes, but don't worry. Everything is all right.' We were not left in peace, however. We returned to Mother's the next day, but the requests to return for more interviews were made of us repeatedly.

I received permission to visit my home town of Krolevets where I had been to school. I went back to the street where we once lived, but there was now a new house standing where the front yard used to be. The old house had gone. I remembered how I had hidden my diaries in the roof of the house. Together with my past life, they too, had gone. A man came out and asked us what we wanted. I told him, but his next statement was very abrupt:

'I've bought this place, and it's my house!'

'So, all the work and care I spent on it before I was taken away had been for nothing,' I thought to myself. Nonetheless, I thanked him for coming outside.

I then went to visit a friend called Vera with whom I had spent the winter of 1941-42 when the house we lived in had no heating. We survived that winter on a meagre diet and concocted dishes from whatever food we could find. She greeted me with surprise and unease. She was now nursing her first grandchild, and told me that her sister, who was also with us that winter, had been killed in a train accident. She had lived alone after having divorced her husband. I gave her a bottle of perfume and asked her about our school friends. Of course, I had to ask her about my first infatuation, Nicholas, whom I had always remembered. She told me that he lived by himself and had never married. His mother had died and his sister was married and living in another town.

'Are you going to see him?' She asked.

'No,' I answered, 'there's nothing between us that could possibly pull me to him.'

'I see,' she added, 'that might explain why he never married.'

I smiled and said: 'I would love to see him, but not now.'

I did not yet know it, but I would never see Nicholas again. We parted and Vera was glad to have seen me, but I did notice that she was also frightened. I was an intruder from a forbidden world and she might yet be questioned by the KGB about my visit. Later, I wrote some letters to her, but I never received a reply.

The day reflected my mood. It was grey and it rained. We returned to see my old school which was once beautifully painted yellow and had stood amongst the white birches and green pine trees. It was now painted green and looked small and neglected, and most of the trees had gone. Opposite the school, I walked to where the beautiful Church of St Nicholas had once stood. I remembered the ruins, and the statue of Lenin which replaced it. When the Germans came the statue was knocked down and replaced by a gallows to hang the locals. Two tall pine trees now grew there. I touched them: two beautiful trees – surviving gifts of God's creation. The park where we once walked, and danced, and met was neglected – overgrown with wild shrubbery and weeds. There was now a new school in the centre of town, with new monuments, but I did not want to go there as it meant nothing to me. My youth, my childhood, and my home – the most beautiful places of my teenage years, had all gone now. They were all I had wanted to see, one final time.

We went to visit some relatives in the neighbouring village where the people were simple and loving. They showed kindness and hospitality and displayed no fear or suspicion. We then returned to Mother's that same day as it was one of the conditions of my visit. I had no permission to visit Ivan's family so I did not even think about it, but Ivan's brother Mykhailo and niece Maria, were allowed to come to Mother's house later on.

I stayed for the whole month, and whilst I was there I met many people, but they were all so poor. I could tell just by looking at their clothing. One day, Auntie Chrystyna cut her leg, so Mother called for the doctor.

'You will meet our doctor,' she told me with pride.

An elderly lady in a dark skirt, blouse and scarf came. I would never have thought she was a doctor. She looked much like everyone else from the village, but when she wrote the prescription I noticed that it was written in Latin. We went to the hospital – which was in the old church house. I admired the big windows, high walls and large rooms. The smell of carbolic, however, overpowered everything. Nurses in white coats gathered round us, and after learning that I was a nurse in England they asked me many questions. I explained that carbolic was no longer used in England, but I did not mention that our disinfectant did not smell: that would have offended them.

Those summer days were beautiful and everybody who did not work on the collective farm was usually busy – perhaps weeding on their own small piece of land. There was a plague of Colorado beetles which everybody wanted to see destroyed.

'Come and help us,' Nadiya said, but I didn't go.

'So why didn't you come and help us weed the potatoes?' she asked when she returned, 'are you afraid you'll dirty your hands?'

'No. I've been clipping Auntie's nails,' I replied.

'And she's done them ever so well,' added Auntie Chrystyna. 'You never do them for me.'

I did go and work outside. I had earlier heard a story about a woman from our Ukrainian community in Bradford who went to visit her mother in a village. She had dressed up like a lady and wore her expensive clothes, but she soon discovered that nobody wanted to know her. I had therefore packed some simple dresses and tried to look very modest. I gave away my best blouses and best dresses to my nieces.

One evening, after helping on the field, a neighbour persuaded me to go to the theatre to see a modern play with professional actors from Kyiv. I went reluctantly, as the theatre was in our old church. We sat on a bench at the back and I looked at the building. It had all changed. The small, narrow hall had been painted a grim dark-grey, and the side aisles and altar spaces had been made into separate rooms. Pictures of Lenin, Marx, Engles and Stalin seemed to look down mockingly. There were slogans in large letters everywhere commanding everyone to "WORK!" I thought of how people had laboured though the Five-Year Plans. Once, this had been a large and rich village. Now everybody was poor and dressed in simple and similar clothing, and there was no church. During the interval, the lights came on and I noticed that all the eyes were upon me.

'So, how do you like it here?' asked a man sitting in front of me.

He looked friendly, and I smiled back at him and asked: 'Can you tell me why everything is so dull and grey in here?'

'Well,' he said with a sigh, 'you can see for yourself, we have neither taste nor paint.'

I smiled at him again, but said no more. I could see the people's kindness and warmth in their eyes. Perhaps my presence had reminded them of our earlier times.

After the play finished, I went out with my neighbour. It was a windy and dusty evening and dark clouds drifted quickly across the unsettled sky. I felt cold and uncomfortable. The huge trees by the church waved their branches, scraping at the heavens before bending down low, as though in despair. I exchanged a few words with a few people but they were too frightened to talk to me openly. I was glad to return to Mother's clean and tidy, little house. She kept the lamp alight in the corner where Father used to pray. It was a Saturday night, and here at least, the atmosphere was relaxed and uplifting.

I continued to witness how people were living under the current Soviet regime. People were people, and they had to find their own means of survival.

One day, a remembrance service was held at a neighbour's house in memory of their mother, and I was invited to go along. Long planks of wood were laid across stands to form a table in the little garden outside. A strip of black paper was put across the middle. The people sat there on benches. A young daughter-in-law, plump and red-faced, brought some food out. Spoons, forks and fingers were used, but there were no knives. I was told that all of the best steel had been taken to build Kyiv's "Baba" or "Iron Lady" – the huge war memorial overlooking the Dnipro River, and it had been deliberately erected to be the city's highest structure.

'Someone said: 'They asked Brezhnev not to allow it to be higher than the churches, but he would not agree.'

'That's why Chornobyl exploded,' added a ginger-haired man who had had a lot to drink and was no longer frightened of speaking out.

'Death unites everyone,' said an old man, digging at a piece of small, dry fish with his fingers. 'Communism will also die.'

'Just be quiet!' snapped his elderly wife. 'Your tongue is much too long!'

'It's true. I'm not frightened of death. One day I'll be free from all of them.'

The plump daughter-in-law brought more food which everyone ate eagerly. There was still a food shortage in the town and local area. You could not buy fruit or vegetables in the market, except for onions, garlic, pickled gherkins, cabbage and tomatoes. There was also a shortage of clothing, but most of all, there was a shortage of money. If you wanted to buy a car you had to wait for years. Even household utensils were expensive and most people could not even afford those. The shops in the town were, at best, half empty. People tried to live as well as they could, but there was no end of hospitality in the homes to which I was invited with my mother and sister. People baked and cooked their favourite food for us, and they treated us kindly and very politely. Was it because I was their former priest's daughter, or was it because I had come from England? Of course, the answer was neither. It had always been Ukrainian nature to share such kindness with others, regardless of who they were.

I enjoyed talking to everyone and explained everything I could from my life's experience. I gave them presents – scarves, blouses, and sometimes dresses. I was not sorry to part with anything because they were my people, and I loved them. Auntie Chrystyna told me off for giving some things to complete strangers, but I was happy to give. People seemed to be so well-natured and friendly, despite the stories that Nadiya and Auntie Chrystyna would tell me about them. Mother never said anything bad about anyone and made no comments about my behaviour. She seemed to rise above it all and remained silent and dignified. Women came to visit us. They were from the choir, which Mother had kept going, despite the closure of the church. They sang prayers so beautifully in the graveyard where Father was buried that I taped them. It was a moving and emotional link that took me back many years. Sadly, the recording was deleted by customs officials on my return journey to Bradford.

One Sunday, we went to the Desna River in the neighbouring village. The Desna has a powerful undercurrent so Nadiya pleaded with me not to go swimming. She told me that a swimming instructor had drowned there recently. Even though I was a strong swimmer, I did not want to take my younger sister's advice. I jumped into the water and started to swim, and the current was indeed so strong that it carried me far from the place where I had started.

'You are right,' I said to her. 'The current is indeed very powerful. I'd rather not try that again!' We gathered flowers in the valley, and enjoyed the whole day out. On the way home, I wanted to see the place where the church had stood, next to our little, stone cottage.

'Why do you want to go there?' Nadiya asked. As far as she was concerned, the past had long since died. She had no idea that I had longed to visit so many places in the years I had been away. But I could not find the place where the church had stood. Trees and bushes were growing everywhere, and I was lost. I saw an elderly man who was walking along the path, so I stopped him and asked:

'Excuse me! There used to be a church here. Do you know exactly where it stood?' He had a dark, sunburnt face and looked back at me through his friendly, blue eyes. He asked me who I was. When I told him, he smiled and said that he had known my father and identified him as the priest who had buried his mother. He sighed and began to lift a heavy burden from his heart:

'That was quite a church we had. A new official recently came from the Village Council and said, "What fool could ruin such a church? Now we have to pay from what little we have to rebuild historic buildings". He was right, you know. Who could replace a church like the one we had?'

'The people can,' I replied spontaneously, 'and if not you, then your children.' He looked at me, and then pointed:

'Go up there, that way, and you will find the place, but there's nothing left to see there now.'

I thanked him and found the place where our church had stood. There were red bricks left from the foundations, now overgrown with weeds and shrubs. Twenty-four years had passed since the church was destroyed in 1954. I quietly looked around and placed my bunch of flowers on the bricks.

I made my way back to the bus stop through what had once been the garden of the church, but this too, was overgrown and running wild. I saw men sitting on the grass drinking vodka. Some were singing and others were swearing. They were drunk. As we travelled back to Mother's I noticed that people sat outside their homes on the benches. They were well-dressed as it was Trinity Sunday. At least I could see that many had remained faithful and were celebrating festive days in their own way.

I became friendly with the women who worked on the collective farm. They told me about their labour, and how they had been told to weed a small plot of beets by hand. Their work had to be finished by a certain time. They were

349

pensioners and received fifteen roubles a month – it was a very small pension. They told me that their children did not want to work on the collective farm and had run away to the town. There were subsequently no people left in the village to work on the farm. As a countermeasure, children, students and office workers were sent out from the town to work in the villages. As if to prove this, my beautiful, young niece came and told me how she had been sent to weed the beet. I could not imagine how she and her white, manicured fingers could cope for a whole day.

'Have they not given you any gloves?' I asked.

She laughed: 'We never see anybody wearing gloves. Fancy that! Weeding with gloves on! No, they never give us anything.'

'Do they give you any food, then?'

'No. We have to bring our own.'

'That's strange,' I said, 'I would have thought they'd at least give you something to eat.'

My niece laughed again: 'There's no such thing here, and we have to walk to the fields. Oh, yes, and that's by foot.'

To encourage young people to work on the farms, cottages were built and offered to young couples, but the cottages remained empty as nobody was interested.

Forty-five years had passed since the collective farms were first imposed. People had been forced to work on them but they were inefficient. On some farms there were crops; on others there were orchards, but everything was controlled and directed from above. There was a Five-Year Plan, and workdays for which payment was only ever made in the autumn. Knowing about large, cultivated farms in England, I still could not believe how badly this particular system was run. Food had to be bought in from abroad before the end of the harvest. Once upon a time, Ukraine's famous black soil had fed Europe: now, it could not even feed its own people.

'Enjoy yourselves boys, America will give us bread!' This was a common call made by the younger ones as they set off for work. I said nothing. I was an outsider; a visitor; just an observer.

Whilst visiting some of my mother's friends, I was equally amazed by the wonderfully-kept gardens and allotments which belonged to each family. They were their

350

real source of food for the year. Every collective farm worker owned a small piece of "private land" on which they were allowed to grow their own potatoes, beets, carrots, cabbage, corn, beans and other vegetables and fruit. The plots were properly looked after, watered and weeded, although that work had to be done before or after work on the collective farm. These plots were a source of income and staple food for the people. It was a limited private initiative. People could survive with it, but they still struggled.

Mykhailo came to see me. He was tall and handsome, and when we walked through the village everybody looked at him admiringly and said a friendly "Good day!" in Ukrainian. Maria was a tall, pretty young woman whose large, dark eyes shone with her kindness. She was up before sunrise one morning to go into Mother's garden to kill off the beetles. She came back with a bucket and broom, wet and breathless, yet she smiled as if it was natural for her to do such work. We spent happy days together by going to the river to swim, sunbathe and admire the wildflowers. The days remained sunny and warm. The air was pure, and the trees and grass around the village were green and aromatic. It began to feel as if there had been no Germany, no camp life, no illnesses, and no England. I had reconnected to my childhood and teenage years.

Unforgettable as the summer was, I had to go back. I said goodbye to all of my new friends in the village and my dear, frail auntie whose only job was to feed the chickens. I tried to see the funny side. She shouted at them and had a fight with the cock every time they were fed. Mother came with us to the station. It was a perfectly normal journey, but then suddenly the wind blew very forcefully and covered everything with a layer of sand and dust. The sand went into our mouths and nostrils. I had never known such a gust before. Poplar trees, growing nearby, spread their seeds like layers of white cotton wool on the ground and created the illusion of a carpet of summer snow. I asked Mother to give me her blessing, and as we parted she made the sign of the cross over me. We hugged and kissed each other, not knowing if we would ever see each other again. The wind continued to blow and pushed dark clouds in from the East. We cried and nature cried with us.

351

I boarded the train with the other members of my family. The rain now lashed at the windows. Lightning then lit up the carriage and the thunder overpowered the sound of the train from the outside. It was a hurricane which blew down trees and flooded roads across the region. By the time we reached Kyiv it was calm again.

We spent the night in a hotel, after which I helped the others buy their tickets. I registered mine for the journey back. We visited the "Kashtany" shop where I bought another fur hat for my brother-in-law, scarves for my nieces, and presents for my mother and sister. I used up my last roubles. In the afternoon, we parted and I boarded the train back to England. Tears came to my eyes once more. I had not seen as much of my beloved homeland as I would have liked, but when the light faded from the windows and darkness crept in, a lady passenger kindly comforted me on the journey to Warsaw.

It was an express train, so it didn't stop at any of the smaller stations, but it stopped for ages in Bialystock. The wheels had to be changed to fit Europe's narrower tracks. It was two o'clock in the morning. I enquired about the belongings which had been confiscated on my way into Ukraine. The conductor simply replied that it was now night and everything was closed. I could get off the train and wait until morning and then get another train. It would probably have been a waste of time. I did make further enquiries, but it was of no use.

I had no more baggage checks and arrived home safely. It had been a daring, brave and naïve journey, yet I had taken it and fulfilled my wishes. I knew I would not return again, and Ivan was particularly adamant about it, no matter how lovingly my mother would ask me to come back. Three years later, in 1981, she died of a stroke. It was on the 24th of June – again the same day that Anatoly died.

My mother had gone to the river as it was a hot, sunny day, and whilst she paddled in the water she suddenly fell. A soldier who was crossing a bridge saw her and took her to the hospital where she died nine days later. I received the news in a letter from Nadiya, and it came as a very hard blow. I had hoped to see her again, at least one more time.

Ivan and I decided to book a holiday to Penzance, but

when we arrived I felt restless and wanted to travel on. It did not matter where. Anywhere would do, just as long as I could continue travelling. We took a ferry to France and went to Le Mont Saint Michel a small peninsula with a castle on a hill. We only spent the day there, but I felt spiritually compelled to buy a picture of the Mount. It acted as a reminder of my dear mother, and of the strength and dignity which she had always shown us.

Chapter 37

I retired in 1983, and was given a wonderful leaving party by the staff of the hospital. Ivan came and I was finally able to introduce him to the doctors and operating theatre staff. He was elegantly dressed and before long he was busy chatting with all of them. I could see the world of difference between the two. Ivan had received a good education and had earned his professional status, but he had lost it through no fault of his own. His subsequent life in England had consisted of poorly-paid, menial jobs, but he never once complained. He was happy just to be alive. As he stood alongside the doctors, I could see he was in the company of his true, academic peer group. We enjoyed the party, and by the end of the evening I said my last goodbye to hospital life.

I began my retirement by collecting and rewriting my short stories in Ukrainian. I then made arrangements to have them published in Canada and posted them to a friend in Scotland who was about to travel there. He would then deliver them by hand. However, they did not arrive before his departure. In fact, I was later told that the parcel with my stories had never arrived at all, and no matter how hard I tried to recover them, I would never find them. It was another severe blow for me. I was heartbroken, and I compared my loss to that of a mother losing a baby. I had some rough draft copies and worked on them later, but I had no real chance of ever getting them finished. I then decided to start writing in English. I felt it was just as important to tell my English friends something about the beauty of Ukraine and our traditions, and where I was from. I also had to say something about our recent history – about life under the Soviet regime, and about the suffering that so many of us had gone through in the hands of the Germans.

I spent my days doing the housework and in the evenings I relaxed with Ivan. We would talk and watch programmes of interest on the television. Ivan would go to bed at ten o'clock and would leave me alone downstairs. I would then light my table lamp which had a green shade, and I would sit and write for many hours, filling one exercise book after another. I began to relive my life on paper. I filled at least twelve exercise books and then began to type my writing again on a small, portable typewriter. I then put the text away, hoping that one day I might find an editor, or someone to simply correct my English. Meanwhile, in Ukraine, events were beginning to unfold that would change our lives for the final time.

The Old Guard Soviet Communist leaders began to fall like flies. They had been the leaders of a political system that had taken millions of lives and had ruined countless millions more. In November 1982, the former president of the Soviet Union of eighteen years standing, Leonid Brezhnev, died of a heart attack. He was succeeded by Yuri Andropov, the chief of the KGB, but he was only fit enough to lead for 15 months. The community hated the KGB and Andropov was feared as he had a track record of crushing dissidents. Konstantin Chernenko, aged 73, was his replacement, but his reign did not last long, either. He died on the 10th of March 1985.

The quick succession of deaths paved the way for a youngster by Soviet political standards – Mikhail Gorbachev who was then aged 54. He was a reformer, well-educated and open-minded, and he aimed to reduce the enormous stockpile of arms in the USSR. Nonetheless, he was still a Communist, and despite offering Ukrainians freedom of speech, our desire to have total freedom still remained. We had always wanted to see a free and independent Ukraine, and we never lost hope that a proclamation of independence would eventually arrive; perhaps we would even live to see it. Our belief was then fuelled when we saw Ukrainians beginning to visit their lost relatives in England with increasing frequency.

Earlier, in 1979, Ivan had suffered a blow when his other brother Yoseph – a former professor at the University of Uzhhorod – suddenly died of a heart attack. He left a wife and two young sons Yuri and Yoseph in Southwest Ukraine.

Ivan kept telling me that the boys were like twins, although they weren't. They just looked alike and had always been the best of friends when they were young. Yuri was devastated at the loss of his father, so he decided to come and visit us in England. Such a visit was unheard of at the time as similar requests had been forbidden, but he was determined. After cutting through endless amounts of red tape, he finally received a visa – probably because of the changes in Soviet policy. He came to stay with us in the spring of 1984. It was a great a joy, not only for us as a family, but it was great news for everyone in Bradford's Ukrainian community. Yuri was one of our first visitors from Ukraine, and now everyone began to believe that they, too, could reunite with their loved ones.

One of my distant nieces then arrived with her husband. They were a young and charming couple. They delighted everybody, and like Yuri, our friends admired them and gave them presents. My own niece, Vera, followed in 1989 and arrived with her five-year-old daughter, but this time they could stay for a few months. She joined our circle of friends and went to the church with us. We were all very happy to welcome them. Then finally, in 1991 my sister Nadiya came to stay with us. She brought great joy, and together, from a distance, we watched television and saw the final weeks of the collapsing Soviet Union. We took her everywhere and when she returned by train, she willingly took many suitcases bulging with presents, as I had once done. She had also caught up with her history lessons.

Hitherto, Ukraine's national movement had been suppressed. Its activists had been placed behind bars. They had been forcibly sent to Siberia for hard labour, or had even been killed. Everything was now out in the open. In February 1989, the Society for Ukrainian Language was formed and it united the nationally conscious people to prevent any further Russification. Then, one of the greatest sights in Ukrainian history took place on the 21st of January 1990 when the People's Movement of Ukraine formed a human chain from Lviv to Kyiv. They held hands over a distance of 500 kilometres that had once taken me 24 hours to travel by train.

On the 17th of March 1991, a national referendum was held in which the vast majority of Ukrainians voted for

Ukraine's independence from the Soviet Union, Soviet Communism and Russia. Then, on the 24th of August 1991, Ukraine was free.

With this news, all Ukrainians in Great Britain finally felt they could go home and planned visits to see their relatives. In the summer of 1992 Ivan and I had the necessary documentation and flew to Kyiv, except on this occasion we knew we were free and we felt it. The searching, the checking and the questioning had now gone. We simply filled out a customs declaration to state how much money and jewellery we had with us, and that was it.

We had a happy reunion, and many of Nadiya's friends also welcomed us into their homes and showed us their kind hospitality. Each visit was like a banquet and we were made to feel very special. We were happy everywhere we went. The whole atmosphere had changed: everything. Dignity had returned and everyone could be seen wearing well-kept clothing. I insisted on going to the Desna River again to see the woodlands and all the beauty spots. I had longed to see them so many times and dearly wanted to show Ivan the places where we had played as children.

It was sad that my father and mother were no longer there, and my auntie had passed away too. We prayed for them in the church, which had been reconverted from the theatre immediately after independence. Portraits of my father and my mother were now hanging on the memorial wall. Everybody talked about them with love and respect. I shed tears with my sister at their graveside where I kissed their crosses. I then found Anatoly's name which had been engraved on the war memorial.

We went by train and bus to visit Nadiya's son Oleksander and his family. He now had four beautiful children and proudly showed us the garden where he grew vegetables and fruit. His yard was full of poultry, and in a sty his pigs grunted as they rolled lazily on the straw. For sixty years, this simple existence had not been allowed. Oleksander's wife, Halyna, welcomed us and joined us in our outings. She prepared the meals which we ate at a table in the yard. A really huge tree outside the house acted as a stand-alone playground. The children played on its swings, rope ladders and gymnastic bars which were carefully built into the trunk. We enjoyed our stay there. It was a happy and unforgettable time, and it was like a reward and resolution for the many years of homesickness and longing.

We set off by train to Ivan's home in Transcarpathia. The journey was long but we made friends on the train and talked to them freely and openly on all sorts of subjects. It took almost twenty-eight hours to reach Uzhhorod where Yuri met us with his son. They took us to his house where all their relatives had gathered to meet us. Some of them were young, and we had never met them before, but love united us and made us into one happy family.

Yuri took us to the town of Hust where Ivan was born and where his brother Mykhailo and sister Karolina still lived. After fifty-three years it was an emotional return and reunion for the whole family. Karolina had a family who were doctors, and his two brothers also had well-established households. Other distant relatives also gathered to greet us, and they too, all had tears in their eyes. We stayed with Ivan's niece Maria, her husband and their beautiful daughter Myroslava, and visited the others every day. I became very fond of all of them. They were sincere, friendly, honest and hardworking people who welcomed us as though we had always been with them as part of their family unit. We went to the beautiful church that Ivan's father had built and met many people who remembered Ivan. They welcomed him back with open arms.

Ivan's nephews then took us by car to the Tysa – a fast-running mountain river, deep in the valleys and woodlands. We picnicked there, swam in the river and enjoyed the scenic beauty of the Carpathian Mountains which were covered with fir trees, oaks, maples and beeches. Hazelnuts were growing on the lower slopes. There were also private orchards with ripening fruit trees, and summer berries. There were picturesque villages with white houses and coloured roofs, and churches with beautiful steeples which could be seen in every direction we travelled.

We returned to England safely, and everyone who had also been to Ukraine shared their experiences with us. It was a time of rebirth. Subsequently, Ivan and I returned to Ukraine every year, and we were happy there because we had always treasured freedom. It was now ours to enjoy, but we kept England as our home. England was the country that had always given us the shelter we needed to survive. We had fled from persecution and oppression, and although Ukraine had reached independence, not all things there would change for the better overnight. Our life in England, on the other hand, had always been relatively normal and stable. I expect it shall continue that way.

Over the years, I learned to love England – its political system and its welcoming people. I lived free from the fear of being arrested or of being put to death because of suspicious whispering, or because of false testimonies. I knew I would never be sent to a labour camp, or be forced into slavery, or be put into a cell to be cruelly tortured by sadistic officials. I knew I could work and save without having my property confiscated for no reason at all. My aim, to learn and to succeed, and to do so without creating harm, could be fulfilled here. Most of all, the right to lead a peaceful life had been given to me, and never once had it been taken away. May that way of life continue for all those who continue to live here.

Aiming to join the European Union, Ukraine is now similarly free and many small miracles have been seen across the country. Churches have been rebuilt and thousands of new buildings have sprung up everywhere – luxurious apartments, offices, restaurants, supermarkets and open markets with goods from all over the world. The massive political turnaround from Communism to Capitalism has brought many difficulties, but the hardworking people of Ukraine have been finding their way through this transition. Long may they continue to rebuild their country – especially their schools, colleges and universities. And long may they find a future that is safe and secure. Most of all, may they never have to experience the hardships that my generation so silently and painfully endured.

Printed in the United Kingdom
by Lightning Source UK Ltd.
135876UK00001B/169/P